Responsible
Behavior

Teaching Responsible Behavior

Developmental Therapy—
Developmental Teaching
for Troubled Children
and Adolescents

FOURTH EDITION

Mary M. Wood
Constance A. Quirk
Faye L. Swindle

An International Publisher

8700 Shoal Creek Boulevard
Austin, Texas 78757-6897
800/897-3202
Fax 800/397-7633
www.proedinc.com

© 2007 by PRO-ED, Inc.
8700 Shoal Creek Boulevard
Austin, Texas 78757-6897
800/897-3202   Fax 800/397-7633
www.proedinc.com

The Developmental Therapy–Developmental Teaching Service Mark, THE DTORF–R, and
the PEGs graphics are used with the permission of the Developmental Therapy Institute, Inc.

Permission is granted to the user of this material to make copies of the forms on the CD–ROM
for educational purposes.

Library of Congress Cataloging-in-Publication Data

Wood, Mary M.
Teaching responsible behavior : developmental therapy–developmental teaching
for troubled children and adolescents / Mary M. Wood, Constance A. Quirk,
Faye L. Swindle.—4th ed.
    p. cm.
  Revised ed. of: Developmental therapy–developmental teaching. ©1996.
  Includes bibliographical references and index.
  ISBN-13: 978-1-4164-0134-6
  ISBN-10: 1-4164-0134-2 (softcover : alk. paper)
  1. Mentally ill children—Education.   2. Problem children—Education.   3. Children
with social disabilities—Education.   4. Developmental therapy.   I.   Quirk, Constance.
II. Swindle, Faye L.   III. Wood, Mary M. Developmental therapy–developmental teaching.
IV. Title.
LC4165.D47 2006
371.94—dc22

                                                                    2005034130

Art Director: Jason Crosier
Designer: Nancy McKinney
This book is designed in FairfieldLH and Futura.

Printed in the United States of America

1 2 3 4 5 6 7 8 9 10   10 09 08 07 06

Development continues ... from age to age ... throughout life.
Ages: 1 to 100

Contents

CHAPTER 1

Students and the Competencies They Need   1

CHAPTER 2

Snapshots from Early Childhood Through the Teen Years   29

CHAPTER 3

Assessment of Students' Competencies   59

CHAPTER 4

Decoding Behavior: From the Seen to the Unseen   91

CHAPTER 8

Getting Started in Your Own Classroom 201

CHAPTER 9

Effectiveness 237

Appendixes

List of Figures

List of Tables

Developmental Therapy– Developmental Teaching in Brief

Developmental Therapy–Developmental Teaching is a developmentally based system proven to be effective in teaching troubled children and teens to be increasingly responsible individuals. The general goal is social, emotional, and behavioral competence. It has four content areas that are widely recognized as essential for success in school and at home: *behavior, communication, socialization, and cognition.*

Within this framework, the approach provides teachers, other professionals, and parents with procedures for establishing learning objectives and matching instructional practices to a student's current developmental profile. The content follows typical developmental sequences through five distinct stages of children's lives. These stages define general instructional practices for use with preschoolers, school-age children, and young teenagers, with or without disabilities. Instruction is then refined and adapted for the individual needs of each student. When these practices are used in conjunction with other academic and social skills curricula, options for simultaneously enhancing both academic achievement and responsible behavior are greatly increased.

Several measurement instruments provide an evaluation component for this approach. The *Social–Emotional–Behavioral Quick Profile* (S–E–B *Quick Profile*) is an initial screening procedure with indicators of a student's current stage of development. The *Developmental Teaching Objectives Rating Form–Revised* (DTORF–R) is used for an in-depth assessment of a student's social, emotional, and behavioral development. Results become the foundation for instructional planning. For students in special education, the DTORF–R is used to obtain a functional behavioral assessment and a behavioral intervention plan (BIP) as part of an Individualized Education Program (IEP), Individualized Family Service Plan (IFSP), or Individual Transition Plan (ITP). Repeated DTORF–R assessments document a student's annual yearly progress (AYP) during a school year.

Two companion instruments broaden the scope for program evaluation. The *Developmental Teaching: Rating Inventory of Teacher Skills* (DTRITS) provides a measure of a teacher's skills in applying specified practices. It can be used as a self-monitoring tool by an individual teacher or paraprofessional for self-directed skill enhancement, or as a guide for mentoring beginning teachers. Extensive research during the development of the DTRITS indicates that it is a reliable and valid measure of a teacher's proficiency. It can also document the quality of the intervention provided to students. A supplement to this measure is the *Administrative Support Checklist*, which contains administrative elements associated with high levels of teacher performance and overall program quality.

Cumulative evidence from research over a number of years resulted in three separate validations for program effectiveness from the U.S. Department of Education. The first study documented significant gains of children who were severely emotionally disturbed. The second study validated the effectiveness of the Developmental Therapy–Developmental Teaching in-service training program for significantly improved classroom proficiencies of participating teachers and student teachers, with documented student gains as a corollary outcome. The third validation resulted from a broader study of students with developmental, speech/language, and social, emotional, or behavioral disabilities. Students made significant gains whether they received the program in general education, partially inclusive, or in special education settings. These findings provide additional confidence that Developmental Therapy–Developmental Teaching, skillfully implemented, will result in students with increased social, emotional, and behavioral competence.

Preface

Teaching children and teens about responsible behavior is no simple matter. First, teaching responsible behavior requires teachers and parents to understand what "behaving responsibly" means for different age groups. Next is the matter of understanding how responsible behavior is acquired, how it affects academic achievement, and which instructional practices are effective in guiding its development. The National Research Council (2002) articulated these ideas in its standards-based reform proposal "to make explicit the link between standards, assessments, accountability, instruction, and learning" (Elmore & Rothman, 1999, pp. 3–6). This system reflects the Developmental Therapy–Developmental Teaching approach to improved outcomes for students, illustrated in Table P.1. This approach is also imbedded in federal regulations for the reauthorized IDEA legislation of 2004 and the No Child Left Behind Act of 2001 (U.S. Department of Education, 2002).

As a practical guide for putting these standards into practice, we offer the revised edition of *Developmental Therapy–Developmental Teaching*. This approach is intended for general and special educators who have students with challenging behaviors. It also includes material for parents concerned about how to help children become increasingly responsible for their own conduct—in school and in life. There are applications for childcare providers, paraprofessionals, student teachers, and mental health practitioners. For those who are new to this approach, the material is introduced gradually, step by step. Those who currently use Developmental Therapy–Developmental Teaching will find many familiar instructional strategies, as well as new insights for connecting applications to research and underlying theory. This should be of help when demonstrating the practices for others and for documenting student progress toward increasingly responsible behavior and school achievement.

While the practical applications and the growing body of scientifically based research evidence about the effectiveness of this approach make Developmental Therapy–Developmental Teaching directly relevant to teachers in their classrooms, the universally recognized theoretical foundations are what enhance its authenticity (Wood, Brendtro, Fecser, & Nichols, 1999). Theory provides the basis for practices. Over many years, theorists, researchers, and educators have expanded our understanding about successful education of children and youth. They have described intricate interrelationships among the developmental processes that produce social and emotional competence. They offer explanations about how relationships are formed and responsible behavior is acquired. They explain the role of emotions, emotional memory, and mental energy in learning; and how values become motivating forces in behavioral choice. Theories also expand our understanding of anxiety and its pervasive role in learning.

Among major theories that have been translated into practice in this approach are the seminal works of Erik Erikson on identity formation and Jean Piaget's constructs about cognitive scaffolding. We include Table P.2 as an introduction to the way stage theories are reflected in Developmental Therapy–Developmental Teaching. Works of other major theorists are integrated throughout the book, including Robert Selman's model for how interpersonal understanding develops, Lawrence Kohlberg's work on moral development, Eliott Turiel's formulations about social development, and the rich insights of Fritz Redl and David Wineman about aggressive children. Additionally, this approach builds on the constructs developed by Albert Bandura about how behavior is learned, Jane Loevinger's synthesis of personality development, Anna Freud's studies of developmental lines and children's anxieties, and the extensive research contributions of Mary Ainsworth, James Bowlby, Michael Lewis, and Margaret Mahler for greater understanding of the emotional lives of children.

Combining learning theory with transactional, sociological, and clinical orientations provided greater understanding of how social and emotional development of children and teens affects their behavior and their learning. With or without disabilities, children need certain universal benchmarks for social, emotional, and behavioral competence. These critical milestones

Table P.1

Developmental Therapy–Developmental Teaching Meets NCLB/IDEA Standards-Based System To Improve Instruction

	Components of Developmental Therapy–Developmental Teaching
Standards	• Standards of social, emotional, and behavioral competence for students, identified from research and theory about healthy personality development, for increasingly responsible behavior at school and at home. • Key indicators aligned with benchmarks to the general education curriculum. • Specified instructional standards for teachers and paraprofessionals linked to gains in student competencies.
Assessments	• Student's general developmental profile (*Social–Emotional–Behavioral Quick Profile*) • A functional behavioral assessment (FBA) of a student's individual pattern of competencies, achieved and missing standards, for precise IEP objectives and a behavior intervention plan (BIP). (Developmental Teaching Objectives Rating Form–Revised; DTORF–R) • In-classroom ratings of a teacher's proficiency in demonstrating the specified standards. (Developmental Teaching Rating Inventory of Teacher Skills; DTRITS)
Accountability	• Students demonstrate adequate yearly progress (AYP) in social, emotional, behavioral, and learning competencies specified for their individual stage of development. (DTORF–R Progress Record) • Teachers demonstrate specific proficiency levels in applying the practices indicated in their students' IEPs. (Teachers' DTRITS proficiency scores) • Schools demonstrate that teachers and students have the necessary administrative support for student progress. (Administrative Support Checklist) • Improvement in schoolwide indicators of a mentally healthy school environment.
Instruction	• Sequentially planned academic lessons and other learning activities matched to student's current learning objectives and capacity to achieve in school. • Learning material that challenges students to increased levels of competence. • Flexible scheduling and timely adjustments in individual student's programs. • Motivating curriculum content relevant to students' experiences. • Instruction and behavior management strategies matched to students' learning objectives.
Student learning	• Carefully aligned educational intervention programs that result in high levels of motivation and willing student participation in achieving the selected learning objectives. • Students with gains in expected standards for social, emotional, and behavioral competence, with increased participation, personal responsibility, and academic achievement.

Table P.2.
Developmental Therapy–Developmental Teaching Parallels Theories About Stages of Personality Development

Erikson's Stages of Psychosocial Development	Piaget's Stages of Cognitive Development	Typical Age When Stage Ends	Developmental Therapy–Developmental Teaching Stages and Goals		Associated Developmental Anxiety
Intimacy versus isolation	Dialectic reasoning	Young adult		Know personal reality in relations with others	Search for personal identity
Identity versus role diffusion	Late formal operations / Formal operations (abstract thinking)	About age 16	Stage Five	Apply individual and group skills in new situations	Search for role identity as independent person
Industry versus inferiority	Transition: late concrete to early formal operations	About age 12	Stage Four	Invest in group membership	Conflict between need for independence and for others' approval
Initiative versus guilt	Concrete operations	About age 9	Stage Three	Achieve skills for success in peer group	Guilt for failing to measure up to others' expectations
Autonomy versus shame and doubt	Preoperations	About age 6	Stage Two	Respond with success	Personal inadequacy and punishment by powerful forces
Trust versus mistrust	Sensorimotor	About 18 months	Stage One	Respond with pleasure and trust	Abandonment and deprivation by others

encompass psychosocial and cognitive skills in successive phases of human development. Each individual's pattern for acquiring these skills reflects a unique cultural, familial, emotional, and developmental history. Therefore, standards must be age appropriate, reflect the cultural values of their families and communities, and match their individual stages of development.

Teachers, parents, and peers play key roles in the lives of children. They shape a child's learning, behavior, personality, and emotions in intensely interrelated ways at each age and stage of development. Institutions outside of school and home, government policies, law enforcement, community recreation, religious affiliations, health services, and childcare also contribute to the persons children are and the persons they will become. When learning environments at school, at home, and in the community reflect this interrelationship by using developmentally and emotionally appropriate behavior management and instruction, the outcomes are increased student competence in learning and greater personal responsibility for behavior.

In this new edition, the central theme concerns teaching students social and emotional competence to achieve responsible behavior for success in school. The approach is to use strategic instructional strategies carefully matched with the individual's unique needs at every stage of development.

Each chapter contains a topic that is essential to this mission. Chapter 1 introduces typical and troubled children in three age groups: early childhood, elementary school age, and teens. These brief vignettes portray authentic children with very real problems and with behaviors that are familiar to most teachers and parents. Their individual characteristics and stages of development shape the way they learn. These descriptions are used for the content in the chapters that follow. Chapter 1 ends with a summary of how this approach contributes to planning for a tiered system of school-wide management with a positive learning climate for all students—those who are troubled, those whose conduct presents discipline problems, those with severe emotional or behavioral disabilities, and those at risk.

The focus in Chapter 2 is on snapshots of how we use Developmental Therapy–Developmental Teaching with children and teens at each age and stage of development. The snapshots summarize general learning goals for each stage of development and specify the competencies students need to achieve these goals. Also included in the summaries are learning characteristics, central concerns, anxieties, and values that motivate students in different ways as they mature. Students in each age group have changing views of authority, and they go about problem solving in different ways. Their education must be responsive to their individuality, age- and stage-related needs, their family and cultural backgrounds, and their developmental accomplishments. Each snapshot concludes with information about how teachers' instructional practices are matched with students' developmental and learning characteristics. The applications are relevant for students who are developing typically, for those who are troubled or at risk, and for those with serious delays in social, emotional, or behavioral development.

Chapter 3 contains practical details for obtaining a comprehensive functional assessment of a student's social, emotional, and behavioral competencies as the basis for teaching responsible behavior. The manifest indicators of these competencies are contained in two assessment tools: the *S–E–B Quick Profile* and the *Developmental Teaching Objectives Rating Form–Revised* (DTORF–R). These measurement instruments are included on CDs at the back of this book. These instruments provide reliable and valid information about each student's individual learning differences and are the basis for planning specific interventions. For students in special education, this information becomes part of an Individualized Education Program (IEP), Individualized Family Service Plan (IFSP), or Individual Transition Plan (ITP).

This assessment system is used for assessing behavior, communication, socialization, and thinking competencies of children from birth to age 16, and can be used for completing a functional behavioral assessment (FBA) and a behavioral intervention plan (BIP). Detailed rating and scoring directions are provided, along with an example of how the assessment is used to identify instructional objectives, to plan effective instructional interventions, and to document student outcomes. The chapter ends with information about how validity and reliability were established for the DTORF–R.

Chapter 4 extends comprehensive assessment into areas that are present, but unseen, in every student. This process, called *decoding behavior,* is essential for understanding how learning and behavior are influenced by forces that are not always observable. Decoding is a way to understand what a student's words and actions signal about his or her unique needs. The first section describes several unseen resources to stimulate learning and responsible behavior: *mental energy, emotional memory,* and *motivating values.* The second section reviews ways individuals attempt to maintain psychological defenses against stress and anxiety and how these defenses effect learning and behavior. Topics include *developmental anxieties, defense mechanisms,* and *maintaining emotional balance.* A separate section follows with a focus on the *existential crisis* and how students' views of authority and responsibility change as they develop. There is a discussion of *group dynamics,* which can dominate behavior in a classroom. This includes students' roles in a group, their forms of social power, and ways to change group dynamics for an improved psychological climate in the classroom. At the end of the chapter, there is a summary form for combining the DTORF–R assessment results from the previous chapter with information gained through decoding as you plan an individual student's program.

Strategic behavior management strategies are described in Chapter 5. Use this chapter as a guide when selecting interventions for the students in your classroom. The first topic is an overview using a developmental frame of reference to help determine how much independence students at varying ages should be given for making behavioral choices—with the freedom of choice to succeed or fail on their own. The overview also provides a quick summary chart for selecting and modifying specific strategies for each age group. The second section is a review of widely used management strategies familiar to most educators and parents. It describes how each strategy can be applied for maximum effectiveness. There is a discussion of the issues of punishment, rewards, and when to ignore misbehavior. The chapter ends with a summary of specific applications for students who have severe behavioral problems associated with thought disorders, passive aggression, physical aggression, and violence.

Chapter 6 extends the topic of behavior management to focus on talking with young or developmentally delayed students to help them learn to manage their feelings and to behave in ways that bring about the results they desire. This chapter describes how to teach them to use words instead of actions to deal with frustration and crises in positive ways. This process is the *abbreviated* LSCI, which is an adaptation of the widely used *Life Space Crisis Intervention* (LSCI), simplified for students who have not yet developed the necessary readiness skills for benefiting from LSCI. The chapter outlines the three-part process and provides a guide to determine when to use the abbreviated form rather than the full LSCI. There is a section that describes how this process also becomes a strategy for teaching specific DTORF–R learning objectives for students in Stages One or Two, preparing them for future participation in a full LSCI. Specific examples illustrate how to conduct an abbreviated LSCI and what to look for in each phase. The transcript of an actual situation with sobbing, inconsolable 5-year-old Sam is provided at the end of the chapter.

Chapter 7 is organized around core knowledge and skills needed by teachers to maintain a developmentally and emotionally healthy learning environment in general or special education. The first section reviews phases of skill development for teachers (and student teachers), lead and support teachers as a team, teachers' power to influence students' actions, personal characteristics that shape the teacher's effectiveness, and how teachers gain needed skills.

In the last section, there is a description of two tools for teachers to use independently when learning to apply the specified practices—the DTRITS and *PEGS for Teachers.* The DTRITS is a reliable and valid rating inventory for teachers to check themselves on their use of specified practices. It also can be used to document proficiencies of teachers in applying the practices. Separate versions—for teachers in Birth-to-three programs, early childhood programs, elementary school, and middle school—are included in the CD at the back of this book.

PEGS for Teachers is a series of three interactive programs on CD-ROM offering simulation games for teachers to experiment with different intervention strategies for responding to challenging behaviors of student characters during typical school activities.

Chapter 8 explains how to begin using the practices described in the previous chapters in your classroom. There are two important issues to consider before you begin: how your beliefs about teaching fit with this approach, and a realistic appraisal of how much change these practices will require of you. This discussion is followed by a general review of basic content for getting started with students of any age or stage of development in any educational setting.

There are specific planning guidelines about how to use assessment and observational information about your students, establish learning objectives, group students for strategic instruction, plan lessons that target the objectives, choose learning content and materials to target objectives, unify lessons around a central theme, use reading and writing lessons to accelerate competence, and structure teaching for an effective lesson. The chapter ends with suggestions about how you might extend developmental practices school wide. Although the chapter focuses specifically on applications in general and special education classrooms, the same processes apply in childcare and community mental health settings. Parents who are home schooling also should find useful applications.

In Chapter 9, there are summaries of several scientifically based research studies that resulted in recognition of this approach as an "Educational Program that Works" by the U.S. Department of Education. These studies provide evidence of progress made by students receiving Developmental Therapy–Developmental Teaching. There are also summaries of the gains in classroom skills made by the teachers and teaching assistants who participated in in-service training to use this approach.

A section with additional studies reports the sustainability of students' gains one and two years after the intervention, and briefly reviews a study involving the training of university interns who received the same inservice training as the teachers. The chapter ends with performance data from replication sites. The cumulative results add to the growing body of evidence about significant, positive effects of this approach on teachers' skills and on the progress made by the students they teach.

There is an Epilogue to describe an encouraging international consortium that is networking to improve the education of troubled children and youth worldwide. With it comes a vision of greater opportunities for educational excellence across boundaries. By forming institutes that offer access to information and training in Developmental Therapy–Developmental Teaching, educators and parents can learn and then adapt the practices to local cultures, languages, and educational standards. This international movement has been accelerated with formation of the Institute for Developmental Therapy–Developmental Teaching–Europe (Institut fuer Entwicklungstherapie/Entwicklungspaedagogik—ETEP–Europe) and the Developmental Therapy Institute–USA. As a result, locally adapted Developmental Therapy–Developmental Teaching practices are becoming increasingly inclusive and highly effective for the education of troubled students with behavioral problems and mental health needs.

At the end of this revised edition, you will find a CD that contains the instruments we use in evaluating program effectiveness. These measurement tools, with established reliability and validity, provide a way to evaluate and document (a) student outcomes, (b) teachers' skills in implementing the specified practices, and (c) the extent of administrative support for a program. The CD can be downloaded and duplicated.

We encourage you to use these instruments to conduct your own field research. The need for research continues to be an urgent priority. Questions remain about how students' experiences at school and outside of school—past and present—shape their academic achievement and conduct. Also, little is known about how the size and membership of instructional groups affect students' performance. Other questions remain about the effect of teachers' personality and behavioral variables on students' performance. The questions are legion! Every well-conducted research study adds to the expanding knowledge base. For all of us, greater understanding continues to be the goal as we assist young people of all ages to gain social and emotional competence and responsible behavior.

M. M. Wood
C. A. Quirk
F. L. Swindle

Acknowledgments

Two very special individuals, Betty Tate DeLorme and Debbie Huth at the University of Georgia, helped birth this revised edition. They are the anchors that held our team together when the intensity of workloads, deadlines, and competing demands for training in this country and abroad pulled us in many other directions. Without their steadfast belief in the value of the effort and their enthusiasm for Developmental Therapy–Developmental Teaching, this book would still be a work in progress. Their vision of its potential is evident throughout the manuscript. With a commitment to supporting teachers, parents, foster parents, and grandparents, they helped us see new ways to extend beyond a focus on schools and classrooms. In a very real way, this is their book.

The history of the Developmental Therapy–Developmental Teaching movement is a story of individual talents, shared vision, and team efforts. Those who contributed to past editions are recognized again in the appendix of this revision because each successive version has built on their work. Among that group are those who continue to provide current leadership for technical assistance, program evaluation, preservice teacher preparation, and in-service staff development for this approach. These include Dr. George Andros, Dr. Marita Bergsson, Dr. Dan Burns, Carolyn Combs, Dr. Susan Galis-White, Dorothy Hollenbeck, Betty Martin, Dr. Bonnie McCarty, Rosalie McKenzie, Dr. William Swan, Geraldine Williams, Sara Williams, and Wanda Wright. The results of their contributions have been a steady expansion of knowledge and applications about how to provide the best possible education for troubled children and youth.

To these gifted individuals, a new group is added: certified Regional Trainers for Developmental Therapy–Developmental Teaching. They are providing in-service training and demonstration programs to improve the quality and expand the pool of skilled teachers and other service providers in many state and local programs. These Regional Trainers include Judith Bondurant-Utz, Patricia Copeland, Adrea Criste, Sandra Davis, Helen Eberlein, Cynthia Edwards, Andrea Gillen, Barry Ginnis, Kim Henderson, Kelley Simmons-Jones, Scott Jones, Linda Middleton, Billie Navojosky, Mary Perkins, Pam Spinner, Suzan Wambold, and Wendy Watts.

From this impressive talent, we have lost several dearly treasured friends and dedicated colleagues. These include Larry Beye, Charleen Cain, Karen Davis, Bonnie Eninger, Julie Hendrick, and Joey Thomas. Their superb skills when teaching troubled children and their vast knowledge about Developmental Therapy–Developmental Teaching were only surpassed by their life-long commitment to improving the lives of children. Each has left a profound mark.

The support and collaborative teamwork of those at the University of Georgia have made this expanded demonstration and outreach possible. In particular, Dr. Sharon Nickols, Dean of the College of Family and Consumer Sciences, Dr. Gordhan Patel, Vice President for Research, and colleagues in their offices have been hugely supportive in making university resources available to continue the research and development efforts. In our own office, Kim Bradley and Tangela Bernius have made invaluable contributions to our continuing field research efforts. Similarly, the Georgia Department of Education provided a level of professional collaboration that exemplifies what coordinated efforts can produce for the benefit of students and their teachers. Additionally, John O'Connor and Susan McKenzie, with the Georgia State Improvement Grant (SIG) and the Georgia Psychoeducational Services Network continue to be invaluable sources for guidance with their insights and leadership.

Acknowledgments would not be complete without recognition of the lively artistic contributions to this edition by Arlette Revells at Great Works Creation in Athens, Georgia and by Kendra Bradley, Dave Smellie, and Adrienne Robson on the art staff at LetterPress Software, Inc. in North Logan, Utah. Guidance from the publishing staff at PRO-ED has also been of immense help. Their belief in the value of Developmental Therapy–Developmental Teaching has continued since 1986—a remarkably lengthy association. In particular, Kathy Synatschk, Chris Anne Worsham, Dolly Jackson, and Sue Carter provided the encouragement and vision that brought this new edition into being.

Without grant support provided by the U.S. Department of Education's Office of Special Education Programs and the Georgia Department of Education to build an exemplary demonstration and outreach program for children and youth with severe emotional and behavioral disabilities, Developmental Therapy–Developmental Teaching would not stand today as a recognized "program that works."

Finally, we gratefully acknowledge the contributions made by teachers, parents, students, and professional colleagues, nationally and internationally, who are part of the ever expanding circle of effort to improve educational opportunities for all children.

M. M. Wood
C. A. Quirk
F. L. Swindle

Students and the Competencies They Need

In order for us to nurture our children's diverse talents and interests and to provide them with the greatest chance of future success and fulfillment, individualized and personalized treatment must itself be a standard in educational practice, and the concept of fairness in education must reflect the reality of idiosyncrasy.

Theodore Sizer (2004, p. 209)
Professor Emeritus, Brown University
Visiting Professor of Education, Harvard and Brandeis Universities

Teaching and learning have the same end goal for students: meeting the expectations set by others while fulfilling their own needs in satisfying ways. This is the task for acquiring responsible behavior—changing at every age and stage of life. It is not an easy task to learn, especially for those who lack social, emotional, or behavioral competence. For them, success seems to slip further and further away as they become increasingly challenging to teach or difficult to discipline. These students are found in every classroom and at every age. They come from all socioeconomic groups, races, religions, and educational backgrounds. They may or may not have mental health problems but their lack of social and emotional skills affects the way they behave, communicate, relate, think, and learn.

This chapter begins with brief introductions to children from preschool through high school, whose actions are familiar to most teachers. The characteristics of these troubled children and their needs for instruction are described. There is also a discussion of social and emotional competence as a foundation for responsible behavior. A section follows with an overview of the Developmental Therapy–Developmental Teaching practices that address these needs. The chapter ends with a summary of how this approach can be expanded in a school-wide effort for increased competence and responsibility of students through prevention, targeted, or intensive intervention programs.[1]

Focus on the Students

The young people introduced in this section represent a range of life experiences,[2] competencies, and challenging behaviors for their teachers. These students are trying to express, in whatever way possible, their own needs, thoughts, and feelings, while also responding to the expectations of others to be successful in school. To do this, they need social and emotional competencies as well as thinking skills. If their teachers know how to help them accomplish

[1] The term *therapy* may be unsettling to some educators. However, when used in a *teaching* context, Developmental Therapy–Developmental Teaching refers to educational practices based on theories about how personality develops, how competence can be expanded, and how the mental health of children and youth can be maintained and strengthened by strategic instruction.

[2] As you continue through the book, refer back to these case studies to practice applying developmentally based teaching methods.

this, disruptive behavior decreases and participation increases, which, in turn, bring about increasingly responsible behavior and success in school.

Meet Several Preschool Children

Belinda—Age 3

A shy, cautious girl, Belinda spends much of her time watching other children in her group. When she sees them doing something that interests her, she comes closer to their activities and watches or plays by herself nearby. She likes puzzles and the toys in the homemaking area, especially the baby dolls and stuffed animals. Her play is imaginative and she often pretends to read to the dolls. In group activities, she seldom volunteers or answers adults' questions. But when she is by herself with an adult she speaks quietly and spontaneously about her dolls at home. She also talks about her grandmother's cats and the good things Grandma cooks for her.

Her grandmother has taken care of Belinda since birth. Grandmother does the cooking and housekeeping for the family. Belinda's mother is an emergency room nurse who works long shifts. Her father is a retired policeman with a work-related disability. Belinda's father is interested in her doing well at home and at school. He encourages her reading by spending time talking about picture books with her. He also takes her to the public library for a storytelling program every Saturday. She seems to miss time with her mother and cries for her when she goes to bed before her mother gets home from work.

Before she began preschool this year, Belinda's grandmother insisted on her taking daily afternoon naps. She still tires easily around noon, and frequently falls asleep during rest time at school. Around other children she is shy and cautious. Her parents report no serious discipline problems with her, except that she cries when corrected. Generally, they tell her "no" when she is not allowed to do something, and she will do what she is told. Sometimes they use time-out, but never spank her, and they rarely need to raise their voices to her.

Leon—Age 3

Leon is a very thin child who lives with a foster family. He is enrolled in a childcare program several days a week. When he arrives, he looks for his favorite toy—a fuzzy bear—and then wanders around the room, clutching the bear. The teachers have never heard him speak. When they come close to him, he hugs the bear and looks away. When distressed, he makes strange sounds that no one understands. He does the same thing when other children come close, so they ignore him. The teachers are very concerned. He is not interested in any activity, and does not appear to be developing like a typical 3-year-old. When Leon is afraid, he will slowly rock back and forth and begin pacing. When he hears loud voices or noise, he looks startled, covers his ears, and makes strange sounds of distress. He seems to have impaired memory, gets confused easily, is extremely withdrawn, and has the physical appearance of a child about 18 months old. He rarely talks at home, and when he is corrected, he will cover his ears and scream in a high pitch. He then begins rocking back and forth, still screaming.

The health department records show that Leon's mother had a history of alcohol and cocaine use at the time of his birth. His father is unknown. A visiting nurse instructed his mother on how to bathe and feed Leon, but he did not thrive. Over the course of several visits, the nurse became concerned about the lack of healthy food and cleanliness in the trailer where Leon and his mother lived with several other unrelated adults. The nurse also reported that the infant appeared neglected, and his mother seemed to be unable to care for him. Since that time, his mother has found a part-time job and is also occasionally attending an alcohol rehabilitation program. However, there was concern that Leon was being abused by his mother's visiting male friends, and he was recently placed with a foster family.

Ann—Age 4

A bright, outgoing child, Ann participates in Head Start group activities with enthusiasm and follows directions carefully. She entertains other children in her group with storytelling and likes to pretend to be the teacher. She also has made friends with children in the kindergarten classes. On the playground she sets the pace for the games and tells the other children what to do. Sometimes they complain about her being "bossy." However, when another child is upset, Ann responds with sympathy and concern. She is among the first children to finish a task and wants to show her work to everyone else. If the other children are not interested in her work or fail to admire what she has done, Ann turns to the teachers for reassurance. Her favorite activity at school is Storytelling Time.

Ann's mother is an office manager, and her father is in the Army, stationed in Europe. Ann has an older sister in the fourth grade and a brother in sixth grade. Ann's sister has taken great interest in caring for her since her birth, and spends time reading to her and playing school with her. Her brother is protective and includes her in some of his backyard sports like T-ball. She can ride a small bike, jump rope, walk a balance beam, and swing by herself. Last summer, she participated in a community swimming program and has almost learned to swim alone.

Cayla—Age 4

Cayla's severe temper tantrums upset her teachers and the other children. When she cannot have her way, she screams or cries for long periods of time. The more attention she gets, the more she screams. Ignoring her at these times does not seem to work either. Nothing seems to make her stop until a teacher takes her outside the door where she can see what she is missing in the room. Cayla often says she needs for her mother to call. She seeks approval and assistance in every activity and constantly gets up to find a teacher who will admire her work. Any criticism upsets her, and she responds by complaining that her stomach hurts or that she has a fever and needs to go home. When group activities begin, she insists on sitting by the teacher and being first to have a turn. She seldom listens to directions and then pouts when the teachers remind her about how she must do a task. On the playground, she stays by herself or stands close to the adults. She refuses to eat the food at lunch and brings snacks from home. Cayla is most attentive and easiest to manage during Storytelling Time.

During Cayla's first 2 years of life, her mother attended school while her grandmother cared for Cayla. After her grandmother's death, Cayla was enrolled in the first of four different childcare programs. Her mother travels frequently on business and is gone several days each week. Cayla's aunt, who watches her at night when her mother is away, says that Cayla cries herself to sleep most nights, calling for her mother. She has frequent nightmares and occasionally sleepwalks. Now she is also becoming increasingly difficult to manage, with more angry outbursts and tantrums.

Brad—Age 5

Brad is a handful for his parents and teachers at his kindergarten. He tries to be the center of attention in every activity. Teachers report that he talks constantly and cannot sit still or stick to any activity for long. Impulsive and unpredictable, Brad uses obscene language and is abusive to the other children. Many of them are afraid of what he does and try to stay away from him. Recently his teacher found him attempting to poke a pencil down the throat of the pet rabbit in the classroom. The "Time Out" chair does not seem to be effective with him. When he was sent there for smearing paint across another child's work, he exploded violently and threw the chair at another child.

According to his teachers, Brad seems most interested in school activities when using the computer or when allowed to spend time alone with picture books. During storytelling time, he also becomes thoroughly engaged, sitting quietly and attentively. He is the first to answer questions about the story and its characters. He also tries to be first in role play with the story.

His mother warned the teachers that "He'll give you trouble. He's not like his sister, who is an angel and a blessing from heaven." His father brags about Brad's older sister's achievements and calls her "my honey," while joking about Brad as "the monster from hell that we found under a rock somewhere." His mother claims Brad inherited his "rough ways" from his father's side of the family and she is worried about his "mean streak." She described his attempts to strangle a neighbor's puppy and set fire to a cat. She is apologetic about his behavior and expresses concern that it is all her fault.

Brad usually refuses to eat what is prepared and screams at his parents if they come into his room. His mother says that no punishment works. His father has used harsh discipline, denying him food for the day while making him sit tied in a chair, watching the family eat their meals. His father has also made him run laps around the house for an hour and then locked him in his room. When Brad's behavior "pushes me over the edge," his father reports that he spanks him and then locks him in his room.

Carlos—Age 5

Carlos is a quiet boy from the Hispanic community where English is a second language. He has been in the Head Start program for several months now and seems unsure of himself. The teachers find him to be attentive but shy and hesitant to volunteer his ideas. He follows the rules, and responds carefully to directions from adults. His teachers are having a hard time identifying his real interests. He is difficult to motivate and they are not sure if he understands what is expected of him. Sometimes it seems that he deliberately resists participating and pretends to be confused. They are also concerned that he often seems to be daydreaming. Although he seldom participates spontaneously in class, on the playground he shows leadership skills and seems to have the respect of the other boys. His teachers hope that he will begin to make friends among the other children.

Carlos is the oldest of three boys. The youngest baby was born recently, and Carlos expressed great pride in showing the baby to his teachers. His family shares a home with the family of his father's brother, who has four children. Two of these children are in elementary school and two are in high school. Carlos' mother speaks no English, and his father is a silent man who speaks with a heavy accent and limited English vocabulary. The seven children sleep in the same room and get along reasonably well, according to Carlos' father. The two teenagers are responsible for supervising the younger children, maintaining discipline, and directing the work given to the children at home.

According to his parents, Carlos was an easy baby to raise. He seldom needs discipline and obeys quietly. They say he does not like to go to bed at night, preferring to stay up and watch TV with his parents and older cousins. At a recent parent–teacher conference, his teachers noticed that his ways of speaking and relating to others are quite like that of his father. His parents want Carlos to do well in school and are concerned that his recent readiness test scores show that he is behind the other children in his group, especially in reading and writing.

Meet Several Students in Elementary School

Marcus—in 3rd Grade

A bright, eager student, Marcus is 9 years old. He is quiet in class and respectful toward adults. His above-average abilities and good study skills are reflected in his grades. He has been on the school honor roll for 2 years. Marcus responds more quickly to teachers than he does to other students. Occasionally, he volunteers a comment and participates in group activities if the teacher organizes them. His teachers recommended that he be tested for possible enrollment in an accelerated academic program, but when the results were discussed with his parents, they chose to keep him in his current classes. They believe Marcus needs time for his independent musical interests. They also expressed the hope that he would become interested in school sports as a way to make friends. On the playground, Marcus tends to go off by himself or stands alone to watch when other children play games. But when invited to join in, he responds as a good team player. He has complained about the behavior of children who ride the school bus with him, and frequently asks his parents to take him to school.

Marcus' family spends time with him on his homework and encourages his musical interests. They say he is a well-behaved child, and usually does what is asked of him. They reward him with plenty of attention and support. His entire family is musical, and Marcus shows similar interest and talent for playing the piano. His parents are active volunteers in school programs.

Clint—in 4th Grade

A restless 9½-year-old, Clint has the best attendance record at school. He has attended the same elementary school since kindergarten. His steady academic progress is reflected in excellent grades in all subjects. However, reports from his teachers contain numerous statements of concern about his conduct. He attends a class each day for gifted and talented students in creative writing, but is not doing well. He tries to be the center of attention. His teachers report that he talks constantly and cannot sit still or stay at his desk. Impulsive and unpredictable, Clint uses obscene language and is verbally abusive to the other students. Many of them are afraid of him and try to ignore him. He argues with the teachers and tries to tell them how to conduct lessons. Yet he seldom finishes assigned work and has not completed a homework assignment this year. Last year, he was suspended briefly for threatening other children. Recently, he exploded violently toward a teacher, knocking everything from her desk, throwing her chair, and storming out of the room, shouting that she was incompetent and stupid. His parents met with the principal the next day and blamed the school for failing to provide a challenging program for him.

After that episode, his mother took him to a private counseling center for a psychiatric and educational consultation. A meeting has been scheduled at school for his mother, teachers, and the school's special services team to review the results and to plan an individualized education program. Clint's mother described him as "Hard to love, hard to discipline, headstrong, and willful." She had hoped for a girl when he was born because "Girls are fun to raise." However, she speaks with pride about his "giftedness" and previous achievement record. She would like to see the school offer year-round programs and is quick to blame Clint's current difficulties on the school's lack of attention to his needs and talents. Two years ago a baby sister was born. This caused Clint considerable conflict. He talks about taking care of the baby, who "screams a lot." His parents separated last year, and Clint spends weekends with his father. According to Clint, the baby stays with their mother because his father thinks the baby is "disgusting." Clint tells his teachers about the adult movies he sees with his father every weekend. He also speaks with anger about his mother's friends who "hang out at the house all the time." A divorce is now pending, and there is so much anger between the parents that they refuse to talk to each other. They only communicate through Clint. Both parents actively try to do whatever Clint wants and attempt to outdo each other in meeting his demands. They rejected counseling as a means to help Clint adjust to their separation.

Brenda—in 4th Grade

Among the most outgoing students in the school, Brenda has just turned 10 years old. Her friendly but independent attitudes toward adults and other children make her well liked by all. In her 4th-grade class she works casually on her assignments, preferring instead to visit with other children. This gets her in trouble with her teachers. They encourage her to take more time and be more careful with her classwork, but her grades reflect her difficulty staying on task. Brenda's parents are convinced that she should go to college, and put her on restriction when she brings home bad grades. She responds by vowing to study harder. She has also found several friends who help her out with difficult assignments; they have started exchanging notes frequently in class.

Alice—in 4th Grade

The teachers are very concerned about Alice. Almost 11 years old, but small for her age, she does not seem to listen in class and rarely participates spontaneously. In class, she fidgets constantly. She often looks off into space with a blank expression. She seldom speaks. When teachers speak to her or come close, she twitches and looks away. She also whispers sounds that no one understands. Alice does the same thing when other children come close to her, so they ignore her. She has received special education services each year since 2nd grade. She can now read basic primary words and sentences, write simple sentences, and do basic addition and subtraction computations. She responds to comforts like soothing sounds, food, and materials that are gently arousing. When she is stressed, her instinct is to withdraw or whisper to herself. Her teachers are concerned because of her inability to remember and her resistance to participating.

When Alice was about 3 years old, Protective Services reported concern about her extensive bruises and a dislocated shoulder. After that, her mother voluntarily put Alice in foster care. At that time Alice was poorly nourished and using baby talk. Her foster parents are concerned about her development. She never shows emotion about her mother's absence and displays no reaction to pain when she hurts herself or goes to the doctor for shots. The whereabouts of her mother are unknown at present.

Amy—in 5th Grade

One of the youngest students in the 5th grade, 10-year-old Amy complains frequently to the teachers that she has a headache from staying up so late at night and needs to go home. Her grades indicate difficulties with subjects every year, especially reading. Her report cards consistently contain unsatisfactory grades and notes from teachers about her need to work harder and to do her homework. In class, she struggles unsuccessfully to keep up with the assignments, and tries to hide her failing efforts from the other children. Her teachers have found her copying from other children's work, which she vigorously denies. She has also accused other children of copying her work. Amy seeks approval and assistance from teachers for every task she works on and constantly gets up to find the teacher. When group activities begin, she often asks to visit the restroom. At other times, she asks to visit the school counselor or the front office, where she expresses concern that she may have a fever. She complains about the food at lunch and brings snacks from home and offers them to other children.

Amy's mother describes her as "just like other girls her age," but expresses concern about her occasional baby talk when she wants something. According to her mother, "Amy usually gets her way." Her mother worries that she will not be able to afford the things Amy needs and wants as she gets older. There is also concern about Amy "staying out of trouble with boys," the influence of TV on Amy's attitude about sex, and the amount of violence Amy has seen at home. Although eager to help Amy, her mother is also defensive about her own troubles and is emphatic that she has her own life to live.

Luisa—in 5th Grade

Luisa recently arrived in this country and has just celebrated her 11th birthday. Her teachers find her English to be somewhat limited but clear and concise. They describe her as hard working even though she is shy and unwilling to volunteer her ideas. She follows school rules and responds carefully to directions from teachers while frowning frequently. Her academic achievement is generally at 4th grade levels, except in math, in which she excels. Homework seems to be a problem for her, and her incomplete or incorrect work appears to embarrass her. Her teachers are having a difficult time identifying her real interests. Luisa hesitates to participate spontaneously in class, but on the playground she talks freely with other students. At a recent parent–teacher conference, her teachers noticed that Luisa's shy ways of relating to others is quite like that of her mother. Although Luisa's mother appears to be concerned about her daughter's grades, her own difficulties with English make it hard for her to be of help to Luisa.

Tony—in 5th Grade

Slow-moving, 11-year-old Tony has no friends and seeks none. At school he fails to do homework. He never turns in assignments or makes up work he has missed. His teachers believe that he is capable but irresponsible and unmotivated. When asked about his failure to complete assignments, he simply shrugs and says he did not do it. He prefers to be alone, makes negative comments about the other children, and never participates in group activities. A few months ago Tony was suspended briefly for bringing razor blades to school. During that time, neighbors reported him to the police for wandering in the neighborhood at night attempting to steal from garages and mailboxes. Lately, his attendance at school has dropped to a few days a week, and his anti-social behavior outside of school is increasing.

Tony lives with his parents, one younger brother, and one teenage brother. His father retired early on disability and is at home most of the time. They are part of a large, extended family in a predominantly Hispanic community. There have been numerous deaths in the immediate family recently. Both of his grandparents, with whom Tony was close, died within a year of each other. His mother's younger sister was killed in a car accident the previous year. This event was a great tragedy for the family and the community. Because of concern about Tony's continuing preoccupation with violence and death, and on the recommendation of their family's priest, his mother took him to the neighborhood mental health clinic.

Tony told the counselor that his dog and a close friend both died during the past year. He also talked repeatedly about his father's heart attack. Before this event, Tony says he felt safer, because they could "handle trouble" together. Now he sees himself as having to protect his mother and younger brother. He is also concerned about gang violence and people breaking into their home. His mother believes that these concerns are too difficult for him to handle and he simply "shuts down." Tony's mother tells the school counselor that he is now refusing to go to school. He locks himself in the bedroom when friends or family visit. She says he talks constantly about the violence he has seen at school and around the neighborhood. She also reports that his older brother receives threatening phone calls, but she doesn't know why.

Tony expressed negative attitudes toward his teachers and the school. He said the classes were boring and too crowded. He also was concerned because other students "are always watching me." He mentioned feeling sick at his stomach frequently, being tired, and having sweaty hands. He also has bad dreams and worries about what his mother would think when he gets into trouble. A consulting psychiatrist prescribed medication to relieve symptoms of depression and disoriented thinking. At first Tony appeared to be more relaxed, but now he refuses to take the medications because he does not like the way they make him feel.

Meet Several High School Students

Aleesa—Age 15

Aleesa is a straight "A" student. Teachers are pleased to have her in their classes. They report that she is always willing to help. If there is a group project, she is reliable. She helps other students get involved, and the project gets done. Aleesa is clearly a leader with many friends from diverse backgrounds. She was selected to be a junior varsity cheerleader. She is also in student government and secretary of her class. This is a big honor. The school has a service club, where she is active. Club members visit a nursing home two Saturdays each month.

The guidance counselor has this to say about Aleesa: "I don't see her often, except when we have student government meetings. She knows how to be a good member. She doesn't have a lot to say, but when she speaks up, she usually gets the attention of the other council members. I think she is a very positive influence for the standards of conduct we try to maintain in this school. I remember one time when she was quite outspoken about some of the bullying that was going on. I think our student government had a lot to do with turning that problem around. Now there are very few problem kids trying to dump their own feelings on others."

A close friend describes Aleesa with genuine admiration this way: "When I first met Aleesa I just wanted to hang out with her because she always had a lot of guys hanging around her. But then I found out that she is a really nice person, and we've been friends ever since. It doesn't matter how pretty she is; it's her personality. She never says anything mean about anybody, and she's nice to people of every race."

Other girls in her classes speak about Aleesa this way: "She's a lot of fun. We go to the movies together and spend the night at each other's houses on the weekends. Aleesa's there for you if you get stressed out, and she can always see a good side to things, no matter how awful."

Boys in her classes talk about Aleesa this way: "Some girls act like they can't stand you. Aleesa's not one of them. She always seems interested and she's easy to talk to. Sometimes she is too straight, and mostly, she keeps her ideas to herself. But if she doesn't like what someone is doing, or disagrees with what you've said, she lets you know it—without making you feel stupid."

Aleesa describes her own life this way: "My parents divorced when I was in fourth grade, but they are on friendly terms. I see my dad on weekends, but that sometimes gets unpleasant. He has his own ideas about dress code and curfew hours. He doesn't understand that there has to be some give and take in high school. He has a lady friend he wants me to like. She's not the type I would choose, but he's the one who has to live with her. My mom seems to understand me better. She gives good advice and encourages me. Mom also sticks to her rules, which I don't mind. When we have arguments, she'll listen, but she also tells it like she sees it. She's sort of like a sister. I wish I had a brother and sister. I think both of my parents are proud of me and expect me to go to college. I don't know how they can afford it. Maybe I can get a scholarship."

BB—Age 15

The math teacher describes BB this way: "I can't figure out BB. Last week he was in a rage and screamed at me for giving him a 'D.' The next minute he apologized and calmly asked if he could discuss it with me. He wanted to do something to raise the grade to a 'C.' When I told him there was no extra credit offered, he snapped into a rage again. I had to call in a hall monitor to escort him to the principal's office. He threatened me with things like, 'You'll be sorry ...' and 'Just wait!' These incidents happen every week. He just can't seem to settle down. I talked with him about getting some help to manage his anger. He smiled, thanked me, and said he was seeing a counselor and was trying to get his life in order. I found out 2 weeks later that he hasn't tried to find help anywhere."

BB is a frequent visitor to the principal, who describes BB this way: "It seems that BB is in my office every day with a referral from a teacher. He's always in trouble for fighting kids and cursing teachers. I've been trying to talk with him about this problem. He apologizes and says he'll change, but after he started a schoolwide fight this week, I think he needs professional help. BB went up to one student and said,

'I think you're ugly!' The other guy said something back like, 'You're a jerk!' Then friends on both sides started shoving, and everyone else got into it."

The guidance counselor also has many concerns about BB: "He can't sit still when he comes into my office. He paces the floor and has a hard time staying on one subject. One minute he's all smooth smiles and agreeable. Then he jumps up because he doesn't like where the conversation is heading. A few times he opened up to me. He told me that his parents fought all the time and divorced when he was seven. He chose to live with his father because his father told him that if he lived with his mother 'She'll make you a sissy boy.' His father thinks he is doing a good job as BB's parent. BB says his dad 'roughs him up to make a man of him.' His father buys beer for him, to teach him 'how to drink like a man,' and his friends tell BB he has 'a cool dad.' But BB doesn't ever cross his dad because if he did his dad would beat him. He's learned to lie to stay out of trouble with his dad and still get his way."

His best friend is loyal but makes it clear that he does not want to make BB angry: "BB was a star on the baseball team, a great player and very popular. But one day at a game the umpire made a call he didn't like, and BB threw the bat, walked over to the guy, and started to scream at him. The guy yelled back, and BB picked up the bat and hit the umpire across the face. It broke his jaw. BB was kicked off the team, and our team has been losing ever since. BB's a cool guy to hang out with and he's one of my best friends, but I don't cross him! Most people are terrified of him, especially 'cause he's smart."

A friend of BB's girlfriend, Celeste, describes BB this way: "BB is very popular, with lots of friends. I guess that's why Celeste fell for him. She's always telling me about the romantic things he gave her when they first started seeing each other. I was jealous, but that faded when Celeste came over to my house with black and blue bruises on her face, saying that she and BB had gotten into a little fight. He's real nice with her until she gives in to him. Now he thinks he owns her, but Celeste doesn't see it. She tells me, 'He can be so sweet!'"

On one of his visits to the office, BB describes his own life to the principal: "I see my mother every now and then, but I don't stay long. She has a boyfriend—a jerk. He likes to pick fights with me. He makes sarcastic remarks like, 'Did you beat up anybody today?' So, I have to let him know he's going to get it, too, if he doesn't watch his mouth. Then he badmouths my dad with dumb remarks like, 'You're just like your old man—not worth much except to fight.' I'm not letting him get away with that!"

Caron—Age 16

Caron has average ability for academic work but is not living up to her potential. This year she is passing most of her classes, as compared with less than half of them last year. Her grades could be better, but she is not interested. Her attendance has improved, but she continues to be upset by the actions of others. Caron frequently asks to use the restroom during class discussions. She wants teachers to do things for her or to grant her special privileges. She does not seem to have any close friends, probably because she's so manipulative. She participates in class projects but quits if she cannot get her way. She usually ends up having her way, because she annoys everyone so much with her whining and complaining.

Caron received a psychoeducational evaluation 2 years ago for a possible learning disability when she appeared to be having problems listening, paying attention, and problem solving. However, the results indicated that she was not eligible for special education services at that time. The evaluation also indicated that although she has intellectual ability in the average range, her achievement in math calculations, math reasoning, and spelling are about 5 years behind that of her peers. After hearing these results, her grandparents got a tutor for her.

The guidance counselor reports on Caron's situation this way: "Caron is an only child who has lived with her grandparents for the past 8 years. Her mother killed herself when Caron was 4 years old. To my knowledge, she never sees her father. Nobody likes this girl. She borrows others' personal things, doesn't seem to bathe often, and eats all the time. She is constantly whining and trying to get other students to feel sorry for her. She talks about her mother's suicide to anyone who will listen. She sees a therapist weekly after school.

She is now taking medication for depression and tells me this is why she feels so bad and has such erratic behavior. Last year during spring break, she overdosed on the medications, 'to get high' and 'forget my problems.' I see her frequently because she drops in at my office and always seems to have some health concern. She complains about headaches, cramps, cold sweats, difficulty breathing, and numerous possible diseases."

A classmate describes Caron this way: "She uses her background to get attention and to get teachers to help her. She told them her dad tried to kill her mother, but I heard that her mother killed herself. Caron tries to get people to believe she's been abused and discriminated against. I think she's just a pathological liar. She tells crazy stories. Once she told me, 'I had surgery. One of my kidneys had to be removed. I gave it to a popular cheerleader last year.' Another time she said she was 'part royalty and related to the Duchess of Germany.'"

Caron describes her own life to the guidance counselor: "It's hard being me! I think I may have early diabetes. I can't sleep, and when I lie awake I think of why my mother killed herself. I try to make friends, but no one is nice to me. I don't know why. I do everything I can to be friendly. Maybe it's because I have to live with my grandparents and they're too old fashioned. They won't even let me stay home when I'm sick. And they won't let me watch my favorite TV shows very often. I'm thinking of going to acting school. I'd like to be on television, but they laugh at me. When I ask them for spending money they don't give it to me. They don't know how much clothes and makeup cost now. So the clothes I have to wear are gross. And the food is so terrible at school that I have to buy stuff at the store to eat at school. Sometimes I think I'll be just like my mother."

Victor—Age 16

Victor's homeroom teacher has this to say about him: "Sometimes I worry about Victor. He is a new student and so reserved that I can't tell whether he is really understanding the material or not. I don't think his low grades reflect what he really knows. He certainly tries in class. He completes assignments, although not always correctly, is attentive, and is always polite. He seems to hang back from getting involved with the others but responds to the students when they initiate exchanges with him. I noticed that in PE, the boys seem to have accepted him and seem eager to have him on their teams. I am concerned that Victor is falling behind in his studies. When I talked with the guidance counselor about him, she suggested that we have a parent conference to review the files from his previous school and plan ways to help Victor keep up with the class."

The guidance counselor also has concerns: "The standardized achievement test scores from Victor's previous schools indicate that he has steadily fallen behind a little each year since third grade. His test scores show that he has low–average ability and should be able to do the academic work, but it may take some additional tutoring. Our school has a mentoring program that might be able to provide this help. It may be that Victor also has some problems with English, because Spanish is the only language spoken at home. His parents have agreed to Victor's meeting with the teacher who has classes in English as a second language. We'll know more about how to help Victor after we meet with his mother."

One of the students in a literature class describes Victor: "He's okay. He doesn't say much, but that's not all bad. There are plenty of other guys who have too much to say. He knows how to stay out of trouble. Maybe girls like quiet types like Victor. He may be lucky that way."

Victor has this to say to the guidance counselor: "School's okay. There are some great guys here. The girls are pretty nice, too—most of them. Home? Well, they don't speak much English. They want me to be a good student. My mother and my father, they neither one went to school much. But they can read good in Spanish. They want me to go to college. That's a dream! I want to get a job."

Beth—Age 17

Beth's homeroom teacher describes her this way: "Beth is so quiet you hardly know she is in the room. She is an average student, is never a discipline problem, and tries hard to do what is asked of her. She has trouble in basic algebra and biology but is doing much better in American lit. She actually gets enthusiastic about some of the reading assignments. She does fairly acceptable book reviews but is still having a hard time with spelling and grammar, especially punctuation. She and I had a talk recently, and she opened up a bit about how concerned she is about graduating. Schoolwork seems to be really hard for her. We talked about spending more time on assignments, but she said she stays up until after midnight every night trying to get it all done. She seems chronically tired to me."

The guidance counselor is sympathetic but uncertain about how to help Beth. This is how she describes the situation: "Beth has an after-school job that seems to be interfering with her studies. She doesn't get off work until 9 o'clock. Then she comes home, too tired to put much effort into her assignments. She says she uses her study hall at school to start the work, but that isn't nearly enough time. We talked about dropping her job, but she says she has to work. Her single mother doesn't earn enough to support the two of them. Beth and I met with her mom to talk about how to help. Her mother expressed concern but said, 'Beth is how we keep food on the table.' Beth's mother talked about getting a better paying job but says she has to go back to school to do this. We discussed reducing Beth's course load, recognizing that it will take Beth longer to finish high school. Apparently Beth's mother wants her to graduate but thinks it is unlikely. 'It's hopeless. There's nothing we can do about it.'"

A girl in Beth's American literature class describes her this way: "I don't think I've ever seen Beth enjoying herself. She's okay to be around but not very interesting. She hangs around our group. I guess she needs friends, but she doesn't have much to talk about. Once she told us about how there was a robbery where she worked and how she almost got shot, and everyone was impressed. She wears clothes that are a put-off. No wonder she doesn't have any boyfriends."

When boys in her homeroom are asked about Beth, they say things like this: "Beth? Beth who? Oh, that one who always has her nose in her books. Yeah, her locker is near mine, but she never speaks or even looks over my way. You might say she has looks, but not with those old clothes she wears. And I don't know who she hangs out with."

Beth describes her own life this way: "I never have any fun. All I do is work. It would be nice to have a close friend—someone I can talk to. I don't know why I have all the bad luck. I guess I'm lucky to have a job, but the guys there make crude remarks to me. I'd like to slap them, but I know better. I had a boyfriend there for a while, but he started pushing me about sex and smokes and that sort of thing. No thanks!"

Jameel—Age 17

Jameel has never been a problem in class, but his lack of interest in his schoolwork and his lack of friends have started to worry his homeroom teacher. When he comes to school, which is infrequently, he sits and daydreams. He is failing all his classes now and claims he does not care. Jameel also talks about feeling useless and has mentioned suicide. He has shown his classmates scars on his wrist and says, "Nobody would care if I'm dead." His homeroom teacher suggested that he see the guidance counselor to discuss his problems.

The guidance counselor reports on Jameel's situation this way: "Jameel has a history of low achievement and absenteeism from school. Last year, a psychoeducational evaluation concluded that Jameel met eligibility criteria for special education services through the emotional/behavioral disordered program. The evaluation summary also indicated that he should be referred for mental health and psychiatric services. However, his mother never agreed to these recommendations. When I try to talk with Jameel, he is somewhat secretive, but he seems to want others to know how bad things are for him. He is aware of the difficulties he is having at school and describes the classes as 'boring, too crowded, and noisy.' He also feels that students are talking about him in the cafeteria and halls. Jameel has told other students that he has a police record, and he talks to me about his two arrests last year for buying drugs from a dealer who hangs out in his neighborhood. Apparently, he is trying to escape from his situation by solitary drinking and drug use. I've tried to contact his mother but can't reach her."

A student in one of his classes speaks about Jameel this way: "He is really freaky. Everyone is scared off by his weirdness. He never mentions school parties or sports or friends. He always talks about being worthless, and he's shown me scars where he says he cut himself. Jameel is drifting down to the hard-core drug users at school, but if you come up alongside of him and start talking, he's very responsive. I told him once, 'I'm on your side. You've been through hell.' He told me then that the only way he has fun is to cut himself. He probably does it for attention."

Jameel describes his own life to the guidance counselor: "Yeah, I know I'm not going to graduate. I have bad dreams. Sometimes my hands sweat a lot. My dad's in jail. My mom's at work all the time. I just do my own thing, and nobody bothers with me. If I'm not home when Mom gets back from work, she doesn't worry. She figures I'll get back sometime. She's so burned out. Once I got hired part time to help make hamburgers. I got some spare cash, but it didn't work out."

Troubled and Troubling Students— At School and at Home

Labels are not needed to recognize troubled[3] or potentially troubled students. Behavioral indicators, such as those in Figure 1.1, help to identify troubled students. Teachers may call these students difficult, lazy, unmotivated, anti-social, delinquent, hopeless, or a discipline problem. Their lack of responsiveness, failure to participate, or general disregard for educational activities cause their teachers enormous frustration. At home they are frequently hard to live with or difficult to reach. Parents anguish over what to do about their kids' unmanageable behavior, mood swings, defiant attitudes, or volatile emotions. Peers also use derogatory terms to describe them such as *mean, weird, off-the-edge, crazy, freaky, strange,* or *someone to stay away from.* With reputations like these, troubled students' positive attributes often go unnoticed and their constructive and acceptable behaviors are often overlooked because of the troubling effects of their disruptive behaviors.

Frequently, troubled students have labels such as disruptive, conduct problem, oppositional, defiant, reactive attachment disorder, anxiety or adjustment disorder, learning disability, communication disorder, substance abuse, attention-deficit/hyperactivity disorder (ADHD), schizophrenia, depression, Tourette's or Asperger's syndrome, autism, or other pervasive developmental disorders (Forness, Walker, & Kavale, 2003; Mattison, Gadow, Sprafkin, & Nolan, 2002; National Institute of Mental Health, 2000). Although the type of problems they exhibit may vary, it is widely recognized that they have academic deficits (Nelson, Benner, Lane, & Smith, 2004).

Some children and teenagers do not have clinical diagnoses but also have difficulty learning and adjusting to school. They need special assistance to continue to benefit from education.

[3]The term *troubled* is a reminder that the problems these children and teens generate for others are also major burdens to themselves. This term was first used in the ReEducation approach developed by Nicholas Hobbs and associates (1994).

- Talks or behaves like a much younger child
- Frequently unhappy, overly sensitive, sad, or irritable
- Very short attention span, restless, or hyperactive
- Listening difficulties
- Repetitive or unusual motions
- Impertinent, defiant, resentful, negative
- Avoids adults
- Unusual language
- Frequent temper tantrums or uncontrolled rages
- Sudden or pronounced change in behavior
- Harmful acts to other children or animals
- Extreme confusion or incoherence
- Evidence of substance abuse
- Sudden changes of academic grades
- Avoidance or abandonment of friends
- Angry or tearful outbursts
- Self-destructive behavior
- Inability to eat or sleep
- Overly concerned with own health or health of a loved one
- Giving away important possessions
- Depression
- Threat of suicide or preoccupation with suicide

FIGURE 1.1. Indicators of a troubled youngster at any age.

They may have educational labels such as emotional and behavioral disorder (EBD), emotional disturbance (ED), or severe emotional/behavioral disability (SED, SEBD; Bradley, Henderson, & Monfore, 2004; Cullinan, Evans, Epstein, & Ryser, 2003). Typically behind their peers in academic achievement, they are frequently identified with learning disabilities (Forness, 2005). Some have designations of externalized or internalized behavioral characteristics (Achenbach, 1992; Kaiser, Hancock, Cai, Foster, & Hester, 2000; Nelson, Babyak, Gonzalez, & Benner, 2003; Sprague & Walker, 2000). The behavior of others is described as reactive or proactive aggression (McAdams & Lambie, 2003). These are psychological and educational terms used to describe students' characteristics that impair their ability to function socially, academically, behaviorally, or emotionally.

To a lesser degree, there are students with mild conduct or learning problems. Their challenges are often typical of a particular age: transient problems they may outgrow. Other students' behaviors may indicate unrecognized mental illnesses (Lewis, 1990). There are also students at risk for developing social, emotional, or behavioral problems because of difficult family conditions or lack of supports as they attempt to cope with the challenges of learning and living (Anthony, 1976; Cummings, Davies, & Campbell, 2000; Feil, Walker, Severson, & Ball, 2000; Robins & Rutter, 1990).

Sometimes teachers and parents mistakenly assume that a student who sits quietly and does the assigned schoolwork is an invested, committed learner. They may wonder why a student does not pay attention, ignores directions, or fails to remember from one lesson to another. They may wonder why a student is disinterested or careless, lacks confidence, and resists assignments, becoming a discipline problem at school or at home. And they may be concerned about the student whose learning has gone "in one ear and out the other." These are all indicators of students' failure to achieve the social and emotional competencies needed for their age. Such behavior should alert educators and families to pay attention to the link between emotions, learning and living. Figure 1.2 provides three basic guidelines for judging the potential seriousness of a child's behavior at school or at home.[4]

[4]Not all problems require special help. But if even one troubling behavior interferes with a student's progress in school or at home, pay attention!

- Depth: severity, intensity
- Duration: length of time it has persisted
- Development: extent of delay to typical development

FIGURE 1.2. To judge the potential seriousness of a student's behavior, use the "Three Ds of Disturbance."

Why Does Disruptive, Difficult Behavior Happen?

Disruptive, difficult behavior in children and youth cannot be attributed to any single cause. Both environmental and biological forces appear to influence how it develops (Farmer, Goforth, Leung, Clemmer, & Thompson, 2004; Hyman & Snook, 2000; National Institute of Mental Health, 2000). Figure 1.3 provides examples of ways behavior is acquired.

Problems often begin in small ways when children are young. For example, a child may not understand something and will make a mistake. Sensitive to this lack of success, the child may refuse to try again or will use devious means to avoid criticism. If these defensive patterns continue, they usually become part of a child's behavioral style. Then, when the child becomes a student, such defensive responses can interfere with learning, distort views of reality, or impair logical thinking (Kagan, 2002). Without assistance in changing such potentially destructive pathways in development, defensive behaviors become sources for severe disruption to the educational process for the child, family, and community (Bandura, 1986; Bowman & Stott, 1994; Cosmos, 2002).

- Direct experiences with others that have a successful outcome.
- Attention to the modeled behavior of others.
- Observation of actions and feelings of others.
- Content of play, stories, pictures, TV, drama, and movies.
- Examples set by others.
- Memories of past experiences.
- Vicarious experiences of others' successes and failures.
- Social status in the peer group.
- Self-reinforcement, self-reward, self-censure, and self-disengagement.

FIGURE 1.3. Behavior is acquired in many ways.

As they fail to learn, troubled students become increasingly disconnected from the mainstream of healthy childhood experiences. They communicate their troubles and needs with words and actions—in school, with family, at play, and with peers (Dwyer, Osher, & Hoffman, 2000). Their behaviors may be attempts to relieve stress, displace anger, deal with anxiety, or satisfy longings. Or, they simply may be responding with behaviors they have learned from others (Bandura & Walters, 1963). Frequently, their actions are cover-ups that are quite difficult for their teachers and parents to deal with or to understand. Difficult behaviors may also result in unintended consequences that create new and even more severe problems. Without skilled intervention, school failures may result in severe forms of delinquency as troubled students mature. Examples of such potential negative outcomes are listed in Figure 1.4.[5]

Neuroscience reveals how emotional circuitry, the limbic system, brain chemicals, and neurotransmitters such as serotonin influence rage reactions, stress reactions, impulsivity, and aggression. Damage to the central nervous system from injury, infection, poor nutrition, or exposure to toxins can influence neurological functions, including behavior and learning. How does this work? The brain is continuously developing elaborate systems of interconnected circuits, neurons, and synapses. This process of forming and organizing brain structures while dropping unused neural connections is dependent upon experiences for activating and strengthening existing pathways in the brain and for creating new ones (Damasio, 2003; Hebb, 1949).[6]

[5]Use of alcohol and drugs, sexual activity, and violence are indicators of students at high risk for school failure.

[6]Experiences can re-shape existing brain circuitry and alter biological elements like brain chemistry and brain tissue.

- Tardiness
- Class cutting
- High absence rate
- Physical conflicts among students
- Bullying
- Robbery and theft
- Vandalism
- Alcohol and drug use
- Possession of weapons
- Trespassing
- Verbal and physical abuse of teachers
- Racial tensions
- Gangs

FIGURE 1.4. If ignored, students' unacceptable behavior can result in these behaviors. *Note.* From *Indicators of School Crime and Safety, 2005*, National Center for Education Statistics, 2005.

New research with brain imaging offers other ways of understanding what may have gone awry in typical development when mental health issues become evident (Toga & Mazziotta, 2000). Research with gene mapping suggests that damage to certain genes may contribute to some learning and behavioral disorders, poor impulse control, and aggression (Giedd, 2000; Giedd, Blumenthal, & Jeffries, 1999; Giedd & Yurgelun-Todd, 2004). There is also recent evidence that although dynamic changes occur in the typical patterns of brain structure of children between ages 5 and 20, there may also be atypical patterns associated with various forms of childhood psychopathology such as childhood schizophrenia, autism, bipolar disorders, and violence (National Institute of Mental Health, 2000; Gotay et al., 2004).

Intense and traumatic events or repeated negative experiences can have profound effects on the actual structure of the developing brain during a child's early years and these events can remain pervasive influences throughout life (Greenspan, 1997; LeDoux, 1996; LeDoux & Phelps, 2000; National Clearing House on Child Abuse and Neglect, 2003; Stien & Kendall, 2004). Thus, in an important way, "experiences shape not only what information enters the mind, but the way in which the mind develops the ability to process that information" (Siegel, 1999, p. 16).

Family characteristics also play a significant role in developing personalities and behavior (Arllen, Gable, & Hendrickson, 1994; Bowlby, 1988; Cummings, Davies, & Campbell, 2000; Parke, Burks, Carson, Neville, & Boyum, 1994). Research on origins of delinquency and violent crime in adolescent boys indicates increased risk for boys in families with low levels of discipline, lack of monitoring of their activities, little structure in routines, limited cohesion as a family, and shared deviant beliefs. Low levels of communication, family discord, lack of warmth, and disturbed parent–child relationships are also reported to be associated with violent behavior, mood disorders, and alcohol and substance abuse in children and youth.

In contrast, factors such as high emotional warmth among family members, clear limits and expectations, family cohesion and communication, and concerned but not overbearing parents were evident in families of boys least likely to be involved with violent and nonviolent forms of delinquency. These boys also had significantly higher educational aspirations (Gorman-Smith, Tolan, & Henry, 1999; Gould, et al., 1998; Henry, 2000).

What About Students At Risk?

Educators and parents are not only concerned about students with diagnosed social, emotional, or behavioral problems, but also for those who are at risk and in need of special assistance to prevent the development of learning and behavioral problems. Many children have been pushed aside by the contemporary lifestyles of adults who talk about responsible behavior but fail to care for their children. Some parents have such heavy burdens themselves that they are unable to actively raise their own children. Others seem to have abdicated their responsibilities. Parents who received little positive attention themselves as children have an added challenge as they try to provide for their own children in supportive ways.

It is a tragic commentary on life today that so many children are at risk and vulnerable to neglect or abuse. Poverty, lack of health care, out-of-home placements, and homelessness are among the conditions that make a child "at risk." Approximately 1 in 25 children live with neither parent. These children are found in alternative living situations such as correctional or mental health treatment facilities, foster care, or care with grandparents or other relatives. Among foster children, there are many behavioral, intellectual, educational, social, developmental, and adaptive difficulties, which are challenges for their foster families and teachers (Children's Defense Fund, 2004).

Children are also maltreated every year by physical or psychological abuse. According to the National Clearinghouse on Child Abuse and Neglect (2003), about 906,000 children are abused and approximately 1.8 million others receive preventive services. Abuse frequently leads to withdrawal, depression, conduct disorders, impaired functioning, posttraumatic stress, delinquency, school failure, and later unemployment (National Center for Education Statistics, 2005; National Institute of Mental Health, 2000).[7]

In short, these troubled and potentially troubled young people need certain basic conditions to thrive at school and at home. It is the responsibility of teachers, parents, and communities to provide these essentials:

- the comfort of a predictable routine
- a safe and healthy environment
- abundant success when trying
- supportive relationships with adults
- satisfying times with peers
- acceptance as a contributing group member
- time to explore ideas and experiences

Needed: Social and Emotional Competence for Responsible Behavior

Everyone seems to agree that students should receive the best education possible. Teachers and parents want students to achieve in school with solid study habits, good grades, high test scores, and acceptable behavior. Yet, in the drive to emphasize academic achievement, it is easy to overlook the essential characteristics that make academic achievement happen: social, behavioral, communication, and emotional competencies (Rogers-Adkinson & Hooper, 2003; Salovey, Bedell, Detweiller, & Mayer, 2000). As shown in Figure 1.5, these competencies are necessary tools for success at school and in life.

To acquire social and emotional competence for responsible behavior that leads to success, students need skilled instruction and abundant positive experiences in a social context. The following section presents an overview of how Developmental Therapy–Developmental Teaching addresses the need of students for instruction that results in competence and responsibility.[8]

- Defines how well a student copes with the tasks of learning and life.
- Shapes responsible behavior.
- Transforms everyday experiences into what a student becomes.
- Continues to expand as a lifelong part of a student's personality.

FIGURE 1.5. Social and emotional competence.

Developmental Therapy–Developmental Teaching

Developmental Therapy–Developmental Teaching is a way to teach that fosters increasingly responsible behavior, social and emotional competence, and academic progress from early childhood through secondary school. The idea is to systematically base instruction on a student's existing competencies and to teach new ones as needed. The developmental map for guiding this process is the sequences of key competencies that are typically acquired from birth through

[7]Feelings of helplessness, blame, and inadequacy resulting from physical or psychological abuse promote fear and anxiety in children. Children experience realistic fears (Be careful or it will happen!), remote fears (It could happen!), and symbolic, mystical fears (This terrible thing is going to get me!).

[8]Larson and Brendtro (2000) specify the need for external and internal assets for healthy social and emotional development. Similarly, Howard Gardner (1999) uses the term "personal intelligence" and Daniel Goleman (1995, 1998) refers to "emotional intelligence" to define intra- and interpersonal attributes needed to be competent. See also the SEARCH Institute (1998).

the teen years. These sequences reflect familiar developmental stages in a child's maturation, and they gradually expand the capacity to behave in responsible ways. The tree illustrated in Figure 1.6 (an image taken from the CD-ROM that accompanies this text) shows this progression in ages and stages of development, with four major components (developmental domains) as branches making the tree whole and strong.

Each stage of development has a general goal and specific subgoals in four developmental domains: DOING (behavioral competencies), SAYING (communication competencies), RELATING (socialization competencies), and THINKING (cognitive–learning competencies). These four domains each contain a sequence of key competencies needed by children at various stages of development from early childhood through the young teenage years (refer to Figures 1.7–1.10).[9]

The ways in which a student acquires these competencies is uniquely individual, influenced by age, gender, ethnicity, endowed attributes, life experiences, relationships, culture, and family values. Each personality takes shape and is reshaped as these competencies are acquired, usually in a fairly predictable sequence (Bowlby, 1988; A. Freud, 1973; Whittmer, Doll, & Strain, 1996). However, before new competencies can be achieved, readiness skills must be in place.

By following developmental sequences in each domain, you can identify which competencies a student has acquired (the student's strengths), which ones are missing (the gaps), those

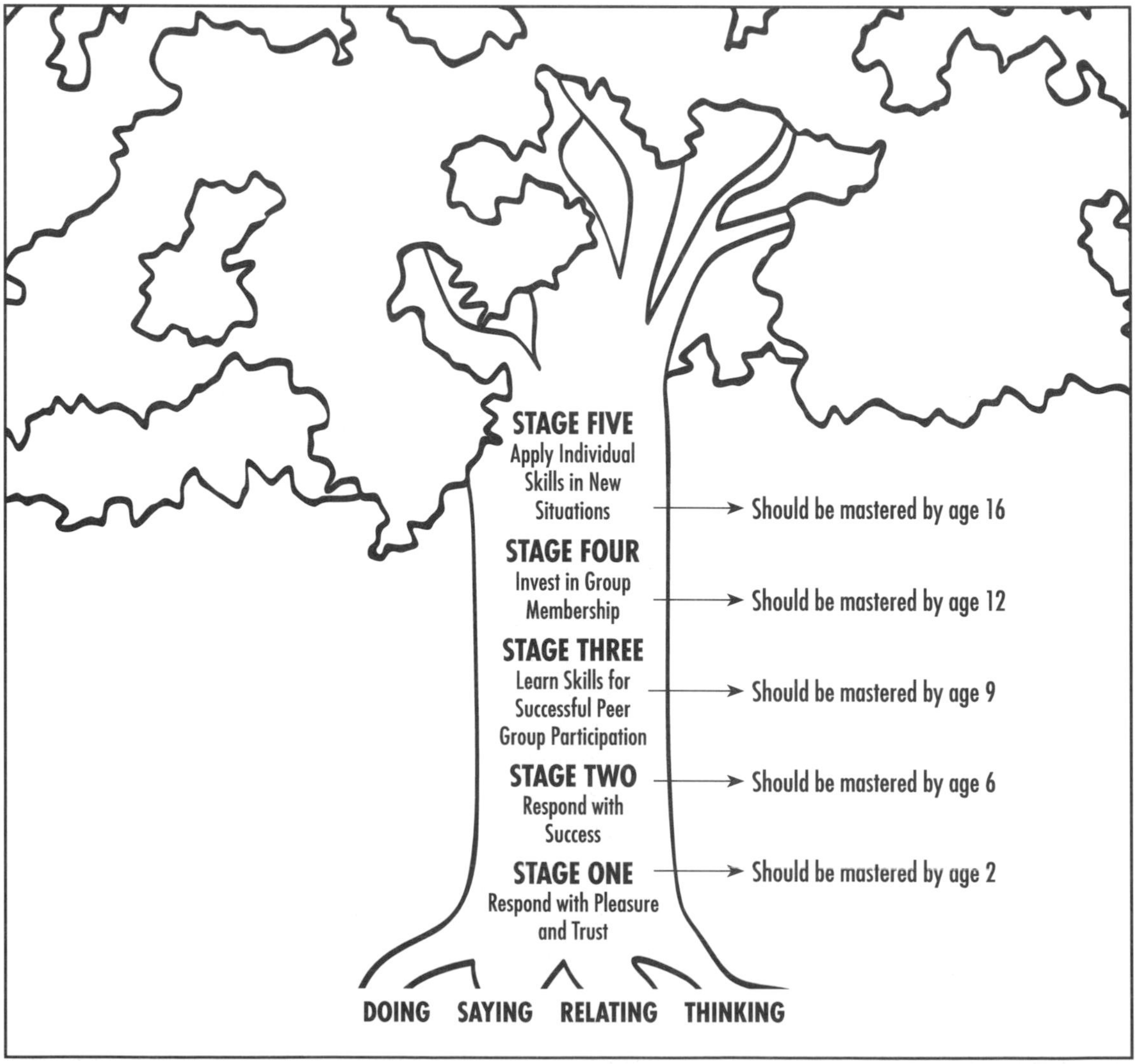

[9]For a concise review of the benefits of blending developmental theory with classroom practice, see Selman (2003).

FIGURE 1.6. The content areas of Developmental Therapy–Developmental Teaching change as students mature.

that arc "stumbling blocks" (the problem behaviors), and which competencies will be needed in the future. This is the way to specify individualized learning objectives, customize learning experiences, organize instruction, and use developmentally appropriate behavior management practices to help students acquire needed competencies.[10]

[10]Chapter 2 provides snapshots of how each stage is matched with instructional strategies that are developmentally appropriate for individual students. Use the remaining chapters as a how-to-do-it guide for putting this approach to work in your own classroom.

Early Childhood	• Attend with awareness • Respond to others • Respond to play materials independently • Use materials appropriately • Follow routines • Control impulses • Participate spontaneously in learning experiences
Elementary School	• Complete work independently • Understand rules and expectations • Regulate own behavior • Imitate positive behavioral role models • Use control when provoked • Accept responsibility for own behavior • Contribute to group solutions
Secondary/High School	• Seek new skills • Recognize need for law and order • Participate in group governance • Regulate own behavior with values • Seek solutions to personal problems

FIGURE 1.7. DOING: Key behavioral competencies.

Early Childhood	• Convey needs with preverbal speech • Use simple words with others • Listen with receptive language • Respond with spontaneous language • Describe characteristics of self and others • Convey intentions and information to peers
Elementary School	• Describe experiences • Dialogue in groups • Express feelings of self and others • Explain reactions of others • Express feelings in words to peers • Initiate relationships • Support others
Secondary/High School	• Use figurative speech • Offer conciliatory responses • Recognize others' contributions • Discuss values • Maintain relationships

FIGURE 1.8. SAYING: Key communication competencies.

Early Childhood	• Recognize and trust adults
	• Form attachment and dependency
	• Form a sense of independent self
	• Participate in play with others
	• Use imagination
	• Seek adults and peers
	• Participate in organized activities
Elementary School	• Cooperate with others
	• Recognize basic values of right and wrong
	• Value oneself
	• Become an accepted group member
	• Form friendships and a social self
	• Identify with adult heroes
	• Recognize others' opinions
	• Draw inferences from social situations
Secondary/High School	• Understand and respect others
	• Interact successfully
	• Form personal convictions and self-understanding
	• Make choices based on values
	• Sustain relationships with values

FIGURE 1.9. RELATING: Key socialization competencies.

Early Childhood	• Form sensorimotor responses
	• Imitate actions of others
	• Form object permanence and memory skills
	• Coordinate body movements
	• Process visual perceptions
	• Form and sequence concepts
	• Understand relational concepts
	• Recognize basic symbols
Elementary School	• Acquire academic tools of primary grades
	• Explain actions and feelings of fictional characters
	• Write to communicate
	• Develop game skills
	• Solve abstract measurement problems
	• Acquire academic tools of upper grades
	• Use rules and logic for problem solving
Secondary/High School	• Seek opinions of others
	• Evaluate ideas
	• Distinguish process and results and cause and effect
	• Follow current issues
	• Use analysis and logic for personal problem solving
	• Use academics for independent life skills

FIGURE 1.10. THINKING: Key cognition competencies.

Begin instruction at the point where a student has sufficient mastery of prerequisite skills to be successful with the tasks at hand. Gradually introduce new skills and knowledge by following the increasingly complex sequences of development. Design specific learning objectives, lessons, and activities to teach the needed competencies. As a student achieves increasingly complex competencies, change your instructional strategies to adapt to these developmental changes. Then, systematically monitor and chart the student's progress. In this way, you will also be able to document program effectiveness.

Using this approach, you can track typical development. Ages, stages, and school levels are outlined in Figure 1.11. Instruction for the youngest children starts in Stage One to teach competencies generally acquired by typically developing toddlers during the first 24 months of life. The goal is to teach them to respond with pleasure and trust. By the time the preschool years are completed, most children have the readiness skills associated with Stage Two competencies—they can respond with success. By completion of third grade, at about age 9, typically developing students have the competencies needed for success in Stage Three. They have acquired skills for successful peer group participation. As they enter Stage Four, instruction for preteens in upper elementary and middle school focuses on skills that result in students who value group membership. For young teens in high school, Stage Five teaches competencies that allow them to apply individual and group skills in new situations.[11]

[11]As students achieve key social and emotional competencies at each sequential stage, responsible behavior increases. They also develop thinking skills that lead to academic successes.

	Age Range in Years	Stage of Development	School Level
Infants and toddlers	0–2	Stage One	Infant and toddler programs
Preschoolers	3–5	Stage Two	Preschool and kindergarten
Middle childhood	6–9	Stage Three	Primary grade school
Preteens	10–12	Stage Four	Upper elementary and middle school
Young teens	13–16	Stage Five	Secondary school

FIGURE 1.11. Stages of Developmental Therapy–Developmental Teaching follow typical development.

Developmental Practices for a Successful Schoolwide Program

Developmental Therapy–Developmental Teaching provides a framework to guide schoolwide practices across a multi-tiered plan for comprehensive programming, as shown in Figure 1.12. The range of applications for developmentally based teaching extends from inclusive general education programs to special education settings and from clinics and residential programs to intensive, concentrated intervention programs provided by school systems. Developmental Therapy–Developmental Teaching is also used in home schooling, community programs, by foster parents, in residential schools, and in special education all-day or half-day sessions, resource rooms, special classes, and vocational or transition programs (Bergsson, 1999a, 2001; Berscheid, Cooley, & Dier, 1998; Wood, Davis, & Swindle, 1998).[12]

To customize instruction that is matched to individual needs, ages, and stages of development for every student in a school, there must be broad, schoolwide involvement. Provision must be made to identify those students who require individualized education programs (IEPs). Equally important is the need for flexibility in programming, so that services can be adjusted to students' changing needs as they make progress. With a developmental framework, successful

[12]Chapter 9 contains summaries from classroom-based research about the effectiveness of this approach. Appendix A is a summary of publications documenting its expansion over three decades.

schoolwide support can be provided for every student. The result will be increasingly successful school experiences, improved academic achievement, and greater responsibility for behavior such as shown in Figure 1.13.[13]

[13]Chapter 3 provides a guide for assessing social, emotional, and behavioral competencies with the Developmental Teaching Objectives and Rating Form (DTORF–R). Results are used to plan strategic instruction.

- Assess a student's current social, emotional, and behavioral status, in collaboration with parents and other teachers.
- Select strategic learning objectives and instructional strategies that are emotionally and developmentally appropriate.
- Plan interventions to change the physical and psychological classroom climate in positive ways.
- Systematically and sequentially teach each missing competency by building on existing competencies.
- Track students' progress with repeated assessments at intervals during the school year.
- Use tracking results to change instructional objectives as competencies are acquired.
- Monitor your own skills and strategies daily.

FIGURE 1.12. Use Developmental Therapy–Developmental Teaching as a framework for these tasks.

- New actions and words (*behaving* and *speaking*).
- Positive results (good *feelings* in *relating* to others).
- Expanded understanding (*thinking*).

FIGURE 1.13. Things that successful school experiences produce.

When planning a schoolwide student support system to meet the educational needs of students with varying degrees of problem behaviors, educators widely recognize three levels of intervention as essential. These include *preventive, targeted,* and *intensive* programming (George, Harrower, & Knoster, 2003; Peterson, Miller, & Skiba, 2004; Sugai & Horner, 2002). This section summarizes how such program diversity can be provided schoolwide with Developmental Therapy–Developmental Teaching as the framework. The chapters that follow provide details about how this is done at each level of service.

Prevention

Consider a typical school with 600 students. An estimated 80–90% of the students will develop in typical ways while also facing the transient troubles typical for their ages. This calls for a schoolwide *prevention* program (Sugai & Horner, 2002, p. 38). A school environment that provides support and sensitive management for typically developing students can prevent problems from developing (Carr et al., 2002; Larson, 2000.) If effective support and management are provided, the number of serious discipline or mental health issues will be reduced. Because of its focus on teaching key competencies needed by all students, Developmental Therapy–Developmental Teaching has broad applications in general education programs focused on prevention of discipline problems.[14]

[14]All students need a healthy school climate that promotes learning, teaches competence, and encourages responsible behavior.

Targeted Interventions for Troubled Students

Using the three-level approach to programming illustrated in Figure 1.14, approximately 5% to 15% of the students in a typical school will experience mild to moderate problems that interfere with their learning (Sugai & Horner, 2002). This translates into 30 to 90 troubled students with challenging behaviors who require *targeted* interventions to address missing com-

INTENSIVE INTERVENTION NEEDED

TARGETED INTERVENTION NEEDED

FIGURE 1.14. In a typical school with 600 students, approximately 10% of the students need targeted intervention, and about 4% need intensive intervention. *Note.* Each figure represents five students.

petencies and to avoid more serious, chronic problems in learning. For these students, teachers blend developmentally based interventions into existing academic programs.[15]

Developmentally based Individualized Education Programs (IEPs) are "portable" and not dependent on any particular academic curriculum or organizational structure. Each program can be carried out in whatever setting is judged to be most effective for that student's learning. Sometimes the programs are in a fully inclusive setting where developmental practices are added to an existing general education curriculum. Intervention may be provided in a modified cluster plan for partial inclusion, sometimes called "pull out" or "resource room" plans. Reverse inclusion with typically developing peers also offers the benefits of inclusion, as does a social program plan in which special groups have scheduled opportunities with typically developing peers. These various forms of inclusion are options for each student's IEP, IFSP, or ITP.[16]

Inclusion provides troubled students with opportunities such as those listed in Figure 1.15. Inclusive programs offer appropriate peer models, a chance to practice new skills in open settings, and participation in the general education curriculum. Inclusion should also result in acceptance by peers. Failure to be accepted can become an emotional and developmental

[15]For students in special education programs, individual Developmental Therapy– Developmental Teaching programs are a part of their IEPs, IFSPs, or ITPs.

[16]When this developmental approach is used in residential school settings or in home-based programs by parents, opportunities for inclusion with typically developing peers must be provided.

- Successful academic instruction.
- Meaningful social relationships.
- Positive developmental outcomes.

FIGURE 1.15. Things that inclusion should provide to a student.

disaster for a troubled student. Lack of competencies for interacting successfully with peers often results in greater failure to participate or engage in learning.

Intensive Interventions

A school must also have a program to meet the instructional needs of about 3% to 5% of students with serious and debilitating mental health problems (Sugai & Horner, 2002). The 18 to 30 students in a typical school will need *intensive intervention,* skillfully implemented, to reverse the downward cycle of chronic failure to learn. Small groups with a low teacher–pupil ratio offer intensive assistance. In a small group, the teacher is able to control and change group dynamics for positive outcomes in social exchanges between students and teachers. When a student is also failing in academic achievement or has significant learning disabilities, a small group offers intensive attention to instructional needs. With a skilled, accessible teacher, students also receive help in understanding and managing the behaviors and emotions that disrupt their lives. As a student makes progress in a small group, opportunities for inclusion are gradually increased. In whatever grouping is provided, the purpose of intensive interventions for these very troubled students is to help them achieve the social, emotional, and behavioral competencies they lack.[17]

Mental Health for Learning

Schools must keep the mental health of their students as a top priority because mental health is a necessary condition for successful academic performance. The results of mentally healthy students arc participation in productive learning, fulfilling relationships with other people, and ability to cope with distress, adversity, and new situations.

For a school's program to maintain a mentally healthy climate, specific behavior management skills, group behavior management, and general classroom management for instruction must be in place at all levels of intervention. To achieve these conditions, teachers should focus systematically on both physical and psychological environments during planning.

Interventions and management in the physical environment include some fairly straightforward ways to guide learning and student behavior. Rules can be instituted, along with associated rewards and consequences, as well as more subtle procedures (structuring choices, organizing learning experiences and procedures, designing motivating academic lessons, providing positive feedback, and planning for effective use of space).

Intervention in the psychological environment is much more subtle and is often more difficult to provide. It requires integration of information from every dimension of a student's world—school, home, and community, past and present. It requires knowing about the student's cultural heritage, academic strengths and weaknesses, learning style, significant prior experiences, social roles in peer groups and family groups, attitudes, self-concepts, values, emotions, concerns, and behavioral defenses. It takes into account a student's age, view of authority, developmental anxieties, sources of anger, and need for dependence or independence in relationships with adults. All of this information is synthesized to reveal a student's profile of socioemotional competence, including specific strengths, gaps, and goals.[18]

When academic instruction is blended with teaching for social, emotional, and behavioral competence, learning will occur. This dynamic and ever-shifting synergy between academic achievement and social, emotional, and behavioral competence provides the learning model for instructional practices, which are described in detail in the following chapters.[19]

Practice: Can You Identify Key Indicators and Competencies?

In this chapter, you have met, very briefly, students of various ages. Among those in the age group most familiar to you, review the descriptions and look for behaviors that are indicators of troubled students, using the list provided (Figure 1.1). Then rank the students from least

[17]Chapter 4 contains a section describing group dynamics and how they are used in Developmental Therapy–Developmental Teaching programs.

[18]Chapter 4 describes how to gather information relevant for planning ways to intervene effectively in a student's psychological environment.

[19]The developmental perspective offers a systematic, sequential way to teach competence, step by step, through developmentally and emotionally appropriate learning sequences.

troubled to most troubled. Use the "Three Ds of Disturbance" (Figure 1.2) to help you make these estimates.

When you have identified one student as "most troubled" in the age group you selected, check the charts of key competencies to find what that student has already achieved in DOING, SAYING, RELATING, and THINKING. Consider the competencies that remain for the student to acquire for that age. Finally, choose one competency that the student needs to achieve *first* in each of the four domains.

This exercise illustrates the process used in Developmental Therapy–Developmental Teaching. The four selected competencies (one in each area) would become the instructional goals and objectives for the student's educational plan. If you want to carry it further, repeat the process for every child described in the age group you selected. Then, think about how you might plan instruction to meet each child's individual educational needs.

Snapshots from Early Childhood Through the Teen Years

CHAPTER

This approach emphasizes the healthy pathways of development in children and youth and builds systematically to ensure a positive outcome to each learning experience. Because behavior, personality, and intellect evolve from the sum of small, daily experiences with others, teachers must consider every moment instructional. With each success, more responsible behaviors and attitudes emerge, and old, maladaptive responses fade. This is how social-emotional competence and learning occur.

M. M. Wood
in the introduction to
Developmental Therapy (1975, p. xii)

Educating students of any age begins with an understanding of how their social, emotional, and behavioral development is unfolding in comparison to their age peers. They may be typically developing students facing the ordinary challenges of growing up. Some may be at risk because of difficult circumstances in their lives. Others may be students who are having severe mental health or behavior problems that interfere with learning. Regardless of how mild or severe a student's problem may seem, the foundation for effective teaching and learning is a developmentally and emotionally appropriate learning environment. With meaningful instruction and positive behavior management strategies—customized to match each student's age, stage, and individual profile of skills and gaps—teachers are able to provide strategic instruction for maximum effectiveness in learning.

The brief snapshots in this chapter outline developmental pathways for healthy social, emotional, behavioral, and cognitive competencies of learners at each age and stage of development. This framework identifies ways for teachers to provide instruction for young children, school-age children, and teenagers. Refer to Figures 2.1 and 2.2 for snapshot summaries of learning goals in each stage of development and the competencies students need to achieve the goals. Also included in these summaries are learning characteristics, central concerns, anxieties, and values that characteristically motivate students; the ways they go about problem solving at different ages; and their changing views of authority. Each snapshot concludes with a review of variations in teachers' roles to match students' developmental characteristics.

These are the general principles that guide Developmental Therapy–Developmental Teaching of children or teens with and without disabilities. The material is relevant for students who are developing typically, for those who are troubled or at risk, and for those with serious delays in their social, emotional, and behavioral development. Life experiences shape children and teens in distinct ways. Their programs must be responsive to these personal experiences, their age-related needs, their family and cultural backgrounds, and their developmental accomplishments.[1]

[1]The goal for each student is to acquire needed competencies for successful learning, so that school prepares the student for life.

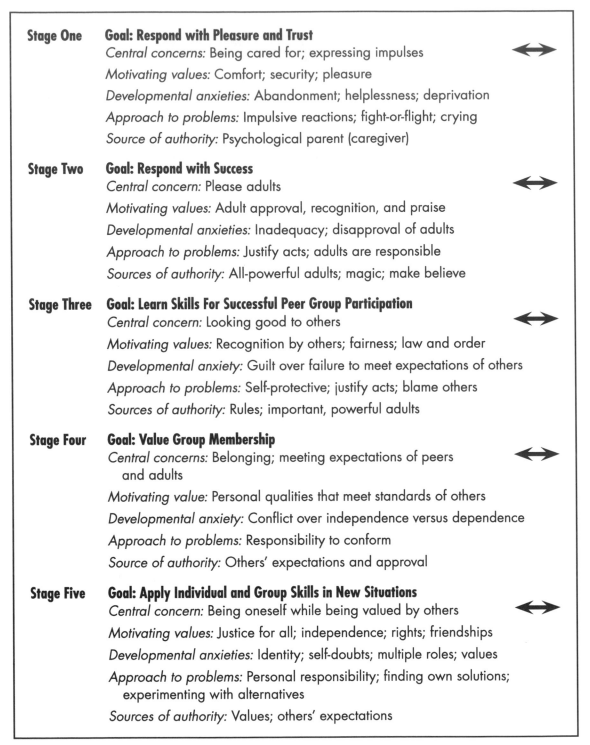

Stage One **Goal: Respond with Pleasure and Trust**
Central concerns: Being cared for; expressing impulses
Motivating values: Comfort; security; pleasure
Developmental anxieties: Abandonment; helplessness; deprivation
Approach to problems: Impulsive reactions; fight-or-flight; crying
Source of authority: Psychological parent (caregiver)

Stage Two **Goal: Respond with Success**
Central concern: Please adults
Motivating values: Adult approval, recognition, and praise
Developmental anxieties: Inadequacy; disapproval of adults
Approach to problems: Justify acts; adults are responsible
Sources of authority: All-powerful adults; magic; make believe

Stage Three **Goal: Learn Skills For Successful Peer Group Participation**
Central concern: Looking good to others
Motivating values: Recognition by others; fairness; law and order
Developmental anxiety: Guilt over failure to meet expectations of others
Approach to problems: Self-protective; justify acts; blame others
Sources of authority: Rules; important, powerful adults

Stage Four **Goal: Value Group Membership**
Central concerns: Belonging; meeting expectations of peers
   and adults
Motivating value: Personal qualities that meet standards of others
Developmental anxiety: Conflict over independence versus dependence
Approach to problems: Responsibility to conform
Source of authority: Others' expectations and approval

Stage Five **Goal: Apply Individual and Group Skills in New Situations**
Central concern: Being oneself while being valued by others
Motivating values: Justice for all; independence; rights; friendships
Developmental anxieties: Identity; self-doubts; multiple roles; values
Approach to problems: Personal responsibility; finding own solutions;
   experimenting with alternatives
Sources of authority: Values; others' expectations

FIGURE 2.1. Learning characteristics of children and teens at each stage of development.

For Children in Stage One ⟷	*Your task:* Teach them to respond and trust *Your role:* Care and nurture; encourage responses; make good things happen *Learning environment:* Consistent routine; luring rather than demanding *Developmentally appropriate materials:* Exploratory materials with enticing sounds, colors, and textures *Management strategies:* Stimulating materials; organized structure and routine; comforting feedback; redirection; controlled vocabulary; supportive physical proximity
For Children in Stage Two ⟷	*Your task:* Teach them basic skills for success *Your role:* Lead them to abundant success *Learning environment:* Active exploration; participation *Developmentally appropriate materials:* Exploration; imagination; themes of adults caring for children and kindness to others *Management strategies:* Abundant encouragement to participate; positive feedback; verbal redirection; reflection of positive words and actions; model desired actions
For Students in Stage Three ⟷	*Your task:* Teach them to participate successfully in peer groups *Your role:* Be the group leader, benign sheriff, and motivator *Learning environment:* Group focus and team work *Management strategies:* Positive feedback about individual contribution to group; motivate with success-producing lessons; redirect behavior and attention; reflect positive words and actions; connect actions to feelings; positive rules; individual Life Space Crisis Intervention (LSCI)
For Students in Stage Four ⟷	*Your task:* Teach them to care about being contributing members in groups at school, with peers, and at home *Your role:* Group facilitator, advocate, counselor, role model, reflector of reality *Learning environment:* Reality-oriented group focus *Management strategies:* Positive feedback from peers and adults; help student interpret behavior and feelings; group and individual LSCI
For Students in Stage Five ⟷	*Your task:* Teach them to use their skills in new situations independently *Your role:* Supportive teacher, mentor, counselor, advisor *Learning environment:* Natural teen settings for independent use of competencies and selected values *Management strategies:* Positive feedback and encouragement, preferably from peers; interpretation; LSCI; remind student to consider values and consequences

FIGURE 2.2. Customize your instruction to match students' social, emotional, and behavioral needs for learning.

Developmental Practices in Early Childhood

Most toddlers and preschool children are developing competencies specific to Stages One and Two. Then, as they near first grade, they begin to learn a few of the early Stage Three competencies.

Children in Stage One

Stage One: "My needs are everything!"
The Learning Goal: Respond with pleasure and trust.

Developmental Characteristics for Learning

Children who are in Stage One of development have not yet mastered sensorimotor skills or expressive language—the basic tools needed to participate in human events. They are dependent on adults for care and emotional security. Whether they are typical infants, young children at risk, or teens with profound developmental delay, they must rely totally on others to help them become social beings. They need assistance to learn that the world is a satisfying place to be and that people can be trusted to provide the comforts they need (Cummings, Davies, & Campbell, 2000).

Children of any age, with or without disabilities, who are in Stage One learn primarily through sensory channels. This is the basic source of pleasure for them and a powerful motivation for learning (Piaget, 1937/1954, 1952). Most of their intentional actions are directed toward increasing comfort and reducing discomfort. This quest for security and pleasure is the foundation for a child's motivation to learn and to trust during Stage One and the motivation can be channeled into successful learning if the results bring comfort (Erikson, 1972).[2]

For children in Stage One, associating with a significant person (the psychological parent) as the comforting caregiver is the initial step in development (Hughes, 1998; Mahler, Pine, & Bergman, 1975). When an infant looks at the caregiver with awareness, a first competency is achieved. Awareness leads to recognition and association of the caregiver with pleasure. Older children with severe developmental delays also must acquire this competency. The result is a primary relationship called the first attachment (Ainsworth, 1973; Bowlby, 1982/1997, 1988; Maccoby, 1980; Mahler, 1968/1987). Its success or failure becomes the foundation for future development that will shape the pathways for learning.

Trust, formed from a satisfying first attachment, becomes the essential ingredient for responding to life's experiences with continuing mastery of social, emotional, and behavioral competencies. Erikson (1959/1980) built his psychosocial theory of life stages on the emergence of

[2]Children in Stage One cling to sources of pleasure and retreat from discomfort.

trust during this first stage of life. Trust, he writes, implies not only that individuals have learned to rely on sameness and continuity from their caregivers, but also that they may trust themselves. This first trust, built from dependency and attachment, is the foundation for self-esteem and for later capacity to develop and maintain interpersonal relationships. Trust culminates in the ability to form mature love relationships as an adult (Bretherton, 1987; Erikson, 1977; Kagan, 1982; Loevinger, 1976, 1987). Because of its importance for healthy personality development, trust is the first major learning goal in Developmental Therapy–Developmental Teaching. Figure 2.3 illustrates how a child forms trust during Stage One.[3]

As children in Stage One learn to tell the difference between what is pleasant and unpleasant, a typical developmental anxiety about aloneness or abandonment also emerges. Anxiety is a sign of acute awareness of surroundings and concern about possible abandonment or deprivation. Children whose essential support systems break down through neglect, abuse, illness, or denial of affection, are at risk and vulnerable to this anxiety. If this happens, a child's emotional and sensorimotor energies are deflected away from learning and toward survival. These children are often upset and anxious about anything that is new or changed. There is an absence of constructive, self-directed activity. Rage reactions are typical, and resistance to participation in any new activity is common. Further relationships with adults are fragile, if formed at all. These reactions are expressions of fundamental emotional insecurity and have a powerful effect on the child's continuing learning and development (Bowlby, 1989; Edward, Ruskin, & Turrini, 1992; Osofsky, 1994).[4]

Children's Instructional Needs During Stage One

The rudimentary competencies children in Stage One must acquire include social, emotional, and behavioral milestones of typically developing children during the first 2 years of life (see Figure 2.4). These are basic competencies for a healthy foundation in Stage One and are also essential for success in the next stage of development, where skills become more organized and increasingly complex.[5]

An effective program for children in Stage One provides them with experiences that are pleasurable, supportive, and reassuring. The goal is to teach them to trust that the world can be a comfortable, pleasing place. Pleasure-producing activities within a consistent, familiar routine promote this basic trust. Engaging materials and manipulative toys that involve all of the senses—color, texture, sound, movement, and taste—stimulate learning. Above all, a Stage One learning environment must be a satisfying place for a child to be. With these elements in their programs, children respond with a sense of psychological security, pleasure, and physical well being. In this climate, trust abounds and learning occurs.

The most frequently used intervention strategies include pleasurable feedback from nurturing, caring adults. When attention wanders, children are redirected by touch or by the compelling quality in the voice of the adult. This helps increase their impulse control and attention to activities. Sometimes it is necessary to help a child move physically through a motion to teach the movement pattern.

A carefully selected, limited vocabulary is used to help children make connections between objects, sounds, and actions. The words that are chosen are ones that have functional usefulness for the child. By consistently using the same sounds and words, the adult is able to increase a child's receptive and expressive vocabulary. This controlled vocabulary also serves to expand the child's awareness of events and people and to express needs with words.

Educational Settings for Children in Stage One

At home, in childcare, or at preschool, the program for a child in Stage One should be provided in a natural setting. During the first year of life, this is usually the responsibility of parents or other family members. With toddlers and very young children, a developmentally focused program can also be offered in childcare settings or in early intervention programs. For older students with disabilities who are still in Stage One, the program can be part of inclusive

[3]The natural dependency of Stage One children requires a bond of attachment and trust with caregivers, which is the foundation for future relationships with others.

[4]The psychological parent—provider of care, nurture, and comfort—is the source of emotional security, the buffer that protects young children from the experience that "no one cares." Those whose jobs are to care for very young children must provide this protection.

[5]A summary of needed competencies is in Chapter 1. Chapters 3 and 4 contain information on how to assess children to identify the competencies they have achieved and those that are needed.

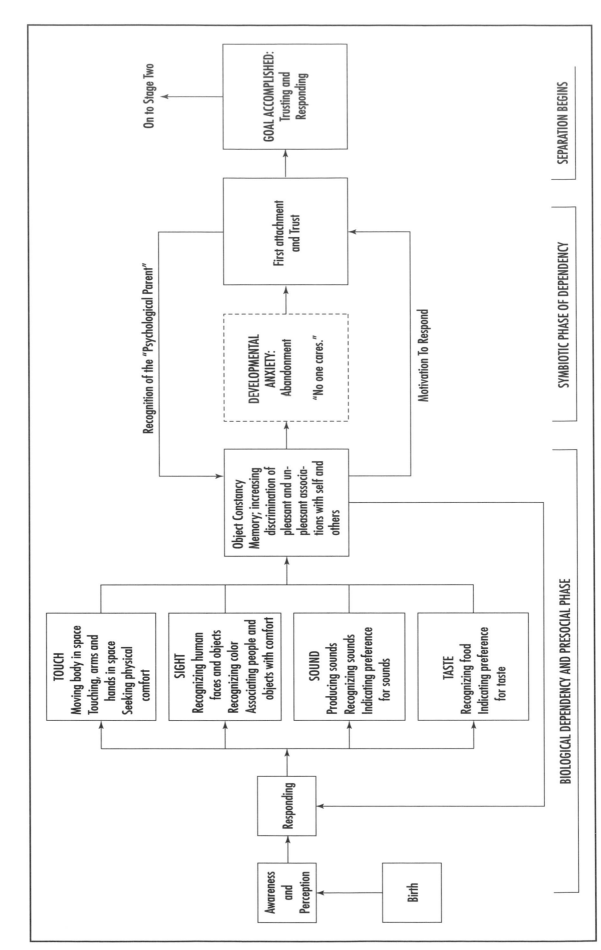

FIGURE 2.3. Key processes of typical social and emotional development in Stage One. The dotted lines indicate the inner life of thoughts and feelings.

For Doing	Look at other people.
	Assist in self-help.
	Seek play materials spontaneously.
	Remember routines.
For Saying	Listen to others speaking.
	Use words to respond to children and adults.
	Use words in sequence.
For Relating	Watch others.
	Respond to name.
	Respond to request to come.
	Play in organized ways spontaneously.
	Seek contact with familiar adults.
For Thinking	Remember familiar places, toys, people, and activities.
	Imitate adults' actions.
	Name objects.
	Match and group objects and pictures.
	Recognize details in pictures.
	Name objects in pictures.

FIGURE 2.4. Examples of competencies children need for success in Stage One. *Note.* From *The Developmental Teaching Objectives for the DTORF–R*, Developmental Therapy Institute (2001/2005).

special education in schools or day treatment settings. Wherever the program is provided, dysfunctional behaviors and significant delays in development are *not* the focus. Instead, programs are organized to teach children in Stage One new responses that bring comfort to themselves and pleasing attention from valued adults.

Some Guidelines for Teaching a Stage One Program

We summarize the essentials of instruction for children in Stage One with these guidelines:

- Select arousing materials that hold the attention of all children in the group.
- Design activities that are stimulating and evoke pleasurable responses. Try to involve several senses in each activity.
- Provide motivation and leadership for every activity.
- Conduct each activity so that it has a clear beginning and ending. Announce when a previous activity is over and a new one is beginning.
- Limit waiting for turns to an absolute minimum.
- Extend an activity if involvement is at its maximum, and then end the lesson before interest and motivation lag.
- Watch for positive actions by each child in an activity and respond with abundant praise and encouragement.
- Sequence each small step in the learning process. Sometimes it may be necessary to physically guide a child through the motions of an activity until the response is mastered.
- Know when to accept a particular response and when to expect a higher level response. This information comes from understanding how sequences for social, emotional, and behavioral competency are developing for each individual.
- Make some form of contact with each child frequently. Without this, a child in Stage One may become disoriented, lose interest, or revert to meaningless behavior.

- Recognize a child's feelings, and then communicate the necessary reassurance that the situation is under control.
- Maintain a calm activity for others while responding to a child in crisis.
- Expect every child to participate in cleaning up after each activity. The cleanup directions can consist of only four words: "Time to clean up." You may have to teach the actual physical motions employed in bending, reaching, grasping, and putting things away.
- Plan for the systematic transfer of learning by connecting the same communication and motor skills learned in one activity to other activities. A simple weekly unit theme helps in planning for these connections.

A Teacher's Role with Children in Stage One

To be effective in fostering learning for children in Stage One, a teacher must mobilize them to respond to materials, people, and activities in spontaneous ways, with pleasurable results. These teachers are quick to recognize the sensory preferences of each individual, and they select materials and activities that tap these preferences. As the child responds to the teacher and to the activity, the result brings delight. From these exchanges, the relationship that develops between teacher and child is warm and responsive, providing comfort and pleasure. At the same time, the teacher is careful to pull back as the child develops competency for sustained attention to an activity independent of adult support. When a pattern of warm, spontaneous interaction is established between them, the child begins to make rapid gains in acquiring the remaining competencies for Stage One. These successes result in achievement of developmental goals for Stage One, summarized in Figure 2.5.[6]

[6]For children in Stage One, adults are the lifelines for learning. Adults provide care, pleasurable sensory experiences, and nurture. They create the experiences that bring satisfaction and comfort.

- Respond to objects and people with basic motor skills.
- Use words to gain needs.
- Trust an adult sufficiently to respond to requests.
- Explore surroundings spontaneously with basic mental and motor skills.

FIGURE 2.5. Abilities of children who achieve the Stage One goal and view the world with pleasure and trust.

Children in Stage Two

Stage Two: "I can do it!"
The Learning Goal: Respond with success.

Developmental Characteristics for Learning

At the beginning of Stage Two, children have limited skills. They have little self-confidence, a limited awareness of cause and effect, and ineffective responses to adults and peers. Although they typically have functional speech, they are limited in language skills and need abundant opportunities to communicate. They are also restless, have short attention spans, and are generally disorganized.

As they progress through Stage Two, children are learning to talk, think, relate, and play in increasingly complex ways (Parten, 1932; Whittmer, Doll, & Strain, 1996). It is a dynamic time for learning that is full of exploration. However, new activities can cause anxiety and resistance, so they tend to cling to whatever is familiar. Impulsive behavior is characteristic, and frustrations are usually directed toward adults. Kagan calls this phase of development "the impulsive self" (1982, pp. 363–381; 1983, pp. 134–135; see also Kegan, 1982). If navigated successfully, this stage prepares young children for the developmental hurdles ahead when they enter elementary school. Figure 2.6 illustrates the processes that lead to success in this stage.

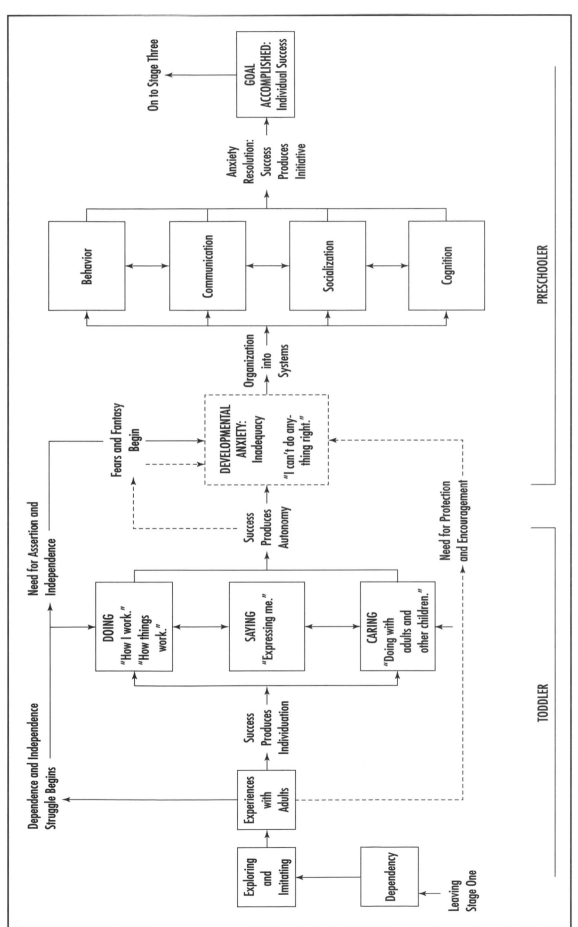

FIGURE 2.6. Key processes of typical social and emotional development in Stage Two. The dotted lines indicate the inner life of thoughts and feelings.

During Stage Two, children usually develop competencies in a fairly predictable sequence (A. Freud, 1973). However, lack of social, emotional, and behavioral skills often keep children in Stage Two from receiving the adult approval they crave. Many have been told again and again: "Don't act so stupid. You can't do anything right. You're a bad kid. Hurry up—here, let me do it! How can you be so ugly (mean; no good; a nothing)?" Missing competencies also keep them from interacting successfully with their age peers. The fewer skills they have, the more negative comments they receive from both peers and adults.

If children are also at risk for social, emotional, behavioral, or learning problems, these competencies may be difficult for them to achieve (Beckman & Lieber, 1992). With or without disabilities, children who are at risk have hurdles to overcome as they mature in their capacities to learn and to function successfully. They need to be reassured that they can be successful, good will conquer evil, they will not be overwhelmed by bad forces, and that they can use their own skills to give and receive kindness from others. They also need confidence that good behavior is rewarded (Erikson, 1959/1980, 1972; A. Freud, 1965; Selman, 1980; Turiel, 1983, 1994).[7]

Children's Instructional Needs

Children respond to learning during Stage Two in different ways, depending upon their age, prior experiences, and the competencies they have previously acquired. Yet, there is a set of fairly well recognized general growth outcomes to be achieved in the areas of communication, socialization, cognition, adaptive behavior, and motor skills (Brazelton, 1994; Piaget, 1951/1962, 1967; Wolery, 2000). With all that must be accomplished during Stage Two, the instructional program helps children gain the competencies shown in Figure 2.7, which are essential foundations for future learning in the primary grades.[8]

Carefully designed lessons and activities guarantee success, alleviate failure, and give order to their lives. Learning experiences focus on movement, exploration, and participation. Uncomplicated but enticing instructional materials and activities encourage action and language. Imagination provides opportunities to explore the world through stories, play, and imagination. In this way, fears and anxieties are safely considered and resolved. The National Center

[7] A pervading anxiety for children in Stage Two is the sense of inadequacy—"I can't do anything right." Chapter 4 reviews the developmental anxieties all children experience.

[8] A Stage Two program is designed to turn around self-defeating beliefs children have about themselves. Where they may have seen themselves as failures and unable to "measure up," the program helps them see themselves as adequate and esteemed individuals who can be successful.

For Doing	Use toys and materials in acceptable ways. Stop briefly to wait for instructions from teacher. Participate in play and learning activities spontaneously. Accept praise with self control.
For Saying	Answer questions. Ask questions. Describe characteristics of self and others. Share information with teachers and other children.
For Relating	Use imagination in play. Interact with others spontaneously. Participate in sharing activities with others. Cooperate with peers in organized activities.
For Thinking	Use motor skills for school readiness tasks. Classify objects and shapes. Recognize details and meanings in pictures. Recognize basic words and number concepts. Sequence pictures into stories.

FIGURE 2.7. Examples of competencies children need for success in Stage Two. *Note.* From *The Developmental Teaching Objectives for the DTORF–R,* Developmental Therapy Institute (2001/2005).

for Clinical Infant Programs (1992) suggests an emphasis on fostering confidence, curiosity, intentionality, self-control, relatedness, capacity to communicate, and cooperativeness. The Council for Exceptional Children's Division for Early Childhood (CEC/DEC) offers extensive guides to practices and standards that will accomplish these Stage Two goals (Bredekamp & Copple, 1997; McLean, Snyder, Smith, & Sandall, 2002; Sandall, McLean, & Smith, 2000; Sandall & Ostrosky, 1999; Smith et al., 2002).

As they progress successfully through Stage Two, children begin to rely more on their own initiative and good feelings about themselves and less on adults. If their experiences with adults, peers, and the world around them are successful, learning occurs. This, in turn, brings greater self-confidence, more independence, and increasingly responsible behavior (Erikson, 1959/1980; Lickona, 1985; Loevinger, 1976; Piaget, 1932/1960).

Educational Settings for Children in Stage Two

A natural educational setting is usually best for children ages 2 through 5 years who are developing in typical ways or who have mild to moderately challenging behaviors (Odom, 2000). The program may be in neighborhood day schools, childcare programs, pre-K, Head Start, early childhood school-based programs, kindergartens, or at home. In the primary grades there will also be troubled students with mild to moderate behavior problems who need to acquire many of the same Stage Two competencies of typically developing preschool children. An inclusive classroom is an effective setting for them to achieve the needed competencies.

Older children and teens are seldom in Stage Two unless they have severe disabilities such as thought disorders, pervasive developmental disabilities, profound neurological damage, depression or other mood disorders, serious substance abuse problems, or autism. Little that they do produces success and without success, they feel bad about themselves. They may communicate by screaming, cursing, kicking, resisting adults, attacking others, or destroying property. Sometimes they turn inward, masking their feelings, talking very little, avoiding others, passively resisting, or threatening self-destructive acts. These are responses of extremely angry, confused, or alienated children who have given up and do not like themselves or the world around them. For them, a customized Stage Two program in a special education setting can begin to help them gain competencies that will change the directions of their lives.

Some Guidelines for Teaching a Stage Two Program

The following instructional guidelines for this stage of development apply whether the child is a typically developing preschooler or an older child in need of a Stage Two instructional program.

- Insist on the participation of every child in every activity.
- Design activities so that every child in the group will enjoy participating and will feel successful.
- Avoid activities requiring long waits for a turn and have unison activities so that children have abundant opportunities to participate.
- Redesign group games and activities so that there are no losers.
- Select learning activities and materials that their age peers are using and redesign them as needed to guarantee success.
- Design all activities with opportunities for each child to talk; convey the expectation that talking is part of participating.
- Provide brief and simple demonstrations of each activity or material so that the children have a model to imitate successfully.
- Encourage children's involvement with each other by pairing them in activities.
- Select content themes in which characters are in situations similar to the personal experiences of each child in the group.
- Always ensure that there is a satisfactory resolution at the end of a story or creative play.

- Be flexible, improvise, and redesign a planned activity when their responses indicate that it is not sufficiently motivating or is too difficult to ensure success.

A Teacher's Role with Children in Stage Two

Children in Stage Two see adults as all-powerful—able to solve problems, meet needs, and provide emotional security. They need to be reassured that adults make good things happen. Because they crave recognition from adults, it is not surprising that pleasing adults is their central concern. Children value this approval so totally that it motivates almost everything they do and learn. They depend on adults to help when events become too difficult, to assist when something is challenging, and to teach them to be successful.[9]

The essential responsibility for a teacher of children who are in Stage Two is to be a trusted adult. For this to happen, the teacher must remain alert to each small sign of growth, avoid negative statements, and encourage every independent effort to succeed. Then, the effort must be recognized. Abundant encouragement and praise, such as "The Four As" shown in Figure 2.8, motivate children to try. This is the way they gain basic competencies that bring success and achievement of the Stage Two developmental goals listed in Figure 2.9.

[9]For children in Stage Two, adults are responsible for taking care of things and maintaining order. Refer to Chapter 4 for information about the preexistential phase of development and the way children view adult authority during this stage.

Developmental Practices in Elementary School

In elementary school, most students will be in Stages Three or Four, but a few will continue to need a Stage Two program.

During the Primary Grades, Typical Students Are in Stage Three

Stage Three: "I'm an okay person!"
The Program Goal: Learn to participate successfully in peer groups.

Students' Characteristics for Learning

Typical students in the primary grades are beginning to give up a self-oriented view so that they will be recognized by and approved of by others—teachers, family, and peers (Lickona, 1985, 1991; Selman, 1980, 1989, 2003). The 6- through 9-year-olds in this stage of development are learning to modify their intensely self-centered orientation of early childhood to obtain acclaim from others at school and at home (Barbour & Seefeldt, 1993). Learning the concept of "giving up in order to get" is a difficult idea for many primary grade students to understand at first. Because it is often hard for them to make this change, they rely on rules and routine for

- Attention
- Affirmation
- Approval
- Admiration

FIGURE 2.8. Children in Stage Two gravitate to teachers who provide "The Four A's."

- Participate in routines and activities with success.
- Use words to affect others in positive ways.
- Spontaneously seek ways to participate with others.
- Engage in activities with motor coordination, language, and school readiness skills.

FIGURE 2.9. Things that children can do when they achieve the Stage Two goal of participating with initiative and confidence.

a sense of security. They also express great concern when others fail to conform. Beneath this concern about the behavior of others is a fundamental defensiveness about their own rights and feelings as individuals (Coles, 1997; Kohlberg, 1981, 1984; Kohlberg & Hersh, 1977; Piaget, 1932/1960; Saarni, 2000).

Equally important is the need to be recognized as successful in what they do. So, when their own actions are criticized, students in Stage Three usually react defensively, frequently blaming others, denying involvement, or vehemently justifying what they have done (Turiel, 1983, 1994). Such self-protective reactions make it difficult for them to accept change easily or to see how their actions cause others to react to them in negative ways. When success eludes students during Stage Three, the result is usually an enormous sense of personal failure. Their emotional protection against failure is usually defensive behavior. They want to hold others responsible, yet are equally aware that they have not met the expectations of others. This is a complicated process. There is a gradual change in attitude from self-protection to self-judgment and then to self-esteem (Erikson, 1959/1980; Loevinger, 1976). If change is successful, social and emotional competence grow. Figure 2.10 shows how this happens.[10]

Stage Three also brings the beginning of a difficult transition, sometimes identified as the "existential crisis." During this phase of development, a student's view of authority gradually changes. There is an emerging self-reliance and independence. With increasing competence and mental maturity, students become less dependent on teachers and other adults (Piaget, 1967, 1977). They begin to recognize that adults cannot (and should not) be responsible for solving all of their problems and providing for their successes. As this shift in viewpoint occurs, they are uncertain about how to behave. Their dilemma is whether to continue to look compliantly to adults for direction or to act independently. They may comply and then suddenly protest. They try to conform and then pull away for fear of failing. Gradually, they learn to rely less on teachers for the regulation of behavior and begin to see their own responsibility for what happens.[11]

Perhaps for the first time at school, they also actively attempt to establish roles for themselves within their groups (Erikson, 1968, 1977). These roles may not be conscious, but usually they are efforts by students to protect their own interests. Conflict between group members is inevitable. The emotional and social dynamics between individuals are dominant forces in the day-to-day management of any classroom with students who are in Stage Three.[12]

Troubled older students in elementary school may also need a Stage Three-type program because they lack the social, emotional, or behavioral competencies of their own age peers. They have many of the same developmental characteristics of younger students. Similarly, older students in middle or high school who have moderate to severe mental health or behavioral

[10]Typical students in Stage Three are anxious to be viewed as acceptable. Worry over failure to obtain approval creates guilt. This developmental anxiety is discussed in Chapter 4.

[11]The "existential crisis" described in Chapter 4 occurs during Stage Three in response to the uncertainties a child feels about whether to assume personal responsibility or to continue to be directed by others.

[12]See Chapter 4 for a discussion of how to use group dynamics and roles of students in groups to help them acquire the competencies they need to succeed.

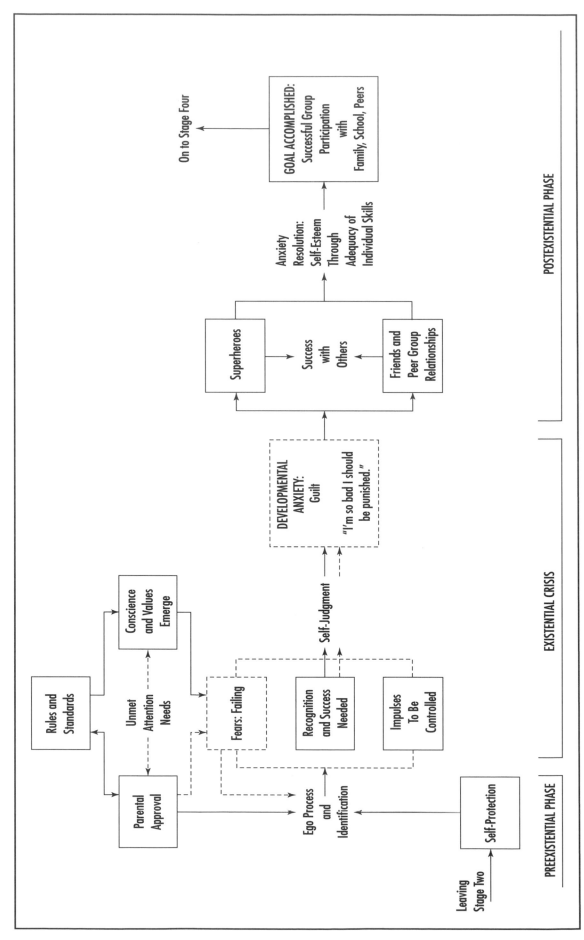

FIGURE 2.10. Key processes of typical social and emotional development in Stage Three. The dotted lines indicate the inner life of thoughts and feelings.

problems will lack essential competencies that are the foundation for success in Stage Three. The skills they need to learn for success as participating members of peer groups are similar to those needed by younger students in Stage Three. Examples of these competencies are shown in Figure 2.11.

For Doing	Finish what is started. Be part of making rules for the group. Participate when others are group leaders. Maintain acceptable conduct without reminders.
For Saying	Spontaneously talk with others about personal experiences. Contribute to group discussions. Make positive remarks about self and others. Recognize feelings of others. Express pride in personal and group achievements.
For Relating	Share spontaneously, without reminders. Recognize positive values in situations. Encourage friendships. Suggest standards of conduct for peers. Accept suggestions from peers.
For Thinking	Use primary academic skills successfully. Write about own ideas. Tell about stories from readings. Apply academic skills to problems of daily living.

FIGURE 2.11. Examples of competencies students need for success in Stage Three. *Note.* From *The Developmental Teaching Objectives for the DTORF–R,* Developmental Therapy Institute (2001/2005).

Instructional Needs of Students in Stage Three

As shown in Figure 2.11, achievement of primary academic skills is essential for success during this stage. Lessons are designed to catch and hold students' attention, give them confidence to try, encourage spontaneous participation, and minimize competition. Instruction is provided with a carefully planned group emphasis so that there are daily opportunities to learn how to be a participating group member. Content has personal and cultural meaning for everyone in the group, and each member is encouraged to contribute. Team projects, peer pairs, and games are used to simultaneously teach content and the competencies needed for success. The idea is to help them learn that acclaim comes from working together for *group success.*

Effective instruction assists students in learning to regulate their own behavior with decreasing needs for outside controls and greater self-direction. They must learn to use words as a substitute for physical reactions to anger, stress, or conflict. They are taught how to talk with adults about ways to handle crises and solve problems. *Life Space Crisis Intervention* (LSCI; Long, Wood, & Fecser, 2001) provides an effective strategy through which students learn to recognize connections between their own disruptive behaviors, their feelings, and the way others react to them.[13]

Motivation is intensified when lessons are about heroes and bigger-than-life characters who face challenges in which right wins over wrong. Themes of epic adventure and courage allow students to identify with winners and the forces of good. As they connect with heroes who triumph, their own fears and guilt about failing to meet expectations of others become less potent. They also learn ways to face their own problems with greater assurance.[14]

[13]LSCI is a strategy that teaches students to talk it out instead of acting it out. See Chapter 5 for more information about this strategy.

[14]Chapter 5 describes ways to adjust rules to students' stages of development.

Educational Settings for Students in Stage Three

Inclusive programs in general education with typically developing peers are essential if students in Stage Three are to acquire needed competencies. However, *experiences with age peers in inclusive settings must be successful*. Without skillful teachers to assure that each student experiences success, school may become a series of failures. Such experiences inevitably arrest further development. In contrast, a skillfully conducted inclusive program provides a student with ways to successfully achieve academic work and to participate as a contributing member of a peer group (Margolis & McCabe, 2003).

For some troubled students who are just beginning to work toward Stage Three competencies, an inclusive placement may not provide sufficient instruction for successful group membership. For these students, a smaller group in a controlled learning climate provides opportunities for targeted or intensive interventions in social skills. The programs also may offer intensive academics and include instruction in art, music, dance, library, or physical education. These small groups may be organized in counseling rooms, learning labs, resource rooms, or media centers. In whatever way small group learning opportunities are provided, they offer school experiences leading to successful inclusion later (Lane, Mahdavi, & Borthwick-Duffy, 2003; Ya-Yu, Loe, & Cartledge, 2002).[15]

Some Guidelines for Teaching a Stage Three Program

Here are essentials of Stage Three instruction for students of any age:

* Design lessons so that every student in the group participates and feels successful.
* Plan activities requiring short waits and taking turns, so students know that each person will be treated fairly with opportunity to participate.
* Establish a few basic rules, stated positively, and apply them consistently to all.
* Select learning materials age peers are using, and redesign them as needed to guarantee individual participation and success.
* Design group lessons that are culturally relevant, so that every student has opportunities to contribute successfully to the group effort.
* Emphasize benefits that result from group participation.
* Provide simple instructions and brief demonstrations of tasks, so students have models to imitate successfully.
* Select content in which successful heroes have feelings that students recognize as their own, or in which children and their friends triumph over evil together.
* Encourage group discussions about topics in which they share a common interest or experience.
* Redesign games and activities so that teams, rather than individuals, win and compete against their own team record.
* Be flexible, improvise, and redesign a lesson when students' responses indicate that it is not sufficiently motivating or is too difficult to ensure success.

A Teacher's Role with Students in Stage Three

Typically developing students at this stage look to teachers to enforce rules, treat them with fairness, and provide expert solutions to problems they cannot handle by themselves. They also need teachers to structure group involvement and praise individual contribution to mutual effort. Yet, troubled students are frequently angry with teachers and parents because the students have concluded that adults have failed them. They need explicit assurance that adults respect them and will not expect more than they can comfortably handle. Confidence is the basis for building trust in teachers, the program, and each other.

These expectations from students are challenges that require teachers to take on several different roles when working with students of any age who are in Stage Three. As students become convinced that a teacher or parent respects them, will be fair, will not set expectations too

[15]Chapter 8 contains information about various grouping options and how they are customized for the developmental and emotional needs of individual students.

high to meet successfully, and will not embarrass them in front of peers, they become more willing to cooperate. And when the activities are personally and culturally relevant, each student will participate with increasing enthusiasm, involvement, and self-confidence. The result is evident in the students' achievement of the developmental goals for Stage Three, shown in Figure 2.12.[16]

[16]Teachers must be group leaders, enforcers of rules, referees, and motivators for students during Stage Three. Check Chapter 7 for more on these roles.

- Use acceptable behavior in a group.
- Use words to express themselves constructively in a group.
- Find satisfaction in group activities.
- Participate in primary grade academic groups successfully.

FIGURE 2.12. Students who participate successfully in peer groups have achieved these Stage Three goals.

In Upper Elementary School, Typical Students Are in Stage Four

Stage Four: "I have friends; we look out for each other!"
The Program Goal: Learn to value group membership.

Developmental Characteristics for Learning

Students in Stage Four are typically upper elementary age students, between 9 and 12 years old. Coopersmith's (1967) classic study about the origins of self-esteem in fifth graders, ages 8 through 10 (typical beginning Stage Four students) contributes to an understanding of their developmental pathways. This is the period when their central concern is belonging—being accepted by friends, peers, and admired adults. They have reached a point in development when they are eager to be a member of a peer group. When students in Stage Four make behavioral choices, they generally imitate friends and those who belong to their own peer group. Loyalty to others is a dominant value. As they mature during this stage, quarreling and demands for competitive testing to prove themselves against others diminish in favor of conciliatory actions and acceptance as group members (Erikson, 1964, 1968; Loevinger, 1976).

Stage Four is also a time when new cognitive skills are developing and problem-solving abilities are increasingly important (Piaget, 1967, 1977). They are learning to use academic skills and abstract thinking processes to expand their own social competence and to understand ideas other than their own. Because of the newly acquired mental capacity to see another person's point of view, they also increase their abilities to establish and maintain friendships (Buhrmester, 1990; Mussen, Conger, Kagan, & Huston, 1990). These newly developed skills, shown in Figure 2.13, also encourage them to attempt solutions to their own problems and to consider values to live by (Selman, 1980, 1989).

- *Comprehending:* interpreting ("encoding"); advanced perception and understanding.
- *Remembering:* recalling experiences, observations, and understanding others.
- *Producing ideas:* generalizing; problem solving with inductive, inferential, and creative approaches.
- *Evaluating:* considering the quality of one's own thinking.
- *Reasoning:* deducing; using rules to solve problems.

FIGURE 2.13. During Stage Four, students develop new thinking skills.

During Stage Four, students learn that they have qualities that can make them valued members of a group. Their interpersonal, social, and gender role models are real people, in contrast to the superhero, larger-than-life idols from the previous stage of development. Parents, teachers, other admired adults, friends, and real-life heroes typify the people they would like to become. They need positive peer role models, friendships, and experiences with admired adults to be successful in achieving the competencies expected during this stage of development. With these needs met, they become increasingly willing to conform to expectations set by others.

The standards by which students in Stage Four judge themselves often create inner conflicts between independence and dependence. They are pulled in two ways: between the need to become independent individuals and the need to cling to the security of their previous childhood behaviors. They dream great dreams of accomplishment, but the limitations of their abilities defy their aspirations. They may fantasize about their ideal selves but are faced with accepting themselves as others see them. Family members, valued adults, friendships, and peer groups are all significant influences in this process (Aronfreed, 1968). By sifting through their own concerns and those of others, they learn that people differ in their values and points of view. And as they learn more about others, they learn more about themselves. In short, students in Stage Four are developing a comfortable, temporary balance between their inner needs and the expectations of others. Figure 2.14 illustrates how these forces compete, with conformity temporarily winning as a by-product of acceptance in a peer group.[17]

Instructional Needs of Students in Stage Four

Refer to Figure 2.15 for a list of the developmental competencies that are essential for students during Stage Four. In the previous stage, they acquired individual skills for participating successfully in groups when direction is supplied by teachers. They learned to abide by rules to avoid bad consequences. Their understanding of the reasons for rules increased. And they gained insight into consequences when rules are broken, although they were not always able to conform. The program teaches them how to be valued, contributing members in groups at school, at home, and in the community. In Stage Four, with this solid foundation of skills, they are prepared to become increasingly invested participants, able to accept greater responsibility for their own behaviors and to express concern for others.

A student-focused approach to instruction in Stage Four stimulates students' involvement in group experiences and obtains their commitment to increasingly responsible behavior. Figure 2.16 highlights activities that offer opportunities to teach group skills. Students are increasingly on their own, with less dependence upon adults for direction. They need affirmation in their efforts to speak out and encouragement to express their individuality. They also need acclaim for independent ideas, especially when their suggestions are used in group instruction (Beyda, Zentall, & Ferko, 2002).

Students in Stage Four must learn to set realistic individual goals. They also need encouragement to participate in developing and enforcing group rules. Although their program provides opportunities for them to make behavioral choices, they are also expected to conform to group standards, or experience the natural consequences of their actions. By having both negative and positive rules as choices—"Things we can do" and "Things we can't do"—and by understanding the potential consequences, students in Stage Four learn that *they* must make decisions about their own actions. When consequences happen, disruptive actions should not deter a valued teacher from providing positive support, guidance, understanding, and advocacy.

Stage Four competencies are especially difficult for troubled students to achieve. Stressful situations can trigger a flood of emotional memories and unresolved anxieties that break out in the form of immature, angry, hostile, or disruptive behavior. Whether emotionally generated behavior originates from incidents at school or is brought into class from outside, the behavior must be addressed.[18] In the process, be ready to provide increased structure and support, sometimes temporarily resorting to Stage Three management strategies. This may include the repeated use of individual LSCI: talking through a crisis to gain insight into how emotions influence the student's actions. Most students in Stage Four respond to this approach. They can talk

[17]Conflict between one's own wishes and the expectations of others is a primary developmental anxiety associated with Stage Four. These developmental anxieties are described in Chapter 4. The culmination of successful social, emotional, and behavioral development during this stage is a resolution of the conflict between independent resistance to conformity and satisfactions in belonging (Erikson, 1959/1980). Belonging wins—temporarily!

[18]See Chapter 4 for a discussion of emotional memory and its impact on learning and behavior.

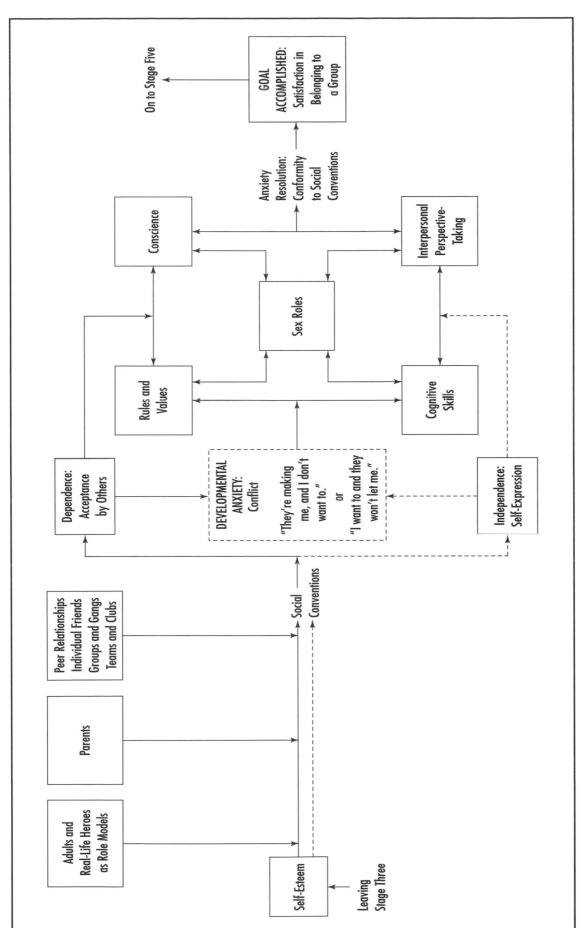

FIGURE 2.14. Key processes of typical social and emotional development in Stage Four. The dotted lines indicate the inner life of thoughts and feelings.

For Doing	Convey awareness of own progress. Participate in new experiences with flexibility and self-control. Use new ways of behaving. Use self-control when provoked by others. Accept responsibility for actions. Contribute to solving group issues in acceptable ways.
For Saying	Express feelings in acceptable ways. Describe connections between own behavior and responses from others. Expand verbal skills to make and keep friends. Be supportive of others and recognize their accomplishments.
For Relating	Explain characteristics of admired heroes. Become involved in activities with peers spontaneously. Recognize opinions and values different from one's own. Suggest solutions to problems. Indicate understanding of reasons for others' actions.
For Thinking	Express ideas in writings. Read for pleasure and information. Explain behavior and motivations of fictional characters. Use grammatical rules in writing. Identify differing social values. Use academic skills to solve problems of daily living.

FIGURE 2.15. Examples of competencies students need for success in Stage Four. *Note.* From *The Developmental Teaching Objectives for the DTORF–R,* Developmental Therapy Institute (2001/2005).

- Planning group learning experiences.
- Resolving conflicts.
- Evaluating their own performance in the group.
- Acknowledging successes—their own and those of others.

FIGURE 2.16. Active group participation is expected of everyone in a Stage Four group during these activities.

through their issues and explore alternative behavioral choices. If there is a group that threatens the rights of others or the learning climate, a lesson may be stopped to explore the issue with everyone. In this way, children learn to understand themselves and others and to conform to the rules, constraints, and consequences that apply to all.[19]

Educational Settings for Students in Stage Four

For students in upper elementary school, participation in general education classes is the preferred option where their peers provide positive models for acceptable standards of behavior and the academic curriculum is within their capacity to achieve. However, if students are behind their peers in academic achievement, they will also require individualized instruction. Small group study sessions and team projects offer good alternatives and individualized instruction can focus on achieving missing competencies.

In upper elementary and middle school older students may also have emotional or behavioral problems. Although they have many characteristics of their age peers, they frequently lack prerequisite skills for success. Programs for these students can be provided in several ways. For a few, an inclusive setting may be appropriate, if there is more than one teacher and both teach-

[19]Chapter 5 describes both individual and group LSCI in more detail, and Chapter 6 contains information about how to adapt the LSCI for students with developmental delays.

ers are highly skilled in teaching troubled students. However, unless the student makes measurable progress, continuing an inclusive placement is questionable. As these students get older, it becomes increasing difficult to meet their educational needs in large groups. It usually takes intensive intervention in small groups to give them the learning experiences they need. Consider a range of special educational options in which their instructional programs can be provided more effectively. This may be in a resource room, a scheduled pull-out class, a special education class with age peers, community day treatment, a mental health program, a psychoeducational program, after school, or in a special residential school.[20]

Some Guidelines for Teaching a Stage Four Program

An effective program for students who need Stage Four competencies must blend academic content with socially and emotionally appropriate instruction. Here are basic guidelines for their teachers:

- Involve students actively in individual and group goal setting.
- Encourage the group to participate in designing and conducting lessons so that everyone has input and feels successful in contributing to the effort.
- Expect each student to participate in all learning activities with the group.
- Provide lessons that connect to their real-life, cultural, and age-related interests and concerns.
- Include students in developing principles to guide their own behaviors.
- Encourage them to make choices that have natural consequences, but help them anticipate outcomes before choices are made.
- Plan daily activities for expanding their friendships and peer relationships.
- Be flexible. Encourage the group to improvise and redesign a planned activity when it is not as successful as they would like it to be.
- Involve students in individual and group evaluation of results.
- Encourage students to support and recognize each other's progress.

A Teacher's Role with Students in Stage Four

The major responsibility of a teacher providing Stage Four instruction is to teach students how to be effective group members. As students learn how to plan activities, rules, and procedures as a group, the teacher is the bridge to help them consider their decisions in relation to each other and to possible consequences. To do this, teachers reflect reality, suggest alternative actions, and assist the group in utilizing the abilities of each member. Less structure and control are required of teachers, except in instances when the group fails to function constructively or to benefit an individual student.

When teaching students in Stage Four, you will needed to help resolve conflicts between individuals and the group. Apply your knowledge of the group dynamics and be sensitive to providing insights while allowing the natural consequences of students' actions to unfold. As group facilitator, you may have to set limits sometimes. Involve students in decision making, yet maintain the boundaries of what is possible and acceptable. Because they have decision-making responsibilities, they sometimes make poor choices in the process, often with very real consequences. This is when they really need assistance. Avoid authoritarian attitudes; guide instead of direct, and encourage and inspire instead of confronting.[21]

Although a teacher's personal characteristics are powerful influences on the behavior of students in Stage Four, *genuine respect* is the essential attitude they need from adults. With their heightened sensitivity toward others, they are able to look closely at how teachers behave in their relationships with other adults and with other students.

They do not look to teachers for solutions to problems as often as they did in previous stages. However, they need to know that their teacher will be authentic in encouragement, responsive to their own individuality, and give straight answers. They will test less frequently and usually accept guidance if they see the teacher as someone who represents fairness and justice

[20]In any setting, the educational focus for students in Stage Four must include teaching them to be increasingly successful with their age peers. Chapter 8 describes small group options for offering either targeted or intensive interventions for students in Stage Four.

[21]Teachers of students in Stage Four must guide, facilitate, advocate, counsel, reflect reality, and be role models. Chapter 7 outlines these responsibilities and includes suggestions for building healthy relationships between teachers and students.

for all. The important point is that to assist students achieve the Stage Four goals, summarized in Figure 2.17, effective teachers must be people with personal characteristics students admire and can emulate.

- Contribute to group success.
- Communicate understanding of connections between feelings and behavior.
- Participate spontaneously as accepted group members.
- Use elementary academic skills for successful problem solving and social understanding.

FIGURE 2.17. Things that students who achieve Stage Four goals can do.

Developmental Practices in Middle and High School

When Young Teenagers Reach Secondary School

Stage Five: "Who am I, and what will I become?"
The Learning Goal: Use skills in new situations independently.

Developmental Characteristics for Learning

A typically developing young teen is characteristically beginning Stage Five. This is a period when some of the most dynamic changes occur in the entire course of human development (Benson, 1997; Blos, 1979; Lerner, 1993; Loevinger, 1976, 1987; Rogers & Ginzberg, 1992). These changes are shown in Figure 2.18. It can be a long and sometimes painful journey from

---

- Physical growth.
- Brain growth.
- Sexual maturity.
- Competing moral values.
- Advanced mental development.
- Enhanced self-awareness.
- Pending entrance into the adult world.

FIGURE 2.18. Example of the powerful changes that affect teenagers during Stage Five.

a conforming individual at the beginning of adolescence to an independent individual with personal identity and an integrated self by the end of Stage Five.

In this new developmental phase, a student is a self-confident 12-year-old,[22] comfortable with others, emotionally secure, and eager to be a part of the teen scene. However, complacency rapidly dissolves with the advent of puberty, when teens are forced to respond to the dramatic changes associated with adolescence. They must cope with new dimensions—mentally, physically, socially, spiritually, and sexually (Coles, 1990; Erikson, 1964, 1977; Piaget, 1967, 1977). Advances are also occurring in mental development, brain structure, and the ability to organize and think in abstractions (Giedd, 2000; Giedd, & Yurgelun-Todd, 2004; National Institute of Mental Health, 2004). Key changes during this process are shown in Figure 2.19.

The signature themes for young adolescents are *experimentation* and *identification* with new roles, new ideas, new values, and new behaviors. They have many competing options. Because of rapid body growth and sexual maturity, they are experiencing physical revolutions within themselves. They become concerned about how they appear to others, often in contrast to what they feel about themselves. Selman (1989, p. 412) describes two major motivations of young adolescents as they attempt to define themselves in relation to others. First, they have a need to share experiences with others; and, second, they have a need for independence to negotiate their interactions with others on their own terms. Both of these needs directly influence their learning.

Research suggests that parents and peers have influence on the development of teenagers, but in different ways (Youness & Smollar, 1985). Peers may be the greatest influence as teens form physical, social, and sexual identities. They also turn to peers for relief from emotional needs. However, parents and other valued adults are reported to have greater influence on teens' emerging ideals, values, morals, and ethical characteristics (Brittain, 1968; Brown & Gilligan, 1992; Feather, 1979; Selman, Beardslee, Schultz, Krupa, & Podorefsky, 1986). This seems to be a consistent finding whether the issue is political opinion (Gallatin, 1980); values and moral development (Arnold, 1984; Eisenberg, Miller, Shell, McNalley, & Shea, 1991); social knowledge and interpersonal perspective taking (McCarty, 1992; Selman, 1989, 2003); occupational choice (Kandel & Lesser, 1969); or parent–youth relationships (Lam, Powers, Noam, Hauser, & Jacobson, 1993; Patterson, 1988).

Among the challenges teens face are the large numbers of individuals, groups, and institutions with whom they interact. In addition to parents, relatives, mentors, friends, peers, and members of the many groups in which they participate, teens are influenced by public figures, sports heroes, and prominent entertainers. Every contact has potential for impact on their developing personalities, both negatively and positively (Cooper & Cooper, 1992; Mussen, Conger, Kagan, & Huston, 1990, chaps. 13, 14). Sifting through each experience for meaning and personal relevance takes them a number of years and many encounters with all sorts of people. In the process, they modify their thinking and actions while expanding their value systems for a new emphasis on personal goals, personal responsibility, social responsibility, fairness, and justice for everyone (Benson, Williams, & Johnson, 1987; Erikson, 1968, 1977; Kohlberg, 1981; Selman, 1989, 2003). Examples of these values and principles are shown in Figure 2.20.

The views of young teens about a vocation also change as they mature (see Figure 2.21). They first fantasize about a wide range of careers, usually glamorous ones that imitate admired adults' careers. As their self-appraisal becomes more realistic, they begin to consider a match between their personal likes and dislikes. With increasing maturity, they use their own values to guide career alternatives. Eventually, they begin serious consideration of the transition from high school either to work opportunities or to higher education (Ginzberg, 1972; Vondracek, 1993).

Instructional Needs of Typical Students in Stage Five

Just as in previous stages of social and emotional development, successful instruction of students in Stage Five requires attention to behavior, communication, socialization, academics, and thinking processes (Myers, 1993). As they acquire the needed competencies, shown in

[22]Age 12 is a rather arbitrary division between typically developing students in Stages Four and Five. Although biological adolescence begins at about age 12 for girls and a few years later for boys, there is much individual variation around this age. In addition, psychological adolescence is also a function of previous experience.

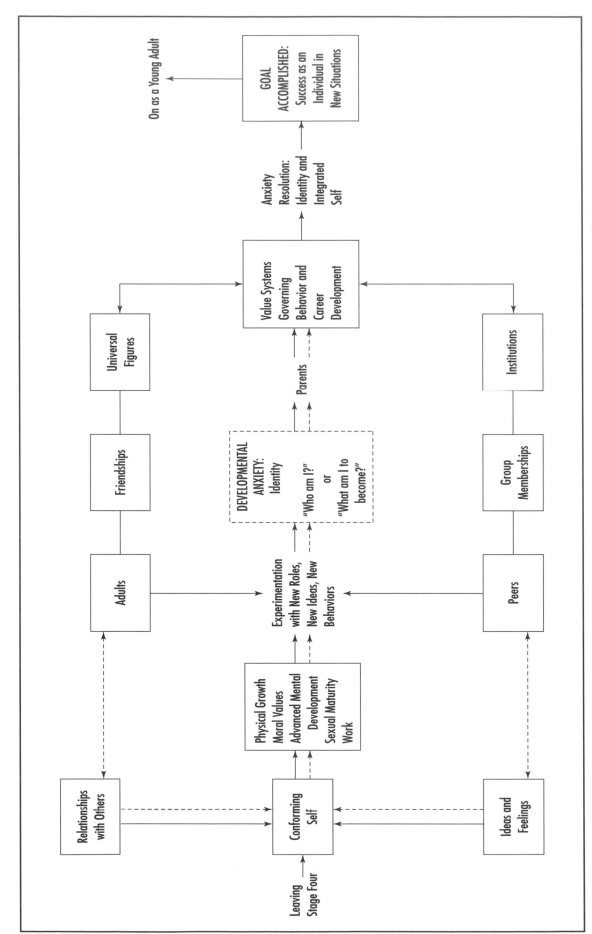

FIGURE 2.19. Key processes of typical social and emotional development in Stage Five. The dotted lines indicate the inner life of thoughts and feelings.

- Act in ways that express your own beliefs.
- Think for yourself.
- Think of others' needs.
- Choose friends with similar views.
- Be trustworthy.
- Expand personal goals.
- Express personal ideas.
- Take personal responsibility.
- Be a moral person.

FIGURE 2.20. Values and principles of Stage Five teenagers guide them in making choices.

1. Fantasy about careers.
2. Interest in many different careers.
3. Self-appraisal used as a guide.
4. Values guide career alternatives.
5. Transition from high school to higher education opportunities.
6. Realistic exploration of life's work and personal attributes.

FIGURE 2.21. During Stage Five, teenagers' ideas about a vocation typically evolve in this sequence. *Note.* From "Toward a Theory of Occupational Choice," by E. Ginzberg, 1972, *Vocational Guidance Quarterly,* 20, pp. 169–176. Copyright 1972 by the American Personnel and Guidance Association. Adapted with permission.

Figure 2.22, students achieve the overall goal for this stage—to be independently effective in new situations requiring both individual and group skills.

The curriculum should include courses that expand students' understanding of other people's behavior and the circumstances that shape behavior. This is essential information for them to have. Considerable amount of content for a Stage Five program can come from general academic courses and from the students themselves—from their own experiences and ideas about these experiences. See the examples in Figure 2.23.

Students in Stage Five learn to recognize the necessity for rules that benefit all. They are learning to associate natural consequences of rule violations as inevitable results of their own actions or those of others. Avoid presenting rules as restrictions. Rather, encourage students to develop rules that help them make connections between what they want to happen and the principles and values they want to follow. In this context, rules made by students in Stage Five are decision guides, generated by their own aspirations that empower them to be increasingly responsible for their own lives.

During a successful Stage Five phase of development, students become competent, responsible individuals, equipped to face the challenges ahead as adults. Instruction has helped them develop a sense of self-respect and the optimistic confidence that they can make personal contributions for satisfaction and purpose in their lives. Guided by their personal beliefs, feelings, values, and an inner confidence in their own competence, these students are on the brink of adulthood.

Instructional Needs of Troubled Adolescents

In contrast to their typically developing peers, troubled students in secondary schools often lack key skills for school or job success. They are physically, mentally, and sexually teenagers, with many of the same needs and competencies of their typically developing peers. But

For Doing	Polish social and work skills.
	Establish a positive reputation in various groups.
	Understand and accept law and order in school and community.
	Participate in group self-governance.
	Solve personal problems in constructive ways.
For Saying	Use complex, figurative statements.
	Support others by recognizing their contributions.
	Describe multiple motives and values in social situations.
	Express values and ideals spontaneously.
	Respond to provocation with positive verbal responses.
	Use communication skills to maintain positive interpersonal and group relationships.
For Relating	Understand and respect the feelings and beliefs of others.
	Interact successfully with others in various roles.
	Make personal choices based on values and principles.
	Indicate self-understanding by describing goals and characteristics.
	Sustain relationships with individuals and groups.
For Thinking	Apply clear thinking to solve personal problems.
	Use academic skills in school, home, and community.
	Suggest conciliatory solutions to provocation.
	Seek the ideas and opinions of others.
	Distinguish fact from fiction.
	Separate logical from illogical arguments.
	Understand multiple motives and values in social situations.
	Express values and ideals spontaneously.

FIGURE 2.22. During Stage Five, students must acquire sophisticated competencies. *Note.* From *The Developmental Teaching Objectives for the DTORF–R*, Developmental Therapy Institute (2001/2005).

- Biology
- Childcare
- Current Events
- Driver Education
- Drug and Alcohol Abuse Prevention
- Ecology
- Economics
- Ethics
- Health and Nutrition
- History
- Human Physiology and Sexuality
- Introductory Psychology
- Media
- Money Management and Finance
- Political Science
- Sociology
- Women's Studies
- Vocational and Career Education

FIGURE 2.23. Examples of courses in which students in Stage Five learn about human behavior, themselves, and life.

missing skills have disrupted their developmental progress, school achievement, and relations with others (Carter, & Wehby, 2003; Selman, & Schultz, 1990). For example, just like students in Stage Four, troubled teens may want independence but lack responsibility for their own actions. Or, like younger students, they may still have a unilateral view of obtaining fairness for themselves in an attitude typical of students in Stage Three: "Do to others what they do to you" (Kohlberg, 1981, 1984). It is the juxtaposition of their adolescence with delayed development that makes them such a challenge for their teachers, families, and future employers.[23]

To determine if students have the necessary prerequisite skills to begin acquiring the Stage Five competencies of their typically developing peers, assess their social, emotional, and behavioral competencies and the degree to which lower stage skills are lacking. Then, customize instruction to target achievement of the missing competencies. General teaching guidelines for previous stages apply, but adaptations must be made for their age-related interests and their differences in physical, mental, and sexual maturity. Adaptations can be done many ways, depending upon the severity of a student's problems.[24] If students are limited in their interests, try to provide academic content that is pertinent to their own experience and to that of their peers. Internet and television offer unlimited resources for content about current happenings and the lives of prominent individuals whom they admire.

Educational Settings for Stage Five Instruction

The question is frequently raised about whether a troubled teenager should receive educational services in an inclusive, general education program or in a special education class. Learning experiences that occur naturally in school and community provide the climate for mastery of competencies in Stage Five. Sports, recreational programs, and community service groups are additional resources that provide natural environments in which Stage Five programs can be conducted. A special group setting is not required when students have the prerequisite skills to achieve the competencies needed in Stage Five. A special program should be a supplement, not a substitute, for a general curriculum. However, in middle and high school, many troubled teens lack the competencies of Stages Three or Four, even as their adolescent needs also make them like their peers in Stage Five. The determining factor in selecting the right educational setting is the opportunity to receive a developmentally and emotionally appropriate educational program that provides successful experiences with typically developing peers.

Within the general education curriculum are many ways to offer the necessary instruction, such as special education resource rooms, counseling groups, work-study programs, vocational classes, or related community service programs. In a typical middle or high school, a program can be offered in any place that offers flexible scheduling—a counseling office, resource room, or learning center. A student's IEP or ITP will specify the most advantageous setting.

Some students benefit from one resource room class period each day. Others will need more assistance. A few students completing special education or mental health programs may be scheduled once a week or on a drop-by-as-needed basis for follow-up support. Resource room programs also offer assistance in inclusive settings for students with psychiatric disabilities returning to school from hospitals and residential treatment facilities.

A well-designed class in a resource room can offer considerable help to troubled students in secondary programs. Resource rooms can also be adapted for at risk students who are not enrolled in special education but are in need of special help. Resource rooms give students opportunities to participate successfully in a small group as well as time to focus on individual goals for academic and personal growth. Small groups foster exchanges of ideas and different points of view. Many times, these special peer groups are the means for students to "find themselves"—to validate their new, emerging identities and new social roles in the group. There are also opportunities for dealing with old anxieties that may have remained unresolved in the past.[25]

[23]Troubled teens are vulnerable to a range of potentially life-altering problems such as substance abuse, early pregnancy, automobile risks, suicide, violence, unemployment, and crime.

[24]Chapter 3 provides details of the assessment process that will reveal a student's profile of competencies and lags.

[25]See Chapter 4 for a discussion of how students deal with stress and use social power to influence peers and adults.

It is important to recognize that a small-group resource room program does not substitute for the natural friendships and peer relationships that typically develop in a secondary school. In a resource room, relationships with peers are usually transient but can provide a way to practice interpersonal skills (Selman & Schultz, 1990). There is insufficient time in a resource room to build a genuinely cohesive group. Close friendships and other significant relationships usually occur in homeroom, classes, clubs, home, neighborhoods, and sports and leisure groups. However, because such independent experiences are not always successful, it is important to be available for crises and have a drop-in arrangement for students seeking support or guidance.

Some Guidelines for Teaching Students in Stage Five

Here are suggestions for teaching students in Stage Five:[26]

* Involve students in analysis of their own competencies.
* Assist students to formulate personal and cultural values for setting goals and making decisions.
* Encourage contributions that draw from their daily experiences.
* Use established courses in the general curriculum to explore human issues.
* Emphasize culturally and personally relevant themes.
* Plan lessons that concern human behavior and the institutions that regulate it.
* Select materials and activities that expand the students' understanding of other people and themselves.
* Provide daily opportunities to expand skills for communicating effectively.
* Encourage group planning of lessons and projects to foster interpersonal competencies and successes with age peers.
* Design lessons that help make connections between school and their own real-life experiences.
* Provide opportunities for every student to develop individual, creative ideas.
* Guide them to broader understanding of people and diversity.
* Encourage personal responsibility for themselves and others, using the values and principles they have chosen.
* Be available for support, reflection, and affirmation.
* Share knowledge, expertise, and insights as a mentor and advocate.

A Teacher's Role with Students in Stage Five

Students who are in Stage Five of social and emotional development need little direct management but considerable guidance. They benefit from the experience and insight offered by their teachers. They also profit from the affirmation of themselves that comes when a teacher shows genuine respect. For this reason, accessibility is vital, and intervention typically focuses on listening and reflecting. This is often enough for teens who are attempting to resolve their own crises.

A teacher who is effective with teens in Stage Five must be a mentor, skilled teacher, counselor, and advisor. The essential characteristics are those that convey respect for students, recognition of their potential, and encouragement. However, a mistake that some teachers make is misunderstanding what constitutes an appropriate adult–teen relationship, whether it is as teacher, coach, mentor, parent, relative, or counselor. The fact that a teacher is identified by a student as someone to listen to, confide in, respect and emulate should not imply a buddy relationship. A teacher with admired qualities can guide and help, but a line must clearly define the teacher–student relationship for the guidance and mentoring aspects of a teacher's role with teens in Stage Five.

High school teachers are subject to scrutiny by their students. Teens respond to adult coercion and manipulation negatively, as do most individuals in every stage of human development. In contrast, respected teachers are imitated and become personal role models. Students seek teachers with qualities they value. They admire friendliness, sociability, looks, style, mannerisms, warmth, or power, among a number of traits. They are also responsive to teachers who have expertise and share it with them. Teachers with insight into the psychology of human behavior are seen as experts by their students. They are also admired for work-related skills, creative talents, sports skills, or social knowledge. Teachers also have great credibility when they show students how to play guitars, drive cars, help them to find summer jobs, or suggest ways to make and secure friendships.[27]

During Stage Five, if students have role models among their teachers and mentors, their developmental trajectories are invariably strengthened. They gain new competencies for responsible behavior and learn to apply these new skills independently. In the process, major developmental goals for behavior, communication, socialization, and cognition are achieved. These are reviewed in Figure 2.24.

- Respond to school and community with constructive, responsible behavior.
- Use communication skills to establish and enrich relationships.
- Initiate and maintain reciprocal friendships.
- Use advanced academic skills for personal enrichment and successful life skills.

FIGURE 2.24. The Stage Five goals are achieved when a student uses competencies independently in new situations to do these things.

Practice Thinking Developmentally!

With these brief snapshots of teaching and learning as references, select an age group among the children or teens introduced in Chapter 1 and answer these questions about each individual in that group:

1. What typical stage of development would you expect from a student this age?
2. Based on the limited description of each student, which developmental stage describes the student's general level of social, emotional, and behavioral competence?
3. Is the student just entering the stage, well into it, or about to finish it?
4. What adult role should you convey to enhance the student's continuing development?
5. As the teacher, what can you do to communicate this role?
6. What lessons and activities might be used to catch the student's interest and promote greater social, emotional, and behavioral competence?
7. What other information do you need before planning an educational program for this student?

Summary

In this chapter, basic characteristics of learners from toddlers to teens are summarized to provide an overview of developmentally based instruction. Each phase and stage of life brings new perspectives to children about what is important, how they see themselves, and how adults contribute to this developmental process of learning and living. Figure 2.25, "A Child's Expanding Spirit," catches the essence of the complexity, the interactions, and the outcomes that can occur when an adult's role is in synchrony with a child's development. It is a good way to close this chapter.

[27]Chapter 7 contains a discussion of characteristics of teachers who are effective in working with troubled students. This discussion includes a review of forms of adult social power that influence the behavior of their students.

What's Important to a Child	⬇	The Adult's Changing Role
"My needs"	"I am what I am given." (Infants and Toddlers)	Satisfier of needs
"Please adults"	"I can do, so I am what I will ... with your help." (Preschool Children)	Teacher of standards Provider of approval
"Be fair"	"I am what I can imagine I will be." (School-Age Children)	Upholder of authority Director of behavior
"Fit in ... and be responsible"	"I am what I can learn from others." (Middle School Children)	Social role model Group facilitator
"Do what's right and care for others"	"This, I believe ... so I can stand tall." (Teens)	Counselor Advocate Confidant

FIGURE 2.25. A child's expanding spirit. *Note.* From "Vibes, Values, and Virtues," by M. M. Wood, 1996b, *Reclaiming Children and Youth,* 5(3), p. 17. Copyright 1996 by Compassion Publishing. Reprinted with permission.

Assessment of Students' Competencies

The Developmental Teaching Objectives and Rating Form–Revised (DTORF–R) is a practical, reliable, easily administered ordinal rating scale consisting of 171 sequentially arranged items organized into four related subscales representing key competencies for healthy social, emotional, and behavioral development of children and youth from birth through age sixteen.

Buros Institute (2002, p. 218)

When increasingly responsible behavior is a goal for a student, it is necessary to include learning objectives that target specific social and emotional competencies. This chapter reviews the procedures used in Developmental Therapy–Developmental Teaching for doing this. The process is a research-based functional behavioral assessment (FBA) system to meet requirements in the reauthorized IDEA federal legislation, P.L. 108-466, which is The Individuals with Disabilities Education Improvement Act of 2004 (IDEA), Part A, Section 614 (b)(6) and (d) and Part D, Section 664 (c) (Congressional Research Service, 2005; National Association of School Psychologists, 2005; National Association of State Directors of Special Education, 1998).[1] The FBA process, explained in this chapter, assesses competencies needed by all students for success in school. Four broad domains of development are assessed in this system: behavior, communication, socialization, and cognition. By providing a way to identify a student's current and missing competencies in a developmental framework, the process provides objectives for an Individualized Education Program (IEP), Individualized Family Service Plan (IFSP), or Individual Transition Plan (ITP) that are appropriate for a student's stage of development, instruction, and behavior management. Because the progression of key behavioral milestones indicates competencies needed by all children and teens to be successful in school, this system brings assessment of children with special needs into alignment with universal standards, a goal of the federal reauthorization of the Elementary and Secondary Education Act, known as the No Child Left Behind Act of 2001 (NCLB; U.S. Department of Education, 2002).

[1]Part B of IDEA authorizes early intervention to avoid having children "wait to fail" before receiving special services.

Comprehensive Assessment

Two instruments are described in this chapter: the *Social–Emotional–Behavioral Quick Profile (S–E–B Quick Profile)* and the *Developmental Teaching Objectives Rating Form–Revised (DTORF–R)*. With these, you can obtain a comprehensive assessment of development for children from birth to age 16, with or without special needs. The process establishes developmentally relevant learning objectives, instructional strategies, and a behavioral intervention plan (BIP). It also documents student progress over time. Detailed rating and scoring directions are included. There is an example of the completed process with Tony, an 11-year-old student. Information is also included about how the DTORF–R was developed as a valid and reliable way to assess a student's current strengths and instructional needs.[2]

S–E–B Quick Profile

The profile is simply a form to use during the "get acquainted" period with a new student. It requires very little time to complete and is a way to estimate the general goals and competencies that the student has already achieved and those that may be needed. It also gives the teacher initial information for assigning the student to an instructional group.

As you begin planning, review all available information about the student in school, in the neighborhood, and at home. Gather test scores, grades, attendance records, psychological and educational assessments, examples of schoolwork, notes from previous teachers, and any other information that broadens your understanding of the student. With this information as a base, meet with parents, teachers, and other service providers to complete the *Profile*.

The Quick Profile Rating System

Figure 3.1 is an example of the way the *Profile* rating was completed for Tony, a student introduced in Chapter 1. Each column indicates a domain goal, presented in developmental sequence. In each domain, an area of strength is marked *A* (the goal is 100% achieved) or *B* (approximately 80–99% mastery of the goal). The first goal statement in each domain needing current instructional focus is marked *C* (approximately 20–79% achieved). The *C* areas become the general developmental focus for social–emotional–behavioral instruction in a student's current program. Areas beyond a student's current developmental needs are marked *D* (approximately 1–19% mastered) or *N* (goals too advanced for the student currently) and are not included in the initial instructional plan.

It is important to consider all of the information you may have available about a new student as you complete the *Profile* in consultation with others who are a part of the student's educational program. The consensus of those involved in a student's instruction determines the *S–E–B Quick Profile* grades. It is also necessary to observe and judge the student's behavior through a "developmental lens." To do this, keep in mind typically developing children or teens associated with that student's age. Also consider the behavioral expectations and standards placed on students at that age and the amount of adult support usually provided.

For example, take the Stage Two Behavior goal: "Participate in routines and activities with success." Generally, typical children in this stage are between ages 2 and 6. The expectation for their participation is simply to be involved with the activity—to try. The quality and length of their participation is not judged. The same expectation should be used when determining if an older student has achieved this Stage Two goal. Ask yourself, "Will this student get involved in an activity, even if the participation is not up to the standard I expect of students this age?" If the answer is *yes,* consider that goal mastered and move on to the next goal in the column. Why? Because the next goal in the sequence builds on this simple base and will add an increased expectation for performance.

By moving a student on to the next higher goal, you will be able to target a higher performance level with an instructional focus that avoids misjudging the student's capacity as lower than it actually is. However, the opposite mistake can also occur if you set expectations beyond a student's current capacity. If the student is judged to be ready for a higher goal before the prerequisite competencies are mastered, there may be a lack of progress, an increase in behavior problems, and increased resistance to learning.[3]

[2]The *S–E–B Quick Profile* and the complete DTORF–R are included in the accompanying CD and can be reproduced. The electronic version of the DTORF–R with a system for record keeping and reporting is available online through *www.dtorf .com*

[3]A student's stage of development is seldom the same across the four competency areas, so a profile is essential if you want to target instruction precisely.

S–E–B Quick Profile

Student: _Tony_ DOB: _(11 years old)_ Date: _(example)_

Start with *Behavior*. Read down the column and enter a letter for each competency. Then go to the first competency in *Communication* and repeat the process, working down the column. Continue rating each competency until you have a grade in each of the 20 boxes. Use this scale: A = *Fully mastered*, B = *Most of the time*, C = *Some of the time*, D = *Occasionally*, NR = *Not ready to do this*. Instruction begins with the first competencies graded B and C in each column. When mastered, the next competencies become the focus.

Stage	Behavior (Doing)	Communication (Saying)	Socialization (Relating)	Cognition (Thinking)
Respond with Pleasure and Trust				
One	Respond to objects and people with basic motor skills.	Use words to gain needs.	Trust an adult sufficiently to respond to requests.	Explore surroundings spontaneously with basic mental and motor skills.
	A	A	A	A
Respond with Success				
Two	Participate in routines and activities with success.	Use words to affect others in positive ways.	Participate in activities with others.	Engage in activities with motor coordination, language, and school readiness skills.
	B	A	B	A
Learn Skills for Successful Peer Group Participation				
Three	Use acceptable behavior in a group.	Use acceptable words to express ideas in a group.	Find satisfaction in group activities.	Participate in primary grade academic lessons.
	C	C	C	A
Invest in Group Memberships				
Four	Contribute to group success.	Communicate understanding of connections between feelings and behavior.	Participate spontaneously as an accepted group member.	Use elementary academic skills for successful problem solving and social understanding.
	NR	NR	NR	C
Apply Individual Skills in New Situations				
Five	Respond in school and community with responsible behavior.	Use communication skills to establish and enrich relationships.	Initiate and maintain reciprocal friendships.	Use advanced academic skills for personal enrichment and successful life skills.
	NR	NR	NR	NR

Signatures of Raters: _____

_____

FIGURE 3.1. Example of a *Social–Emotional–Behavioral Quick Profile.*

Consider Tony's *Profile*. It reveals that his strength is in the cognition domain, with grades of *A* for achievement of goals in Stages One through Three. His instructional goal for this area appears to be in Stage Four, using his academic skills to help him problem solve successfully and increase his social understanding. This strength is especially significant in helping Tony with his relationships as a participating member of his class. This is where he has the greatest delay, as shown with the grades of *B* for Stage Two in Behavior and Socialization domains. (You may recall in the previous chapters that Stage Two includes competencies typically achieved by children before they begin first grade.) Tony's grades of *A* for Communication in Stages One and Two indicate that he has achieved early childhood competencies necessary for success in school. But he currently needs Stage Three instruction in Communication (graded *C*) to use acceptable actions and words for successful participation as a group member.

It is clear from this preliminary profile that Tony will be a challenge for his teachers. Although a bright student (Stage Four in Cognition), he has extremely immature relationships and an inability to be a successful group member (grades of *C* in Stage Three for Behavior, Communication, and Socialization). Overall, this *Profile* suggests to Tony's teachers and parents that Stage Three instruction will be needed for Tony's program.[4]

As a new student enters a group, behavior frequently changes. It may take some students several weeks to adjust. For others, the behavior shown on the first day is what continues. As soon as you believe you have a realistic and consistent picture of a student's strengths and weaknesses, conduct a functional behavioral assessment using the DTORF–R to obtain a comprehensive measure of development as the foundation for planning the student's IEP and BIP.

The DTORF–R

After a student's preliminary profile of goals and overall stage of development have been estimated with the *Quick Profile,* as described above, and the student has made an initial adjustment to the classroom, a functional behavioral assessment is needed. In keeping with federal requirements, the DTORF–R is used for assessment, establishing specific learning objectives for a student's program and the beginning point for planning customized learning experiences strategically matched to the student's needs. In this way, learning experiences and lessons are prepared with precise developmental and personal relevance, and a student's progress can be tracked over time.[5]

The DTORF–R is a criterion-referenced assessment instrument used in Developmental Therapy–Developmental Teaching for a comprehensive assessment. There are 171 items hierarchically organized in four ordinal subscales: *Behavior* (DOING, 33 items), *Communication* (SAYING, 35 items), *Socialization* (RELATING, 41 items), and *Cognition* (THINKING, 62 items). The items in each subscale are key competencies, stated as sequential learning objectives to achieve specific competencies and broad developmental goals. These sequences are the pathways for through five stages of social, emotional, and behavioral development from birth to age 16 in each competency area. Figure 3.2 shows the relationship of each stage to the chronological age for typically developing children.[6]

The selected objectives are used for a student's individualized educational program (IEP) and behavioral intervention plan (BIP). As shown in Figure 3.3, a teacher selects instructional and management strategies, plans customized lessons and learning experiences, and provides the type of adult role that meets the developmental needs of a student. Repeated DTORF–R ratings during a school year are the basis for new objectives as a student achieves the ones originally selected. Repeated assessments also provide a record of student progress.[7]

Who Does the Assessment?

At least three people should participate in the rating. These should be individuals who know a student well and bring knowledge of the student from different perspectives. The team should include the special and general education teachers who will provide Developmental

[4]When you obtain a preliminary estimate of a student's stage of development with the *S–E–B Quick Profile,* compare the results with the "Snapshot" descriptions of students' learning characteristics and instructional needs in Chapter 2.

[5]The DTORF–R is a versatile, highly practical, and reliable way to obtain a functional behavioral assessment (FBA), identify instructional objectives, plan effective instructional programs, and document student progress. Appendix B contains analyses of the scope and sequence for item content in each subscale.

[6]DTORF–R items represent specific competencies needed by students to successfully accomplish the broad goals identified in the *S–E–B Quick Profile.*

[7]Because the DTORF–R is based on how healthy social, emotional, and behavioral competence develop, it is the structure for strategic instruction to help students achieve competencies in these areas.

- 2-year-olds have mastered Stage One competencies and are beginning to acquire competencies in Stage Two.
- 4-year-olds are acquiring competencies about mid–Stage Two.
- 8-year-olds have mastered all of the competencies in Stages One and Two and many in Stage Three.
- 10-year-olds have all of the competencies in the first three stages and are into Stage Four.
- 12-year-olds are completing Stage Four while adding new competencies in Stage Five.
- 14-year-olds are working on about half of the Stage Five competencies.
- 16-year-olds have achieved about 70% to 80% of the Stage Five competencies.

FIGURE 3.2. Consider competencies of typically developing age peers when assessing a student with the DTORF–R.

- Identify a student's current strengths and weaknesses.
- Select social–emotional–behavioral objectives for a student's IEP, IFSP, or ITP.
- Complete a functional behavioral analysis and develop a positive behavioral intervention plan.
- Identify students in need of referral for additional services such as mental health or other related services.
- Design programs of instruction in the social–emotional–behavioral domains for school, home, or mental health settings.
- Make decisions about placement and grouping individuals for instruction.
- Plan lessons that foster achievement of IEP objectives.
- Document progress of individuals and groups.
- Evaluate program effectiveness.

FIGURE 3.3. Uses of DTORF–R ratings.

Therapy–Developmental Teaching and the teaching assistants who work with the team in the classroom. Others involved with any aspect of a student's program also participate in the assessment. These could include parents or a primary caregiver, family program specialist, or case manager, who provide information about how the student functions at home and in the neighborhood. School administrators, psychologists, psychiatrists, and recreation, music, art, reading, and language therapists are also encouraged to contribute to DTORF–R ratings. This shared understanding of a student's educational and developmental needs promotes communication about the student's program needs and progress once the program is under way (Rock, 2000).[8]

In some programs, older students are involved in their own DTORF–R assessment. Although their participation may be time consuming, this participation has been shown to be effective in teaching them how to set goals and evaluate their own progress. Older students are particularly responsive to this. Their ownership of the selected objectives seems to be stronger, and they learn personal goal-setting skills in the process.

Where To Begin Rating on the DTORF–R Form

The rating team completes a consensus rating by reviewing the extent to which the child demonstrates mastery of each item. There are three forms for recording the rating: one form is used to assess children in early childhood programs; another, with elementary school students; and the third, for those in middle and high school. Because the items are sequenced in order of difficulty and reflect typical ages and stages of development, the three forms provide different

[8]Those who have regular contact with a student should be included on the DTORF–R assessment team. Part A, Section 614(d) of the new IDEA legislation permits development and change in an educational plan by schools and parents without convening a meeting, if alternative communication methods are used.

shaded areas to indicate items not typical for that age group. Items in these shaded areas are not usually rated in an assessment.[9]

A rating begins with the first item in the unshaded section in each subscale. On the DOING subscale, this would be Item 1 for early childhood. For students in elementary school, begin with Item 9, and for preteens and teens start with Item 15. All items in shaded sections prior to the beginning items are presumed mastered. However, if a severe disability is present, rating may begin in a shaded area, with items lower in the sequence.

The DTORF–R Rating System

The rating procedure is summarized in Figure 3.4. Each item is rated in the order in which it appears on the rating form. A check (✓) indicates that the student demonstrates mastery of the item consistently (9 out of 10 times) in all settings—home, neighborhood, and school. Items marked X indicate skills not mastered but currently needed. Items are marked NR (not ready) when developmentally beyond a student's age and stage or when the student has not yet achieved mastery of prerequisite skills and is not ready for instruction on these items. With a completed rating, the missing skills, marked X, become objectives in a student's individualized educational plan (IEP, IFSP, or ITP). Instruction begins at the point where the student has sufficient mastery of prerequisite skills to be successful.

- Select the DTORF–R form that corresponds to the student's age and general school placement:

Birth–age 5	Early Childhood Form
Ages 6–11	Elementary School Form
Ages 12–16	Middle/High School Form

- On any form, begin rating with the first item in the unshaded section of the Behavior subscale.
- Rate every item in one of three ways:
  - ✓ = *Mastered item*
  - X = *Item not mastered—focus for current instruction*
  - NR = *Item not mastered—not yet ready for instruction*
- Rate each item in sequence within the unshaded areas until reaching items in the shaded areas. Do not rate in the shaded areas.
- After four items are rated "X" in a subscale, mark remaining items "NR" except those that have been mastered out of sequence. These can be marked ✓ but not "X."
- Continue ratings for Communication, Socialization, and Cognition.
- Look for the pattern of Xs across the four subscales for instructional objectives.
- Use the stage with the most Xs across the four subscales as the student's overall stage for instruction.

FIGURE 3.4. Rating directions for the DTORF–R.

Items Cross-Referenced Between Subscales

A few items occur in more than one subscale. This indicates that the item should be mastered in both subscales for the sequence of items to be fully accomplished. It would *not* be correct to rate an item mastered (✓) on one subscale while needing to work on it (X) or not yet ready to work on it (NR) in another. If an item has been mastered on one scale, a student should be credited with mastery of the item if it occurs on another. However, it is not unusual for a student's development to be uneven, with noticeable lags on one or two subscales. When this happens, it is possible that a student may be rated NR on a cross-referenced item for one subscale and rated X on that same item in another. This indicates that the student has acquired the necessary prerequisite skills on one subscale but not on the other.[10]

Limit the Number of Instructional Objectives

Every item within the unshaded area of the rating form is assessed in one of three ways (✓, X, or NR). At least 1 but not more than 4 items should be marked X within each subscale during any single rating period. This allows for at least 4 but no more than 16 objectives—a realistic and manageable number for current instructional objectives. Although it is clear that a student will need to acquire additional, higher order competencies at some future time, it is essential that a program be strategically focused to assure that the current objectives are thoroughly mastered before new ones are added. Limiting the number of objectives at any one time avoids unrealistic expectations and keeps the program focused on essentials. Without the limit of 16 maximum objectives at any given time, overload can occur. With too many objectives, students may fail to achieve solid mastery of any of them because the program lacks focus.

The DTORF–R rating system is illustrated in Figure 3.5 with Tony's first rating. Because he is 11 years old and still in fifth grade, the form for elementary school age students is selected. This automatically gives him credit for 100% mastery of all items in the shaded area (Stage One) across the four subscales. The actual rating for Tony begins with Stage Two, Item 9 in Behavior and continues through Item 28. Then, ratings are done for the remaining subscales.

What a Rating Shows About Instructional Needs

The pattern of Xs indicates a student's general stage of development and reveals missing competencies. Use the 20% to 80% rule in Figure 3.6 to clarify a student's current stage for instruction. If a student has mastered at least 20% but not more than 80% of the items in a stage, it becomes the designated stage for instruction. Less than 20% indicates that the student's development has not yet reached that stage and instruction should not be provided at that level. Use the 20/80 rule to judge whether a student is just entering a developmental stage, is well in to it, or close to mastery of the competencies for that stage.

However, when a student has mastered more than 80% of the items in a stage, it indicates that instruction should begin in the next stage. This next higher developmental stage then provides the guide. If several stages have been partially mastered, program emphasis should be directed toward closing the gap between stages by targeting lower objectives while maintaining instructional practices at the student's predominant stage. Similarly, if performance on one subscale is lagging behind others, instruction should strategically target the objectives in that area while continuing to provide instruction in the other competency areas.

> Less than 20% mastery of DTORF–R items within a stage indicates that the student is not yet in that stage. At least 80% mastery indicates that the student has mastered the stage and should begin learning objectives for competencies in the next stage.

FIGURE 3.6. The 20%–80% rule.

Ways To Report DTORF–R Assessments

There are several ways to summarize an assessment. Basic information is the total number of items mastered (✓s). It is helpful to summarize frequency counts and percentages of items mastered in each subscale, for each stage, and for the total rating. The summary of Tony's rating in Figure 3.7 illustrates one way to do this.[11]

Consider the percentage summaries of Tony's DTORF–R. Overall, his score is 108—the total number of items mastered, including the items he received 100% credit for in Stage One.

[10]Several items on each subscale have small triangles to alert raters that a student must demonstrate the item *spontaneously*. This requires a student to use the skill without help or guidance for full mastery. The other items assume that a teacher contributes to the student's performance with verbal cues, prompts, or coaching.

[11]DTORF–R summaries can be prepared for an individual or for an entire group.

DTORF-R: RATING FORM FOR ELEMENTARY SCHOOL AGE STUDENTS

BEHAVIOR (DOING)

Stage I
1. Indicates Awareness
   Tactile / Aud. / Motor
   Taste / Visual / Smell
2. Reacts by Attending
3. Responds by Sustained Attending
4. Responds to Simple Stim./Motor Behav.
5. Responds to Complex Stim.
6. Assists in Self-Help
7. ▲Responds Independently/Play Materials
8. ▲Indicates Recall of Routine

Stage II
9. Uses Play Material Appropriately
10. Waits/No Intervention
11. Participates/Sitting/No Intervention
12. Participates/Movement/No Intervention
13. ▲Participates Spontaneously
14. ▲Accepts Praise, Success with Control

Stage III
15. ▲Completes Individual Tasks independently
16. ▲Conveys Awareness/Expected Conduct
17. Gives Reasons for Expectations
18. Tells Other Appropriate Behavior
19. ▲Responds Approp./Leader Choice
20. ▲Refrains from Behavior/Others Lose Control
21. ▲Maintains Acceptable Behavior in Group

Stage IV
22. Indicates Begin. Awareness/Own Progress
23. Indicates Flexibility/Procedures
24. Participates/New Experience With Control
25. Implements Alternative Behaviors
26. ▲Responds/Provocation With Control
27. Accepts Responsibility/Actions, Attitudes
28. ▲Suggests Interpersonal & Group Solutions

Stage V
29. >Seeks New Work Skills
30. >Seeks Desired Group Role
31. Understands, Accepts Law & Order
32. Participates/Group Self-Governance
33. Solves Personal Problems

COMMUNICATION (SAYING)

Stage I
1. Produces Sounds
2. Attends to Speaker
3. Responds/Verbal Stim./Motor Behav.
4. Responds/Cues/Word Approx.
5. ▲Uses Word Approx. Spon.
6. Uses Word/To Adult
7. Uses Word/To Peer
8. ▲Uses Word Sequence/No Model

Stage II
9. Answers with Recog. Words
10. Exhibits Receptive Vocabulary
11. ▲Commands, Questions/Word Sequence
12. ▲Shares Minimal Information/Adult
13. Describes Characteristics/Self, Others
14. ▲Shares Minimal Information/Peer

Stage III
15. ▲Describes Personal Experiences
16. Shows Feeling Responses Approp.
17. Participates Approp./Group Discussion
18. ▲Indicates Pride in Self
19. Describes Attributes/Self
20. Describes Attributes/Others
21. Recognizes Others' Feelings
22. ▲Verbalizes Pride/Group Achievement

Stage IV
23. Channels Feelings/Creative Media
24. Same as B-22
25. Explains/Behavior Influences Others'
26. ▲Verbalizes Feelings Approp. in Group
27. ▲Initiates Positive Relationship Verbally
28. ▲Praises, Supports Others Verbally
29. ▲Expresses Cause–Effect/Feelings, Behavior

Stage V
30. Uses Complex, Figurative Statements
31. ▲Uses Conciliatory Verbal Responses
32. ▲Recognizes, Includes Others' Contribu.
33. Describes Multiple Motives, Values
34. ▲Expresses Values, Ideals
35. ▲Sustains Interpersonal, Group Relations

SOCIALIZATION (RELATING)

Stage I
1. Indicates Awareness/Others
2. Attends/Other's Behavior
3. Responds to Name
4. Engages/Solitary Play
5. Interacts Non-Verbally/Adult
6. Responds/Request/Come
7. Dems. Underst./ Request
8. Same as C-6
9. Begins Emergence/Self
10. ▲Participates/Parallel Play
11. Same as C-7
12. ▲Seeks Contact/Familiar Adults

Stage II
13. ▲Demonstrates Imaginative Play
14. Same as B-10
15. ▲Initiates Social Movement/Peer
16. Participates/Directed Sharing Activity
17. Participates/Interactive Play
18. ▲Cooperates/Peer./Organ. Times

Stage III
19. ▲Shares Material, Takes Turns
20. ▲Imitates Approp. Behavior
21. Labels Situation/Values
22. Leads, Demonstrates for Group
23. Participates/Activity Suggested by Peer
24. Sequences Own Experiences
25. Indicates Developing Friendship
26. ▲Seeks Assistance, Praise/Peer
27. ▲Assists Others/Conforming

Stage IV
28. Identifies with Adult Heroes
29. Sequences Group Experience
30. ▲Suggests Activ./Peer Group
31. Expresses Aware./Others' Different Actions
32. Listens to Others' Opinions
33. Express Interest/Peer Opinion of Self
34. Suggests Solutions to Problems
35. Discrims. Opposite Social Values
36. Draws Infer. from Social Situations

Stage V
37. ▲Understands, Respects Others
38. ▲Interacts Successfully/Multiple Roles
39. ▲Makes Personal Choices/Values
40. Indicates Self Understanding/Goals
41. ▲Sustains Relationships

▲ = Child must do this spontaneously for item mastery, without direct adult cues or control to elicit the behavior.

Raters **Debbie Huth, Constance Quirk, Mary Wood**

Child **Tony**   Birthdate **Jun** (Month) **1** (Day) **1992** (Year)   Date of Rating **Nov** (Month) **1** (Day) **2003** (Year)

(continues)

DTORF-R FORM FOR ELEMENTARY SCHOOL AGE STUDENTS, Page 2

COGNITION (THINKING)

Stage I

1. ☑ Same as B-2
2. ☑ Same as B-3
3. ☑ ▲Shows Short Term Memory
4. ☑ Same as B-5
5. ☑ ▲Imitates Acts of Adults
6. ☑ Shows Fine, Gross Motor/18 months
7. ☑ Knows Names/Objects
8. ☑ Same as C-4
9. ☑ ▲Same as C-5
10. ☑ Matches Shapes, Objects with Spaces
11. ☑ Identifies Body Parts (4)
12. ☑ Recognizes Detail/Pictures
13. ☑ Sorts Objects
14. ☑ Labels Pictures

Stage II

15. ☑ Recognizes Use of Objects
16. ☑ Performs Body Coord./3 year
17. ☑ Matches Identical Pictures (of 3)
18. ☑ Performs Fine Motor Coord./3 year
19. ☑ Recognizes Different Object (of 3)
20. ☑ Understands 3 Opposites
21. ☑ Categorizes Diff. Pictures/Similar Assoc.
22. ☑ Counts to 4 (1 to 1)
23. ☑ Identifies 4 colors, 3 shapes
24. ☑ Alternates Same, Different Pict. or Object
25. ☑ Counts to 10 (1 to 1)
26. ☑ Performs Eye-Hand Coord./5 year
27. ☑ Discrims. Num., Designs, Upr. Case Letters
28. ☑ Performs Body Coord./5 year
29. ☑ Recognizes Groups to 5
30. ☑ Dem. Rote Memory/5 year
31. ☑ Sequences 3 Pictures

Stage III

32. ☑ Performs Eye-Hand Coord./6 year
33. ☑ Performs Body Coord./6 year
34. ☑ Reads 50 Primary Words
35. ☑ Recogs., Writes Numerals/Groups 1-10
36. ☑ Writes 50 Primary Words/Mem., Dictation
37. ☑ Listens/Story/Comprehension
38. ☑ Explains Others' Behavior
39. ☑ Reads Sentences/Comprehension
40. ☑ Adds, Subtracts/1-9
41. ☑ Identifies Illogical Elements
42. ☑ Writes Sentences About Story
43. ☑ Performs Physical Skills, Games/Elem.
44. ☑ Writes Simple Sentences
45. ☑ Adds, Subtracts/Time/Money
46. ☑ Reads, Explains Meas. Words
47. ☑ Reads, Tells About Stories
48. ☑ Uses Place Value, Regroup, Mult., Seriation

Stage IV

49. ☒ Writes to Communicate
50. ☒ Multiplies, Divides to 100
51. ☒ ▲Reads for Pleasure, Information
52. ☒ Computes Money to $10.00
53. ☒ Explains Fiction Characters
54. NM Uses Grammatical Rules/Writing
55. NM Same as S-35
56. NM Solves Measurement, Logic Problems

Stage V

57. NM Seeks Others' Opinions/Current Issues
58. NM Discriminates Fact/Opinion
59. NM Recognizes, Explains Illogical Behavior
60. NM Solves Word Problems/Fractions, Decimals
61. NM Same as B-33
62. NM ▲Uses Academic Tools/Citizen, Worker

NOTES

DTORF-R SUMMARY (sum √s = items mastered)

Number of Behavior items mastered: **16**

Number of Communication items mastered: **19**

Number of Socialization items mastered: **22**

Number of Academics/Cognition items mastered: **51**

Total DTORF-R items mastered: **108**

Developmental stage: **3**

Chronological age at rating: **11** (Years) **5** (Months)

Parent's Signature   Family Services Coordinator Signature   Teacher's Signature - General Education

Teacher's Signature - Special Education   Additional Signature

FIGURE 3.5. *Continued.*

	DTORF–R Subscales				
	DOING 33 items	**SAYING** 35 items	**RELATING** 41 items	**THINKING** 62 items	**Total** 171 items
Stage One					
Total Items	8	8	12	14	42
No. Mastered	8	8	12	14	42
% Mastered	100%	100%	100%	100%	100%
Stage Two					
Total Items	6	6	6	17	35
No. Mastered	5	6	5	17	33
% Mastered	83%	100%	83%	100%	94%
Stage Three					
Total Items	7	8	9	17	41
No. Mastered	3	5	5	17	30
% Mastered	43%	63%	56%	100%	73%
Stage Four					
Total Items	7	7	9	8	31
No. Mastered	0	0	0	3	3
% Mastered	0%	0%	0%	38%	10%
Stage Five*					
Total Items	5	6	5	6	22
No. Mastered	0	0	0	0	0
% Mastered	NR	NR	NR	NR	NR
Total					
Total Items	33	35	41	62	171
No. Mastered	16	19	22	51	108
% Mastered	48%	54%	54%	82%	63%

FIGURE 3.7. Summary of the baseline DTORF–R assessment for Tony, an 11-year-old, fifth-grade student.
*NR = Not ready for instruction because prerequisite skills have not been achieved.

Among Stage Two competencies, he has 94% mastered (33 of the 35 items). In Stage Three, he has 73% of the competencies (30 of the 41 items). In Stage Four, he has only 10% (3 of 31 items). Applying the 20% to 80% rule, Tony has not yet reached the 80% achievement level for Stage Three in three of the four subscales, even though his age suggests that he should be developing Stage Four competencies. These results indicate that, overall, Tony is developmentally in Stage Three and will need direct strategic instruction at that level to achieve each item rated X.

To understand how a rating can be interpreted, use the steps outlined in Figure 3.8. Notice that in Tony's summary he has one remaining skill to achieve in Stage Two for *Behavior* and *Socialization* although his overall developmental stage for instruction is currently in Stage Three. In addition, he has achieved 100% of the *Cognition* competencies for Stage Three and is ready for instruction on Stage Four competencies in that area. This three-stage spread in development across the competency areas is not unusual, especially for troubled students who are disconnected from interactions with others but also intellectually gifted. However, it is a considerable challenge for his teachers.[12]

[12]Chapter 8 contains information about ways to adjust instruction to cross-stage profiles frequently evident in troubled children and teens.

Step 1: Check for accuracy of rating.
- Birth date and rating date complete?
- One to four items marked X on each subscale?
- Cross-referenced items rated correctly?
- Summary of ✓s completed on back of rating?
- Rating form signed?

Step 2: Check for age–stage–item discrepancies.
- Expected stage based on chronological age?
- Actual stage based on pattern of Xs across all four areas?
- Actual stage on each subscale area?
- Compare items marked X for discrepancy with items marked ✓.

Step 3: Scan profile for strengths and weaknesses.
- Look for highest and lowest items rated X on each subscale.
- Circle one item in each area that may be most easily mastered.
- Consider temporarily omitting the most difficult item in a subscale with wide scatter of Xs.
- Find student's strengths for planning successful lessons.

Step 4: Identify priority areas for program focus.
- Determine *overall* stage goal based on pattern on all Xs.
- Review specific area goals where Xs are clustered.
- Consider subscales that need instructional priority.
- Match student with positive peer models for group activities.
- Identify curriculum that addresses objectives and goals for maximum student motivation.

FIGURE 3.8. Use these steps to review a completed DTORF–R.

In planning Tony's instructional program based on the DTORF–R assessment, the focus is on Stage Three, with the following 15 selected learning objectives:[13]

[13]Chapter 2 contains snapshot descriptions of the way an educational program is designed to meet the needs of students at each stage of development.

Behavior
- Participate spontaneously in group activities without guidance from teachers (Item 13).
- Complete individual tasks independently (Item 15).
- Respond appropriately to peer leaders (Item 19).
- Refrain from unacceptable behavior when others lose control (Item 20).

Communication
- Participate appropriately in group discussions (Item 17).
- Recognize others' feelings (Item 21).
- Verbalize pride in group achievements (Item 22).
- Channel feelings into creative media (Item 23).

Socialization
- Cooperate spontaneously with peers in organized activities (Item 18).
- Participate in activities suggested by peers (Item 23).

- Develop beginning friendships (Item 25).
- Seek assistance and encouragement from peers (Item 26).

Cognition
- Keep a brief daily log to communicate with teachers or counselor (Item 49).
- Read the daily paper for specific information (Item 51).
- Explain fictional characters in stories, movies, and TV (Item 53).

Estimating Severity of Delay

Estimate severity of developmental delay by comparing actual DTORF–R scores to developmental age scores. A developmental age score (DAS) offers an additional way to report a rating. It is used to compare a student's development to that of peers of the same age. Such comparisons reveal the extent to which missing competencies may have delayed a student's overall development. A conversion table for changing DTORF–R scores to DAS is available in the CD and online at www.dtorf.com (See also the *DTORF–R Technical Report* from the Developmental Therapy Institute, 1998a). The conversion table includes all possible scores and the corresponding DAS, calculated for all chronological ages (in months) from birth to 16 years.

To obtain an estimate of the severity of a student's developmental delay, first convert the student's current chronological age into months. Use the DAS column in the conversion table to locate that age and corresponding DTORF–R score for a typically developing student of the same age. Then, divide that age-based score into the student's actual score (total number of items mastered), and subtract that percentage from 100. The resulting percentage gives the extent of the student's developmental delay. It also aids in estimating the length and intensity of intervention necessary for a student to master selected objectives.

Figure 3.9 is a guide for estimating the severity of a student's delay. A 25% developmental lag or less, in comparison with age peers, is a mild delay. These students usually respond quickly to intervention in fully inclusive settings with a preventative focus. A 26% to 74% lag behind peers indicates a moderate level of delay. These students need targeted interventions, often in pullout or resource room settings. When developmental delay is 75% or greater, the missing skills present severely challenging problems. These students require intensive interventions.[14]

[14]Chapter 1 contains a discussion of how levels of severity in students' needs can be addressed in planning schoolwide services. Chapter 8 describes options for grouping students to meet these diverse developmental needs.

25% below age peers	Mild delay
26% to 74% below age peers	Moderate delay
75% or more below age peers	Severe delay

FIGURE 3.9. Use a DTORF–R developmental age score to estimate how missing competencies have delayed a student's development.

Refer to Tony's DTORF–R again as an example of how to calculate this estimate of severity in developmental delay. His overall score is 108 (total items mastered). He is 11 years and 5 months old (137 months). The DAS conversion table provided in the CD indicates that a score of 133 is expected for typically developing students Tony's age. In contrast, his actual score of 108 puts him below that of his peers. The ratio of 108 to 133 is 81% of the expected items mastered, leaving a 19% delay. Thus, Tony's score indicates that his social, emotional, and behavioral development is slightly delayed when compared to his age peers.

It is helpful to use this procedure when considering educational placement and grouping options. For students with scores (and resulting competencies) close to their age peers, fully inclusive placements are preferred. With this information, Tony's teachers and parents are confident that his individualized educational program should be provided in an inclusive, general education setting. However, when there are larger differences between an individual's score and that of age peers, special educational groupings may be needed with more intensive interventions and curriculum modifications (see Chapter 8 for further discussion).

When Questions Arise in Rating

Questions may arise about whether the student has demonstrated mastery of a given item, and whether that item should be marked with a ✓ or an X. Uncertainty about rating an item may indicate that the student is close to mastering it in one setting but not in another. When this happens, review carefully the examples of mastery provided in the DTORF–R subscale assessment booklets (Developmental Therapy Institute, 2001/2005). Then, if a consensus cannot be reached, postpone rating that item until the rating team can gather more information or observe the student in several settings. If uncertainty still persists, mark the item X (err on the side of caution) and keep it as an instructional objective with particular focus on its application in several settings. Within a short time, the student should show mastery of that item. There are also instances when a student's behavior may be viewed as a problem when it is actually quite typical for the student's age group. To minimize ratings that are too high or too low, always consider typical behavior for the item among age peers.

Rating a Student with Severe Sensory or Physical Disabilities

When a student has severe sensory or physical disabilities, alternative ways to respond may be accepted as substitutes for the item's typical response. When it is necessary for a student to use an alternative response to demonstrate mastery, indicate at the bottom of the form that a substitute stimulus or response mode was used. For example, a student with physical disabilities may never be able to master an item requiring specific motor skills. Or, a student with profound hearing loss may not be able to demonstrate mastery of items requiring oral speech but can use alternative forms of communication to demonstrate an acceptable response. In these circumstances, rate the student using the alternative response mode, or omit the item from the rating, go on to the next item, and note the omission or alternative response mode at the bottom of the form.

A Group DTORF–R

After completing individual assessments of each student in a group, use the group form to combine all of the items rated X for the students on a single profile. The steps used to complete a group DTORF–R are described in Figure 3.10, and Figure 3.11 gives an example of Tony's rating and those of other students in a special reading group. For each subscale, the teacher entered the names and rating results of each student in the group as their individual DTORF–R assessments were completed. The resulting pattern of Xs indicates competencies needed by the group collectively and those that are uniquely individual.

As a visual reminder of the targeted objectives for each student, this group profile is an easy way to stay focused on group instruction while meeting individual needs. Teachers using this form find it helpful to post it in easy view while planning and teaching. This reminds them to include the selected objectives for every student in each lesson. They also report that it helps them to avoid overlooking students whose objectives diverge from mutually shared objectives of the group.

Document Student Progress

A baseline rating is not the end of assessment. DTORF–R ratings should be scheduled throughout the school year. With each reassessment, objectives that have been achieved are replaced with new ones, and instruction is adjusted to focus on the new objectives. In this way, a student

---

Step 1: Enter group members' names above each area.
Record only the Xs for each student in all four areas.

Record ages of each student in margin on page 2 of the form.

What is the expected stage(s) based on chronological ages of students?

What is the actual stage(s) for group program planning based on the Xs?

Step 2: What are the group's needs?
Identify stage where most Xs occur, for group focus in program planning.

Identify mutually shared items, marked X for several students.

Consider where to focus instruction for the greatest number of X objectives.

Consider smaller groups with shared objectives for intensely focused instruction.

Step 3: What are the individual needs within the group?
Look for the highest and lowest items marked X in each area, for special attention.

Consider how to modify strategies for individual needs among "outlying objectives."

Step 4: Compare student profiles for maximum information.
Identify students who seek security by relying on adults.

Identify those who need positive peer models.

Identify those who do and do not participate (talk, show interest in others).

Select peer models for group activities from those who do.

Plan lessons to include every student as a contributing member of the group.

FIGURE 3.10. Use these steps to complete a group DTORF–R.

[15]Both NCLB and IDEA legislation require measurable and rigorous indicators to report students' annual yearly progress (AYP) toward achieving stated goals.

moves through an increasingly complex series of objectives to achieve the needed competencies. Repeated assessments also provide a way to document a student's progress in achieving IEP, IFSP, or ITP goals and objectives (U.S. Department of Education, 2001, 2005).[15]

The diagram in Figure 3.12 illustrates a practical, criterion-referenced approach to documenting student progress following an initial assessment, which is the baseline for repeated ratings during the school year. This documentation is designed to answer the question, Has the student acquired the specified learning goals and objectives while participating in the program?

Annual Yearly Progress (AYP)

Repeated ratings provide information to answer this question and to make continued refinements in instruction. The process identifies objectives that have been achieved since the previous rating and replaces them with new, more advanced objectives as the student acquires competencies. In this way, a student's program is accelerated as rapidly as possible. Instruction does not continue to focus on an objective after it has been mastered.[16]

[16]The DTORF–R is used in both formative and summative evaluations for planning and guiding each student's educational plan.

To use this evaluation system, rate each student to obtain an accurate baseline assessment (just as in the previous example with Tony). This establishes the foundation for documenting student progress. Then, specify a yearlong schedule for repeated assessments. Ratings should be repeated *at least* three times during a 10-month school year or quarterly in a year-round program. Most teachers and administrators prefer that reassessments follow grading periods.

(*text continues on p. 76*)

GROUP DTORF–R

BEHAVIOR (DOING)

	Tony	Student 1	Student 2	Student 3
Stage I				
1. Indicates Awareness				
2. Reacts by Attending				
3. Responds to Sustained Attending				
4. Responds to Simple Stim./Motor Behav.				
5. Responds to Complex Stim.				
6. Assists in Self-Help				
7. ▲Responds Independently/Play Materials				
8. ▲Indicates Recall of Routine				
Stage II				
9. Uses Play Material Appropriately				
10. Waits/No Intervention				
11. Participates/Sitting/No Intervention		X		
12. Participates/Movement/No Intervention		X		
13. ▲Participates Spontaneously		X		
14. ▲Accepts Praise, Success with Control				
Stage III				
15. ▲Completes Individual Tasks Independently		X		
16. Conveys Awareness/Expected Conduct				
17. Gives Reasons for Expectations				X
18. Tells Other Appropriate Behavior				
19. ▲Responds Approp./Leader Choice			X	
20. ▲Refrains Behavior/Others Lose Control			X	X
21. ▲Maintains Acceptable Behavior in Group			X	X
Stage IV				
22. Indicates Begin. Awareness/Own Progress	X			
23. Indicates Flexibility/Procedures				X
24. Participates/New Experience With Control				X
25. Implements Alternative Behaviors				
26. ▲Responds/Provocation With Control				
27. ▲Responds/Provocation With Control				
28. ▲Suggests Interpersonal & Group Solutions				
Stage V				
29. ▲Seeks New Work Skills				
30. ▲Seeks Desired Group Role				
31. Understands, Accepts Law & Order				
32. ▲Participates/Group Self-Governance				
33. Solves Personal Problems				

COMMUNICATION (SAYING)

	Tony	Student 1	Student 2	Student 3
Stage I				
1. Produces Sounds				
2. Attends to Speaker				
3. Responds/Verbal Stim./Motor Behav.				
4. Responds/Cues/Word Approx.				
5. ▲Use Word Approx. Spon.				
6. Uses Word/To Adult				
7. Uses Word/To Peer				
8. ▲Uses Word Sequence/No Model				
Stage II				
9. Answers with Recog. Words				
10. Exhibits Receptive Vocabulary				
11. ▲Commancs, Questions/Word Sequence	X			
12. ▲Shares Minimal Information/Adult				
13. Describes Characteristics/Self, Others				
14. ▲Shares Minimal Information/Peer				
Stage III				
15. ▲Describes Personal Experiences		X	X	
16. Shows Feeling Responses Approp.		X	X	
17. Participates Approp./Group Discussion	X		X	X
18. ▲Indicates Pride in Self				
19. Describes Attributes/Self				
20. Describes Attributes/Others				
21. ▲Recognizes Others' Feelings	X		X	X
22. ▲Verbalizes Pride/Group Achievement	X			X
Stage IV				
23. Channels Feelings/Creative Media	X			
24. Same as B-22				
25. Explains/Behavior Influences Others'				
26. ▲Verbalizes Feelings Approp. in Group				
27. ▲Initiates Positive Relationship Verbally				
28. ▲Praises, Supports Others Verbally				
29. ▲Expresses Cause-Effect/Feelings, Behavior				
Stage V				
30. Uses Complex, Figurative Statements				
31. ▲Uses Conciliatory Verbal Responses				
32. ▲Recognizes, Includes Others' Contribu.				
33. Describes Multiple Motives, Values				
34. ▲Expresses Values, Ideals				
35. ▲Sustains Interpersonal, Group Relations				

SOCIALIZATION (RELATING)

	Tony	Student 1	Student 2	Student 3
Stage I				
1. Indicates Awareness/Others				
2. Attends/Other's Behavior				
3. Responds to Name				
4. Engages/Solitary Play				
5. Interacts Non-Verbally/Adult				
6. Responds/Request/Come				
7. Dems. Underst./ Request				
8. Same as C-6				
9. Begins Emergence/Self				
10. ▲Participates/Parallel Play				
11. Same as C-7				
12. ▲Seeks Contact/Familiar Adults				
Stage II				
13. ▲Demonstrates Imaginative Play				
14. Same as B-10				
15. ▲Initiates Social Movement/Peer				
16. Participates/Directed Sharing Activity				
17. Participates/Interactive Play				
18. ▲Cooperates/Peer/Organ. Times	X		X	
Stage III				
19. ▲Shares Material, Takes Turns		X	X	
20. ▲Imitates Approp. Behavior		X	X	X
21. Labels Situation/Values		X		X
22. Leads, Demonstrates for Group				
23. Participates/Activity Suggested by	X			
24. Sequences Own Experiences		X		
25. Indicates Developing Friendship	X			X
26. ▲Seeks Assistance, Praise/Peer	X			X
27. ▲Assists Others/Conforming				
Stage IV				
28. Identifies with Adult Heroes				
29. Sequences Group Experience				
30. ▲Suggests Activ./Peer Group				
31. ▲Expresses Aware./Others' Different				
32. Listens to Others' Opinions				
33. Expr. Inter./Peer Opinion of Self				
34. Suggests Solutions to Problems				
35. Discrims. Opposite Social Values				
36. Draws Infer. from Social Situations				
Stage V				
37. ▲Understands, Respects Others				
38. ▲Interacts Successfully/Multiple Roles				
39. ▲Makes Personal Choices/Values				
40. Indicates Self-Understanding/Goals				
41. ▲Sustains Relationships				

▲ Student must demonstrate item spontaneously without help or guidance.

(continues)

FIGURE 3.11. Example of a group DTORF–R for four students with special needs in an inclusive fifth-grade program.

GROUP DTORF-R, Page 2

COGNITION (THINKING)

Stage I

	TONY	STUDENT 1	STUDENT 2	STUDENT 3
1. Same as B-2				
2. Same as B-3				
3. ▲Shows Short-Term Memory				
4. Same as B-5				
5. ▲Imitates Acts of Adults				
6. Shows Fine, Gross Motor/18 months				
7. Knows Names/Objects				
8. Same as C-4				
9. ▲Same as C-5				
10. Matches Shapes, Objects with Spaces				
11. Identifies Body Parts (4)				
12. Recognizes Detail/Pictures				
13. Sorts Objects				
14. Labels Pictures				

Stage II

	TONY	STUDENT 1	STUDENT 2	STUDENT 3
15. Recognizes Use of Objects				
16. Performs Body Coord./3 year				
17. Matches Identical Pictures (of 3)				
18. Performs Fine Motor Coord./3 year				
19. Recognizes Different Object (of 3)				
20. Understands 3 Opposites				
21. Categorizes Diff. Pictures/Similar Assoc.				
22. Counts to 4 (1 to 1)				
23. Identifies 4 colors, 3 shapes				
24. Alternates Same, Different Pict. or Object				
25. Counts to 10 (1 to 1)				
26. Performs Eye-Hand Coord./5 year				
27. Discrims. Num., Designs, Upr. Case Letters				
28. Performs Body Coord./5 year				
29. Recognizes Groups to 5				
30. Dem. Rote Memory/5 year				
31. Sequences 3 Pictures				

Stage III

	TONY	STUDENT 1	STUDENT 2	STUDENT 3
32. Performs Eye-Hand Coord./6 year				
33. Performs Body Coord./6 year				
34. Reads 50 Primary Words				
35. Recogs., Writes Numerals/Groups 1–10				
36. Writes 50 Primary Words/Mem., Dictation				
37. Listens/Story/Comprehension		X		
38. Explains Others' Behavior		X		
39. Reads Sentences/Comprehension				
40. Adds, Subtracts/1–9				
41. Identifies Illogical Elements		X		
42. Writes Sentences About Story		X		
43. Performs Physical Skills, Games/Elem				X
44. Writes Simple Sentences				
45. Adds, Subtracts/Time/Money				
46. Reads, Explains Meas. Words				
47. Reads, Tells About Stories			X	X
48. Uses Place Value, Regroup, Mult., Seriation			X	X

Stage IV

	TONY	STUDENT 1	STUDENT 2	STUDENT 3
49. Writes to Communicate	X			X
50. Multiplies, Divides to 100			X	
51. ▲Reads for Pleasure, Information	X		X	
52. Computes Money to $10.00				
53. Explains Fiction Characters	X			
54. Uses Grammatical Rules/Writing				
55. Same as S-35				
56. Solves Measurement, Logic Problems				

Stage V

	TONY	STUDENT 1	STUDENT 2	STUDENT 3
57. Seeks Others' Opinions/Current Issues				
58. Discriminates Fact/Opinion				
59. Recognizes, Explains Illogical Behavior				
60. Solves Word Problems/Fractions, Decimals				
61. Same as B-33				
62. ▲Uses Academic Tools/Citizen, Worker				

Date: _EXAMPLE_

Class Stage: _EXAMPLE_

Teacher: _EXAMPLE_

FIGURE 3.11. *Continued.*

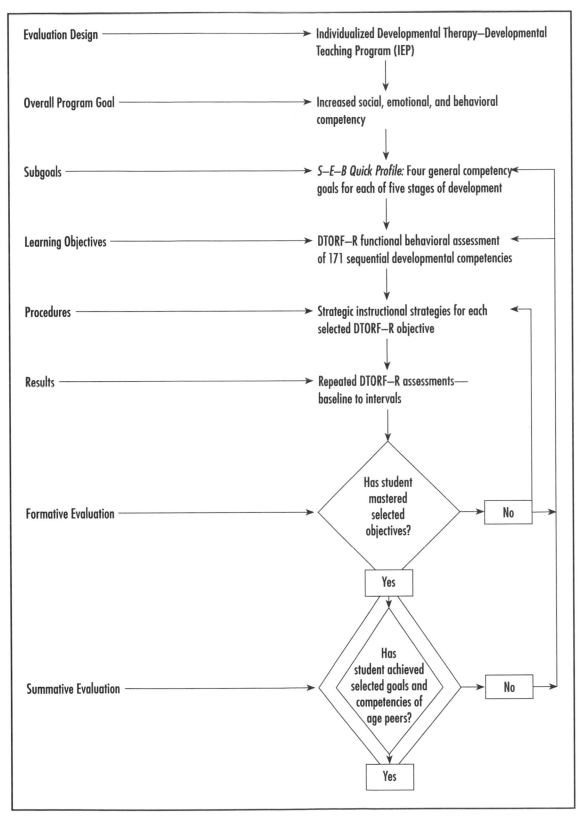

FIGURE 3.12. Follow this diagram to evaluate student progress.

By completing ratings on a schedule that corresponds to a school's grading periods, parents receive DTORF–R information regarding the progress of their child toward IEP goals and objectives along with other *Quick Profile* information.

There are numerous ways to summarize repeated assessments. The usual way is to record the number of items mastered (✔) on each of the four subscales and the total for each repeated assessment. These scores can be compared and gains calculated. Individual scores can also be pooled to obtain an average and range for gains by an entire group. When group gains are combined, be certain that the data for all students reflect the same time period between assessments.

Interpreting Results of Repeated DTORF–R Ratings

After more than two assessments, DTORF–R data can provide trends over time. When interpreting repeated assessments of a student, first consider the actual time between ratings. For example, if 10 weeks have passed since the student's baseline rating, several objectives should have been achieved, although gains may not yet be evident among items that are more difficult for the student. If the rating represents an entire school year, notable gains should be evident on each subscale, reflecting progress in every competency area. If this does not occur, either the program has somehow failed to meet the student's needs or something extraordinary has occurred in the student's life to produce regression and a negative effect on learning.[17]

No student can sustain dramatic increments in learning without periodic plateaus—to practice and assimilate. Typically, a large gain on one subscale will be followed by a plateau period for that competency area, and no additional gains in the domain should be anticipated during the following weeks. During these periods, mastery of additional competencies is usually minimal. View this next period as a practice phase to solidify item mastery because practice is essential to sustain gains. Also, anticipate gains on other subscales during this time. With strategic instruction, a student can often make gains in other competency areas where there has been little previous progress.

Consider Tony's mid-year DTORF–R assessment after 10 weeks, shown in Figure 3.13, and the comparison between his first and second ratings, summarized in Figure 3.14. Patterns of gain or lack of gain across the four subscales can help refocus his instruction during the next rating period. His greatest gains are on the Behavior subscale, where his achievement of behavioral competencies indicates that he learned to participate, work independently, and maintain control without assistance from his teacher when others were misbehaving (Items B-13 mastered in Stage Two and B-15 and B-20 in Stage Three). These gains suggest that he is ready for more instruction in the Stage Four behavioral area where he spontaneously achieved one additional competency: showing flexibility in modifying procedures to satisfy changing needs of the group (Item B-23). With these key milestones achieved in a relatively short period, Tony's teachers choose to continue their focus on Stage Three instructional strategies. The intent is to provide him with behavioral successes during the next 10-week period and to be certain that these gains are maintained. This will also give him time to achieve the remaining two objectives he needs in Stage Three (B-19 and B-21). These objectives will be particularly hard for him to achieve because they involve interaction with peers—his greatest difficulty.

Recognizing that successful interaction with others is an increasingly significant competency as children mature, Tony's teachers decided to shift their emphasis from objectives in *Behavior* to *Communication* and *Socialization*, where he had made little notable progress. His only gains in these areas were a Stage Two *Socialization* objective (S-18: Cooperates with peers spontaneously during organized class projects) and a Stage Three *Communication* objective (C-17: Participates appropriately in group discussions and cooperates with peers during organized instructional time). In Stage Three, he had failed to achieve any of the previously selected objectives, continuing to avoid interacting with peers and making no attempt at friendships (Items S-23, S-25, S-26).

Tony's teachers knew that achievement of the Stage Three objectives were necessary to his eventual accomplishment of the broad Stage Three developmental goal: participating successfully

[17]Analysis of a student's rating also reveals what has happened since the last rating and what to expect during the next rating period.

(text continues on p. 79)

DTORF-R: RATING FORM FOR ELEMENTARY SCHOOL AGE STUDENTS

BEHAVIOR (DOING)

Stage I
1. Indicates Awareness
   - ✓ Tactile ✓ Aud. ✓ Motor
   - ✓ Taste ✓ Visual ✓ Smell
2. Reacts by Attending
3. Responds by Sustained Attending
4. Responds to Simple Stim./Motor Behav.
5. Responds to Complex Stim.
6. Assists in Self-Help
7. ▲Responds Independently/Play Materials
8. ▲Indicates Recall of Routine

Stage II
9. Uses Play Material Appropriately
10. Waits/No Intervention
11. Participates/Sitting/No Intervention
12. Participates/Movement/No Intervention
13. ▲Participates Spontaneously
14. ▲Accepts Praise, Success with Control

Stage III
15. ▲Completes Individual Tasks independently
16. Conveys Awareness/Expected Conduct
17. Gives Reasons for Expectations
18. Tells Other Appropriate Behavior
19. ▲Responds Approp./Leader Choice
20. ▲Refrains from Behavior/Others Lose Control
21. ▲Maintains Acceptable Behavior in Group

Stage IV
22. Indicates Begin. Awareness/Own Progress
23. Indicates Flexibility/Procedures
24. Participates/New Experience With Control
25. Implements Alternative Behaviors
26. ▲Responds/Provocation With Control
27. Accepts Responsibility/Actions, Attitudes
28. ▲Suggests Interpersonal & Group Solutions

Stage V
29. >Seeks New Work Skills
30. >Seeks Desired Group Role
31. Understands, Accepts Law & Order
32. Participates/Group Self-Governance
33. Solves Personal Problems

COMMUNICATION (SAYING)

Stage I
1. Produces Sounds
2. Attends to Speaker
3. Responds/Verbal Stim./Motor Behav.
4. Responds/Cues/Word Approx.
5. ▲Uses Word Approx. Spon.
6. Uses Word/To Adult
7. Uses Word/To Peer
8. ▲Uses Word Sequence/No Model

Stage II
9. Answers with Recog. Words
10. Exhibits Receptive Vocabulary
11. ▲Commands, Questions/Word Sequence
12. ▲Shares Minimal Information/Adult
13. Describes Characteristics/Self, Others
14. ▲Shares Minimal Information/Peer

Stage III
15. ▲Describes Personal Experiences
16. Shows Feeling Responses Approp.
17. Participates Approp./Group Discussion
18. ▲Indicates Pride in Self
19. Describes Attributes/Self
20. Describes Attributes/Others
21. ▲Recognizes Others' Feelings
22. ▲Verbalizes Pride/Group Achievement

Stage IV
23. Channels Feelings/Creative Media
24. Same as B-22
25. Explains/Behavior Influences Others'
26. ▲Verbalizes Feelings Approp. in Group
27. ▲Initiates Positive Relationship Verbally
28. ▲Praises, Supports Others Verbally
29. ▲Expresses Cause–Effect/Feelings, Behavior

Stage V
30. Uses Complex, Figurative Statements
31. ▲Uses Conciliatory Verbal Responses
32. ▲Recognizes, Includes Others' Contribu.
33. Describes Multiple Motives, Values
34. ▲Expresses Values, Ideals
35. ▲Sustains Interpersonal, Group Relations

SOCIALIZATION (RELATING)

Stage I
1. Indicates Awareness/Others
2. Attends/Other's Behavior
3. Responds to Name
4. Engages/Solitary Play
5. Interacts Non-Verbally/Adult
6. Responds/Request/Come
7. Dems. Underst./ Request
8. Same as C-6
9. Begins Emergence/Self
10. ▲Participates/Parallel Play
11. Same as C-7
12. ▲Seeks Contact/Familiar Adults

Stage II
13. ▲Demonstrates Imaginative Play
14. Same as B-10
15. ▲Initiates Social Movement/Peer
16. Participates/Directed Sharing Activity
17. Participates/Interactive Play
18. ▲Cooperates/Peer/Organ. Times

Stage III
19. ▲Shares Material, Takes Turns
20. ▲Imitates Approp. Behavior
21. Labels Situation/Values
22. Leads, Demonstrates for Group
23. Participates/Activity Suggested by Peer
24. Sequences Own Experiences
25. Indicates Developing Friendship
26. ▲Seeks Assistance, Praise/Peer
27. ▲Assists Others/Conforming

Stage IV
28. Identifies with Adult Heroes
29. Sequences Group Experience
30. ▲Suggests Activ./Peer Group
31. Expresses Aware./Others' Different Actions
32. Listens to Others' Opinions
33. Express Interest/Peer Opinion of Self
34. Suggests Solutions to Problems
35. Discrims. Opposite Social Values
36. Draws Infer. from Social Situations

Stage V
37. ▲Understands, Respects Others
38. ▲Interacts Successfully/Multiple Roles
39. ▲Makes Personal Choices/Values
40. Indicates Self Understanding/Goals
41. ▲Sustains Relationships

Raters **Debbie Huth, Constance Quirk, Mary Wood**

Child **Tony**   Birthdate **Jun** (Month) **1** (Day) **1992** (Year)   Date of Rating **Jan** (Month) **10** (Day) **2003** (Year)

▲ = Child must do this spontaneously for item mastery, without direct adult cues or control to elicit the behavior.

(continues)

FIGURE 3.13. Example of a repeated DTORF–R rating for Tony.

DTORF-R FORM FOR ELEMENTARY SCHOOL AGE STUDENTS, Page 2

COGNITION (THINKING)

Stage I

1. Same as B-2
2. Same as B-3
3. ▲Shows Short Term Memory
4. Same as B-5
5. ▲Imitates Acts of Adults
6. Shows Fine, Gross Motor/18 months
7. Knows Names/Objects
8. Same as C-4
9. ▲Same as C-5
10. Matches Shapes, Objects with Spaces
11. Identifies Body Parts (4)
12. Recognizes Detail/Pictures
13. Sorts Objects
14. Labels Pictures

Stage II

15. Recognizes Use of Objects
16. Performs Body Coord./3 year
17. Matches Identical Pictures (of 3)
18. Performs Fine Motor Coord./3 year
19. Recognizes Different Object (of 3)
20. Understands 3 Opposites
21. Categorizes Diff. Pictures/Similar Assoc.
22. Counts to 4 (1 to 1)
23. Identifies 4 colors, 3 shapes
24. Alternates Same, Different Pict. or Object
25. Counts to 10 (1 to 1)
26. Performs Eye-Hand Coord./5 year
27. Discrims. Num., Designs, Upr. Case Letters
28. Performs Body Coord./5 year
29. Recognizes Groups to 5
30. Dem. Rote Memory/5 year
31. Sequences 3 Pictures

Stage III

32. Performs Eye-Hand Coord./6 year
33. Performs Body Coord./6 year
34. Reads 50 Primary Words
35. Recogs., Writes Numerals/Groups 1-10
36. Writes 50 Primary Words/Mem., Dictation
37. Listens/Story/Comprehension
38. Explains Others' Behavior
39. Reads Sentences/Comprehension
40. Adds, Subtracts/1-9
41. Identifies Illogical Elements
42. Writes Sentences About Story
43. Performs Physical Skills, Games/Elem.
44. Writes Simple Sentences
45. Adds, Subtracts/Time/Money
46. Reads, Explains Meas. Words
47. Reads, Tells About Stories
48. Uses Place Value, Regroup, Mult., Seriation

Stage IV

49. Writes to Communicate
50. Multiplies, Divides to 100
51. ▲Reads for Pleasure, Information
52. Computes Money to $10.00
53. Explains Fiction Characters
54. Uses Grammatical Rules/Writing
55. Same as S-35
56. Solves Measurement, Logic Problems

Stage V

57. Seeks Others' Opinions/Current Issues
58. Discriminates Fact/Opinion
59. Recognizes, Explains Illogical Behavior
60. Solves Word Problems/Fractions, Decimals
61. Same as B-33
62. ▲Uses Academic Tools/Citizen, Worker

NOTES

DTORF-R SUMMARY (sum ✓s = items mastered)

Number of Behavior items mastered: **20**

Number of Communication items mastered: **21**

Number of Socialization items mastered: **23**

Number of Academics/Cognition items mastered: **53**

Total DTORF-R items mastered: **117**

Developmental stage: **4**

Chronological age at rating: **11** (Years) **8** (Months)

_____   _____
Family Services Coordinator Signature   Teacher's Signature - General Education

_____   _____
Additional Signature

_____   _____
Parent's Signature   Teacher's Signature - Special Education

FIGURE 3.13. *Continued.*

	DTORF–R Subscale Items Mastered				
	BEHAVIOR	**COMMUNICATION**	**SOCIALIZATION**	**COGNITION**	**TOTAL**
Stage One					
1st Rating	8	8	12	14	42
2nd Rating	8	8	12	14	42
Gain/Loss	NCE	NCE	NCE	NCE	NCE
Stage Two					
1st Rating	5	6	5	17	33
2nd Rating	6	6	6	17	35
Gain/Loss	+1	NCE	+1	NCE	+2
Stage Three					
1st Rating	3	5	5	17	30
2nd Rating	5	6	5	17	33
Gain/Loss	+2	+1	0	NCE	+3
Stage Four					
1st Rating	0	0	0	3	3
2nd Rating	1	1	0	5	7
Gain/Loss	+1	+1	NR	+2	+4
Stage Five*					
1st Rating	0	0	0	0	0
2nd Rating	0	0	0	0	0
Gain/Loss	NR	NR	NR	NR	NR
Total					
1st Rating	16	19	22	51	108
2nd Rating	20	21	23	53	117
Gain/Loss	+4	+2	+1	+2	+9

FIGURE 3.14. Summary of Tony's repeated DTORF–R assessment after 10 weeks. NCE = No change expected. *NR = Not ready for instruction because prerequisite skills have not been achieved.

in peer groups. When reviewing his achievements on the *Cognition* subscale during this 10-week period, his teachers noted that he had been quick to demonstrate creative writing skills for mastery of Item 49. He also responded with success to reading assignments, often searching for additional books on a subject (Item 51). With this information, the teachers developed a revised plan to help Tony with his "people skills." They selected *Cognition* objective 53 (Explain fictional characters) and used writing assignments to create stories about how people cope with their problems. The teachers also planned current events projects to study challenges in the lives of others and how they problem solve. Science projects and lab assignments were designed to emphasize student teamwork, which structured students' interactions with each other. Physical education activities and games were redesigned so that individual competition was not a factor. The emphasis was on each individual's contribution to team success. The goal was to close the gap between Tony's competencies in *Cognition* and other areas of his development.

Using DTORF–R Gains as a Guide to Regrouping Students

Students who make solid gains in achieving the selected objectives need to move forward. For them, regrouping with higher-functioning students usually accelerates learning. Without this regrouping, they can actually lose skills recently acquired. On the other hand, being placed with advanced students may also keep success out of reach.[18]

If a student is not progressing as rapidly as expected, or is not progressing at all, consider modifying instructional content, learning materials, and management strategies to target the specific objectives more intensely. Also, consider the developmental profiles of the other students in the group. Sometimes another student will have a powerful negative influence on a particular group of students. In these situations, reassigning the student to another group should be an option. Occasionally there is unhappy chemistry between a student and a teacher. This requires thoughtful review of the match between the student's needs and the teacher's instructional strategies. If adjustments cannot be made, it may be necessary to find a different teacher.[19]

Accounting for the Effect of Maturation on Students' Gains

When reporting student progress, it is necessary to consider possible maturation effects. One approach is to use a student's preintervention rate of item mastery to estimate a projected DTORF–R score as if that same mastery rate had continued without intervention. The estimated score is then compared to the actual score the student achieves after the implementation of the program. To do this, divide the baseline score (total number of items mastered) by the student's age in months. This calculation provides a preintervention rate of item mastery for each month of life in the past, assuming an even rate of mastery. The preintervention rate is then multiplied by the months the student is in the program from the baseline assessment to the next rating. This gives the estimated number of items that the student might achieve during that time, assuming that the student continues to master objectives at the preintervention rate. The resulting number is then added to the actual baseline score to provide an estimated no–intervention score expected at the second rating. A comparison is then made between the estimated score and the actual score achieved with intervention. The difference is the proportion of change attributed to the intervention (Cook & Campbell, 1979, pp. 195–196; Developmental Therapy Institute, 1998a).

Tony's repeated DTORF–R ratings illustrate this calculation (refer again to Figure 3.14). When his baseline score of 108 is divided by his age of 137 months, the preintervention item mastery rate is .79. This indicates that he achieved less than one item per month during his past development. If his program is implemented for 10 weeks (approximately 2.5 months) assuming the old preintervention rate, his estimated score would be 110 (.79 × 2.5 months = 1.98 items achieved + 108 baseline score = 110).

After Tony completed his first 10 weeks of developmental instruction, the DTORF–R assessment was repeated. He had gained 2 competencies in Stage Two, 3 items in Stage Three, and 4 items in Stage Four, bringing his new score to 117 (108 baseline score + 9 items gained = 117). The difference between the score he actually achieved (117) and the estimated score (110) confirms that the program contributed to Tony's achievements with a rate of item mastery greater than what would have occurred had he continued at the preintervention rate of development. The same procedure also applies to obtaining group data. Dependent *t*-tests can be used to determine statistical significance of the difference between estimated and actual group mean scores.[20]

This procedure is valid to the extent that three assumptions are accepted:

- First, a student's preintervention rate of item mastery is evenly distributed across prior months of development, thus permitting the DTORF–R score to be divided by the

[18]Periodic ratings can be used to regroup students, so that those who are progressing can be moved into peer groups with competencies more comparable to their newly developed skills. Chapter 8 has a discussion about regrouping.

[19]Chapter 8 contains suggestions for ways to avoid or overcome many of the potential difficulties between students and teachers.

[20]A statistical test comparing estimated scores with actual scores is useful for documenting program effectiveness to administrators and policy makers.

chronological age at baseline. The hierarchical structure of the items supports this assumption.

- Second, without intervention, the student's preintervention rate of development would continue to affect item mastery at a similar rate in the future. This permits multiplying the "old" rate of development by months between ratings to obtain an estimated score.[21]
- Third, other threats to validity are considered, such as student and teacher characteristics, possible regression, reliability of rater judgments, changes in conditions, or the Hawthorne effect (Shadish, Cook, & Campbell, 2002, pp. 54–61).

Davis (1992) used this approach to document program effectiveness with 112 special education students, ages 2 through 12 years, in six different schools in four states. These students received Developmental Therapy–Developmental Teaching programs for one school year (range = 6 – 12 months). Their DTORF–R scores indicated that statistically significant gains occurred on each subscale ($p < .000$). To rule out the possible effect of maturation on this finding, scores were calculated to estimate what the students might have achieved as a result of maturation without intervention. These scores were then compared with their actual scores. Results showed that student achievement was greater on each subscale than what was estimated with their preintervention rate of mastery had they not received the programs.[22]

Proportional Change Ratio

Another way to compare rates of item mastery before and after intervention is to obtain a proportional change ratio (PCR). Ratios greater than 1.0 indicate that item mastery was greater during intervention than before, a PCR of 1.0 indicates no change in mastery rates before and during intervention and, a ratio less than 1.0 indicates that the rate of mastery was less during intervention than before (Simeonsson, Huntington, & Short, 1982). Average PCRs for groups of students can be compared for statistical significance with dependent t-tests. However, Wolery (1983, p. 170) advises that such ratios are of limited usefulness for comparing individual students but acceptable for comparing rates of item mastery among groups of students.

Goal Attainment Scaling

Goal attainment scaling (GAS) is a procedure for solving evaluation problems associated with individual differences when documenting program effects on groups of individuals receiving an intervention (Cardillo & Smith, 1994). GAS is a mathematical procedure using T scores for "assessing the amount of relevant change brought about by participation in a treatment program, educational experience, or other intervention" (Smith, 1994, p. 5). GAS procedures have been developed and refined over the past 30 years for applications in the mental health and clinical fields. They also have been used for evaluation of populations of young children with disabilities (Maloney, Mirrett, Brooke, & Johannes, 1978; Roach & Elliot, 2005; Simeonsson, Bailey, Huntington, & Brandon, 1991; Simeonsson, Huntington, & Short, 1982). GAS can be a useful procedure when pooling gains data for students at different stages, with different program objectives and rates of learning, in varying locations, for different disabling conditions, and with a range of problem severity. GAS scores allow comparisons of relative success of a group of individuals in achieving their individual program objectives. Procedures for converting DTORF–R scores to T scores or developmental age scores when calculating GAS are described in the *DTORF–R Technical Report* (Developmental Therapy Institute, 1998a).

A Bar Graph for Visual Summaries

A color-coded bar graph is a visually effective way to show changes with repeated assessments. This form provides places for ratings at least three times during a school year—baseline, midyear, and end-of-the-school-year. The example in Figure 3.15 summarizes Tony's midyear reassessment after 10 weeks. Each cell in the bar corresponds to a DTORF–R item. The cells with items mastered (✓) are lightly shaded. Items selected for current instruction (X) are darkly shaded. Those not ready for direct instruction (NR) are left unshaded. This shows clearly how

[21]Although it is certain that students experience uneven spurts in maturation and an even rate of item mastery might not be accomplished during any given time period, such variations are equalized when rate of mastery is aggregated and distributed over a number of years and for a group rather than for an individual (Wolery, 1983).

[22]Chapter 9 provides additional information about comparing preintervention rates of development with gains during intervention.

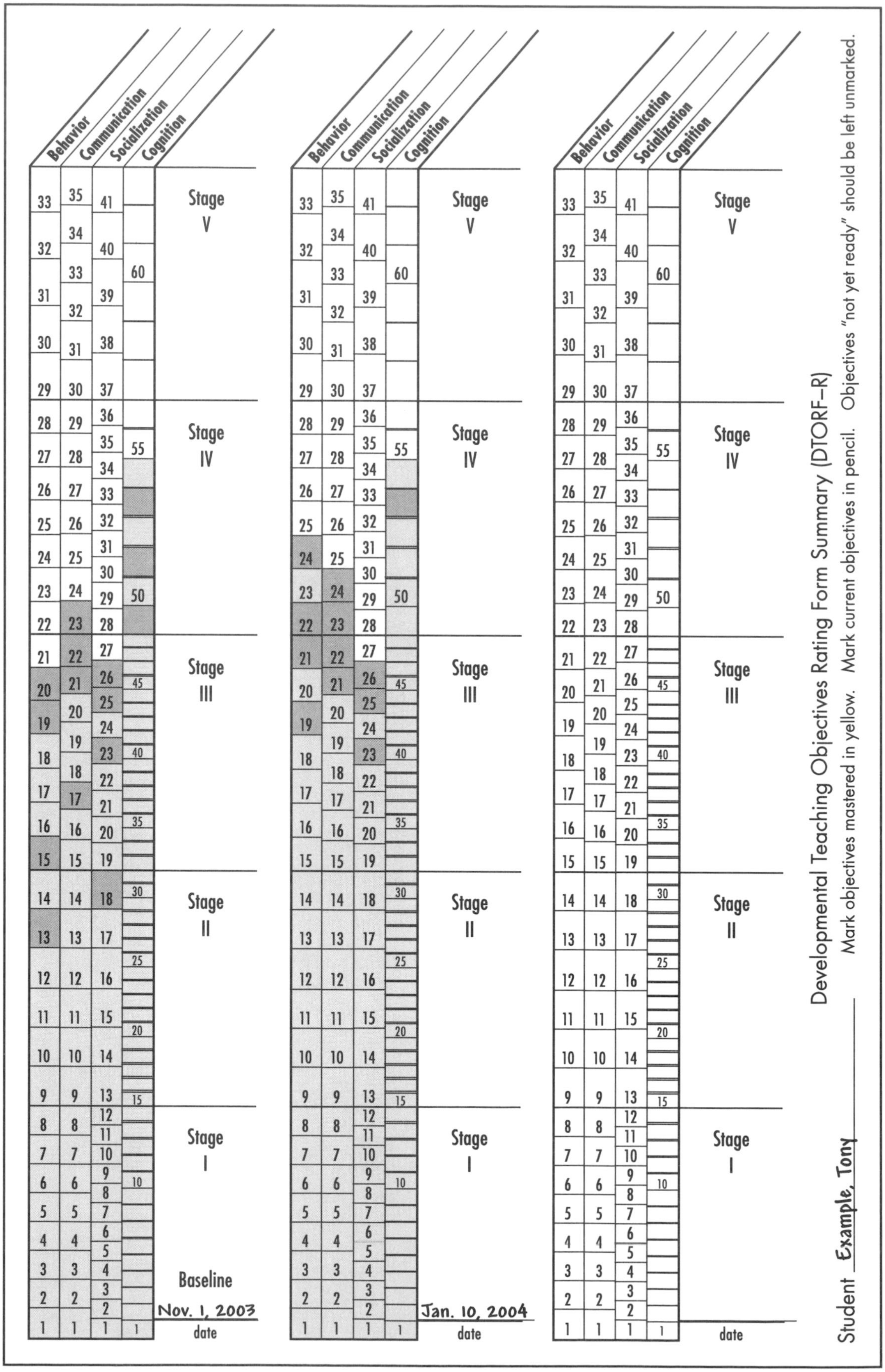

FIGURE 3.15. Bar graph summary of two repeated DTORF–R ratings for Tony.

Tony is progressing and in which areas. It also illustrates the solid foundation of prerequisite skills and the uneven pattern of achievement as the competencies become more complex. Color variations can also be used to indicate a student's progress in achieving the missing competencies. Parents and students respond favorably to seeing the "success" portion of the bar graphs get taller at each reporting period. Older students have also been able to make these bar graphs themselves to track their own progress.[23]

Electronic Summaries of Student Progress

Evidence of student progress and program effectiveness can be summarized easily using the Web-based electronic version of the DTORF–R system. Repeated ratings can be stored, summarized, analyzed, and reported for individuals and for groups. This electronic version also contains a form that automatically prints the selected social, emotional, and behavioral learning objectives to include with IEP, IFSP, or ITP formats already in use at school. Figure 3.16 shows the information calculated by the system and Figure 3.17 uses Tony's baseline DTORF–R rating to illustrate a printout titled "Summary of Selected Instructional Objectives." With these stored data, it is possible to obtain descriptive and inferential statistics when group data are pooled.[24]

As an option, the electronic system can also generate a behavioral intervention plan with specific management strategies selected to match a student's current developmental status. There is an example in Figure 3.18 showing the strategies selected jointly by Tony's teachers and parents during the IEP meeting. These strategies are among those reviewed in Chapter 5.[25]

How the DTORF–R Was Developed

The DTORF–R was developed with scientifically based research methods as defined in the No Child Left Behind Act of 2001, Section 9101 (37) (U.S. Department of Education, 2005). This act requires procedures to meet acceptable standards for measurement validity and reliability, as well as to provide a practical tool for classroom-based education. Because of this latter priority, the DTORF–R is not administered as a strictly standardized testing procedure, nor does it produce scores for comparison with a normative group. Rather, it emphasizes the direct application of each item to instruction.

To document program accountability or to conduct experimental or quasi-experimental evaluations, several statistics can be used to analyze DTORF–R scores of groups of students. Dependent *t* tests compare changes in group means. Growth curve analysis examines changes in skill acquisition with repeated measures, and multivariate analyses explore interaction effects of teachers, schools, and student characteristics on student outcomes (Curran, 2000; Curran & Hussong, 2001; Shadish, Cook, & Campbell, 2002). Each of these options for data

[23]The bar graph form for summarizing repeated DTORF–R ratings is included in the CD and may be reproduced.

[24]The Web-based electronic version for storing and summarizing DTORF–R ratings is available from www.dtorf.com.

[25]Computerized data make it practical for a school or school system to build local normative tables for comparisons between groups of students by age, race, classes, stages, teachers, severity of problems, or by areas of competence and lags.

- Time in months between ratings
- Age in months at time of each rating
- Projected number of objectives that should be mastered based on age
- Actual number of objectives mastered
- Developmental age score
- Actual gains as a percentage of expected score
- Net gain (or loss)
- Gains or losses at repeated ratings

FIGURE 3.16. Data that the online electronic version of the DTORF–R automatically calculates. *Note.* The electronic DTORF–R system is available online at http://www.dtorf.com.

Summary of Selected Instructional Objectives for IEP Planning

Student Name: **Example, Tony**   Student ID: **002**

School/Site: **DTT**   Evaluation Date: **Nov 01, 2003**

Developmental Goal for Behavior Subscale: APPLY SKILLS TO INDIVIDUAL SUCCESS AS A GROUP MEMBER.

☒ PARTICIPATES VERBALLY AND PHYSICALLY IN ACTIVITIES, SPONTANEOUSLY, WITHOUT PHYSICAL INTERVENTION. Verbal support or touch may be used. Student expresses personal initiative to participate. Transitions not included for mastery of this item.

☒ COMPLETES SHORT, INDIVIDUAL TASKS WITH FAMILIAR MATERIAL INDEPENDENT OF ANY ADULT INTERVENTION.

☒ RESPONDS APPROPRIATELY TO CHOICES FOR LEADERSHIP IN THE GROUP. Student accepts not being selected and being selected leader.

☒ REFRAINS FROM UNACCEPTABLE BEHAVIOR WHEN OTHERS IN THE GROUP ARE LOSING CONTROL. Verbal support may be provided by adult.

Developmental Goal for Communication Subscale: USE WORDS TO EXPRESS ONESELF CONSTRUCTIVELY IN GROUPS.

☒ COOPERATES INDEPENDENTLY WITH PEER DURING ORGANIZED ACTIVITY AND PLAY. Is involved actively. Verbal support may be provided for item mastery.

☒ PARTICIPATES WITHOUT INAPPROPRIATE RESPONSE IN ACTIVITY SUGGESTED BY PEER. Adult structure may be used for item mastery.

☒ INDICATES DEVELOPING FRIENDSHIP BY PREFERENCES FOR A PARTICULAR STUDENT OR STUDENTS. Adult structure may be used for item mastery.

☒ SEEKS ASSISTANCE OR PRAISE FROM A PEER SPONTANEOUSLY.

Developmental Goal for Socialization Subscale: FIND SATISFACTION IN GROUP ACTIVITIES.

☒ PARTICIPATES IN GROUP DISCUSSIONS IN WAYS NOT DISRUPTIVE TO THE GROUP. Adult guidance of discussion is acceptable for item mastery.

☒ RECOGNIZES THE FEELINGS OF OTHERS. Student makes comments spontaneously or in response to questions.

☒ SHOWS PRIDE IN GROUP ACHIEVEMENTS. Student indicates identification with the group's success and conveys this through use of the plural and possessive pronouns (we, ours, etc.)

☒ CHANNELS FEELINGS OR EXPERIENCES THROUGH CREATIVE MEDIA SUCH AS ART, MUSIC, DANCE, OR DRAMA. Student does not need to give explanations for creative efforts.

Developmental Goal for Cognition Subscale: PARTICIPATE IN AN ACADEMIC GROUP SUCCESSFULLY, USING PRIMARY ACADEMIC SKILLS, LANGUAGE CONCEPTS, AND SYMBOLIC REPRESENTATION OF EXPERIENCES.

☒ WRITES TO COMMUNICATE INFORMATION, EVENTS, OR FEELINGS. Work should show basic spelling, understanding of punctuation, and rules of grammar but 100% accuracy is not necessary for item mastery. Assistance from adult may be provided.

☒ READS FOR PLEASURE AND FOR PERSONAL INFORMATION. Adult encouragement may be used.

☒ DESCRIBES CHARACTERS AND EXPLAINS MOTIVES OF FICTIONAL CHARACTERS FROM READING, TELEVISION, OR MOVIES. This item can be mastered in oral or written form. Emphasis is on understanding human behavior and the motivations of others.

FIGURE 3.17. The electronic DTORF–R system provides a summary printout of instructional objectives selected for IEP planning.

Positive Behavioral Intervention Plan (BIP)

Student Name: _Example, Tony_   School/Site: _DTT_   Evaluation Date: _Nov 01, 2003_

Based on Current Functional Behavioral Assessment Using the DTORF–R

The purpose of a BIP is to minimize disruptive or destructive behavior, teach acceptable alternatives, encourage participation, and provide a safe, orderly learning environment.

Developmental Goal: Learn Skills for Successful Peer Group Participation (Stage Three)

Major Positive Behavioral Strategies to be Used *Extensively* in All Settings

- ☑ Provide positive feedback to encourage individual participation in group effort.
- ☑ Motivate with lessons, materials and activities that are valued by the individual and group to encourage engaged group participation.
- ☑ Shift attention back to a task or activity with verbal cues to remotivate, modify a task, or redirect actions for acceptable behavior.
- ☑ Verbally mirror words, actions, and feelings to reflect what is said or happening in supportive, nonjudgmental ways.
- ☑ Talk about feelings suggested by observed actions.
- ☑ Model expected behavior and relationships for successful interactions with people.
- ☑ Establish a few positive rules to consistently guide behavior in both individual and group situations.
- ☑ Use steps in "Life Space Crisis Intervention" (LSCI) to talk through a crisis for resolution and greater understanding of self and others.

Additional Positive Behavioral Strategies to be Used *Frequently* in Various Settings *as Needed*

- ☑ Clearly organize lessons, activities, space, pace, time, and schedules.
- ☑ Clearly explain procedures and expectations.
- ☑ Move close to signal awareness.
- ☑ Provide opportunities for independent control of materials, supplies, and equipment while assuring that there will be satisfactory outcomes.
- ☑ Use physical proximity to show interest, convey authority, avert unacceptable behavior, refocus attention on task, communicate support, or show approval of acceptable behavior.

Selected Positive Behavioral Strategies to be Used *Occasionally, as Needed*

- ☑ Reprimand or convey disapproval of words or actions that could bring negative results and encourage alternatives for more satisfying outcomes.
- ☑ Apply firm but supportive physical containment for out-of-control behavior to gain control and to consider more acceptable alternatives.
- ☑ Remove from the room for "cooling off."
- ☑ Exclude from an activity with brief time out to calm down.

Additional Strategies to be Used

FIGURE 3.18. The electronic DTORF–R system provides a summary printout for a Behavioral Intervention Plan (BIP) based on a functional behavioral assessment (FBA) with the DTORF–R.

analysis has been used during development of and refinements to the DTORF–R. These research activities are reported in the section that follows and expanded upon in Chapter 9.[26]

During the original phase of constructing the DTORF–R, nine criteria for validity were established. Every item had to meet these standards to be included as a potential developmental indicator:

- Reflects a strength rather than a deficit
- Represents a desired functional skill
- Describes a key developmental competency for social, emotional, or behavioral development between birth and age 16
- Occurs in a logical sequence of increasing complexity
- Has internal consistency among the selected indicators across domains
- Conveys clear meaning to teachers, paraprofessionals, and parents from diverse backgrounds
- Contains sufficient specificity to document accomplishment
- Contributes to a broad, comprehensive assessment
- Facilitates repeated measures of student progress and program effectiveness at regular intervals

In the process of verifying these standards, both construct and content validity were rigorously examined.

Construct Validity

Among the first activities for DTORF–R development, an extensive review was undertaken to identify psychological processes widely recognized as constructs of social, emotional, and behavioral competence. In doing this, four major developmental domains were evident: *Behavior* (DOING), *Communication* (SAYING), *Socialization* (RELATING), and *Cognition* (THINKING). From the findings of 164 theorists and researchers who described specific characteristics within these domains, a large pool of indicators of healthy personality development was formed. The descriptors were then organized into sequential developmental pathways for specific ages and stages within each domain from birth to age 16. These characteristics were defined in operational terms as observable items and sequenced into four subscales. Finally, to verify that every item had validity for the four subscales, each selected item was referenced directly to the original domain analyses.[27]

Content Validity

To evaluate the relevance of the selected items for children and youth with challenging behaviors, educators, mental health professionals, and parents were asked to independently review each item for importance to the education of students of different ages and types of social, emotional, and behavioral disabilities. They also reviewed the scope of selected items to suggest content that may have been overlooked or excluded. The educators were experienced in general and special education, and included early childhood specialists. The parents were those who had firsthand experience with mental health needs in their families. Among the mental health professionals were social workers, psychologists, psychiatrists, paraprofessionals, and community service volunteers working in clinical settings.

This review for content relevance resulted in the first version of the instrument. A field test was then conducted for 6 months to evaluate the sequence of items in each subscale and to prepare specific examples of mastery for each item. The resulting revised version was then used for 5 years by similar groups of educators and mental health professionals for the purpose of continuing to refine the sequence, clarity, and relevance of items (Wood, 1975, 1986, 1996a).

The field review resulted in additional changes in the instrument. Several key aspects for infant development were added. New items were also included to reflect the characteristics of children with autistic-like behavior or pervasive developmental delay. The upper limits for the four subscales were also extended to include new research findings concerning moral development, interpersonal perspective taking (social knowledge), and values through the teen years. These additions expanded the instrument to its present 171 items representing essential aspects of social, emotional, and behavioral competence from birth to age 16.

DTORF–R Item Difficulty

A Guttman-type scalogram was used with the first version to determine if items were ordered sequentially within each subscale. In that analysis, 87 students with severe emotional disturbance were rated on the instrument at 5- and 10-week intervals over a 9-month period. No sampling procedure was used, as all students in the program were included regardless of age and diagnostic classification. Results indicated that the order of items on each subscale was generally similar to a statistically accurate order reflecting increasing item difficulty (Huberty, Quirk, & Swan, 1973). The few items found to be out of order were those also identified as problematic by the staff. The resulting revision reflected these analyses, and again incorporated suggestions from professionals in educational and mental health programs.

A later study of item difficulty used the Rasch model to statistically reexamine item difficulty on each of the four subscales (Rasch, 1960; Snyder & Sheehan, 1992). Logit values were calculated for every item on each subscale using 300 entry level DTORF–R ratings of students with severe emotional–behavioral disabilities, ages 3 to 14 years. Results indicated that the correct statistical sequence was present for 91% of the items on the *Behavior* subscale, 94% of the items for *Communication*, 88% for *Socialization*, and 79% for *Cognition*. The few items found to be out of order were subsequently reordered (Weller, 1991).

Additional Content Validity

Because a lower percentage of correctly sequenced items occurred primarily in the early childhood stage for *Cognition*, a further content analysis was conducted for this subscale. A panel of six expert preschool teachers and teacher educators conducted an item-by-item comparison of DTORF–R items with other early childhood developmental inventories, assessment scales, and curriculum. These included the *Bayley Scales of Infant Development* (Bayley, 1969), *Battelle Developmental Inventory Screening Test* (Newborg, Stock, Wnek, Guidubaldi, & Svinicki, 1988), *Brigance Diagnostic Inventory of Early Development, Revised* (Brigance, 1991), *Developmental Diagnosis, Third Edition* (Gesell & Amatruda, 1975; Ilg, Ames, & Baker 1981/1992), *Developmental Profile II* (Alpern, Boll, & Shearer, 1986), and *Learning Accomplishments Profile–Revised* (Sanford & Zelman, 1981).

All of the *Cognition* items for Stages One and Two were located among these other guides. Each item was compared for wording similarities, item difficulty, and place in the developmental sequences. Where indicated, DTORF–R items were reworded for greater clarity and a few items were reordered to correspond with prevailing judgments about relative item difficulty. The result was improved confidence that the content of this subscale has validity for early childhood assessment.

Inferred Construct Validity

Because social, emotional, and behavioral competence are complex and interdependent, no single behavior can be a valid indicator of achievement in these areas. Competence must be inferred by the combined mastery of skills such as those identified in the content analyses described above. In addition, the behavioral progress of troubled students who have received repeated DTORF–R ratings over time contributes to the accumulating evidence that the collective content is a valid indicator of social, emotional, and behavioral performance. The DTORF–R has been used with thousands of troubled children and teens of all races, ethnic backgrounds, personalities, socioeconomic levels, and geographic areas, both urban and rural. It has also been used to assess the developmental competence of students with a range of disabilities including autism, intellectual delay, and language, hearing, or visual disabilities and with those who have multiple disabilities, no disabilities, or are gifted (Davis, 1995; Quirk, 2002; Wood, Davis, & Swindle, 1998).[28]

[28]Chapter 9 provides summaries of these research studies using the DTORF–R to document program effectiveness.

Culturally Sensitive Content

Those who have used this approach in other countries find that the developmental competencies and instructional practices have compatible applications. Multicultural and multiracial comparisons of similarities and differences among troubled children and youth, as measured by the DTORF–R, have been the subject of several professional international conferences and much informal exchange. Educators from Canada, China, Germany, India, Italy, New Zealand, Norway, Peru, Puerto Rico, Russia, Scotland, South Korea, The Netherlands, and the Virgin Islands have used the DTORF–R and made translations for applications for their own educational programs (Bergsson, 1999b, 2001; Bergsson, Wood, Quirk, & DeLorme, 2003; Berscheid, Cooley, & Dier, 1998).

These educators hold generally similar views about social and emotional development and the necessity for establishing standards for acceptable behavior that is culturally relevant. They report that the DTORF–R allows freedom for cultural diversity in assessing how each student demonstrates mastery of the competencies. They also report that it allows for blending of expectations and values that are unique to individuals, families, schools, and communities while maintaining a direction for learning that fosters socioemotional maturation.[29]

[29]The Epilogue summarizes this international movement. Appendix A has references to the international publications.

DTORF–R Reliability

The first study of agreement between two trained raters using the DTORF–R to independently evaluate 21 students with severe emotional or behavioral disabilities resulted in rater agreement, item by item, of 81%, 84%, and 81% for the *Behavior, Communication,* and *Socialization* subscales. The *Cognition* subscale was not included at that time because it was undergoing revisions. Although these levels of reliability were adequate for a preliminary study, it became evident that a standard training program for raters was needed to assure accurate ratings of individual students and to minimize rater error.

As a result, a rater-training program was prepared. The program included examples of mastery for each item; a user's manual with detailed rating instructions, practice cases, and procedures for obtaining a consensus rating from a three-person rating team; a self-instructional workbook for raters; and a series of video training tapes for verifying rater accuracy in rating. The *DTORF–R User's Manual* (Developmental Therapy Institute, 1998b) includes this training program with specific instructions about how to reliably administer the instrument and score results.

Using these training procedures, reliability analyses then were conducted using two trained raters who independently rated 20 students. Their resulting average agreement overall was 95%. Other measures of rater reliability shown in Figure 3.19 also reflect excellent reliability. These include interrater agreement, item-by-item, for each subscale: *Behavior* = 93%, *Communication* = 94%, *Socialization* = 94%, and *Cognition* = 96%. In another study of item difficulty using 300 DTORF–R ratings, Kuder-Richardson–type reliability estimates of internal consistency among items were greater than .99 within each subscale (Developmental Therapy Institute, 1998a, p. 5).[30]

- Interrater agreement, item by item = 93%, 94%, 94%, 96% (4 subscales)
- Internal consistency = > .99 (4 subscales)
- Standard error = .74 (95% confidence band)

FIGURE 3.19. When teachers have training and practice, their DTORF–R ratings have high reliability.

To obtain a measure of the consistency of individual scores, the standard error of measurement (*SEM*) was calculated for the DTORF–R data (pretest *SEM* = .62, posttest *SEM* = .74) using a 95% confidence band. These measures provide estimates of the variability that would result from an individual's score if it were possible to obtain repeated measures without practice effect or growth by a student. Thus, reliable estimates of a student's true DTORF–R score can be made with considerable confidence.

Summary

The DTORF–R is a well-researched measurement tool that assesses social, emotional, and behavioral competence of students. It is also used to document student progress toward established educational goals. It was designed using scientifically based evaluation methods that meet federal standards defined in the No Child Left Behind Act of 2001 (NCLB) and in P L. 108-466, the reauthorized IDEA legislation (U.S. Department of Education, 1997, 2005).[31]

The 171 DTORF–R developmental indicators identify where an individual student is in the progression from immaturity to maturity in four different areas of competence: DOING (behavioral domain), SAYING (communication domain), RELATING (socialization domain), and THINKING (cognitive domain). These developmental pathways provide rich information for establishing meaningful goals and objectives suitable for each student's current instructional needs. A student's profile of the sequential benchmarks mastered and needed in each domain offers specific entry points for customizing learning objectives. These objectives are the guide for planning academic content and designing individualized lessons and activities precisely matched to each student's current developmental stage. In this way, each student is encouraged to participate in lessons that have been designed with both developmental and personal relevance. Repeated at intervals, DTORF–R assessments also provide annual measures of student progress toward established standards.[32]

Both reliability and validity of this assessment process have been established. Theoretical foundations for construct validity of each DTORF–R indicator was developed from an extensive analysis of how healthy personality develops. The assessment has also had been used by educators internationally because of its adaptability to local standards and cultures. Acceptable mea-

[30]For DTORF–R reliability, at least one member of a rating team should have prior training in the rating procedures and an established reliability score (Developmental Therapy Institute, 1998b). At least 80% interrater agreement, item by item, is recommended.

[31]P.L. 108-466 is The Individuals with Disabilities Education Improvement Act of 2004 (IDEA).

[32]Consider the next chapter, "Decoding Behavior" as an extension of the assessment procedures for the *Quick Profile* and the DTORF–R. This will further expand your understanding of emotional aspects of a student's needs. It also offers a way to summarize the assessment information in an organized way for program planning.

surement reliability was established from extensive field research over several decades. Internal item reliability of .99 has been obtained, with item-by-item interrater reliability of .93, .94, .94, and .96 for each subscale. Finally, several thousand teachers of troubled students from early childhood to age 16 have established the practicality of the DTORF–R and its content validity for classroom use.[33]

[33]Chapter 9 contains additional information about field evaluation studies of program effectiveness using the DTORF–R. Results reveal significant student gains in social and emotional competence and increasingly responsible behavior.

Questions for Review

(Answers are in Chapter 3.)

1. What are six ways the DTORF–R can be used before a student's instruction begins?
2. Can you identify two additional uses of the DTORF–R after a student's program begins?
3. Who should do a DTORF–R assessment?
4. Why rate the items in sequential order?
5. Where should a rating begin for preschool children?
6. Where should the rating begin for elementary school students?
7. For a student in middle or high school, where should the rating begin?
8. Under what circumstances should a rating begin in a shaded area of a form?
9. When there is disagreement on a rating team about how to rate an item, what should be done?
10. Why limit the number of items rated "X" to four on each subscale?
11. What does the small triangle mean when it appears in front of an item?
12. Leon is 3 years old and was placed in a foster family last year when abuse was suspected. Which DTORF–R form would you use?
13. Leon is working on Item 7 in the *Communication* subscale. Can Item 11 on the *Socialization* subscale be marked mastered (✓)? Can Item 11 be rated not ready (NR)?
14. Clint is a restless and volatile 9-year-old in a 4th grade class. Which DTORF–R form would you use?
15. Clint has mastered Item 10 on the *Behavior* subscale. Can Item 14 on the *Socialization* subscale by marked "X"? Can that item be rated not ready (NR)?
16. Alice is an 11-year-old in 4th grade who is receiving special education services. Which DTORF–R form would you use?
17. On Alice's DTORF–R, Item 16 in *Behavior* is marked "NR." Can Item 17 be rated mastered (✓)? Can Item 17 be marked "X" as an objective to work on?
18. Aleesa is 15 years old and a straight "A" student. Which form would you use?
19. Item 32 is the third item marked "X" on the *Socialization* subscale for Aleesa. Can Item 33 be marked not ready (NR)? Can Item 33 be rated mastered (✓)?

Decoding Behavior:
From the Seen to the Unseen

A few discrete emotions emerge early in life, including joy, interest, sadness, anger, fear, and disgust. Another few emotions emerge later in middle childhood as a function of both maturational and social process: these emotions include shame, guilt, shyness, and contempt. Each of these emotions has a unique, adaptive function in motivating, organizing, and regulating behavior ... [and] also plays an important role in the development of personality and individual differences in responding to environmental challenges.

Izard & Ackerman
(2000, p. 253)

Teachers often find it difficult to deal with students' emotions. Perhaps it is because they have little training or experience in using emotional episodes as teaching opportunities. However, it is critical for teachers to understand how emotions shape students' behavior. The process is called *decoding*—making connections between a student's words, actions, and feelings. Decoding helps teachers understand *why* a behavior occurs and *how* it can be changed to benefit the student. When decoding a student's behavior, consider its personal and cultural meaning for the student—emotional memories that have been aroused, developmental anxiety it is protecting, and the defense mechanisms that are being used. For example, consider a student's angry outburst in class. This behavior may be a direct response to a classroom event. But decoding can help a teacher understand that the behavior may also be an expression of complex feelings that have not found immediate expression in any other form and are not connected directly to the classroom event.

Teachers who are skilled in decoding are able to recognize negative, often destructive, self-defeating thoughts, ideas, and feelings that can shape a student's behavior. When they use this knowledge, they are able to help students change their beliefs about themselves, their attitudes, and their emotional reactions to others. As these changes occur, students are increasingly receptive to learning new behaviors that bring better results.

This chapter reviews key forces that are always present but unseen in every student. The first section describes several unseen resources that should be used to stimulate learning and responsible behavior: mental energy, emotional memory, and motivating values. The second section reviews the different ways individuals attempt to maintain psychological defenses against stress and anxiety and how these efforts affect learning, behavior, and developmental competence. Topics include developmental anxieties, defense mechanisms, and maintaining emotional balance. A separate section follows with a focus on the existential crisis (the "X factor") and how students' views of authority and responsibility change as they develop. The chapter ends with a discussion of group dynamics that can dominate behavior in a classroom. This describes students' roles in a group, their forms of social power, and ways to change group dynamics for an improved psychological climate in a classroom. All of this information about decoding students' behavior is essential for understanding how learning and behavior are influenced by forces that are not always observable.

Unseen Resources for Learning

Mental Energy

The term *mental energy* is the fuel that makes learning possible. It influences how a student thinks, talks, relates, remembers, and behaves. Produced in the brain by body chemistry, neurons, synapses, and gray cells, this energy fluctuates with the situation. When activated, it attaches itself to what is most important at the moment. It enables a student to absorb instruction and create meaning from the moment. It also stores and arouses memories—rational and emotional—and recalls situations associated with these memories. In this way, mental energy becomes the catalyst for learning by organizing and expanding a student's networks of knowledge. Every person who has been involved in the life of a healthy, happy child or teen has seen mental energy released for spontaneous participation in life and learning. In contrast, when mental energy is deflected or impoverished, the "get up and go" is gone. Fatigue, chronic worry, anxiety, concerns, or preoccupations reduce mental energy, making a student less mentally available for learning.

Competition for students' mental energy and attention is tough. Students see more intense drama and violence every day on television and in their communities than ordinary curriculum materials can compete against. When they are also struggling with their own emotional, social, or behavioral problems, the challenge to channel their energy into learning is formidable. Such students are sometimes labeled depressed, unmotivated, distractible, or hyperactive. Teachers know how little mental energy these students have for learning in comparison with their peers. No ordinary effort on a teacher's part can hold their attention when it is drawn away from lessons by these powerful emotional forces.

Curriculum offers the best potential for igniting willing participation in learning by these students. Lessons must attract and expand their mental energy, vicariously provide emotional outlets, offer hopes and dreams, and portray human dilemmas confronted and resolved. Figure 4.1 contains suggestions for lesson content that can mobilize mental energy. Words that evoke vivid mental images can attract this energy; so can content that taps a student's real-life concerns. Content should include admired people as role models struggling with and resolving problems and feelings. Action-based projects and activities connected to deeper issues also attract mental energy and can help substitute negative memories with positive ones. When lesson plans are individualized and well designed to include developmental and emotional needs, interests, skills, and values, students become willing and eager to participate.[1]

[1]Consider how much mental energy each student has available and where it is being expended. Then, mobilize and channel that energy through lessons, materials, and learning experiences especially designed to engage that energy.

- Explore what is already known and secure.
- Express new ideas about oneself and the world.
- Try new ideas and new behaviors.
- Experience new feelings.
- Convey concerns without opening oneself to possible hurt.
- Express fears and anxieties safely.
- Expand experiences vicariously.
- Solve troublesome problems.
- Master the immediate environment.

FIGURE 4.1. Lessons should allow students to mobilize mental energy for learning.

Another source for activating mental energy on behalf of learning is the energy force field that can exist between individuals. Anyone in love can vouch for its existence. Young people and musicians call it "vibes." They use it spontaneously and often without conscious effort. People who work extensively with animals use it to communicate; so do actors who want to reach an audience with their "presence." Some successful teachers recognize that such nonverbal communication can sometimes be more powerful than talking with students, and they use this force with dynamic results. They walk into a room and have an immediate effect on the students, even though they say little—or nothing at all. These teachers are generating nonverbal messages that their students receive.

Try sending nonverbal messages yourself. Practice where children are free to respond spontaneously. Or, casually join a group of teens. You will probably learn something about your own ability to communicate in the powerful nonverbal world. When you use this type of communication with deliberation, you convey all sorts of messages that will be "heard" by students who are otherwise tuning out adults' words and ideas. It is a tool for unobtrusively conveying support, affirming the student, and building a relationship. If you fail to put it to work, you may be missing a powerful tool for teaching. You may also be unconsciously conveying your own frustrations, dislikes, or despair to students. Such messages are received, whether intended or not.[2]

Emotional Memory

Emotional memory is an energizing and essential part of learning. Emotional memory is the place where an individual's feelings and emotions about experiences, thoughts, and ideas are stored. It influences the way students learn and how they respond to adults, peers, and daily events. In an individual's private storehouse of memories, previous experiences are filed away with attached emotional notations. Figure 4.2 illustrates how emotional memory works: Real events (involving people, classroom materials, lessons, and activities) trigger highly personalized associations in memory that have attached feelings and thoughts. The same event will evoke different associations for each individual. These associations are not consciously recalled, but through the filter of stored past experiences they tap both cognitive and emotional (affective) memory. As thoughts and ideas (cognition) combine with feelings and emotions (affect), they are transmitted across the perceptual threshold to awareness. These activated mental images and feelings produce responses in the form of knowing, feeling, and behaving in highly personal ways.

When emotional memories are triggered by a troubling event, they are nearly impossible to ignore. They can dominate the student's actions and limit learning (Kagan, 1989). As a student's mental energy is diverted to cope with aroused feelings, the mental energy available for learning diminishes. If intense emotional memories are activated, a student may "shut down," withdraw emotionally, or lash out with hostility or violence. Without reduction in the intensity of aroused emotions, a student's behavioral responses are defensive and usually counterproductive. This compounds the problem, reinforces the strength of the association, and expands the negative associations in stored emotional memory. If negative content, emotional pain, and anger remain in a student's emotional memory bank, these forces will dominate the student's behavior.[3]

How can you change a student's emotional memory bank from negative to positive, especially when teaching those who are abused, troubled, or behaviorally challenged? This should not be left to chance. After each lesson, mention a positive aspect of each student's participation. End with a close-down procedure to teach students to identify positive aspects of the just-completed activity. Every day, be certain that they experience some replacement of negative and destructive memories with feelings of pleasure and confidence. It is a basic process of review and critical appraisal that teaches students to search for their own best moments.[4]

Although traditionally part of good academic instruction, this simple strategy can also gradually change the content of emotional memories. As positive feedback becomes routine for

[2]Skills needed by teachers to build constructive relationships with students are discussed in Chapter 7.

[3]For a theoretical discussion of emotion and memory, see Parrott and Spackman (2000).

[4]Effective educational outcomes are those embedded with emotional memories of success, pleasure, self-confidence, security, and trust.

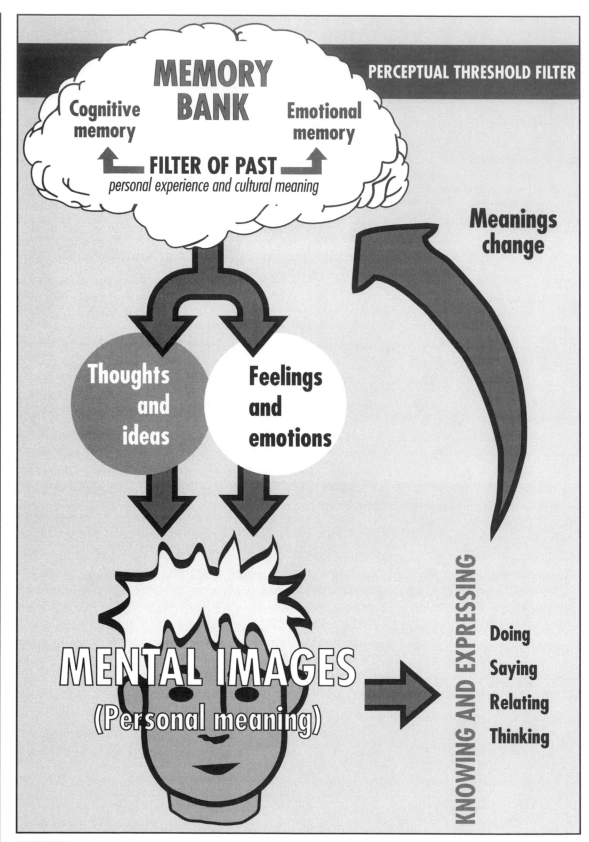

FIGURE 4.2. How emotional memory works.

each activity, students begin to create the feedback for themselves. You will see dramatic changes in students' faces when this happens. They smile more frequently. There is a climate of buoyancy. The message is that they are genuinely successful, and they are aware of these feelings. Their memory banks are taking on positive charges![5]

Values Motivate Students To Learn and To Be Responsible

Values are the internal motivators that hold together the structure of personality and character. They are highly personalized guides that motivate an individual to act in certain ways—to cooperate or not, interact or withdraw, learn or fail. Adults use their values to guide their activities, regulate their behavior, and solve social problems (Eisenberg, 2000; Loevinger, 1976, 1987; Madsen, 1968; Maslow, 1987). Children are much the same. They choose to behave in ways to satisfy their current values and to avoid situations that produce unsatisfying results (Lickona, 1985, 1991). Children without values are angry, volatile, self-serving, or highly anxious. Lack of values also makes them vulnerable to decreased achievement, as well as drug and alcohol addictions, sexual promiscuity, vandalism, violence, truancy, or delinquency. When so many problems come from a lack of values, it is imperative that teachers and parents give attention to how values develop, and what they can do to foster values in children of all ages.[6]

Values provide major motivations for learning. It is a complex process, involving memory, thinking, and every experience that influences an individual. Learning happens when students are motivated by "ownership" of a learning task. They have to believe that their efforts will pay off in ways that they value. If a lesson has no motivational value to them, or is beyond their capacity to complete successfully, it will fail, and so will the students.

Two different forces simultaneously shape students' motivation to learn: individual developmental status and personal values. Both processes change with experience and time. What is important to a toddler will be dramatically different from what an 8-year-old or a 15-year-old values. To motivate students to participate willingly, a teacher must know the stages of development and values that are currently motivating each student. These are deciding factors in how the students will respond to school, to the teacher, and to the curriculum.[7]

Values emerge in a natural sequence as children get older and their experiences increase in complexity. This process is shown in Figure 4.3. Values begin to develop in infancy with the conviction that one's own needs are paramount. Any behavior that meets these needs is satisfactory. Gradually, young children develop values that reflect adult standards. They learn that behavior should conform, to please adults and to avoid punishment. By the time they enter elementary school, most children have expanded their own values to include fairness. By treating others fairly, they learn that they will be treated fairly in return. By the teen years, values of empathy and altruism are added to justice and fairness as values that regulate their behavior (Kohlberg & Hersh, 1977; Kohlberg & Turiel, 1971).[8]

Teachers often ask if values that motivate students include moral values. The answer is "yes." Also called virtues, they are part of the same development continuum. Erikson emphasizes the importance of focusing on virtues as a way to develop responsible behavior. He speaks of *"basic virtues,* with which human beings steer themselves and others through life" (1964, p. 115). He names hope, will, purpose, and competence as fundamental virtues developed in childhood; fidelity as the adolescent virtue; and love, care, and wisdom as virtues of adulthood. By the time most students begin school, they are able to recognize some of these values in their daily experiences, yet frequently they do not know how to deal with them. They understand ideas of right and wrong, fairness and unfairness, justice and injustice, life and death, and truth and untruth. These virtues and values are essential for academic success, personal responsibility, and socioemotional competence.

It is sometimes difficult for teachers to identify specific values that are the keys to motivating a student. Every student can be motivated. But this is not always as easy as it sounds. The difficulty is to determine what motivates each individual. Values may be hidden beneath

[5]More details about how to make changes in emotional memory during a lesson, and a form for summarizing decoding information, are in Chapter 8.

[6]Curriculum offers the best potential for igniting willing participation in learning, but only if it is well designed to meet developmental needs and students' uniquely individual values about what is important.

[7]Appendix C contains a list of major motivators from 20 different theories, organized in developmental sequence to indicate when each motivation is developmentally relevant.

[8]If this progression in the development of values is delayed, a child will have problems in school and in life.

Age Group	Basic Value	Child's View of the Value	Developmental Stage*
Infants and toddlers	My needs	"What I want is important."	Stage One
Preschool children	Please adults	"I do what I'm told so teachers will like me."	Stage Two
Children in primary grades	Be fair	"I do things for others so they will treat me right."	Stage Three
Children in elementary grades	Be responsible	"Be a good person so people will approve of you."	Stage Four
Teens	Care for others	"Others have feelings and deserve respect."	Stage Five

FIGURE 4.3. Use this developmental sequence to identify basic values for motivating students. *When a student nears the end of achievements in one stage, shift your emphasis to the next stage and focus on more advanced values in the sequence.

protective cover-ups. To identify what motivates your students, observe carefully. Listen closely to them during less structured times, such as free play, discussion groups, lunch, recess, and spontaneous conversations during group activities. Role play, dramatic play, drawings, movies, music, television choices, toys, reading material, and leisure activities all tell something of what motivates students. Their friends and the people they admire and imitate also reveal a lot about what they value. Consider concerns and preoccupations. Watch for activities that trigger their imagination or hold their attention without interruption for extended periods. Use all of this information to find what is important to each student. When you provide lessons and activities with connections to an individual's values, you will have a motivated learner.[9]

Perhaps a key to the successful use of values involves the decision whether to continue motivating a student at a current stage in development of values or challenge the student to the next higher value level. Figure 4.4 shows how children can be challenged to use increasingly more advanced levels of values. By emphasizing values at a student's current level, the student will remain in his or her comfort zone. A current level of values assures a responsive student. However, if instruction remains at one stage of development, a student's chance to mature further is jeopardized. Instruction has inadvertently put an invisible ceiling on the student's potential to grow beyond the present. One way to avoid this is to look for every opportunity to reflect a next higher value when you have some confidence that the student will respond positively.

[9]When students see potential for pleasure in a lesson, or find subject content in which they have deep interest, unacceptable behavior is seldom evident.

Psychological Defenses Against Stress and Anxiety

Developmental Anxieties Influence Behavior in Powerful Ways

Developmental anxiety is an active response to a present situation that occurs as a result of the changing interplay between a child's emotional needs and the expectations of others. Developmental anxieties are kept alive by emotional memory; they produce feelings of discomfort, recall past helplessness, and create uneasiness, worry, apprehension, and defensive behavior.

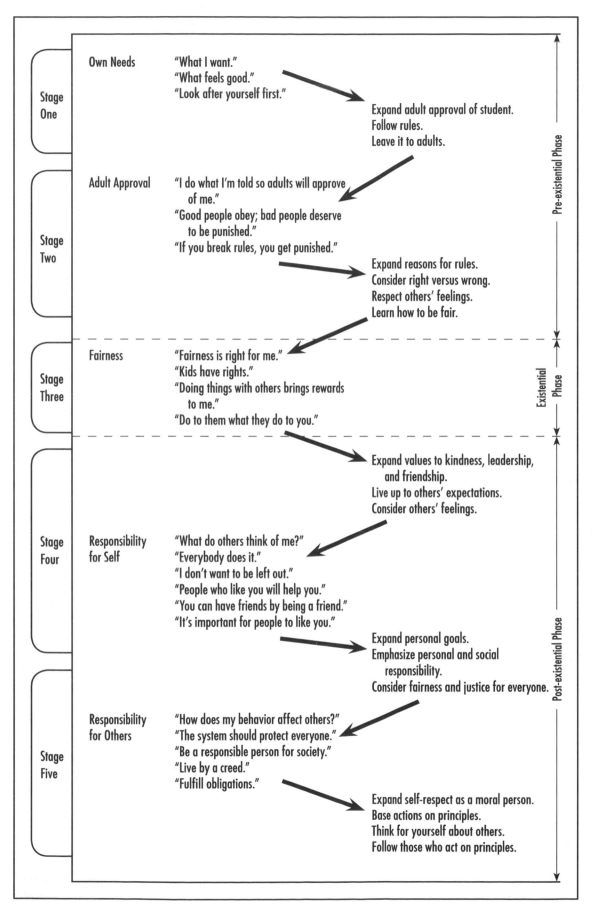

FIGURE 4.4. How values are used in Developmental Therapy–Developmental Teaching to enhance and expand a child's maturity.

When clashes occur between unmet emotional needs and the expectations set by others, the result is a developmental anxiety that demands relief (Brody & Axelrad, 1970/1993, pp. 36–39; S. Freud, 1936; Last, 1993; Lewis & Rosenblum, 1978, p.4).

Age plays an important role in forming typical developmental anxieties in the course of typical development, from birth through adolescence. Each age has its own anxiety-producing conditions. As shown in Figure 4.5, these forces shape an individual's motivation, behavioral defenses, attitudes, values, and views of self and others. Because of this, developmental anxieties typically emerge at predictable ages:

1. During infancy, anxiety about abandonment develops and is typically resolved with loving care and a close relationship with the caregiver.
2. For preschool children, inadequacy is the typical anxiety and is resolved through abundant experiences of mastery and success.
3. For children in the primary grades, guilt emerges as students begin to feel that they have disappointed or failed the expectations others set for them. Resolution occurs with validation that they have indeed met these standards.
4. Elementary and middle school students face anxiety over conflict between being independent or conforming to others' standards—an anxiety that frequently carries over into the teen years when independence gradually wins over conforming.
5. For most high school students, issues of identity predominate with uncertainties about self-image, new roles, and new values. Formation of a satisfying young adult role resolves this anxiety temporarily, as a new, adult life phase begins.

In the course of personality development and achieving adult maturity, every person experiences these developmental anxieties in unique ways. For some, it is a normal progression through each life stage, balancing one's own needs against the demands of others. For those who are troubled or who have had destructive relationships in childhood, the number and intensity of unresolved anxieties increase with age. This makes it more difficult for them to cope successfully with the next stage of development and new expectations from others.[10]

Students bring their developmental anxieties to school every day. Behavior problems and failure to learn frequently result. These are indicators of a student's attempts to protect against being overwhelmed by feelings and unfulfilled emotional needs. Many are caught up in hurried lifestyles that are unpredictable and stressful. Relationships and emotions are often ignored in the push for things, action, and achievement. Some students worry excessively. Others go to extremes to deny any worry at all. Many can navigate a healthy progression through each developmental anxiety with resolution and increased maturation. However, for those with unresolved developmental anxieties, the anxieties do not disappear. They continue into the next stage of development along with a new anxiety typically associated with increased age. And what would have been a "phase" to resolve and pass through becomes a major element in the day-to-day problems teachers have with a student's behavior and motivation for learning.[11]

How can teachers deal with students' developmental anxieties? First, identify a student's predominant anxiety. Age provides the first checkpoint. It gives a framework for understanding a particular situation from the student's point of view. When you know the natural developmental anxiety associated with a student's age and stage of development, you can counter the anxiety with specific curriculum content and intervention strategies. If the student is delayed in social and emotional development, the situation may be further complicated by unresolved anxieties from an earlier age and stage of development. A student's unique history often provides insight into why the behavior is taking the particular form it does in the present.

A language arts curriculum is a particularly effective vehicle for helping students resolve developmental anxieties and the behavioral side effects (Council for Children with Behavioral Disorders, 2003). Think of the potential to resolve specific feelings and problems of students vicariously through reading, storytelling, literature, creative dramatics, role-playing, creative writing, and experience stories. Television and videotapes also are dynamic resources. Fictional

[10]Knowledge about developmental anxieties aids in understanding a student's behavior. It also tells what types of experiences and relationships the student needs with teachers and other students.

[11]Each stage of development has its unique developmental stresses, requiring daily attempts by children to balance the demands of others against their own inner needs.

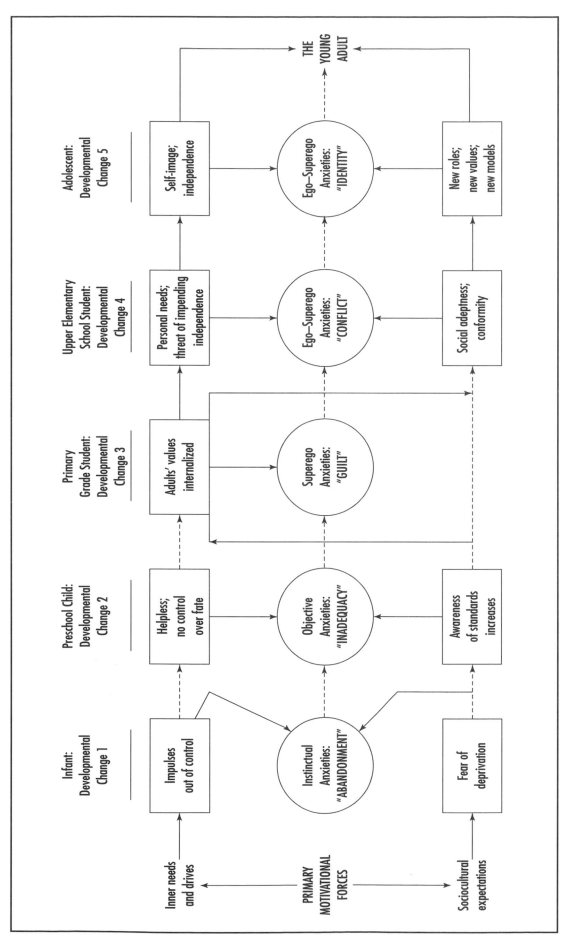

FIGURE 4.5. How typical developmental anxieties emerge. *Note.* Solid lines denote major influences; dotted lines indicate contributing influences.

and imaginary people serve as role models and provide easy identification. When a student "accesses" a character, there is abundant opportunity to learn new ways to behave, to handle crises, and to problem solve through the experiences of others.[12]

This is not as easy as it may seem. You may recall Michael Jackson's popular video, *Thriller*, which was viewed by thousands of children. As the story line progressed to the climax and ending, the message was convincingly clear: "You cannot (and should not) trust anyone, even those who say they love you." *This is not a reassuring message for children.* Instead, the literature selected should always have reassuring resolutions that address students' specific anxieties. *Bambi, Barney,* and *Finding Nemo,* for example, convey an urgent sense of care and nurture needed by young children struggling with the developmental anxiety of *abandonment.* For older students who are anxious about abandonment and being unloved, conflict in the *Star Wars* series is resolved when the evil Darth Vader finally sacrifices his own life for that of his noble son, Luke Skywalker. *The Bill Cosby Show* and *Harry Potter* are other examples of material that deal with resolutions of developmental anxieties, most often conflict and identity. Each episode deals with a conflict between the need to be loved and valued as a member of a family (dependence) and the need for personal identity (independence). The developmental anxieties are resolved in each script with reassurance about care and connection while sanctioning independence and personal identity.[13]

[13]For suggestions of themes for use in a language arts curriculum that address students' developmental anxieties, see Chapter 8.

The point is to reduce or reshape the power of anxiety to dominate a student's life. When curriculum content helps students deal with anxieties satisfactorily, and the learning environment avoids adding unnecessary stress to emotional vulnerability, students begin to participate with new spontaneity. Gradually, they respond with less defensive behavior and reduced anxiety. There is freedom to learn when there is confidence that the classroom will not contribute to their problems.

Psychological Protection with Defense Mechanisms

At any age or stage of life, mental health is a balance between an individual's emotional needs, demands made on the person by others, and the capacity to respond successfully. This requires behavior that is simultaneously protective and responsive. Such behavior, generated for psychological protection, is called a defense mechanism (Cramer, 1990; A. Freud, 1942). The actual form a defense takes does not tell us the nature of the stress or anxiety, only that anxiety is present. The characteristics of these complex behavioral responses are summarized in Figure 4.6. They are defenses against being overwhelmed by anxiety and emotional needs.

Defense mechanisms provide an emotional shield for an individual—a buffer against psychological discomfort or pain. Defenses are used by people of all ages and stages of development, although the form may change with age and increasing maturity. The most frequently used defenses are defined in Figure 4.7. Some provide a retreat from stress. Another group of defenses attack the source of the stress, and a third group simply protects through denial that there is any stress at all. A defense that works well for a person is used repeatedly and often

---

- Behaviors used by everyone to maintain emotional balance.
- Indicators that an individual is in need of emotional protection and is trying to cope.
- Necessary, to avoid being overwhelmed with emotional pain.
- Chosen to meet an individual's unique needs.
- Volatile, when stress and anxiety increase.
- Less necessary when stress and anxieties are reduced.

FIGURE 4.6. Description of emotional defenses.

Defenses Through Denial

Denial. Protects an individual who ignores or refuses to perceive unpleasant aspects of reality.
Examples: A student who has been promised a new bike as a reward for doing well in school fails two subjects. When confronted with his lack of success, he responds with, "I didn't want a bike anyway." Or, a student tells her teacher that she didn't know that the class was scheduled to have a test today.

Projection. Sees own impulses, thoughts, or desires as characteristics in others.
Examples: A child who has failing grades in Social Studies blames his failure on his teacher, who he says is a "terrible" instructor.

Rationalization. Justifies past, present, or proposed behavior with logical, socially approved reasons.
Example: A 7-year-old justifies her failure to do her homework by saying that she forgot to take her book home.

Reaction formation. Prevents unacceptable desires or impulses from entering consciousness or from being expressed by using an opposite action.
Example: A sixth grader who is extremely jealous of a student who received a higher grade on a science project is excessively complimentary to that student.

Repression. Excludes painful or unacceptable ideas or desires from thought, either deliberately or unconsciously.
Example: A high school student involved in a violent fight at school has no memory or recollection of the incident.

Defenses Through Escape

Withdrawal. Retreats from an uncomfortable situation emotionally, physically, or intellectually.
Example: On the playground, a second grader who is uncertain about how to play with others sits under a tree alone, bundled in a coat.

Intellectualization. Gives logical explanations to painful events.
Example: An honor roll student, who fails a final exam, comforts herself with the conviction that the test did not cover important material covered in class.

Regression. Expresses discomfort with less mature responses, characteristic of a lower developmental level.
Example: A 9-year-old boy deals with frustration in school by crying and sucking his thumb.

Defenses Through Substitution

Displacement. Directs bad feelings away from the source to another person or object.
Example: A preschool child, who is angry with the teacher for interrupting his play, picks up a block and hurls it at another child.

(continues)

FIGURE 4.7. Psychological defenses defined (with examples).

Compensation. Emphasizes a desirable trait to make up for frustration or failure in another area.
Example: A high school sophomore who is not doing well in school puts all of his efforts and attention into athletics.

Sublimation. Hides an unacceptable action or idea with a socially approved alternative.
Example: A middle school girl is extremely angry with a friend who embarrassed her in front of others, but she smiles instead of showing her true feelings.

Identification. Takes the characteristics, beliefs, or actions of an admired and respected person.
Example: A fifth-grade student imitates gestures and comments of a famous athlete.

FIGURE 4.7. *Continued.*

[14]If defense mechanisms are successful, an individual achieves a balance between emotional needs and the expectations of others. Students who achieve this balance receive high marks from teachers for acceptable conduct. Those who cannot maintain this balance are identified as having behavior problems.

becomes part of that individual's personality. Defenses that fail to provide emotional relief are usually dropped and different defenses are substituted.[14]

The presence of defense mechanisms alerts us that a student's behavior is an attempt to protect against anxiety-producing conditions, although the cause may not be apparent. Defensive behavior takes many different forms, and it is not always evident why a student chooses one particular defense instead of another. However, when you recognize defense mechanisms in a student's behavior, it is a signal that the student is in need of emotional relief, one way or another.

Maintaining Emotional Balance

Consider the process of maintaining healthy emotional balance, illustrated in Figure 4.8. On an ever-changing continuum, students attempt to balance pressures from within—emotional needs associated with a developmental anxiety—against numerous external demands, each with potential to cause emotional pain and stress. Some form of behavior is used as a shield against the stresses. The behaviors are defense mechanisms. When defenses are working, stresses are deflected, diluted, or avoided, and emotional balance is maintained. It is a constantly shifting effort to adjust and readjust.[15]

[15]Developmental anxieties (abandonment, inadequacy, guilt, conflict, or identity) may be sources of stress, influencing the type of defense used.

These defenses are essential to a troubled student's emotional stability. If one defense fails to provide protection, another will be substituted as long as emotional stress remains. Should these attempts fail to provide relief, a student will shift to more or different defensive behaviors to build a protective barrier, much as an oyster coats a bit of sand to protect itself from abrasion. When several defensive behaviors are observed simultaneously or used frequently, it is reasonable to assume that a student is highly stressed and the defenses are attempts at psychological relief. More intense attempts at protection often result in chronic, neurotic patterns of behavior.

Extended periods with sustained use of defense mechanisms, meant to be protective, actually add to a student's problems. This happens when unrelieved external stresses continue and behavioral defenses fail to provide emotional relief. The result is increasingly distorted perceptions by the student, with intense conflict between with the expectations of others and the student's own emotional needs. To avoid being overwhelmed, the student may be forced to pull away and use defense mechanisms that disconnect from others. The result, illustrated below, has been called many things: cognitive dissonance, distortions in thinking, depression, phobia, obsession, compulsion, conduct disorder, severe withdrawal, and at the extreme, a psychotic break. These conditions are great barriers, built to separate the self from unbearable anguish.

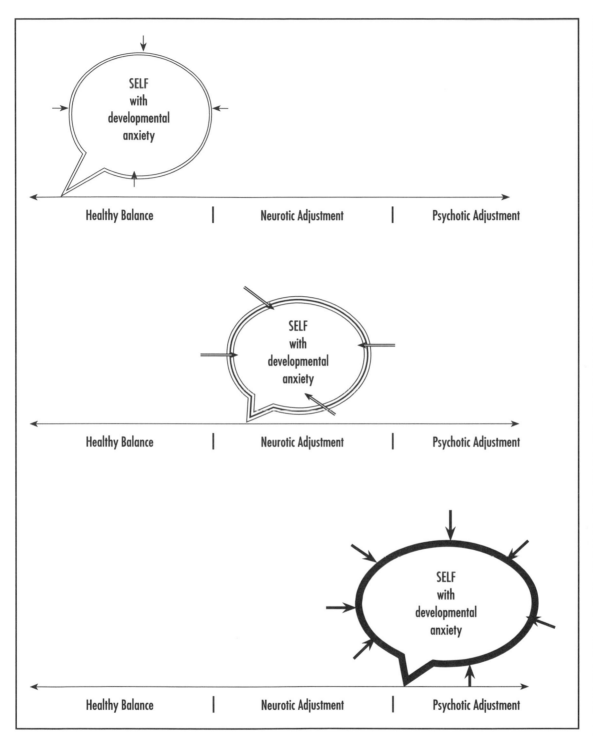

FIGURE 4.8. Healthy emotional balance requires protecting the self from stress by using defensive behaviors. *Note.* Heavy arrows indicate emotionally painful assaults to an individual's inner self. Lines surrounding the self indicate psychological defenses, called defense mechanisms. As stresses increase, greater defenses are necessary.

It is also important to recognize when a defensive behavior is not typical or acceptable for a student's age. The use of defenses that are uncharacteristic of an individual's peer group can indicate high stress and can cause problems by evoking negative reactions from others. The result may be more severe problem behaviors. For example, most young children in the first years of life typically are impulsive, demanding, and self-centered. This behavior is part of the developmental growth process. The defense mechanism is compensation, and it is generally tolerated in children under age 2. However, for a 9-year-old, in addition to compensation, this same behavior would be regression because it is not typical for that age group. Such behaviors are not well received by peers. Unless changes are made in the student's underlying need to compensate for failure-producing behaviors, the student's problems will grow. If the behavior persists at age 13, there will be serious problems because such behavior is a poor choice for a young teen. It typically fails to provide recognition or respect from others, thus compounding the student's problems.

When a student's behavior is unacceptable at school or detrimental to continuing progress, better substitutes must be found. First, consider the possibility that the behavior is defensive—an attempt at self-protection against stress and anxiety. Then, look beyond the observed behavior to consider *what* feelings and anxieties are demanding relief, *which* defenses are being used, *how* effective the defenses are in providing relief, and *what* alternative behaviors can be taught for better results. Use this information to teach the student different behaviors for more successful defenses against the stresses and anxieties.[16]

[16]Chapter 5 describes ways to provide effective interventions that teach alternative behaviors and enable students to be mentally and emotionally accessible for schoolwork.

The Existential Crisis (The "X Factor")

The *existential crisis* describes a developmental shift in students' views about adult authority and responsibility. Recognizing this process and its relevance to instruction is an essential part of decoding students' behavior in every learning situation. All children experience the existential crisis as they mature and gain new doubts about adults' abilities to manage events successfully. In this progression, there is a gradual shift in the source of authority and responsibility from teacher (external controls) to student (internal controls). During this change, children also gain increased awareness of personal responsibility for their own behavior. Typically, students go through this phase slowly during the first 3 years in school. It happens as part of a maturing capacity to carefully observe events and see adults' reactions. Their observations raise questions about who is in charge, who is the authority, and who is responsible for what happens.

For teachers, these questions focus on the issue of their authority in their classrooms and the responsibility of students to behave correctly. There is no argument that students must develop responsibility for their own behaviors. However, personal responsibility does not happen without careful guidance of teachers and parents. Yet many adults simply take the process for granted. They expect students to somehow catch on to what is expected, or they demand acceptable conduct from students without quite understanding how it develops.

Knowing where each student is in the existential progression tells a great deal about response to your authority and how much personal responsibility to expect. The closer your management strategies are to a student's view of authority and beliefs about who is responsible for controlling behavior, the more receptive the student will be to learning to take responsibility for personal actions. Sometimes called the "X factor," this changing paradigm for guiding students through this difficult phase of development is described below.

Preschool Children's Preexistential Views of Authority and Responsibility

Most preschool children are in a preexistential phase of development. That is, they have an absolute belief that adults are responsible for what happens. They see teachers and parents as the authorities who are responsible for keeping things under control. Figure 4.9 contains typical examples of the views of authority held by students in the preexistential phase.

- "Teachers direct things. They solve problems, make rules, and punish kids who mess up."
- "They give treats to kids who do what teachers want."
- "I like teachers who make everyone mind the rules."
- "Good teachers let you know they like you. Rewards are good, too."

FIGURE 4.9. Students with a preexistential view of authority and responsibility see teachers like this. This phase typically ends before age 8.

Every kindergarten and first-grade teacher is familiar with this phase of development. Students want to tell the teacher about infractions of the rules by others: "Teacher! Teacher! He's doing …!" Such behavior is typical for this age. It indicates allegiance to adult authority. It tells us that the children are relying on adults for the regulation of behavior, looking to adults for security, and not yet viewing themselves as able to solve problems on their own.

For these children, a teacher's responsibility is to clearly teach them to behave in acceptable ways that also bring satisfying results. Their teachers need to be caring, expert, and all-powerful adults who provide protection, show them that the world is a good place to be, direct their behavior, handle their problems, and teach them to successfully meet the expectations of others. (These are among the program goals for children in Stages One and Two.)

Primary-Grade Children's Existential Crisis: Who Is Responsible?

During the first 3 years in school, responsibility for regulating behavior gradually shifts from teachers to students. This shift is made as students' views about adults change. There is a growing self-reliance and independence about who has absolute authority and who should be responsible for what happens. As this shift occurs, students first see themselves as increasingly independent, but not yet "responsible." They are also learning that they do not always have to depend on adults to be successful on their own. Yet, when confronted with stress, possible failure, or crises, their anxieties increase. They then become increasingly aware that important adults cannot solve all their problems, which makes them uncertain about how to behave. They have concerns about, "Who's going to handle this?" "Who's in charge?" and "Who will look after my needs?" Awareness of their limitations or helplessness to solve serious problems can be alarming as students realize that they must begin to take responsibility. This is the existential crisis. Examples in Figure 4.10 show how students going through this phase (typically in Stage Three) view teachers, authority, and responsibility. Their dilemma is whether to continue to look to adults for direction or to act independently. And if incidents also reveal how inept adults can be

- "Sometimes teachers act like they know it all."
- "They're always telling you to do this and do that."
- "They have dumb rules."
- "I just pretend I don't know."
- "Sometimes I don't know what they're talking about."
- "Anyway, that's not my problem. I just mind my own business."
- "They don't understand. I want to help out, but they never give me a chance."

FIGURE 4.10. Students in the existential crisis see teachers like this. This phase typically ends between ages 9 and 12.

[17]Children's questions about pretending; the authenticity of Santa Claus, the tooth fairy, and Tinker Bell; and magical solutions are among early signs that the existential crisis is beginning.

in solving some problems, this concern becomes an increasingly powerful factor in how a student behaves.[17]

Students experiencing the existential crisis can be particularly challenging for teachers. Without skills and self-confidence, their insecurity and anxieties increase. Their behavior mirrors their concerns. As they attempt to cope, they may use many different defense mechanisms and their behavior can become volatile. They try to control and test adults, or they use highly unacceptable behavior when their defenses fail to protect them. If life experiences cause some students to be on their own before they have sufficient skills to manage events successfully—and adults fail to guide them—they often fail to resolve the existential crisis. Death and divorce are two common examples of situations faced by young children in which they see that adults are not always able to handle events successfully. Crime, alcoholism, and violence in families also produce the existential crisis, often earlier than is typical. Children in such circumstances may find it very difficult to accept authority because they have learned to fend for themselves. They may seek recognition and approval from adults, but in the process they also learn to resist adult guidance.

If this existential crisis is not resolved comfortably, students can become controlling, untrusting, and manipulative. They seldom take adult direction, yet avoid responsibility for their own behavior. They resist authority and teachers' directions. They seek reassurance, and yet continue to pit themselves against the very adults from whom they seek approval and support. They will continue to be immobilized by this developmental crisis until it is resolved, hopefully through skilled behavior management by their teachers.

As you prepare a behavior management plan, use all available information to see how the student views authority, and whether the student believes that others are responsible for what happens. This will tell you whether the student is experiencing the existential crisis or is beyond it. To guide students successfully through the existential crisis, maintain authority and control through structure in lessons and other classroom activities. Enforce rules of conduct and maintain consequences for rule violations. To encourage good decisions and more self-regulated behavior, use abundant positive feedback and praise. Comment on students' positive words and actions, even when problem behaviors are evident. And spend time talking with students to expand their insight and understanding of their own behavior and that of others.[18]

[18]There will also be times when a teacher should switch to postexistential strategies—when a student begins to show self-control and responsible self-management. Check Chapter 5 for more information on behavior management with students at this stage of development.

Upper Elementary and Secondary Students' Postexistential Views of Authority and Responsibility

Examples of views held by students in the *postexistential phase* are in Figure 4.11. These students have resolved the crisis. Self-confidence and skills for successful actions have brought them gradually through the previous phase of questioning adult authority and their own self-doubts. They continue to respect adults' authority, but in a new way. These students look to teachers for direction but are making the transition to personal responsibility. They have enough self-control and problem-solving skills to be responsible for their own behavior but continue to look to adults for support and help.

Although their new skills are not always sufficient for success, students in the postexistential phase are on a course toward independence and responsible behavior. Much of this growth happens in the process of making independent decisions and exercising self-control. As they turn to peers for behavioral models and affirmation about themselves, they are gradually detaching themselves from psychological dependence on adults. Their behavioral progress through this postexistential phase comes about gradually as daily opportunities for responsibility are provided at school, usually during middle and high school. Each failure increases a student's defensiveness and delays the process, leaving responsibility, authority, and control again to the teacher instead of the student. In contrast, each successful outcome promotes greater independent responsibility by the student.

- "Teachers should let you alone. They should let you be yourself. When I mess up, I'm the one who pays for it. I know what I have to do, and I can handle it myself."
- "Some teachers know how to give you confidence. Maybe it's because they show respect."
- "Sometimes I get in over my head. I have a teacher who's great about that. I don't mind talking it out with her. She's got her head on straight and her ideas usually work out. At least she's fair, and she listens to both sides of an argument. When she sees I'm heading for trouble, she lets me know what's ahead but doesn't try to make me over."
- "She even lets me tell her things about the way I'd run things if I was in charge. And it's not always her way. She's the kind of person I want to be like."

FIGURE 4.11. Students with a postexistential view see teachers like this. This phase typically begins about age 10, but it may vary considerably according to gender and life experiences.

Teachers of students in the postexistential phase help students to see themselves as others see them. These teachers also encourage independent choices for behavior with natural consequences. Teachers who are effective with students in the postexistential phase know how to guide this growth. They have interpersonal styles that promote independence while providing sufficient direction to help students find success among their peers. They serve as role models for effective relationships and teach independence in problem solving. Effective teaching strategies with postexistential students include Life Space Crisis Intervention (LSCI; Long, Wood, & Fecser, 2001), reality therapy (Glasser, 1965, 1968, 1998), affirmation of positive qualities, evaluative feedback with peers and teachers, interpretation of behavior and feelings, group planning for rule making, and use of peers as appropriate social role models.[19]

[19]More information about LSCI is included in Chapter 5.

Group Dynamics

Positive Group Dynamics Can Improve Instruction

The term *group dynamics* describes the ways individuals in a group behave toward each other. Because most instruction is conducted in groups, the challenge for teachers is to use group dynamics to obtain willing participation by every student. It is a complicated endeavor. Yet it is important that all teachers understand how to use this process to create a classroom climate supportive of maximum learning and how to avoid group dynamics that bring chaos to the classroom.[20]

An effective group has several characteristics. First, a group must have a leader. If a positive leader does not emerge among the students, the teacher must provide leadership until skills are developed within the group and a member can fulfill that role. Second, a group is only successful when every member participates. To get this participation, a group must offer something for all members. Without this, a lesson can quickly disintegrate into separate, individual spheres of activity, which opens the way for an increase in unacceptable behavior among individuals and can quickly bring group instruction to a halt. Third, members must value accomplishments of the group and yet be supportive of individual contributions. This implies that competition, criticism, and confrontation between group members should be avoided.

Problems in maintaining group cohesion come from the isolation of some students by other group members. To see oneself as a fully accredited member is not always easy for every individual, and this is particularly true for students who lack self-assurance. It is also difficult for those who feel alienated. Problems in group functioning also come when an individual

[20]The actions and reactions by individuals in a group are attempts to meet their own emotional and social needs by interacting with others.

resists participating or uses distracting behavior to influence others in negative ways. Such actions create a ripple of uncertainty in the group. This allows a student with high social power to step in. If the student's influence is positive, the group will reform. If the leadership is negative, further disruption of the learning climate is inevitable.

When a class or group comes together for the first time, there is little or no group cohesion. Students are venturing into a new social climate, testing themselves against each other and the teacher. As the group settles down, sometimes after several weeks together, the roles of individuals in the group and their forms of social power begin to emerge in a consistent pattern. Then, it is possible to see which students are going to be positive influences, and who will be destructive and counterproductive to a healthy learning climate. If you can identify each student's role and ability to influence the behavior of others (social power), you may be able to intervene and change the group dynamics during this fluid period. The task is to help each student become an accepted, contributing member of the group. This will involve analysis of group dynamics to identify who influences whom in a group.

Students' Roles in Group Dynamics

An individual's group role is the characteristic way that person behaves toward others in a group. Every person is a member of several groups: family, neighborhood, cultural, religious, and ethnic groups; play groups; gangs; fraternities; school classes; sports and work teams; and friendships. Sometimes group members informally assign a role to an individual by interacting with that person in a particular way. Or, one influential group member can determine an individual's role. In other situations, a person actively seeks a particular role.

Nine common roles occur most frequently in groups: instigator, leader, follower, group conscience, bully, clown, scapegoat, baby, and isolate. These roles are summarized briefly in Figure 4.12. As soon as interactions begin among students in a new group, watch for these roles

Instigator	Acts behind the scenes and gets other students to act (Projection)
Leader	Openly organizes and activates group members (Identification)
Follower	Participates in actions that the leader or instigator chooses (Identification)
Group conscience	Reminds group members of rules and responsibilities (Intellectualization)
Bully (Aggressor)	Influences individuals by force or threat (usually Displacement, Reaction Formation, or Projection)
Clown	Gets attention through humor or comic action (Compensation)
Scapegoat	Absorbs the brunt of bad feelings members have toward themselves and each other (Displacement)
Baby	Wants others to take care of things and solve problems, or passively seeks attention from others (Regression, Compensation)
Isolate	Is ignored by all (Denial, Withdrawal, Rationalization)

FIGURE 4.12. Roles of students in groups and the defense mechanism involved.

to emerge. The roles of some students will be quite evident; other roles will be more difficult to identify.

While each student's role is forming, there is increased peer interaction, both positive and negative. This indicates emerging interest in others. There will be conflict between members, unpredictable outbursts, and little or no group cohesion. This occurs because students are venturing into social exchanges with little knowledge about how to behave toward others and how others will respond. They are testing themselves against each other. This is often a difficult phase of group dynamics for teachers to manage. Perhaps the most difficult part of group management at this phase for teachers is to identify each student's current role in the group as perceived by the student and the other group members.

As a group spends time together, students' roles become increasingly clear. It is possible to see those that contribute to positive group interactions and that are counterproductive or destructive. By carefully guiding behavioral changes among key members in a group, new roles and new interactions among group members can be formed. Students find their roles in a group changing for the better when changes in their own behavior result in changes in others' behavior toward them.

Age, maturation, and prior experience determine the point when casual interest in peers changes into intense involvement with one or more individuals in a group. In the primary grades, group roles are not entirely evident. Students' interactions are primarily with the teacher. When students do interact with other members of the group, it is usually in planned activities with structure provided by the teacher. Their limited socialization skills are obvious even though they are interested in having friends. Typically they are unable to provide helpful responses to others because of their own developmental needs. This requires their teacher to be group leader, responsible for building a cohesive group in which most members have positive roles and feel secure and successful with their peers.

By upper elementary school and beyond, students may go to extremes to be noticed by their peers and to obtain reassurance that they have legitimate roles in groups. Becoming secure group members is the essential accomplishment for students during elementary, middle, and high school. They also know the roles of every other student in the group. This makes them extremely vulnerable to group pressure. However, changing roles is more easily accomplished because they have concern about the opinions of others and identify with success of the group. This can lead to new roles among group members.

At any age, students with social, emotional, or behavioral problems have enormous difficulties becoming contributing group members. Verbal and physical forms of aggression among students, including bullying, are typical indicators that they do not feel secure about themselves as individuals and about their roles in groups. Conflict invariably results. Often, a teacher can intervene with individual students to change their roles by helping them see that changes in their behavior will change how others respond to them. This usually results in a change in the student's role in the group, usually for the better.[21]

However, some students are not able to understand the need for change and are unable to adjust their role relationships easily. When a student's role is so negative that it continues to be destructive to the individual's progress and to other group members, it may be necessary to move the student to a new group. Placement in a different group offers a student new associations and opportunities to change behavior and establish a different role.[22]

Students also have roles in their family and in the neighborhood. When working closely with parents and other family members to improve a student's conduct, try to identify which role the child has in the family group. Consider how that role may carry over into school behavior. Child-rearing styles, discipline, cultural and religious values, and family expectations are involved. Understanding the child's roles in the family and community can be helpful in collaborative planning for new, more acceptable interactions in the family, among neighborhood friends, and in school groups.

[21] The roles of some students in a group remain consistent. Roles of others will change as membership in the group changes (as when a new student enters or when a student who is frequently absent returns).

[22] Chapter 5 has suggestions for positive interventions that can help students make positive changes in their behavior and roles with peers.

Students' Social Power

Social power is the ability to influence others to do something that they would not ordinarily do on their own. Social power can be observed in every classroom and in every interaction between individuals. Everyone has some amount of social power—both students and teachers—and it occurs in different forms. There are four general types of social power: coercion, likability, expertise, and manipulation. Refer to Figure 4.13. A person may use one or all types, singly or in combination.

Coercion	**Likability**	**Expertise**	**Manipulation**
Verbal or physical force; overpowering psychological control with implied threat.	Positive personal characteristics that others admire or respect.	Information and skills others want or need.	Covert actions that influence others without appearing to do so.

FIGURE 4.13. Four typical forms of social power used by students. *Social power* is the ability to influence others to do something that they would not ordinarily do on their own.

Coercion is a form of influence that uses verbal confrontation, physical force, or overpowering psychological power to control others. When used by students toward each other, it is usually called aggression or unsocialized behavior and includes fighting, bullying, destroying property, using verbally abusive language, threatening, and taunting. When used by adults, coercion is sometimes called corporal punishment. Coercion usually forces others to respond. Yet the results of coercive actions seldom bring the benefits desired by a student.[23]

[23]Coercion is a common form of social power. For a discussion of social power of teachers, see Chapter 5.

Likability is the ability to have others respond to appealing personal characteristics. Examples include characteristics such as "proper" conduct, kindness toward others, physical looks, bodybuilding, fashion, and the use of slang expressions currently in style. Likability has many positive aspects, such as promoting friendships and interpersonal bonds. It may also have negative consequences when used by a student to gain attention through nonconstructive actions such as being the class clown to make others laugh, displaying genitals to the class for attention, or attempting to buy friendships with gifts or favors. Although positive personal attributes are an important form of social power, a student cannot rely on personal characteristics alone for effective relationships with others.

Expertise is the ability to solve problems skillfully. It comes in many forms and includes abilities that others do not have, but want. For example, students who are viewed by peers as expert may have skill in sports, have information about sex, know the rules that must be followed, have answers to test questions, be sympathetic listeners who can make helpful suggestions, or offer ideas that are attractive. A student who has expertise has potential for considerable social power when the expertise is used around others who feel inadequate. But expertness must be channeled in positive ways or a student with expertise can become a gang leader who sets the agenda and controls the behavior of others in destructive ways. Students in the primary grades and those with challenging behaviors in any grade seldom have sufficient expertness or likability, so they have limited social power for helping other students with their problems. A major task for all students during elementary and secondary school is to expand their expertise and personal qualities for successful experiences with others.

Manipulation is a covert form of social power used to influence others without appearing to do so. For example, a student who encourages another student to break a rule and then watches as the rule breaker is caught and punished is using manipulation. Blaming others for their own mistakes is another common form of manipulation for students who want to avoid responsibility for their own actions. Some students have learned to use personal characteristics (likability), such as helplessness, in combination with manipulation to get what they want from others. This is frequently used when they need help with difficult lessons. They appeal to the teacher, who inadvertently supplies the answers instead of helping them complete assignments themselves. When a student uses manipulation, peers generally do not recognize it and are unaware of why certain social interactions have occurred.

Group cohesion and success are seldom achieved in a climate where students are able to manipulate the teacher, individuals, or the group. Manipulation creates the impression of hidden agendas, in contrast to the openness and directness of coercion. With a skilled manipulator, individuals are not supportive of each other and the group does not function smoothly. No one knows where the manipulator stands in relationship to others. The result is distrust and uncertainty among group members and anger toward the teacher for failing to provide a predictable environment. The manipulator also experiences increased insecurity because the boundaries of power are not clearly defined by the teacher.

Designing a Plan To Change Destructive Group Dynamics

It is a complicated endeavor for a teacher to observe, analyze, and implement changes in a group's dynamics. Figure 4.14 provides five steps to simplify this process. In the first three steps, considerable information is gathered about each student's stage of socialization, role in the group, forms of social power, and the amount of influence (social power) each student has. In the fourth step, identify whom each student interacts with or attempts to influence. These interactions are sometimes referred to as bonds when they occur repeatedly. Bonds can be helpful or destructive. Some bonds link students to each other in mutually supportive ways whereas other bonds are built on active dislike or emotional need. A few are neutral or expedient. Social psychologists call the procedure for analysis of group interactions a sociogram. It is a way to identify the structure of a group's interactions. This is the groundwork for the fifth step—planning how to change the negative relationships, roles, and forms of social power in an instructional group to build positive rather than negative bonds among group members.

---

1. Verify the specific stage of socialization of each group member, using the DTORF–R.
2. Identify the role of each student in the group.
3. Assess the types and amount of social power used by each individual.
4. Chart the negative and positive contacts occurring between group members.
5. Develop a plan to use the above information to change negative relationships among group members by changing the roles and forms of social power group members use.

FIGURE 4.14. For a healthy learning climate in your classroom, use these steps to chart the group dynamics.

Figures 4.15 and 4.16 provide an example with a fourth-grade remedial reading group of six students: Roger, Tom, Sam, Alan, Helen, and Donna. Their teacher first charted each student's role, social power, and amount of influence over group members. She then observed their interactions with each other for several days, making notes about the contacts between them. These were recorded as a sociogram. The solid lines indicate generally positive contacts between students, while broken lines show that contacts are primarily negative. The arrows indicate the direction of contacts, pointing away from a student who initiates the movement and toward the recipient.

From this information about group dynamics, several relationships are evident: There is no clear leadership in the group. Roger, Tom, and Sam have considerable power to influence

Student	Roles in Group	Forms of Social Power	Amount of Power
Roger	Clown, instigator, bully, leader	Likability, manipulation, coercion, expertness	Medium to high
Donna	Follower, scapegoat	Manipulation	Low
Sam	Leader, instigator, bully	Manipulation, coercion	Medium
Helen	Conscience, scapegoat	Manipulation	Low
Tom	Leader, instigator, bully	Coercion, manipulation	Medium to high
Alan	Follower	Likability	Medium

FIGURE 4.15. Analysis of roles and social power in a fourth-grade reading group.

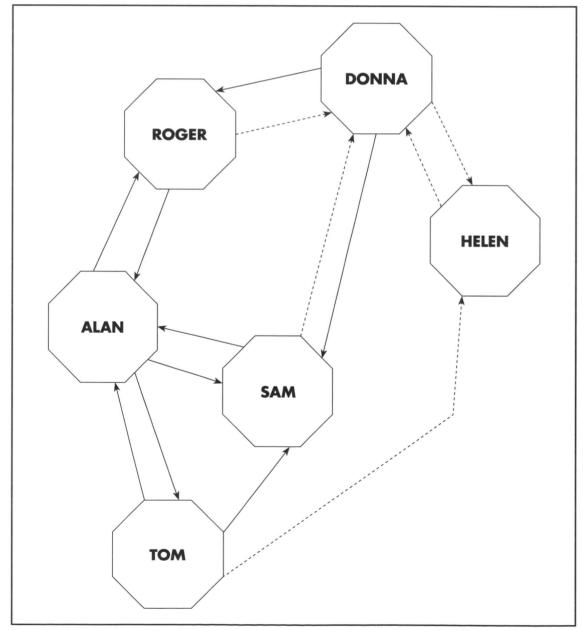

FIGURE 4.16. Sociogram of interactions among members of the reading group. *Note.* Solid lines indicate positive interactions; broken lines are negative interactions. Arrows point to recipients of the interactions.

others, but not always in positive ways. No one interacts negatively with Tom, but Sam and Roger have negative contacts with each other. Tom has negative actions only with Sam and Helen. It is reasonable to assume that Roger is not particularly eager to fight with Tom, so he ignores him. Roger, Tom, and Sam make positive contacts only with Alan, whereas Helen and Donna receive no positive contacts from any of the students.

What Can Be Done with This Information?

It can be used to reduce group conflicts and build group cohesion by planning ways to change the roles, social power, and negative interactions between students. The first step for the teacher is to consider who has the potential to be a positive group leader. When an existing leader is firmly entrenched with coercion as the power base, other students are often hesitant to become involved in group activities where they may be confronted by the negative power of that leader. It may be that the existing leader is the one to remain in that position, if changes can be made in the type of social power that leader uses. Frequently this requires a change from coercion to expertise on the part of the leader. Sometimes it is possible to successfully shift a strong negative leader to a power base of expertise with positive instead of negative interactions with the others. If this happens, the leader's influence for others grows in positive ways, and others respond with increasing respect instead of fear. However, if the decision is to have another student fill the leadership role, the student in the existing leader role must be guided into a different role. Then the student identified as a potential leader is encouraged into this new role by learning to use positive actions toward others.[24]

The Plan for Sam

In the present example, the reading teacher decides that Sam may become the positive group leader if he can be guided toward using his positive personal characteristics (likability), increase his skills for leading the group toward success for all (expertise), and reduce the frequency of his negative interactions (coercion) with Roger and the two girls. It may not be too difficult for Sam to be guided into the leader role, because Donna and Alan already have positive interactions with Sam. However, this strategy requires changes in social power and roles of Roger, Tom, and Helen.

The Plan for Tom

The next step is to identify what alternative roles and forms of social power the others need to learn. The teacher began this process by identifying the student who initiates most of the negative bonds (the disruptive student). In this example, Tom has the most negative bonds, one toward Sam and the other toward Helen. Notice that he has several current roles in the group: leader, instigator, and bully. He also has medium-to-high social power and relies on coercion and manipulation to influence the behavior of others. The teacher believes that he is a destabilizing influence on the others with these types of social power. So, her strategy with Tom is to gradually shift his social power to expertise, anticipating that as he receives recognition from others for his positive skills, he will begin to rely less frequently on coercion and manipulation for his recognition and respect in the group.

The Plan for Roger

In planning for Roger, who is liked by Alan and Donna, the teacher has some concern about which role and social power should be the focus. She sees that Roger shifts among four group roles—clown, instigator, bully, and leader. Clearly, he is trying to establish himself as an influence in the group. She also notices that Sam is the only one who interacts with Roger in a negative way. So, she concludes that Roger's negative interactions with Sam are in response to Sam's actions toward him. With her new plan, she assumes that Roger will no longer be the recipient of Sam's negative interactions. Then, she must decide which form of social power will bring Roger more of what he seems to seek, which is attention, friendship, and a sense of belonging.

[24]For each group member, identify changes in role and social power that should be encouraged, realistically considering which changes could be made most easily.

The Plan for Alan

Regarding Alan, who initiates the most frequent positive interactions with the others, the teacher decides to encourage him to continue as a helpful member of the group (follower) for the present. She does this because he is using likability as his social power, with medium amounts of success with others. She also recognizes that he may have potential to increase his own leadership role in the future as he gains skills in some area admired by the others.

The Plan for Helen

The teacher realizes that there is special animosity between the two girls, both of whom have little to no influence with the others in the group. Helen is the target for negative interactions from Tom, Sam, Roger, and Donna. Considerable effort from the teacher will be required to help Helen learn different ways of behaving that will be received by the others in a more favorable way. The teacher had observed that Helen's standard responses to the others were curt criticisms, complaints about their behavior, and remarks that embarrassed them. The others retaliated by blaming her for everything. The first goal with Helen is to reduce these remarks and substitute positive statements about the others to increase her likability.

The Plan for Donna

There is a different situation with Donna. She admires Sam and Roger and is negative toward Helen. She ignores the others and they tend to blame her. Donna uses manipulation as her only means of getting their attention. She tries to obtain attention by offering candy, answers to test questions, help with reading words, and any other means available. The teacher realizes that Donna wants group recognition, but her attempts are rebuffed by everyone. The challenge for the teacher is to find something that Donna can do that contributes in a positive way to the group effort and brings her the attention she wants.

The Outcome

Changing group dynamics is a slow and deliberate process. Yet it offers a systematic way to bring about changes in the social, emotional, and behavioral competence of your students. These changes will foster responsive learning by reducing group conflict and building group rapport. Here are general guidelines for making group dynamics work in your classroom:

- Plan with students to set group goals.
- Develop group activities together to meet the goals.
- Give students an idea of what the completed project or assignment will be.
- Provide each student with a sense of potential benefits and any emotional hazards ahead.
- Plan ways to increase positive interactions and decrease negative ones between group members.
- Teach students with negative interactions ways to change their behavior.
- Give feedback along the way.
- Be abundant but realistic in your praise.
- Be careful of your criticism; keep it task focused and avoid personal references.
- Recognize each student's role in the progress being made.
- Set aside a time for private exchanges with every student about progress.

Practice: Now, Try Decoding

Decoding behavior is a powerful skill for teachers to use in gaining greater understanding about their students. It is also an essential process for effective instruction. At the end of previous chapters, you selected students in an age group from Chapter 1 and practiced identifying their developmental characteristics. Now, return to the same group of students and practice your decoding skills. Select one individual in the group and use the brief description to decode it for clues about the student's current behavior.

Use this list as a guide to identify

1. Amount of mental energy
2. Types of stored emotional memories, positive and negative
3. Developmental anxiety typical for peers in that age group
4. Developmental anxiety or anxieties for that individual
5. Psychological defenses (denial, escape, substitution)
6. Emotional adjustment (normal, neurotic, psychotic)
7. Motivating values
8. View of authority and responsibility (the "X factor")
9. Social role in a school group
10. Type and amount of social power

Review the results of your decoding and decide how each of the 10 dimensions can contribute to the student's educational plan. Consider what needs immediate attention, and what should be postponed until later. Then, think about how this information can be included in the student's current instruction. You may find the form at the end of Chapter 8 helpful in organizing and summarizing the results of your decoding.

Behavior Management

Management begins with us! A student "reads" us to sense if we are going to respond with compassion or cruelty ... with help or hostility. The message is in our attitudes, values, voice, and body language.

N. J. Long
Director, Life Space Crisis Intervention Institute
(personal communication, 2001)

Effective behavior management is based on positive teacher–student relationships and carefully targeted interventions designed to assist students in achieving their individual learning objectives. The strategic management task for teachers is to maintain a classroom environment that helps each student achieve specific objectives. Before selecting strategies to accomplish this, obtain as much information as possible about each student's competencies or lack of competencies. For a new student, the preliminary information from the *S–E–B Quick Profile* provides a base to begin (see Chapter 3). It is a guide to a student's general stage of development and the strategies that are generally effective at that stage. However, your intervention strategies will have to be adjusted and refined as you learn more about the student. Observe and then decode current behavior (see Chapter 4). This will help you to understand what the behavior signals about that student's unique needs.[1]

After the student's initial adjustment to the classroom, to you, and to the other students, a functional behavioral assessment (FBA) with the DTORF–R will indicate specific social, emotional, and behavioral competencies (strengths). It will also identify behavioral competencies that are missing. These become the objectives for a behavior intervention plan (BIP). For students with behavioral disabilities, a BIP is part of an IEP, ITP, or IFSP. This plan guides your intervention strategies to assist students in achieving competencies they lack. When you select positive behavioral supports (PBS), verify that they are developmentally and emotionally suitable for the individual. Choices must also be made about whether to seek short-term changes or concentrate on long-term results that may require different strategies.[2]

To ensure success, it is also essential to focus on students' strengths. Students are willing to try new ways to behave when they are confident that they will be successful and believe that the results will be something they value (Myles & Simpson, 1994; Schoen & Nolen, 2004; Tobin & Sugai, 1993). Successful behavior management is further enhanced when the selected interventions are consistently the same at school and at home. This is not difficult for teachers using Developmental Therapy–Developmental Teaching strategies, because they have a mutual understanding with parents about their child's development as a result of working together to complete a DTORF–R assessment and to select learning objectives.

[1] To be effective, management strategies must be appropriate for each student's developmental, emotional, and educational needs. Chapters 3 and 4 describe how to obtain this essential information with the DTORF–R and decoding behavior.

[2] Behavior management requires decision making based on a functional behavioral assessment.

Use this chapter as a guide to the interventions you apply in your own classroom. The first topic is a developmental view of behavior management. The second section reviews strategic uses and cautions when applying strategies. It also includes a discussion of punishment, rewards, and when to ignore misbehavior. This is followed by a review of behavior management practices with students who have severe behavioral problems associated with thought disorders, passive aggression, physical aggression, and violence. The chapter ends with a summary for parents and teachers to emphasize the importance of consistency among all of the adults responsible for students' well-being.

A Developmental View of Behavior Management

When To Encourage Students To Make Behavioral Choices on Their Own

Permitting students to make behavioral choices on their own can be an effective strategy for teaching responsible behavior, empowerment, and independent thinking. It also helps promote decision making and self-assertion. But allowing too many choices too early in a child's development may also produce an undisciplined, demanding, difficult-to-manage student who attempts to control others and often fails in the process. It is easy to understand why this happens. For example:

- Adults want to encourage independence and good judgment in a child.
- They want a child to succeed, but mistakenly believe that allowing open-ended choices always provides success.
- They have not given it much thought, but they hear other adults asking children to decide things for themselves.
- They want a child to know that they are totally supportive.
- Their personal stresses make it easier to let a child be self-directed rather than to provide the limits, firmness, time, and guidance needed in order for the child to learn to make good choices.

Responsible behavior is a gradual expansion of an individual's capacity to make positive behavioral choices independently and eventually take responsibility for one's own actions and their consequences. Students must be able to understand what will happen as a result of a choice about how to behave. They must also make informed choices among behavioral options. This requires them to mentally separate the attributes of each alternative and then make a decision with awareness of the result (Joseph & Strain, 2003; Zeeman, 1989). These thinking skills are not fully developed until about age 6 or 7. Before that, students typically rely on impulse, sensory stimulation, or habit to make their choices.

How does a teacher know when to encourage students to make choices independently? A developmental viewpoint is helpful in knowing what types of choices are suitable for a student's age, stage, and individual needs. Figure 5.1 provides a guide to helping students of different ages make behavioral choices. When and how to offer choices is a matter of developmental timing.

By Age 2 (Stage One)

For infants and toddlers, an assertion of needs to obtain pleasure or comfort indicates behavioral choices made independently. For very young children, making choices is essential for acquiring the fundamentals of touch, sight, sound, and taste. They must learn to discriminate

To age 2:	Offer simple choices between two toys, two activities, or two ways to do something. Be sure that both choices will have satisfactory outcomes.
From ages 3 to 5:	Provide up to three satisfactory choices. Talk together about the pleasant results each choice can bring. Let the child choose and enjoy the results of a good choice.
From ages 6 to 9:	Talk together about alternatives—good and bad choices. Discuss what might happen with each choice. Let the student decide. Be supportive but matter-of-fact in your own response as success or failure results from the student's choice. At this age, the student may need assistance if the decision is not a good choice.
From age 10 on:	Encourage students to think about different ways to make decisions and to take responsibility for those choices when they are finally made. Avoid criticism. Let them handle the results. Share enthusiasm when the outcome is satisfactory. Expect them to handle consequences when choices turn out badly. Be sympathetic, but stand firm.

FIGURE 5.1. Use this guide to help students make good behavioral choices.

between the characteristics of different objects. A teacher or parent can encourage this by offering basic choices, usually between two toys. The choices must be between two equally desirable alternatives, and the decision must have a satisfactory ending. Such discrimination skills represent major accomplishments. With this foundation, children begin lifelong learning to make choices with increasing complexity.

Among Young or Developmentally Delayed Students (Stage Two)

Preschool children attempt to do things successfully to receive adult approval. If a choice results in failure, frustration, or adult disapproval, the child's choice was not a good one—neither satisfying nor successful. However, if teachers and parents spend time talking with them about the alternatives and the benefits of each, young children can make good decisions, typically by age 4. Begin by offering just two choices. Combine the choices with talk about the differences and benefits from each. Gradually, introduce more options and a wider range of characteristics to consider when choosing one over another. Successful learning about choices is evident in early childhood programs when children are able to use activity centers independently and purposefully. This indicates that they have learned to make independent choices successfully—a major step toward self-control and increasingly responsible behavior.[3]

Children Entering Elementary School, Typically Around Age 6 or 7 (Stage Three)

With expanded expectations for acceptable conduct in school, students need to know about positive and negative consequences of each behavioral choice they may make. If they have already learned to make thoughtful decisions, their behavior is likely to result in satisfying relationships with other people—both peers and adults. If successful results do not happen, a student's conduct may become an increasing problem. Or, for a student who is unable to make a choice, nothing positive happens. Then, it is a necessary for a teacher to limit the number of choices a student has, and provide guidance for making decisions that lead to better results.[4]

[3]Learning to compare results from different choices is essential for making good decisions.

[4]During 3rd and 4th grades, there is an increased rate of office referrals for conduct problems. This may reflect the expanded opportunity students have for making behavioral choices independently, but not always successfully.

Students in Upper Elementary or Middle School and Beyond (Stages Four and Five)

Because they have the ability to behave in almost any way they choose, making good behavioral choices is essential for older students who are learning to participate as successful group members. When guiding them in their choices, first ask yourself, How much does this student really value the outcome of one choice over another? If a student deliberately selects one alternative to obtain a satisfying result or to avoid painful consequences, the student is using rational thinking and connecting personal behavior to the reactions of others. If this process is not evident, the student will need assistance to develop it. A useful strategy for this is talking with the student to explore together the ramifications of various behavioral alternatives. (More about this strategy later in the chapter and in Chapter 6.)

Observe the Details When Problem Behaviors Occur

Make precise observations as a problem behavior occurs. Give careful attention to what the student says. Consider the physical and psychological events that occurred before, during, and after the event. Look for elements that might have provoked the student to behave that way. Also, think back to previous situations (antecedents) to help understand the significance of the event to the student because it is important to understand how a student sees an incident. It may be quite different from the way others see it.

If a direct connection can be made between an event and a student's behavior, the behavior is situation specific. This means that the behavior has occurred as a direct result of the incident. Selection of an appropriate management strategy is usually easy. You can respond with strategies that suit that situation and the student's learning objectives. However, some behavior problems happen for no apparent reason and seem to have no obvious antecedent. This a diffused (nonspecific) behavior, meaning that it is unclear why the student responded in a particular way, and the situation itself does not appear to be the real cause of the behavior. This type of problem behavior is difficult to understand and requires considerable knowledge about the student. Management strategies for diffused behavior should be directed toward assisting the student in gaining greater insight into connections between actions and feelings while learning to choose more effective alternative behavior.[5]

Decode Behavior To Understand Its Meaning

In addition to direct observation, decode behavior to fully understand what conditions are interfering with a student's ability to use acceptable behavior. Gather information that helps you to understand the student's unique life experiences. Consider how the student has learned to respond to these experiences in ways that may have produced the troublesome behaviors. Obtain relevant personal history about current family, school, and community conditions. Identify developmental concerns. Use information from test results, clinical reports, and developmental assessments. A student's behavior is a composite of beliefs, feelings, and attitudes toward others and one's self. It is a product of past learning, development, experiences, and the expectations of others. It is also shaped and reshaped by a student's current successes and failures.[6]

As you decode, look for defensive behaviors used by students for emotional protection. Also, identify developmental anxieties, roles and social power in the group, values, interests, and the concerns that motivate their behavior. Determine how they view authority (yours and that of other adults). Their ideas about rules, responsibility, and who is ultimately in charge will influence how each student responds to you.

Also, identify behavior that is uncharacteristic for a student's age. This can be a source for additional stress and disruptive behavior. When a student is "different," peers often react in

[5]Lewis (2000, pp. 269–270) provides an in-depth discussion of the importance of understanding whether emotionally driven behavior is generated by specific events or by preformed responses. In either case, he suggests that cognition plays a major role.

[6]Chapter 4 provides details on how to decode behavior to understand what it signifies to a student. Chapter 8 ends with a summary form to organize the results of decoding for behavior management.

negative ways. This can create more problems and result in additional problem behaviors. However, students with difficult behavior will also have many behaviors that are typical for their age group. Look for these age-related characteristics. They are assets for a behavior management plan.

Consider all of this decoded information and the direct observations you make to determine the extent to which a student's current classroom behavior is meeting developmental needs and providing emotional protection. Identify classroom conditions that may be contributing to the problem. Then, use all of this information to design an individual behavior management plan for each student and select specific intervention strategies.

Match Strategies to Students' Individual Stages of Development

There are many effective management strategies that are familiar to most teachers. To be effective, a strategy must be developmentally and emotionally matched to a student's individual social, emotional, and behavioral needs. These basic strategies are summarized in Figures 5.2a and 5.2b. These charts indicate the extent of use and how each strategy is adjusted to a student's age and stage of development. When choosing specific interventions, use these charts to match strategies with a student's stage of development.[7]

Although almost all of these strategies may be useful in one situation or another, the frequency and form of use varies with a student's stage of development. The bars in the charts indicate these changes. By reading across a row you can follow how a strategy is modified for use with students at different stages. By reading down a column, you can find the pattern of management strategies most frequently used with students in a particular stage. Weights of 3 indicate the major strategies for a stage, weights of 2 show strategies used frequently, and weights of 1 or 0 indicate that the strategy is used only occasionally or not at all for students in a particular stage.

The strategies in Figure 5.2a are positive and supportive. There are four, shown in Figure 5.2b, that are less frequently used, but may be occasionally necessary with students who have severe behavior problems. These latter strategies are generally used (a) after a behavioral incident has occurred or (b) when a student's behavior has become so highly disruptive that it threatens the physical or psychological safety of the student or the group. The last section of this chapter has cautions to consider when implementing interventions if students are out of control and potentially dangerous to themselves or others.

The focus of these strategies is on fostering social, emotional, and behavioral competence of students at varying ages and stages of development. The strategies were originally selected after an extensive review of theories and research about intervention strategies that promote responsible behavior in children and youth. The result was a compilation from psychological, behavioral, and educational orientations, including one of the largest studies concerning classroom behavior management conducted by Martens, Peterson, Witt, and Cirone (1986). Martens et al. surveyed over 2,000 general and special education teachers who had varying philosophies and training in behavior management. They were asked to rate the extent to which they used specific strategies recommended by the various approaches to behavior management. They were also asked to rate the ease in using each strategy and their opinion of its effectiveness. Results indicated that there were few differences in the way general and special education teachers viewed the ease and effectiveness of the strategies, although special education teachers reported more frequent use.

The most frequently recommended strategies from that study were then examined and grouped for developmental appropriateness, by children's stages of development from infancy through the teen years (Wood, Peterson, Combs, & Quirk, 1987). Those that were finally selected are the focus of this chapter. Those that were omitted were judged to be negative or

[7]A developmental framework makes it easy for teachers to match intervention strategies precisely with DTORF–R objectives and the needs of individual students.

Strategy	Stage One	Stage Two	Stage Three	Stage Four	Stage Five
Encourage and Praise	3 From sensory experiences and nurturing adults	3 From adults about individual activity	3 From adults about group activity	3 From peers and adults	2 From peers, adults, and self
Motivate with Interesting Lessons and Ideas	3	3	3	2	2
Assist Students in Getting Organized (Structure)	3	3	2	1	1
Explain Procedures	3	3	2	1	1
Establish or Review Rules	0	2	3 Adult is rule authority	2 Group develops rules	1 Individual uses values as rules
Model Expected Behavior and Relationships	1	3 Response model	3 Group process model	2 Interpersonal model	1
Move Close to Signal Awareness (Proximity)	3 Contact	2 Touch	2 Nearness	1 Signal	0
Redirect	3 Physical assistance	3 Verbal assistance	3	1	0
Reflect Positive Words and Actions (Reflection)	2 Actions	3 Words and actions	3 Words, actions, and feelings	1	1
Connect Actions to Feelings (Interpretation)	0	1	3 Adult interprets	3 Adult helps student interpret	3

FIGURE 5.2a. Match and modify strategies to students' stages of development. ■ 3 = *Major Strategy;* 2 = *Used Frequently;* 1 — *Used Occasionally,* 0 = *Used Seldom or Not Used*

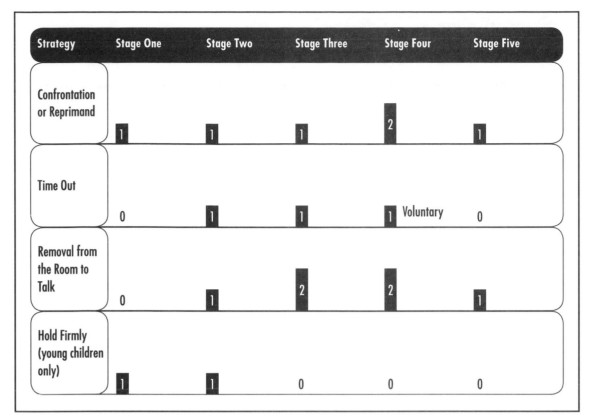

Strategy	Stage One	Stage Two	Stage Three	Stage Four	Stage Five
Confrontation or Reprimand	1	1	1	2	1
Time Out	0	1	1	1 Voluntary	0
Removal from the Room to Talk	0	1	2	2	1
Hold Firmly (young children only)	1	1	0	0	0

FIGURE 5.2b. Less frequently used strategies for managing highly disruptive behavior. ■ 2 = *Used Frequently, if needed*; 1 = *Used Occasionally, if needed*; 0 = *Used Seldom or Not Used*

intrusive in nature. However, four such strategies were included for use only when children are so highly disruptive or out of control that physical or psychological damage is highly likely without strong intervention.

The selected strategies have proven effective in general and special education classrooms. For students with special needs, the strategies have been used successfully in general education, full or partial inclusion (pullout) special education programs, in self-contained settings, and in coordinated home-based programs (Developmental Therapy Institute, 2003a; Quirk, 1993; Wood, 1996a; Wood, Davis, & Swindle, 1998). Figure 5.3 provides general guidelines for behavior management when you have students with special needs of any age or stage of development.[8]

[8]Chapter 9 contains a summary of evidence about the effectiveness of these strategies. The Council for Exceptional Children (2003) has an entire journal issue about the management of disruptive behavior. See also Wolery and Bredekamp (1994) and Wolery and Sainato (1996).

- Match best practice strategies to a student's stage of development.
- Select positive strategies that promote responsible behavior.
- Specify strategies to use frequently and those to be used less often.
- Use strategies that are acceptable in a general education program.
- Include strategies that can also be used by families in home programs.
- Modify strategies as a student improves.

FIGURE 5.3. Management guidelines when you have students with special needs.

Apply Strategies Selectively and Observe Students' Responses

The behavior of an individual student converges at a single point in time, in a particular situation, and with a corresponding set of behavioral expectations in the mind of the teacher. The student reacts to the situation, and the teacher must do something—or do nothing. This is the moment to avoid mismatched strategies such as the examples in Figure 5.4. The strategy choice the teacher makes evokes a wide range of reactions from the student—behaviors and feelings expressed in words and actions. The closer the strategy fits the student's developmental needs, the more likely the response will be positive. In contrast, mismatched strategies will almost always fail.

- Allowing natural consequences to happen to a student who has not yet developed skills for understanding the sequence of events.
- Requiring time on a learning task that is too long or too short for a student's level of development (attention span).
- Isolating a student in "time out" when the student is still in a stage of development where heightened visual or interpersonal stimulation is needed for motivation to participate.
- Attempting to use peer pressure with a student who does not value peers.
- Using individual study booths to separate students when their developmental need is to learn group social skills.
- Rewarding acceptable behavior with tangible prizes or treats when a student has developed to the stage where interpersonal forms of recognition by adults or peers are of greater value.

FIGURE 5.4. *Avoid* mismatched practices like these.

Student participation and satisfying results are the action elements in successful behavior management. Put these ideas into operation by requiring participation of all your students in every lesson and activity. Whether a lesson is structured or "free time," expect each student to participate. With this expectation, establish a rule about participating. State it clearly, and maintain it consistently. If a student cannot—or will not—participate, it is a teacher's responsibility to ensure that participation rule is followed, and the result will be positive. For lasting improvement in behavior, participation must help students to see that participation, with greater self-control, can have outcomes that are desirable. These principles are summarized in Figure 5.5.

As you begin a behavior management program, choose strategies that successfully balance the needs of individual students with the behavioral expectations established for the group, the lesson, and the activity, whether it be a class, the playground, the hall, a group project, a field

---

- Require participation.
- Recognize students' positive actions and ideas.
- Teach students how to participate successfully.
- Convey understanding and respect.
- Keep order with dignity.

FIGURE 5.5. As you apply management strategies, consider these action principles.

trip, or sports. Evaluate the result of every interaction between your strategies and students' responses. Observe their immediate responses. Compliant responses generally indicate acceptance of an intervention. Then, it is reasonable to assume that the strategy you chose provided psychological security and reassurance.

In contrast, exaggerated, defensive, or catastrophic responses by a student may indicate that the intervention has touched an underlying anxiety and, in doing so, has violated the student's psychological boundaries. The student may not be ready for the teacher to know about these feelings, anxieties, or concerns. This may be the result of insufficient trust between student and teacher. When defensive or defiant behavior continues, either the strategy or the analysis of the student's emotional needs is off-target. In either case, the strategy is failing, and changes should be made in the plan.

Use the indicators in Figure 5.6 to judge the effectiveness of your behavior management. At the end of every activity or lesson, ask yourself, "Did I obtain willing participation from every student?" If the answer is yes, your strategies for managing behavior and motivating learners were effective. However, if there are some students who did not participate fully, try other strategies and then observe how each student responds. While you monitor your students' behavior, self-monitor the way you apply a strategy and your own reactions to students. Remember that the goal is to keep *all* students participating in learning. And real success means getting every student to participate enthusiastically.

- Achieve mastery of their IEP, IFSP, or ITP objectives.
- Acquire increased social, emotional, and behavioral competence.
- Take personal responsibility for regulating their own behavior.
- Participate successfully in their school work.

FIGURE 5.6. Judge the long-range effectiveness of your behavior management plans by the extent to which students do these things.

Change Strategies When Necessary

Process evaluation and program adjustment should be an ongoing part of every behavior management plan. Student growth or regression may require changes in management strategies. Watch how each student responds as you apply a strategy. From precise observations of their reactions, you will know when to continue with a particular strategy and when to change it. Negative student responses may indicate that a strategy needs to be changed or discarded for a different approach. However, it is not always productive to change strategies with every negative reaction by a student. Sometimes successful application of a strategy is a matter of skillful repetition of the same strategy. To make this decision to change or continue, understanding of each student is essential.

Daily analysis of students' behavior, at the end of each school day, is an effective way to maintain precision in your management strategies. Some teachers call this "debriefing" (described in Chapter 6). It will help you to stay alert to behavioral and developmental changes as they occur in your students. As part of your daily analysis, always review group dynamics, social power, and students' roles in the group (described in Chapter 4). Reassignment to different instructional groups often changes the dynamics of student behavior. This, in turn, may change the strategies you select and the way you apply them.[9]

In addition to informal daily review of students' responses to your strategies, schedule reassessments to obtain more formal data about each student's gains or lack thereof. To do this, use the DTORF–R at repeated intervals. Then, evaluate the results to make changes when

[9]A student's mastery of new behavior is an ongoing process requiring much practice, encouragement, and repeated successes.

indicated in the management plans for each student. This may also require modifications in your own strategies to meet the changing needs and growth of the students into new stages of development.[10]

Strategic Applications and Cautions

Intervention strategies can promote students' learning or stifle it. When you know which strategies are generally suitable for a student at a particular stage of development, you can respond appropriately to what is needed for a specific situation. Think about the choices this way:

- To *anticipate* and *avoid* problems, use the "A" strategies.
- To keep *behavior* problems from increasing, use the "B" strategies.
- To *control* highly disruptive behavior, use the "C" strategies.

Skilled teachers can choose among these strategies to meet the individual needs of their students in every situation. The strategies are reviewed below.

[11]Be a cheerleader with the "A" strategies.

Anticipate and Avoid Problems: The "A" Strategies

The "A" strategies[11] prevent potential problems by encouraging and praising students in positive ways. Teachers who use the "A" strategies think of themselves as cheerleaders for their students. They encourage their students, promote enthusiasm for the lessons, bring students together, keep spirits high, and generally help students feel good about themselves. When you listen, are supportive, and show respect, students learn that you see the good things that they have done.

There are six "A" strategies, summarized in Figure 5.7.

Encourage and Praise

Encouragement helps students learn good behavior. Give encouragement and praise, not just for what students do (like winning), but for the way it is done. Give encouragement and praise on the positive parts of what students are doing, not just on the outcomes. Let them know that you notice something of real value in what they say and do, even if it is very small. The important thing is to be genuine about your praise. Here are statements to encourage and praise:

With Preschool Children
(A warm, kind tone is important.)
> *Nice colors!*
> *You are being careful.*
> *Look what we did together!*
> *You can do it!*

With School-Age Children
(An admiring attitude is encouraging.)
> *Nice try!*
> *You are really working hard.*
> *You've got the idea!*
> *Wow!*

Encourage and praise	Give feedback that focuses on positive elements in participation, not just on outcomes.
	Let students know you notice something of real value in what is said or done.
Motivate with interesting lessons and ideas	Involve them in participation by providing lessons, materials, and activities that have high interest.
	Weave their interests and concerns into curriculum to create enthusiasm for getting involved and staying on task.
Assist students in getting organized (structure)	Organize space, schedules, activities, and materials to maintain a creative learning environment and a sense of security.
	Encourage independence within boundaries.
Explain procedures	Provide clear expectations and then review the activity or task, step by step.
	Tell how materials will be used and shared.
Establish or review rules	Establish a few concise, positive rules and then be consistent in follow up.
	Ask for suggestions to make a rule that benefits everyone.
Model expected behavior and relationships	Use the same words and behaviors you expect of students.
	Listen and respond with fairness, respect, and interest.

FIGURE 5.7. Strategies to anticipate and avoid problems—the "A" strategies.

With Teens
(A respectful tone in your voice helps.)

> *Looking good!*

> *Great idea!*

> *You've done well with that.*

Caution: Don't constantly repeat the same statements such as "Good work!" or "Nice job." Although students probably like to hear these words, too much of the same thing will lose effect. If you can't think of anything positive to say about a student's behavior, rewards such as candy, money, privileges, or check marks for good behavior may be okay. However, these send a message that the rewards are what are important. If you use these rewards, gradually try to shift away from them by using praise and encouragement when students are behaving in positive ways. Try to avoid using words that suggest competition, such as "You did better than anyone else." Instead, emphasize the value of a student's actions without comparison to others. Also avoid talking about yesterday's failure, such as, "Yesterday you didn't do very well, but today you did better." This is backhanded praise. A more encouraging statement would simply be, "Today you did VERY WELL!"

Motivate with Interesting Lessons and Ideas
To get students to do what is expected, find ways to combine expectations with something really interesting to them. This could come from a favorite TV show, books, story characters, movies, toys, games, heroes, and friends. Students behave better when they are doing things

that they value and will stay on task doing something they like to do, so plan lessons with high interest and appeal. Here are examples of statements that motivate:

With Preschool Children

Is this what the bunny would do?

Show me how the _____ does it.

This is special. You will like it!

With School-Age Children

This is what we'll be using next.

This is neat. Tell how you did it.

Does your friend have to do this, too?

Imagine you were going to tell someone else about this. What would you say?

With Teens

How would you explain this to your friend?

Have you ever used anything like this before?

Think of a way to use this in the project.

This is what you'll need to learn to do to get a job.

Caution: Insensitivity to cultural differences or individual family values may reduce the effectiveness of some lessons, content, materials, or activities. Without being aware of it, teachers sometimes choose activities or things that are more interesting to them than to their students. At the other extreme, allowing them to make choices without guidance can minimize the success of a learning experience. Other problems arise when lessons are too hard to do, too complicated, or confusing. This quickly becomes a turnoff, and students may reject the idea of participating for fear of failing.

Assist Students in Getting Organized (Structure)

Careful planning is always necessary about where a lesson is conducted, what is to be accomplished, the materials to be used, and the time needed. Convey behavioral expectations for the lesson, use of space, materials, activities, time and schedule. Students need to know which materials to use and how to share them with class members. Encourage them to use materials independently, but be alert to times when you should control the materials and supplies. Let them know how much time is involved and remind them as the end of the lesson draws near. This is especially important when a student shows signs of delaying or using things in unacceptable ways. Putting things away when finished is also an important part of every lesson. Here are sample statements:

With Preschool Children

Put it here.

This is what you and your friend can play with now.

Put this away. Then you can have that.

With School-Age Children

This is what we'll be using.

Here is what you need to finish the job.

These are meant to be shared with others.

With Teens

Put the lab equipment away before you leave.

You only have five minutes to get to your next class.
Check through your directions to see what you need for this project.

Caution: This strategy can become a problem if a teacher continues to keep tight control over access to supplies or equipment when students are actually able to use them with increasing independence. Or, a teacher saying, "Let me show you a better way to do this," also can result in a student pulling back and avoiding any further effort to do things independently. However, if teachers fail to take control when students use things in unacceptable ways, behavior problems will increase. The idea is to balance the amount of control with students' abilities to use things in acceptable ways on their own.

Explain Procedures

Provide clear expectations and then review what the activity or task involves, step by step. This gives students a sense of security because they understand what is expected. A motivating introduction at the beginning of each lesson describes the lesson. Then give clear explanations of what you expect of them. When they know this, students are much more likely to try. Use statements like these:

With Preschool Children

Here's what we are going to do.
What comes first?
This is hard, but you can do it.

With School-Age Children

Let's review what we're going to do now.
Here's what to do first.
This is the hard part. Here is how to do it.

With Teens

We need everyone's idea about this.
How do you plan to finish this?
When everyone gets here, we'll plan the project together.

Caution: This strategy can actually be a cause of behavior problems if teachers overorganize to the point that the organization itself becomes more important than a student's own spontaneity and creativity for getting involved. Problems can also result if a teacher has a well-organized lesson but fails to tell the students what is expected.

Establish or Review Rules

Establish a few, concise rules stated in positive ways. Then be consistent in maintaining the rules. Teachers have the responsibility to establish and maintain order. Rules that are *positive* and *doable* help this process and benefit everyone in a class if the rules are fair and consistent. Older children and teens should participate in setting the rules and deciding on fair consequences when rules are broken. When first asked to do this, they may resist or suggest exaggerated rules, stated in negative ways, such as: "Don't push anyone out the window. Don't set the school on fire. Don't forget to come to school (ha-ha)." With redirection, you can help them develop a few rules, stated positively, such as: "Participate. Show respect for others. Do your own work. Follow directions. Respect the property of others." These basic rules apply to everyone—students and teachers alike. Then have some additional rules especially for younger and older children and teens. Always follow through to maintain the rules. While students may need reminders from time to time, even younger children are able to answer the question,

"What is the rule for this?" Then assist them in keeping it, successfully. Here are examples of such rules:

Rules for Everyone in a Class

Be considerate of others.

Be kind and show respect.

Participate.

Rules for Preschool Children

Children do what their teachers tell them to do.

Toys are for playing, not for breaking.

Use words (instead of actions) to let others know what you want.

Rules for School-Age Children

Be on time.

Do your own work.

Listen when others have their turns.

Rules for Teens (posed as questions)

Is there a school rule about noise in the hall?

Let's go over the rules for a group discussion.

What are the safety rules for the lab?

Caution: Rules can easily take on a "crime and punishment" tone. This casts the student as a "criminal" and the teacher (or classmates) as "judge." If this happens, the tone of the learning environment will be changed for the worse. From a place that encourages positive attitudes and participation, the classroom becomes a place that spotlights unacceptable behavior and keeps the focus there. It can create a "them-against-us" attitude among students, where they are the "victims" and the teachers are the "punishers." It is difficult to change these attitudes when students and teachers are in the habit of thinking this way.

Model Expected Behavior and Relationships

Students of all ages watch and imitate adults' actions and words. This strategy is an effective way to teach by example. Set standards for conduct by using words and actions that you expect your students to use. A teacher with a quiet, confident voice will find students imitating that tone. Teachers who smile will find students smiling back. And teachers who listen attentively and ask enthusiastic questions find students doing the same.

When two teachers work together in a classroom, there is an added benefit by being a model of how two people interact and treat each other with kindness and respect. Talk between teachers can teach students acceptable ways to behave toward each other. Use words and actions around students that you expect them to use. Exchange information with another teacher when you want a listening student to hear it. Comments and questions that one teacher asks of another about an activity or lesson can stimulate students' interest in participating. Teacher-to-teacher questions and comments also provide models for students to do the same, encouraging inquiry and listening skills. This sets a positive tone for learning in a classroom. Here are examples:

With Preschool Children

This is new. Try it this way.

Take time. Look carefully at what you are doing.
That's right. Now watch what to do next.

With School-Age Children

When we don't understand, we ask for help.
This is something really different. Here's how it works.
Let's listen to everyone's ideas. Then we can decide how we should proceed.

With Teens

Sometimes people have to do things that seem unreasonable at first.
Two heads are better than one. Let's try to figure this out together.
Sometimes other people disappoint us. Why do you think it happened?

Caution: Some teachers think that behavioral expectations apply only to students, while forgetting that basic standards of conduct apply to everyone. Teachers who fail to listen with attention or interrupt when students speak will find themselves ignored and interrupted. Those who raise their voices when students become loud encourage an even higher noise level from the class members. And students will imitate a teacher's mean tone of voice or critical attitudes toward others.

[12]Be a coach with the "B" strategies.

Keep Behavior Problems from Increasing: The "B" Strategies

The "B" strategies[12] are effective in stopping students' unacceptable behavior before it becomes worse. These strategies help students when they show signs of behaving in unacceptable ways. Teachers who use these strategies think of themselves as team coaches. They notice a student's actions, anticipate what will happen next, call for a different way to "play the game" (do what is expected), and redesign the game plan, if needed. When used in combination with the "A" strategies, these strategies get students back on track for increased participation and more acceptable behavior. The following section provides more information about these "B" strategies, shown in Figure 5.8.

Move close to signal awareness (proximity).	• Signal awareness of what is going on with a look, eye contact, or by moving closer. • Show interest and support without interrupting the task.
Redirect to refocus on task.	• Guide or remotivate when interest lags. • Re-create interest or review steps to simplify procedures.
Reflect positive words and actions.	• Comment on positive words or actions, even if problems are evident. • Offer supportive comments to indicate that you know what is happening and have confidence that a responsible choice will be made.
Connect actions to feelings (interpretation).	• Help connect words and actions to feelings. • Assist in choosing alternative behaviors for better results.

FIGURE 5.8. Strategies to keep behavior problems from increasing—the "B" strategies.

Move Close To Signal Awareness (Proximity)

Indicate that you are aware of questionable behavior by moving closer or signaling to a student quietly. This strategy requires no words and is the least intrusive response you can make when students begin to show signs of restlessness, inattention, or misconduct. It lets them know that you are aware of what is going on, without interrupting the lesson. If a student begins to show signs of misbehavior, a look or a signal can help to avoid greater problems. By standing nearby you show support, interest, and approval (or disapproval) of what the student is doing. By standing near, you can also let a student know you are watching without being intrusive. Words are not necessary. Here are examples of movements to illustrate how this strategy is applied:

When Students Are Doing Independent Work

Quietly move close to show interest in what a student is doing.

A gesture can signal that a behavior is becoming unacceptable.

Catch a student's attention with a glance and a cautionary look.

When Students Are Working Together in Groups

Nod to indicate that you are listening carefully to their ideas.

When two students show signs of a problem developing between them, quietly position
      yourself between them. Words may not be necessary.

Caution: Some students seek teachers' attention, assistance, or approval. Others have an independent nature and want to be left alone. A few are suspicious and negative toward teachers' authority. Consider how each student sees your authority before using this strategy. For some students, any form of individual attention from a teacher is seen as negative. Be careful also that this strategy does not distract students who are focused on an assignment and working independently. Nothing can be more distracting than having someone standing over them when they are involved.

Redirect

When a student begins to misbehave, give additional guidance or remotivate with this strategy. This strategy is effective for students struggling to do something but not having much success. If they are having trouble finishing a lesson, doing homework, or participating in a group activity, they often give up. When this happens, behavior tends to become worse and self-confidence dissolves. This strategy can rebuild interest and confidence to try again. If students are having difficulty with a task, re-create interest in the content by using an approach that is more appealing, or go over the steps again. Clarify, redesign, or simplify the procedure, as shown in the examples below:[13]

[13]Refocus a student's attention on what is expected by reviewing steps or remotivating.

With Preschool Children

You are almost done!

These are beautiful colors. When you finish, we'll put your picture here on the bulletin board.

Let's count the people with blue shirts in the picture.

With School-Age Children

Here is a different way to do it.

This is hard. Try it again another way.

Before you get to the second part of the test, take a short break.

With Teens

Think about other ways you can get this done.

You started out really well. Stick with it!

You've got a good beginning. How will it look when it's finished?

Caution: For some students, overuse of this strategy can create dependency. They may simply wait for your help. When you restructure or redesign a lesson, be clear that it is not a way to get out of doing the assignment. To avoid this misunderstanding, communicate, "Here is a different way to go about it." Also, let the student know that you are confident that the task can be done successfully.

Reflect Positive Words and Actions

As a student begins to show signs of behaving in disruptive ways or losing interest in participating, use this strategy to comment on some positive part of the student's words or actions (past or present). Adults are the mirrors through which children see themselves as good or bad. Be certain that you provide a positive reflection of what they are or can become, even when they begin to misbehave. Your nonjudgmental comments communicate that you see what is happening, yet can be trusted to see that the students have good sides. This strategy is an effective way to create a successful climate for learning. The more positive a teacher's reflections, the more positive students' classroom behavior becomes. Here are statements to illustrate this strategy:[14]

With Preschool Children

You helped put that together.

You know how to take care of the toys.

I see how carefully you are doing that.

It's good that you can do this without help.

With School-Age Children

Even when things are hard to do, you try.

Sometimes it's hard to do, but you stayed with it.

I noticed that you stopped and waited for a chance to talk.

With Teens

It was hard to be kind, but you made a friend that way.

You kept on trying until you got it!

That group needs a leader, and you have leadership qualities.

[14]Comment on a student's positive words or actions, even as problem behaviors become evident.

Caution: It may seem difficult to reflect words and actions in nonjudgmental ways when students are beginning to misbehave. Teachers frequently reprimand students in an attempt to let them know that what they are doing is unacceptable. While negative comments about behavior may seem justified, they are seldom effective.

Carefully balance how much you use this strategy. Too much positive reflection can create a misperception by students that the behavior is really okay, or that the teacher does not really know what is going on. Most students will recognize when positive reflections are undeserved or not genuine and will lose confidence in the teacher. On the other side, too little positive reflection will reinforce students' feelings of inadequacy and alienation.

Connect Actions to Feelings (Interpretation)

This strategy is a way to help students make connections between the words they hear, the feelings they have about what they hear, and how they behave as a result. Because problem behavior is almost always caused by feelings, students need to learn to recognize their feelings as part of learning to control their own behaviors. Some students are quite sensitive to their own feelings. Others are not at all aware of how powerful their feelings are in influencing the way they behave. Without help from teachers, parents, and other concerned adults, few students can make direct connections between how they behave and how they feel. When a teacher makes this connection for them, it is a first step. Then, as they learn to do it themselves, they can make better choices about their own actions. While this strategy is difficult for some teachers to use, it is well worth the effort. When you use this strategy, you are saying that you understand. Here are examples of statements connecting feelings to actions:[15]

[15]Help students see connections between their actions and their feelings. This is a first step toward self-regulation of emotions and behavior.

With Preschool Children

You feel sad about that, so you want to cry.

When she took your toy, you didn't like it.

It's scary, but you are brave.

With School-Age Children

Sometimes it seems easier to give up than to try to do the hard part.

When things go wrong, it can be really upsetting.

They said mean things about you, so you started calling them names.

It's hard to feel like part of a group when others say things that hurt.

With Teens

When there is so much chaos, you feel sort of left out.

Sometimes it makes students uneasy when they are having a hard time and everyone else says it's easy stuff.

Slamming books lets me know that you are feeling bad, but it doesn't really solve the problem.

Caution: This strategy can be harmful if you make wrong connections between a student's behavior and feelings. If this happens, you will see the student becoming defensive. Or, if your interpretations are too close to a sensitive subject, the student will tend to withdraw or become angry. Be sensitive to staying within the boundaries of what is helpful, and respect students' personal space.

Some teachers have the mistaken notion that interpretation involves deep probing into a student's psychological mindset. This idea may make teachers hesitate to talk with students about feelings and behavior, because they think it is not their place to do this. Quite the contrary. When teachers help students make these connections, they are teaching students ways to understand their own behaviors and that of others. However, interpretation requires careful listening without judging what you hear or how you feel about it.

Another common misunderstanding about interpretation is that it helps if teachers share their own experiences with students, such as, "I've felt the same way. I know what you're feeling. When I was your age I had the same feelings." While such statements are not really hurtful, they are not usually helpful. Students may think that teachers are more interested in talking about themselves than their students' feelings.

[16]Be a referee with the "C" strategies.

Control Highly Disruptive Behavior: The "C" Strategies

The "C" strategies,[16] listed in Figure 5.9, stop highly disruptive behavior after it has started. Teachers using these strategies find themselves as referees. They must watch carefully to insure that rules are being followed fairly and by all. Referees stop action, administer penalties, and sometimes are forced to remove players from the game. If teachers depend on these strategies too much, students are less likely to take personal responsibility for their own behaviors. It is also important to remember that when it is necessary to use these strategies, follow them with strategies in the "A" and "B" groups.

Here is more information about the four strategies.

Confront or Reprimand

Use your authority to stop highly disruptive behavior. This strategy is intended to control a student's unacceptable actions or words by reprimanding or conveying disapproval. Success with this strategy depends on three conditions. First, the student must clearly understand that the behavior is unacceptable. Second, the student must know a more acceptable way to behave. Third, the student must believe that you are fair and caring. When you reprimand a student, follow it by redirecting (refocusing) attention on an acceptable alternative. This can increase a student's willingness to stop the unacceptable behavior and conform to your expectations without resentment or anger. If you also remind the student of consequences resulting from continuing the unacceptable behavior, always follow through. Here are sample statements:[17]

With Preschool Children

You must stop that crying! Then we'll find a way to fix the broken toy.

He wants a turn. First it's his turn. Then you will have a turn.

I can't help you when you use bad words. Tell me what you want in a nice way.

With School-Age Children

In this classroom, children do not show disrespect to others.

Making noise bothers the other students. You can be considerate of them by being quiet.

That's his part of the job; yours is over here.

With Teens

You're making a big mistake. You'll have to stop.

That's not respectful. An apology from you is needed.

You know the group rules. No exceptions!

[17]Stop unacceptable behavior by direct order or by conveying your disapproval and the consequences that could occur.

Confront or reprimand.	• Stop unacceptable behavior by direct order to stop or by conveying disapproval (effective only when student is able to independently use another way to behave). • Follow through with *Redirection* for a more acceptable choice of action.
Use time-out.*	• Direct to a place away from others or restrict activity because of unacceptable actions (effective only when student is genuinely interested in activity). • Specify the behavior needed to return.
Remove from the room to talk.	• Talk together, in a quiet place, about a disruptive incident. • Ask student about other behaviors that could have been used.
Hold firmly (for young children only).	• Physically restrain child from destructive behavior by holding firmly, with calm support. • Convey reassurance that you are helping the child regain self-control. • Follow through with *Talk* and *Redirection* to assist student in using more acceptable behavior.

FIGURE 5.9. Strategies to control highly disruptive behavior—the "C" strategies. *Note.* Use these strategies *only* if behavior is out of control and detrimental to the student or to others. *For teens, suggest voluntary time-out to regain control.

Caution: Reprimanding and confronting are frequently overused or misused by many teachers. If this is the major management approach to problem behaviors, it can result in a student seeking ways to "get around" rules and teachers' authority. Continual reprimands can also be destructive with students who already doubt that their teachers like them. If a teacher reprimands students in disrespectful, rough, or mean ways, it puts the students down. They may become so hostile toward teachers that they go to any lengths to defy them. In these situations, reprimands soon result in greater conflicts, leaving the teacher with bigger problems—a challenge to authority and a breakdown in mutual respect.

Time-Out

This strategy is used infrequently and only when it is necessary to remove a student to a place away from others and only when other interventions do not result in improved behavior. Be sure to make it clear why the student has been sent to time-out and specify the behavior the student must demonstrate to return to the group. Here are examples for each age group; notice that each statement specifies what the student must do to end the time-out:

With Preschool Children

The time-out chair will help you remember what you need to do.

You need to stay in the time-out place until you can tell your friend you are sorry.

Sit here, and then tell me what you should do.

With School-Age Children

Stay here until you get yourself under control.

Go to the time-out place, and think about what you should be doing.

Leave the group until you can be respectful to the others.

With Teens

(suggest voluntary time-out to regain self-control)

You need a little time by yourself to think about this.

Stop what you are doing and think carefully about what to do now.

Take time out to think about what's expected of everyone in this class.

Caution: If a teacher sends a student to the office or to another teacher for misbehavior, it is frequently interpreted by students as a sign that the teacher is not able to handle that student in the room. This can create disrespect toward the teacher and insecurity among the other students. An attitude may develop that the teacher is not up to the job.[18]

If time-out seems to be the only solution, try to provide it in the classroom. Some teachers use a timer or clock for time-out. However, while this tells students how long the time out last, it fails to teach the purpose of time-out—learning to take responsibility for using acceptable behavior. With a clock in control, a student may mistakenly believe that spending time is the purpose.

When time-out results in teasing or bullying by others, it should not be used. Nor should it be used for students who want to be left alone. It relieves them of the responsibility of participating and only encourages attitudes such as, "I don't have to do that stupid work now." It is also ineffective when a student knows that getting sent to time-out for showing off will get the attention of friends. Time-out can fosters negative views about the teacher, other students, or the individual, with thoughts like, "Everyone is against me" or "I'm no good."

Avoid lengthy time-outs. If left alone, some students daydream or slip into private fantasies. They may actual enjoy time-out because their private thoughts are more satisfying than what is going on in the classroom. This is not healthy or helpful.

[18]If a student thinks of time-out as punishment, the unacceptable behavior may stop, but the student may fail to learn personal responsibility.

Remove from the Room To Talk

Removing a highly disruptive student from a classroom may be a better alternative than leaving the student to continue to disrupt the learning of the others and talking with the teacher is an essential part of this strategy. A comprehensive guide for using this strategy with students in crisis is available in *Life Space Crisis Intervention* (LSCI; Long, Wood, & Fecser, 2001). An abbreviated version of LSCI for young children or those who have significant developmental delays is the subject of Chapter 6.

Talking together after an incident helps a student (a) to think about his or her actions in new ways and (b) to solve problems with words instead of actions (Dawson, 2003). For this strategy to be effective, a student and teacher need to talk in private, away from others, unless the talk is the result of an incident involving several students. In that situation, a group LSCI is recommended. However, for either the group or an individual LSCI, the process is essentially the same.

For an individual LSCI, a student must have sufficient control to go with you to a quiet place where you can talk together without other students hearing the discussion. If a student is violent and refuses to go with you to talk, or if you have no quiet or secure place to conduct the LSCI, this presents additional problems. Few educational and childcare programs have space available for this type of individual intervention, and most programs do not permit physical forms of intervention when trying to remove a student from a classroom. In such situations, follow your school's procedures.[19]

If the hall is all that is available, plan ahead for how you will manage disruptive behavior. Consider who will provide one-on-one LSCI talks and where they will be held. If you have a teaching team, designate one teacher to go with a student to talk. Because it is unrealistic to expect a highly disruptive student to do a complete turnaround after one LSCI, it is important to plan for repeated sessions with the same teacher. If you are the lead teacher in the classroom, the team may decide that the support teacher will take over the classroom instruction while you spend time with the individual student to talk through the issue, as far away from classroom as possible.

As you begin, encourage the student to talk about what happened and the behavior that necessitated the talk. Encourage the student to describe the situation. Here are examples of statements teachers have used to begin:

With Preschool Children

First we talk about it. Then we can fix it.

Use words, not noise, to tell what happened.

You tell me, so I can understand.

With School-Age Children

Something upset you. Tell me about it.

You were helping and then you got angry. What happened?

With Teens

Let's take a walk to talk about this (followed by statements like these):

Things were not going well for you in there or Let's think about what just happened.

End the talk when the student has a grasp of more acceptable alternatives and agrees to a plan for behaving in better ways in the future. You should decide when both conditions have been met in the talk. If you and the student feel good about the talk, it has been a success.

Caution: Sending a disruptive student out of the room, such as to stand in the hall or to a "time-out" or quiet room, without a talk misses an opportunity to teach more responsible

[19]There is more about behavior management for students who are highly disruptive at the end of this chapter.

behavior. To try to get a student to talk before emotions have cooled down is also futile. Nor will it be successful if a teacher does all the talking or uses the talk as a way to reprimand or lecture the student. A further misuse of this strategy is to allow a student to decide to end the talk before an issue has been resolved or has failed to talk about alternatives and consider different behavior for the future.

Hold Firmly (Young Children Only)

If the only means to stop a young child's highly disruptive behavior is with physical restraint, do so firmly but calmly while communicating that you are going to help the child until he can help himself. There are times that young children require some type of physical intervention to ensure that they don't hurt themselves or others. It is imperative that all staff members know their school's policies regarding physical intervention with children. To use this strategy, prior permission must be established with parents. This strategy is a "last resort" approach when children are so out of control (physically or emotionally) that no other strategies are working and they may hurt themselves or others. It may also be needed if a child tends to run away. When holding or restraining a child, it is not always necessary to say anything while the child is out of control. But it is essential to convey firmness, support, and reassurance with your holding. If words are used, your tone of voice should be calm and reassuring. Here are sample statements, depending on the child's physical position:[20]

If the child is in a standing position when out of control, stand behind and put your arms around the child's shoulders and arms, gently but firmly. Then softly convey calm control, saying:

It's okay. Everything will be all right.

Sometimes kids get really upset, and teachers are here to help.

You'll feel better when you calm down.

If the child is on the playground, intervene to separate the child from others by placing your arm around the child's shoulder. Then walk beside the child to a safe place, saying:

Sometimes kids get really upset, and teachers can help.

I'm going to help you, so you can come back to play with the others.

If you are sitting next to a disruptive child, put your arm firmly around the child's shoulders (be sure you are sitting on the child's left side if you are right-handed or on the right side if left-handed), saying:

I'm going to help you stay here until we can talk—not yell (scream, cry).

When you stop the noise, we can straighten things out.

Think about how we can fix things.

If the child is lying on the floor having a temper tantrum, it is usually a mistake to try to pull the child to a standing position. However, if the child is small enough to be carried from the room to a quiet place, that may be effective. Stay close by, with *little or no talking* and no holding until the child calms down. Then simply say something like this:

You can calm down and get up.

You'll feel better when you calm down.

I don't want you to miss out on what we're going to do now.

When the child gets up, begin talking about a topic that takes attention away from the issue and on to something of interest to the child.

For a violent child, stand in a place where your body blocks the exit to keep the child in a secure area. Don't try touching or restraining unless it is absolutely necessary to keep the child from hurting himself, others, or running away. As the child settles down, calmly say:

It's going to be all right. We'll work this out together.
I'm going to help you until you can help yourself.

Caution: The most frequent misuse of this strategy occurs when a teacher grabs or jerks a child's arm. It is natural to pull away when grabbed. This sets up an unnecessary conflict between teacher and child. Grabbing and jerking also offers a child opportunity to pull free, leaving some question in the child's mind about how capable the teacher is to handle the situation. If a teacher holds a child in a harsh or painful way, the child may stop the unacceptable behavior but seldom views the teacher as someone that can be trusted to help.

Punishment and Rewards

A comment is needed here about punishment and rewards. These two terms are deliberately absent from the list of most frequently used strategies because they are considered by many teachers to be among the least effective strategies over the long term. In fact, they may contribute to restricting a student's development of higher order thinking, self-regulated behavior, and values.

Punishment is generally viewed as inflicting pain or loss as a consequence of unacceptable behavior. Although it may be a natural consequence of misbehaving or making poor choices, punishment can also be a powerful negative force in a relationship between teacher and student or between parent and child. The adult is viewed as a "punisher" and the student as the "victim." This is not a desirable relationship to establish with students. Instead, put a priority on using strategies that focus on successful outcomes rather than on punishment. Success encourages more participation in learning, improved social and emotional competence, and responsible behavior. However, as students mature and gain increased personal responsibility for their actions, punishment can be effective as a natural consequence when a student makes a poor choice or violates an established rule.[21]

Rewards present many of the same potential pitfalls as punishment. Unfortunately, tangible rewards such as food, candy, treats, trips, stars, TV viewing, and toys are used frequently and extensively in schools and families. Some children and teens may need such superficial tokens when they have no other value system. However, these rewards are poor substitutes for a student receiving recognition for personal effort and successful relationships with teachers and peers. If it appears necessary to include a reward system in a behavior management plan, it is equally necessary to include a systematic plan to gradually reduce the reward system and substitute more intrinsic forms of motivation. As long as students work only for tangible rewards, there is doubt that responsible social behavior will develop.[22]

Teachers also ask why *point systems* are not included among the strategies. Points are unnecessary for the successful management of behavior, even for students with severe behavioral disabilities. In the original model development, point systems and tangible rewards were considered but omitted for several reasons. First, there is lack of evidence that behaviors practiced under a point system generalize for students in their daily lives. Second, rewards, punishments, or detailed point-counting systems can communicate to students that a teacher's priority is the system instead of the students. With too much focus on keeping count of successes and failures, the broader meanings of interactions with others can be lost on a student, leading to a view that every behavior has an associated point value. Third, point systems can be easily misused by well-intentioned teachers who reinforce a student's image as "one who cannot do"—a powerful negative message that is difficult for a student to overcome. Finally, externally managed systems of control can contribute to the failure of a student to exercise personal responsibility for behavior.

The same concerns have been voiced over the use of levels and contracts. The essential idea in students' working for increasing privileges by moving from level to level as they progress is theoretically supportable. Levels can be effective as students begin to master goals and objectives typically expected in the primary grades (as students begin Stage Three) and beyond. Levels of accomplishment can provide students with incentives to regulate their own behavior.

[21]For punishment to be effective in changing a student's behavior, it must not result in a breakdown of the relationship between student and teacher.

[22]Chapter 4 includes a review of how students' motivations change with age and development. As you decode students' actions, obtain essential information about their motivations.

Older students (in Stage Four) who participate in self-ratings with the DTORF–R gain a sense of where they are heading and how they are progressing day by day. They see their own actions resulting in progress, and they experience success in achieving valued results that are usually related to peer acclaim, respect, and recognition. If rewards for achieving developmental objectives or fulfilling a contract are age and stage relevant as well as culturally and developmentally appropriate, both contracts and levels can be effective.

When To Ignore Misbehavior

There will usually be at least one student who resists participating in a lesson. Although there are many ways to respond, the best strategy may sometimes be to ignore the student's actions, thereby avoiding unnecessary confrontation, crisis, or the need for disciplinary action. Ignoring disturbing behavior takes away a student's audience. The teacher is also communicating to the student, "I know you can stop that by yourself, and you don't need me to stop you." For example, during an art lesson, a student climbed out on a window ledge and threatened to jump. (It was a ground floor room.) The teacher simply commented in a matter-of-fact tone, "You can join the group." She then proceeded with the art lesson, ignoring the student. He soon joined the group in productive activity. This teacher knew the student well, had a good relationship with him, knew that he had considerable self-control and some insight, and knew that he had a record of success in art classes. Without this information, the teacher would not have chosen to ignore the student's behavior. Had the student continued to stay on the ledge, the gamble would have been lost and the teacher would have had to backtrack to the point of possible physical intervention. But each time a teacher takes a calculated risk and can successfully ignore misbehavior, a student's inner controls are strengthened and the student takes another step toward personal responsibility for behavior.

Although a student who is misbehaving may sometimes benefit from being ignored, there are many situations in which ignoring may be counterproductive. Ignoring students in crisis or out of control is seldom helpful and can be dangerous. Ignoring those who are misbehaving for adult attention may result in intensified behavioral problems. Or students may interpret a teacher's failure to respond as lack of power, uncertainty, or ineptness. The students may believe that the teacher is someone who is not able to keep up with them. Such interpretations (true or not) inevitably produce a series of confrontations as the student attempts to test a teacher's limits. For these reasons, it is important for teachers to ignore misbehavior selectively.

In determining whether or not to ignore a student's actions, be aware of (a) the extent of the student's internal controls, (b) how much the student trusts or respects you, and (c) the degree of interest and motivation the student has for the lesson. The more of these qualities a student has, the more likely it is that ignoring a minor conduct problem will be effective. Conversely, the fewer of these qualities a student has, the more likely it is that ignoring will fuel more negative behavior. A general guideline for ignoring is provided in Figure 5.10: Consider whether or not a student needs your intervention to continue participating in the lesson in an acceptable way. If the answer is *no*, then ignoring the behavior is usually a good alternative. If the answer is *yes*, an intervention strategy is probably necessary.

- Do not ignore a student in crisis.
- Do not ignore a student who is disturbing others.
- Do not ignore a student in need of emotional support.
- Do not ignore a student in need of assistance with a lesson.
- Ignore behavior designed only for your attention.
- Ignore behavior testing your authority.

FIGURE 5.10. Guidelines for deciding whether or not to ignore.

Practice Using These Basic Strategies

When teachers are skilled in using all of these strategies and know how to apply them selectively for each student, they are able to adjust their strategies quickly. As they do so, there is a significant decrease in disruptive, negative behavior from students and an increase in the number of developmental competencies achieved. The *PEGS for Teachers* CD-ROM series offers computer-based independent practice for using these strategies selectively with both typically developing students and those with special needs. Figure 5.11 illustrates the way the CD

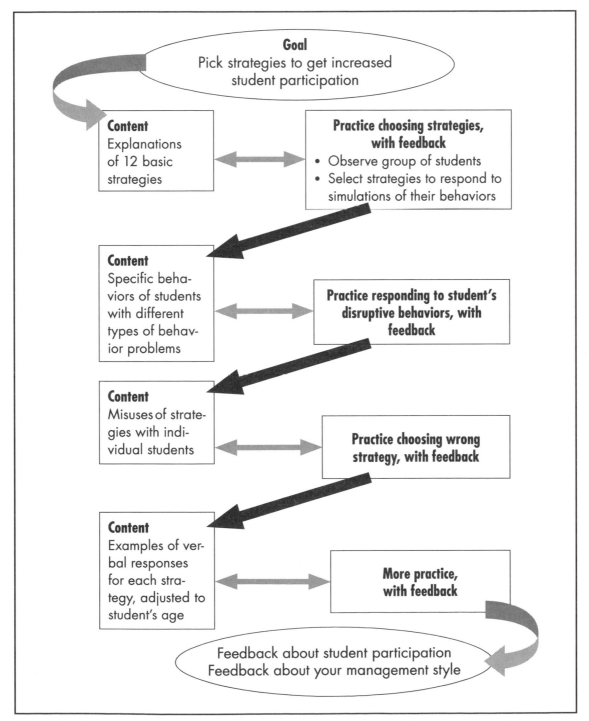

FIGURE 5.11. How *PEGS* CD-ROMs provide teachers with practice in choosing the right strategies for individual students.

[23]Chapter 7 describes the *PEGS for Teachers* CD-ROM series, which offers independent practice with animated simulations of children who have challenging behaviors. Teachers can explore applying these strategies to see how different children respond to various choices. A version for parents is also available.

practice works. There are separate versions for teachers in preschool, elementary, and secondary programs. There is also a *PEGS for Parents* version, providing similar practice opportunities with children in home settings. Research has shown that teachers improve their classroom management skills after using the program and students' negative behavior decreases significantly.[23]

Severe Behavior Problems

Most teachers will face students with severe behavior problems at one time or another. Among the most difficult challenges are those who have thought disorders, use passive aggression, or erupt with physical aggression and violence. As with all students, they also have developmental anxieties, have private emotional memories, hold certain values that may or may not be helpful to them, use psychological defenses, attempt to use social power to influence others, and have roles in their groups. They interact in both negative and positive ways with adults and peers. They also acquire key milestones of development for behavior, communication, socialization, and logical thinking in sequences that may follow the patterns of their age peers, although their skills are usually significantly delayed or uneven in development.

[24]When a management plan is built on a student's strengths, however few there may be, there is a good chance for eventual success.

These students present unique management problems for their teachers. When designing behavior management plans for them, DTORF–R profiles of their social, emotional, and behavioral development are essential (described in Chapter 3). These profiles will indicate what developmental competencies they lack and must acquire and will also reveal skills they have already acquired. Equally important is the teacher's skill in decoding each student's behavior to identify the many emotional needs that shape responses to school, peers, and adults (described in Chapter 4). The following sections focus on management strategies that can be effective with these students when matched to their developmental and emotional needs.[24]

Thought Disorders

Students with thought disorders frequently have language and behavioral patterns unbounded by organizing concepts of time, space, relationships, or logic. These disorders may be the result of erratic neural activity in the brain making it more difficult for the student to organize ideas, respond selectively, or ignore impulses to speak and act irrationally. Because thought and language influence all forms of behavior, impairments in these processes also create challenging problems in psychomotor skills and socialization.

Students with irrational thinking can pose formidable challenges because of their unusual behaviors and the way they view events. The actions and ideas of students with thought disorders are often difficult for others to understand. They think and express information in quite different ways from typically developing peers. Their thoughts are frequently disorganized and fragmentary. Language patterns may be incoherent at times and characterized by loose associations between words, events, and ideas. They may make what appear to be illogical statements or have delusions about what is happening. Sometimes they are extremely excitable and emotionally volatile. They may engage in behaviors that are nonproductive, irrelevant, bizarre, or inappropriate, sometimes with hallucinations.

It is often hard to interest students with thought disorders in participating. Their interests seem so unusual or obscure that it is frequently difficult, if not impossible, to connect their interests to lessons or other school activities. If they show little awareness of what is going on around them, watch carefully for any spontaneous interest, even if it seems irrational. Ask yourself, "What element in that activity caught the student's attention?" When you identify it, plan ways to use this motivation to engage the student in a more productive way.

Students with thought disorders may or may not have significant developmental delay. Those who are delayed will have limited thinking and language patterns, disorganized approaches to tasks, or a tendency to retreat into their own worlds and resist intrusion by others. Observation of their motor patterns and rituals is often the only way to access their thoughts. In contrast, students with thought disorders who are not severely delayed in development will have higher cognitive, language, and social skills. It is not unusual for them to be in a developmental stage similar to that of their typically developing age peers. However, they may talk incessantly and tangentially about topics that have little apparent association with the topic under discussion. They may discuss elaborate fantasies with no distinction made between real and the unreal. Some may insist on using specific rituals at the beginning or end of a lesson. Others may use inner language (self-talk) as a way to avoid or retreat from interactions with others.[25]

Examples of basic practices with students who have these distortions in thinking are summarized in Figure 5.12. First, attempt to redirect them to a new interest. If this does not work, it may be necessary to begin a longer process of interacting with them around their preoccupations. In this private world, they feel comfortable and usually will begin to communicate with you. This eventually builds trust and gradually expands their preoccupations into something more closely resembling reality.

Matt is an example of how this communication is established. His preoccupation is blowing air like an air conditioner. He fills his cheeks with air, puts his hands to his face, and blows air in and out in rapid succession while he makes a rumbling noise. He does this constantly, and with no indication that he is aware of his teacher or the activities in the classroom. After unsuccessful attempts to interrupt this activity and catch his attention, Matt's teacher imitates his blowing actions and sounds. He suddenly stops and looks directly at her. Then he blows at her, and she responds by blowing back. Teacher and student have their first interpersonal exchange. Gradually she is able to hold and increase his attention, without blowing first.

A student's stage of development rather than a diagnosis shapes the way a management strategy is applied. For example, both physical and verbal redirection are used with Rob, a 13-year-old with a diagnosis of schizophrenia, who is delayed in Stage Two. He is absorbed in hallucinations while gazing at the palm of his hand during an art lesson. His teacher puts a paintbrush in his hand and moves it toward the paint jar, saying, "Let's finish this house you are painting." If Rob's DTORF–R assessment indicates that he is developmentally in Stage Three, the teacher would use the same strategy but with emphasis on more complex verbal content, encouraging him to respond to her question, "Rob, what are you painting?" If Rob is in Stage Four, the art teacher might ask, "How are you planning to finish this painting, Rob?"

Here is another example of how several strategies are used. Mandy is in ninth grade and in Stage Three. Although she has many competencies consistent with her age peers, her irrational thoughts, behavior, and comments keep her isolated from her peers. She is very concerned about being "different." When she feels anxious and insecure, especially when faced with something new, she begins to ramble into irrational associations and fragmented language.

Mandy has been able to participate briefly in a class discussion about environmental pollution. Then, someone mentions water pollution, and Mandy begins a rapid, disconnected monologue: "Little drops of water, little drops of rain … falling on my roof … and they all fall down … and no one can put them together again.…"

Her inability to stop talking and the fragmented intensity of her comments turn her peers away. They do not know how to respond, and she does not know when or how to stop. The science teacher recognizes that Mandy wants to contribute to the group, and he builds on this motivation to be a participating and respected group member. He first uses verbal confrontation combined with cognitive restructuring, saying in a firm voice, "Mandy, we are talking about pollution. You are talking off the subject." This catches her attention and stops her verbal outpouring. Then the teacher continues, "Off-subject talk makes it hard to finish the lesson. Think about what the others were saying about river water. What did they say gets into the water to kill the fish?" Mandy mobilizes her thoughts and has the correct answer: "chemicals from a factory."

[25]DTORF–R assessment will indicate a student's stage of development and the associated behavior management strategies, which can be helpful in assisting a student with a thought disorder to stay focused on a lesson.

Maintain a well-organized classroom environment. Classroom order and predictable routines help students develop their own internal organization. Store materials in designated places and in an orderly manner. Use particular areas of the room for specific activities. Follow a consistent schedule to help students recall when and where lessons and activities occur.

Keep instruction clear and to the point. Simple and clear instructions help students as they begin a task or have to deal with large amounts of information. Specified steps aid students in overcoming difficulties with logical sequencing and avoid the tendency to form loose associations that frequently results in irrelevant behavior.

Sequence lessons and activities into short segments. A series of short, simple steps helps students keep track of progression through a lesson. Carefully introduce a lesson, outline the step-by-step process involved, and describe how the lesson will end. Steps can be listed on large cards or on the chalkboard for visual as well as auditory reminders. Older students can help themselves by tracking their own progress through the steps. Younger students can be helped by verbal reflections by the teacher about where they are in the steps.

Regulate the amount of structure you use. Highly structured tasks are necessary during early stages of learning, but as students become more organized it is equally important to loosen your structure so that they learn to manage their own behavior in more typical classroom settings. If they are not able to learn this, they will only be able to function in highly structured, artificial environments, and their efforts to be like their age peers will be thwarted.

Offer verbal cues and signals. Even with medication, a student's mental activity can be so unusual, so scattered, or so unbounded by reality that external supports are needed. Use verbal cues and signals with particular meaning to a student to help maintain organized thought and behavior.

FIGURE 5.12. Suggestions for teaching students with thought disorders.

The teacher follows with a series of private talks with Mandy, using LSCI (see the sections titled "Connect Actions to Feelings" and "Remove from the Room to Talk," described earlier in this chapter). The LSCI focus with Mandy is on how to participate successfully in group discussions. During these talks, she practices ways to monitor her own words, learns to stop herself when her talk becomes jumbled, and listens more carefully to what her classmates say. She learns to imitate expressions and phrases used by her peers. As Mandy becomes more tolerated by them, she sees the changes in their behavior toward her, and recognizes that she can do things herself to be accepted by them.

Careful medical and psychiatric monitoring is essential for students with thought disorders. Symptoms of erratic mental activity, hyperactivity, aggressive behavior, attention deficits, and anxiety can frequently be ameliorated with prescriptive drugs. But these medications can also produce unwanted side effects. As with all drug therapies, careful attention is required to ensure that unexpected effects do not occur and outweigh the advantages.

Passive Aggression

Passive aggression is disguised anger. It is also described as oppositional behavior, a power struggle, manipulation, or setting up someone else (Anthony, 1976; Long and Long, 2001).

Passive aggression is expressed as learned helplessness, deliberate failure, the "innocent by-stander," declared disinterest, and a host of other ways to appear to be uninvolved in events that result in others' discomfort or failure. The most typical role for a passive–aggressive student in a group is that of instigator. The student manipulates situations and other people to control them or to have them act aggressively without the instigator's apparent involvement. Figure 5.13 has examples of students' remarks indicating passive aggression.

- "That's not the way my teacher taught me to do it last year."
- "I was only cleaning up. How was I to know the lid wasn't on the paint?"
- "He doesn't like to be leader, so I took his place."
- "You got it all wrong. I was just trying to break up the fight."
- "My mother says we're going to move away, so I don't have to do this dumb work."

FIGURE 5.13. Examples of passive aggression in the classroom.

It is important to understand that the conflict between a student's need to hide feelings of anger and the need to express the anger is the central issue in passive aggression. Resolution of the conflict is brought about by manipulating people or events so that others express the aggression, bringing relief to the instigator's anger without any apparent involvement. This conflict is typical of the normal developmental anxiety experienced by typically developing students in upper elementary school or beginning middle school. The factors that seem to determine when passive aggression is a severe problem are the amount or intensity of the hidden anger and the extent to which a student feels threatened, abandoned, or betrayed by trusted adults.

If adults fail to identify a student's oppositional actions as passive aggression, it is easy to become increasingly negative toward the student and the group for the conduct problems that result. As this happens, teachers often increase their confrontation, demand strict adherence to classroom rules, and employ punitive measures to enforce adherence to the rules. Gradually, control of the classroom seems to slip away. Punishment, removal of students' privileges, or removal from the group usually results. Punishing students who were manipulated by another student brings cries of "Unfair!" and produces open anger from members of the group. This in turn may generate more anger and rigidity from the teacher. A senseless cycle is created. This type of problem calls for radical changes in management strategies to help the teacher and students redefine limits and plan new expectations for group conduct.

An even more challenging situation occurs when a student is passive aggressive in interactions with adults, usually parents and teachers. This can catch a teacher unaware. The student tries to be "helpful" and rapidly begins assuming the teacher's role and authority. Or, the student verbally controls the classroom instruction, frequently telling teachers that they are mistaken, inadequate, or not up to the standard of a previous teacher. A teacher's natural reaction is to dislike the student intensely and try to smooth things over to avoid confrontation. The approach seldom solves the conflict raging within the passive aggressive student. It is better to address the problem by openly reflecting to the student the underlying conflict and building a relationship based on this understanding. Select management strategies to convey that you are in control, can be trusted, can help the student, and will not allow the student to manipulate you or others, even in the smallest way. Carefully observe the student for any signs of manipulative behavior. Each time it occurs, end it quickly so that the student is not allowed to direct others. At the same time, provide positive feedback to the student during times when passive aggressive behavior is not being used.

With students who are developmentally in Stage One, it is difficult, if not impossible, to identify passive aggression as such. If you suspect its presence, management strategies that bring pleasurable results to the student seem to work best. For example, use physical intervention to ensure participation by helping the student move through an action correctly, or motivate with

[26]This combination of confrontation and interpretation is called "symptom estrangement" (Long, Wood, & Fecser, 2001, pp. 175–176).

materials and activities. For students in Stages Two and Three, structure, highly motivating materials, reflection, redirection, and positive feedback seem to be effective. For students in Stages Four and Five, when relationships have been firmly established between student and teacher, interpretation and confrontation are helpful. The purpose in using these strategies together is to simultaneously make the student aware of the underlying anger (through interpretation) and discomfort with the results of the manipulative behavior (through confrontation). The idea is to increase the student's understanding and motivation to change the behavior.[26]

For students with passive aggression at all ages and stages of development, creative activities provide excellent vehicles for reaching hidden anger. Symbolic material in a creative lesson often redirects the anger (displacement) and can reduce the intensity of the inner anger. However, creative activities must always have a positive outcome if the underlying anxiety and anger are to be reduced.

Questions remain about whether or not passive anger must be expressed openly at some point for mental health. Some authorities believe that anger reduction can occur spontaneously and that anger can simply drain away as positive events occur. Others believe that overt expressions of anger are necessary for a passive aggressive person to be free of the burden of hiding anger for psychological safety. Overt expression of anger can be productive if a student's stage of development is sufficient to allow the student to gain insight into the reactions of others as a result. Students seldom have this ability until they are in Stage Four.

Physical Aggression and Violence

The first responsibility of teachers is to provide all students with protection at school, so that no one is harmed, physically or psychologically. Aggression and violence are completely unacceptable (Gable et al., 2003; Ryan & Peterson, 2004). Follow established school procedures when faced with aggression or violence. The message must be, "At school, no one is allowed to hurt others or themselves." To enforce this principle, careful team preplanning, such as suggested in Figure 5.14, is essential.

Students with highly disruptive behavior can control their aggression by learning that alternative behaviors produce better results. The task is to learn to use words to express themselves and to solve problems in responsible, rational ways, rather than to react physically. They gradually learn this, but it takes time and repeated encounters (Arllen, Gable, & Hendrickson, 1994; Eggbert, 1994; Gibbs, Potter, & Goldstein, 1995; Goldstein, 1997a, 1997b; Redl & Wineman, 1951, 1952, 1957).[27]

Usually a few experiences with physically aggressive students are needed to convince teachers that they can successfully cope with the aggression. Teachers must appear calm, even if it takes considerable inner effort. It is equally important to recognize when a student is really

[27]If a student's behavior is disruptive, communicate your unwillingness to allow the behavior to continue. Your strategy should be to foster acceptable actions by students while maintaining security for everyone.

- Involve the student in goal setting for greater behavioral control.
- Anticipate adequate backup staff needed.
- Plan as a team for the safe management of the student and others.
- Decide which expectations and strategies will be used.
- Identify quiet areas to assist the student who has lost control and for private talks.
- Train all who work with the student to use the same strategies—consistently and skillfully.
- Schedule daily debriefings for the team to maintain consistency and continuity.
- Keep the student's parents and the school administration fully informed.
- Watch for each small gain and give the student encouragement to continue to improve.

FIGURE 5.14. Suggestions for working with a student who is extremely aggressive or violent.

out of control and backup help is needed. Carefully plan ahead for how violence will be handled. This may require identifying "backup" by another adult and a "safe place" where a student can be contained until the behavior is under control.

Look for these emotional phases when a student has lost control and is physically violent: aggression, regression, and compliance. The indicators of each phase are clear and will signal opportunities to change strategies and move the student toward greater self-control and more responsible problem solving. Each phase is described briefly in Figure 5.15.[28]

[28]When a student is bigger and physically stronger, a teacher needs verbal skills for psychological power to control a situation (see Chapter 7).

Phase	Critical Point for Student	Strategy Options
Aggressive	Student needs help for self-control. Emotional intensity is drained off.	Confrontation, removal from group or room (time-out), structure, reflection, redirection, encouragement.
Regressive	Student indicates need for emotional support, understanding, and psychological comfort.	Reflection, interpretation, encouragement.
Compliant	Student begins to communicate rationally about the issue. Problem solving begins.	Encouragement, redirection, interpretation, LSCI.

FIGURE 5.15. As you assist an out-of-control, aggressive student, you will see these phases of behavior.

The Aggressive Phase

In this first phase, aggression may be verbal or physical and may be directed toward other students, at the teacher, or inward by the student toward himself. Verbal aggression is handled best by ignoring the content and redirecting the student's interest back to the ongoing lesson. Confrontation and reprimand for verbal aggression seldom work. This simply shifts the focus away from the precipitating event, and gives the student another target for a second verbal assault. When a teacher engages in verbal battle with a student, the teacher loses authority as the adult in charge (diminished psychological power) and unintentionally encourages further verbal aggression.

It is important to recognize when a student is physically out of control and cannot regain self-control without help. In these situations, there must be a "safe place" where the student can be contained until the violence has ended. It is essential to separate a student from others during this time. When students need help controlling themselves, they may have to be restrained physically. This should be done only in the most extreme circumstances—when they may hurt themselves or you. Never attempt restraint unless (a) it is a practice approved by the school, (b) you are absolutely certain that you can maintain control, and (c) you can maintain control in a nonpunitive manner. Restraining a student with firmness while conveying support takes practice. Grabbing a student's arms is never advisable, as it will only provoke increased resistance or combat. Think of the process as holding to provide support and adult assistance rather than as a confrontation. Remember, a student's aggression should never be allowed to deteriorate into combat between teacher and student, either physically or verbally.

If a student is too violent to move to a quiet place, it may be necessary to have the other students in the group go to another place to continue the lesson while a backup person or the teacher stays with the student who is out of control. *Never leave a violent, out-of-control student without adult supervision.* Although there is considerable resistance to isolation as a means of controlling violent students, it can happen with such intensity that some form of isolation needs to be available. This is when careful preplanning and established school procedures are vital.

The Regressive Phase

In this second phase of an aggressive episode, a student will revert to regressive behaviors usually seen in younger children. The student will seek some form of reassurance, support, or comfort—whining, crying, thumb sucking, rocking, or curling up to withdraw physically. Sometimes a student may reach out physically for support (moving closer to the teacher) or make an initial comment such as "You don't like me." When the student makes such a gesture, it indicates that the intensity of the emotions is decreasing, and the teacher must respond. It is time to convey support. Sometimes silent acceptance of the gesture is the best way to support the student. Occasionally a student will need a reassuring touch. But remember, too much touching or talking can arouse emotions again during this phase. Watch for the time when the student shows signs of ability to talk about what happened. This is the signal that the regression is over and the final phase is beginning.

The Compliant Phase

In this last phase, the aggressive drive is largely diminished. A student is now receptive to some amount of rational talk about the issues. From the student's latest DTORF–R assessment you will know whether or not the SAYING (Communication) competencies for Stage Two have been achieved. This will indicate how fully the student is able to respond to LSCI. If the prerequisite Stage Two skills have not been achieved, use reflection to provide a simple, nonjudgmental statement about the event and the central issue. Then restructure the situation by establishing a few basic actions that the student must make to return to the classroom activity.[29]

Students who are in Stage Three are ready for a basic LSCI. They are learning to use words instead of actions to deal with their own feelings and interactions with others. Talk about the event with sensitivity and understanding. By supplying simple phrases to describe the essential aspects of the event in a noncritical manner, you can help a student learn to describe what happened, even if only in a few phrases. Without concerns about negative criticism, the student's capacity and willingness to talk will increase rapidly.

Students in Stages Four or Five benefit hugely from a full LSCI after an aggressive outburst. It is the preferred way to help them gain greater insight into themselves and the actions of others. For them, this LSCI strategy encourages problem solving, evaluating their options, making responsible choices, and taking personal responsibility for their decisions.

Figure 5.16 summarizes the messages teachers must convey to students who are highly disruptive. When a teacher helps a student through these phases of aggression in a strong and supportive manner, a bond is established. The student learns that the teacher is in control and has the expertise to manage the situation successfully. The teacher learns that there is nothing to fear from a student's aggression, although such experiences are physically and emotionally draining for both the teacher and the student.

[29]The LSCI is described earlier in this chapter under the heading, "Remove From the Room to Talk."

- The student's aggressive behavior has been noticed.
- The behavior will not produce satisfying results.
- Nothing bad will be allowed to happen to the student.
- Nothing harmful will be allowed to happen to others.
- When behavior changes, better things will happen.
- You can help the student make the needed change.

FIGURE 5.16. Messages to convey to students who have highly disruptive behavior.

Summary for Teachers and Parents
School and Home Teamwork

School and home teamwork is essential for parents and teachers as they plan together for appropriate interventions at home and school. Figure 5.17 summarizes strategies familiar to parents and shows how these same strategies should change as young children grow older. Parents can use the list to identify their own management strategies. In this way, they make connections between the discipline and management practices used at home and the intervention strategies selected for their child's program at school. Parents and teachers can discuss how these strategies are applied and gradually change in form, but not in substance, as the child matures. They also can use the list to consider how they might change their discipline practices with their other children.

Begin with these strategies for young children:	Expand the strategies for school-age children:
Convey caring by being close.	Respect privacy; acknowledge feelings.
Encourage and praise.	Show respect and admiration.
Create high interest in activities.	Be positive about events and people.
Model expected behavior, words, and voice tone.	Model positive interactions with others.
Be clear and concise in what is expected.	Discuss reasons and values.
Be organized with routines and activities.	Plan together.
Be consistent with actions, words, and routines.	Encourage talk about ideas, feelings, values.
Reflect positive actions.	Recognize contributions of others.
Redirect behavior into trying again.	Plan success-producing activities together.
Limit rules to a few "dos" instead of "don'ts."	Have rules built on values.
Be firm but calm when correcting behavior.	Reflect consequences of actions.
Remove from room if tantrum occurs.	Encourage talking to problem solve.

FIGURE 5.17. Parents can use the same positive strategies at home when their children's behavior is challenging. Refer to *PEGS for Parents* interactive CDs to help parents practice these strategies.

Steps To Follow for Effective Behavior Management

In summary, when using Developmental Therapy–Developmental Teaching, there are several basic steps to follow for an effective behavior management program. These steps are useful for students of all ages, stages, diagnoses, and behavioral characteristics:

1. Assess a student's functional competencies and stage of development.
2. Decode behavior to understand its meaning for a student.
3. Preplan to ensure that management strategies foster achievement of learning objectives.

4. When problem behaviors occur, observe the details.
5. Select developmentally and emotionally appropriate responses.
6. Observe students' responses and evaluate effectiveness.
7. Make adjustments in the strategies, when necessary.

For Review: Practice Quick Decisions When Intervening

Your fifth-grade students are working on math assignments. You are helping three students work with fractions. Another student, Amy, is frantically waving her arms and calling for you. She says she needs you … **now!** *How do you respond?*

From Chapter 1, you know that Amy is an intellectually average 10-year-old whose academic problems are becoming increasingly severe. If you respond to her using the Developmental Therapy–Developmental Teaching approach, you also know that her age peers have achieved the goals and objectives associated with Stage Three (learning to be a successful group member), and are beginning to work on competencies in Stage Four. However, from Amy's DTORF–R rating and your decoding of her behavior, you know that Amy has not completely mastered the Stage Three goals and objectives for social, emotional, and behavioral development. She seldom completes her work assignments independently. You recognize that she has difficulty with sustained waiting that requires an impulse control she has not yet developed. And because you understand that Amy, unlike most of her age peers, is still in a preexistential phase of development (see also Chapter 4), you know that she relies on adults to help rather than try to solve a problem by herself. You also know that Amy is having difficulties in peer interactions, which she wants badly. Because of this lack of friends and her failing school work, she has little, if any, confidence in her own abilities.

Here is how Amy's teacher responded: "It's hard to wait, Amy. But while you wait, I want you to find that excellent arithmetic paper in your notebook from yesterday. Put a check by the problems that you did correctly, especially if they were very hard. I want to see how they compare with today's problems."

Which management strategies do you recognize in the teacher's response?

1. _____
2. _____
3. _____

A typical 10-year-old can wait for the teacher's help, but Amy's behavior is more like that of a 6-year-old, with distractibility, a baby voice, and low frustration tolerance. She cannot sit still for long without adult attention. This behavior is typical for students early in Stage Three, where they are learning to respond to the environment with individual success.

Now, review how the teacher adjusted his management strategies to Amy's developmental level. Clearly, Amy needs to feel successful and requires more movement activities than a typical 10-year-old. Yet it would be counterproductive to allow her to wander around the classroom or play games until the teacher can give her the help she thinks she needs. For this reason, the teacher does not tell Amy to wait until he finishes working with the other students. Instead, he gives Amy a substitute activity that emphasizes her previous successes until he can help her individually.

Did you notice that the teacher also reflects Amy's feelings before he uses any other strategy? His positive response to Amy recognizes her feelings first, then continues to focus on the arithmetic activity by restructuring the task. By putting words to Amy's frustration, the teacher helps her to recognize feelings and use words rather than impulsive actions to express herself. Additionally, his response meets Amy's need for a dependable relationship with an adult. It reassures Amy that the teacher is someone she can count on. He uses this need for adult approval and assistance to motivate Amy to comply with the expectation to continue the assignment. This is important not only from a developmental perspective but from a learning standpoint as well.

Talking with Young or Developmentally Delayed Students in Crisis

CHAPTER

First we talk about it.
Then we fix it.
Then we smile!

      … Sam, age 5

In its simplicity, Sam's problem-solving "recipe" contains the essence for helping young children deal with crisis. It is equally helpful for those with limited developmental skills. Called the TALK, FIX IT, SMILE process, it is actually an abbreviated form of *Life Space Crisis Intervention* (LSCI; Long, Wood, & Fecser, 2001), modified for children who have not yet developed the prerequisite skills for participating in a full LSCI. With this process, you can help students

- change their views of themselves as responsible people,
- take ownership of solutions to resolve troublesome incidents,
- increase personal responsibility for changing their own behaviors, and
- gain greater understanding of others' actions.

This process is an essential tool for teachers concerned about helping young children become increasingly responsible individuals. As a strategy for support and teaching, it provides a structure to move a child developmentally forward from unacceptable or destructive behavior. By converting emotional responses to an incident into words and solutions, this process teaches a child to talk about the incident, select a resolution, and experience positive results from behaving in more acceptable ways. It also offers a range of opportunities to work on specific DTORF–R learning objectives across all four subscale areas, especially for students who are developmentally in Stages One and Two (see Chapters 2 and 3).

Sam's recipe reflects the essence of the process. It begins with "we," signaling recognition that crisis resolution is the combined effort of two people: the child and the adult. The adult provides support, security, understanding, and guidance. Without "talk," there is no way to work together to transform a crisis into a solution. The child must go beyond the stress of the moment to actively participate in the resolution—talking it out instead of acting it out.[1]

With the "Fix it" statement, Sam shows naive faith in adult omnipotence. We know that there is seldom a quick fix. Yet, young children have a need to believe that when something is wrong, somebody (an adult) can fix it. The point of "fixing it" is to communicate that adults can help children deal with crisis in ways that are within the children's capacities.

[1] A version of this chapter originally appeared in *Life Space Intervention* (Wood & Long, 1991, Chapter 12). It is included here with permission of the authors and publisher. For a comprehensive guide to the current revised version, see *Life Space Crisis Intervention* (Long, Wood, & Fecser, 2001).

The "Smile" in Sam's recipe actually came as he marched back to his classroom to tell the others about how to solve a problem. A smile touches every child's need for optimism and confidence for the future. Things must get better! While this may appear forced to some adults, children must learn to be conscious of what they are feeling—the more positive the feelings, the happier the child. The time immediately following the selection of a new behavior holds promise for successfully sensitizing children to feelings of relief at crisis resolution and pleasure in the results of a new, successful behavior. This learning provides the foundation for future motivation, teaching that changes in behavior can produce desired responses from others. This is what Sam's "smile" is all about.[2]

In this chapter, there is a section about how to tell if a student needs this abbreviated version of LSCI because prerequisite skills are missing. This section also includes a list of developmental skills that can be taught to students who are in Stages One or Two. This is followed by a section that describes the TALK, FIX IT, SMILE process and gives step-by-step directions, including a discussion about when to use emotional first aid. To illustrate, there is transcript of the process that was used with Sam in the "Yellow Towel Incident." The chapter ends with a brief summary of the three phases and a practice section with questions for review.

How To Tell if a Student Needs the TALK, FIX IT, SMILE Approach

Misbehavior is almost always triggered by some specific incident or event. In response, some children lose control. They may shout, become aggressive, curse, have a temper tantrum, or cry. Others withdraw, complain, whine, or argue. They often do not understand the source of their emotional pain, but they feel it acutely. They do not possess sufficient impulse control to curtail expression of intense feelings, and frequently resort to emotionally driven responses. Their behavior may be like that of a much younger child, and they fail to connect their behavior to the way others treat them. Their own needs are paramount (see the values section of Chapter 4). When thwarted in their attempts to gratify their own needs, they can only express outrage. In young children, such behavior is not unusual (although still unacceptable), but the lack of skills is anticipated by adults, who try to teach and intervene in constructive ways. In school-age children, expectations are increased, and such primitive behavior is no longer tolerated. Yet when these students have developmental delay, they usually lack higher functioning coping skills, and some version of LSCI is needed to help them learn better ways to manage their emotionally driven behavior.

There are five essential prerequisite skills needed by a student to participate in a full LSCI (Long, Wood, & Fecser, 2001, p. 10):

- Attention span and memory for listening and retaining what has been said
- Minimal verbal skills to use language spontaneously and with sequential thought
- Sufficient comprehension to understand the meanings of the teacher's words
- Mental reasoning to understand the essence of an incident and the problem it produced
- Trust in the adult

When a student lacks these skills, the readiness process described in this chapter is a suitable alternative. If you are in doubt about whether to use a full LSCI or adapt it to this abbreviated version, do an informal assessment of developmental skills and developmental anxieties (see Chapters 2, 3, and 4). A student who is developmentally unprepared for a full LSCI is one who may have difficulty relating bits and pieces of an incident to a central issue. The student may sequence events in a confused way, tending to focus on one particular aspect of the incident (usually the part that evoked the greatest emotional response). Expressive verbal skills are limited, and the meanings of words and ideas are confusing. Memory is fragmented, and the student may need assistance to reconstruct a simple sequence of events. These students cannot communicate feelings verbally. Nor can they connect their feelings to their own behavior. When you recognize a student like this, who is developmentally unprepared for a full LSCI, use the TALK, FIX IT, SMILE approach to teach the basic readiness skills while dealing with the incident at hand.[3]

Consider Donna, who is described in Figure 6.1. She can benefit from the abbreviated LSCI, even though she has a few of the prerequisite skills listed above. She has sufficient attention span, verbal skills for social communication, comprehension of the meanings of the teacher's words, genuine trust in the teacher, and some awareness of expected behavior. However, Donna's emotions distort her perceptions of events and drive her to behave in ways that fail to bring her the praise and admiration that she wants.

During a music activity, 6-year-old Donna is laughing, giggling, kicking her feet, and squirming. The teacher's attempts to redirect her back to the activity fail. Donna throws her tambourine and tries to snatch rhythm band instruments from the other children. It does not take her long to disrupt the entire activity. She is grinning from ear to ear, but the other children are showing increased anxiousness. When the teacher attempts to take Donna away from the group, she kicks and hits the teacher. As the teacher removes her from the room, Donna makes a last attempt, between kicks and screams, to bite the teacher. Away from the group, she is alternately volatile, hyperactive, threatening, and playful. By holding her in a gentle but firm manner, the teacher is able to help Donna calm down.

Now what?

Should the teacher leave her alone? Go back to the classroom with her? Ignore her? Try to reason with her? Try to build a foundation for future self-control? What should the teacher focus on? The child's laughter? Kicking? Throwing instruments? Or that she was disrupting the others? What can Donna learn from this incident, and what should the teacher try to teach her?

FIGURE 6.1. Donna.

[3]Children as young as age 5 have benefited from the abbreviated LSCI as a helpful strategy for solving or resolving a crisis. They must be able to listen, have some verbal skills for sharing information, understand meanings in words, recognize that there has been an incident with unacceptable behavior, and trust that the teacher is a helping person.

The teacher chooses the TALK, FIX IT, SMILE approach because of its simplicity in encouraging Donna to select better ways to get the praise she seeks. The teacher also recognizes that the regression Donna displays is an indication of her immature emotional needs, which will continue to drive her behavior until they can be replaced with more satisfying outcomes. As they begin the process, the teacher will simultaneously be helping Donna to achieve several missing developmental skills, including sequencing of the events that led to disruption of the music activity. The DTORF–R objectives that can be achieved with this process are listed in Figure 6.2.

If you already use Developmental Therapy–Developmental Teaching, you will recognize many opportunities to include DTORF–R objectives in the process. These are essential skills for students to master as a part of social, emotional, and behavioral development, especially during Stages One and Two. For a child who lacks these competencies, the process then becomes an added strategy for teaching missing skills while learning more responsible ways to respond to disturbing incidents.

Doing
- Recall routine.
- Show awareness of expected behavior through actions.
- Tell about expected behavior using words.
- Refrain from unacceptable behavior when others are misbehaving.
- Explain why an event occurred (cause and effect).

Saying
- Use simple words to answer an adult's questions.
- Use words to describe events.
- Use words to describe characteristics and behavior of self and others.
- Show feelings appropriately through words and actions.
- Make positive statements about self.
- Participate in talk with others.

Relating
- Seek adults spontaneously.
- Initiate appropriate behavior toward another child.
- Interact in acceptable ways with other children in play.
- Cooperate with other children in group activities.
- Share and take turns.
- Imitate appropriate behavior of other children.
- Label events with simple values.

Thinking
- Identify details in objects and people.
- Tell a story sequence.
- Use concepts of "same" and "different."
- Discriminate opposites.
- Categorize things that have the same characteristics.
- Give reasons "why."
- Listen to a story with comprehension of what happened.
- Learn rules of play and participation.

FIGURE 6.2. Children can achieve these DTORF–R objectives with the TALK, FIX IT, SMILE process.

The TALK, FIX IT, SMILE Process

Although there are six steps in the full LSCI, the abbreviated TALK, FIX IT, SMILE process distills the same essentials into three general phases for (a) talking about an incident, (b) "fixing" the problem by finding and practicing a solution, and (c) closing the incident in a positive way that enhances self-esteem. Figure 6.3 illustrates the way the six LSCI steps are condensed into three phases in the shortened version. Sam surely caught the essence of these steps in his recipe.

TALK, FIX IT, SMILE works like this: When there is a crisis incident, take the child aside to talk. If the child is upset or using unacceptable behavior, allow time for the child to quiet down (emotional first aid). Then encourage the child to focus on the incident by asking questions. Listen attentively to the responses (the TALK phase). As a child talks, some comments will be close to what really happened, whereas other remarks may not be accurate. It is not helpful to correct the child's view of the incident during this talk phase, but it is important to get the details of the event, as seen through the child's eyes. As the talk continues, ask ques-

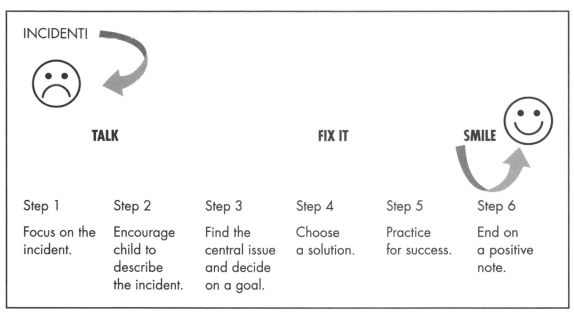

FIGURE 6.3. Use the TALK, FIX IT, SMILE process to help a student resolve an incident.

tions and consider reasons for the behavior. Also, think about how to encourage greater personal responsibility in the future. Have the child list several different ways the problem could have been solved (the FIX IT phase). Together, select one of those options, and make a plan for success with as much input from the child as possible. End the talk by celebrating the resolution of the problem together (the SMILE phase).

Emotional First Aid

Children typically respond to crisis with emotions flooding their behavior. When this occurs, they generally display noticeably regressed behavior. You may see temper tantrums, screaming, crying, sobbing, kicking, spitting, biting, thumb sucking, lying on the floor, waves of "shock" words, or running away.

Many well-meaning adults choose to ignore a child in this condition, using strategies such as, "I'm waiting for you to get it together," or "Time out!" Neither approach is particularly productive if children lack skills to calm themselves without help. It is important for children to settle down before you begin, but ignoring or requiring extended periods of waiting are not usually the best ways to get their attention. Left alone, children who do not understand or have a limited grasp of reality may become increasingly confused or angry. Those who struggle with fears of abandonment may become increasingly anxious (see the section on developmental anxieties in Chapter 4). This is a time to show understanding, support, and your availability to help solve the problem. Let the student know that nothing can happen until things calm down. Be specific that you are looking for some sign of self-control. For example:

"I can tell you're ready to talk when you sit down."
"It's going to be all right."
"I know you are ready to talk when your voice is quiet—like mine."

At first, incidents may be so upsetting that students are unable, or unwilling, to talk. They may retreat into silence, blame others, or even deny that there is a problem. Others continue the unacceptable behavior. Older children, just like younger ones, will need a chance to calm down. Let them know that you are there to talk things through together, but it will be difficult until they begin to act more rationally. Some older children may try to leave. Don't let that happen! Others may try to engage you in verbal combat, but remain calm and avoid arguing with the student. Instead, be a model of mature behavior and continue on with the TALK phase.[4]

The TALK Phase

Step 1: Focus on the Incident

Children are not always eager to face a problem or to talk about it. So, when a student shows any change from regressed behavior, shift the communication away from the behavior. Avoid asking, "What happened?" because a typical response might be

> *I don't know*
>
> *It's his fault!*
>
> *I didn't do it!*
>
> *I don't care!*

Instead, try using a question, with a sympathetic tone, which requires only "yes" or "no" to get the process started. For example:

> *Are you feeling better now?*
>
> *Did someone hurt you (your feelings)?*
>
> *Do you want to solve this problem?*
>
> *Something has upset you. Can we talk about it?*

As soon as the student shows any interest in talking, you are ready for the next step. However, it is not unusual for children to begin to talk and then cycle back to emotional flooding again. When this occurs, just repeat the expectation that they can show you they are ready to talk by a specific behavior. Caution: Don't use a time reference, such as counting "one, two, three," or demanding a specific quiet behavior for a sustained period. These expectations can become ends in themselves, and a child may forget the incident and concentrate on the time demands instead.

Step 2: Encourage the Child to Describe the Incident

Once the student begins to talk, your job is to listen, question, and clarify. Use *who, what, when,* and *where* questions to help the child describe the incident. Together, reconstruct a timeline about what happened. Questions that ask for details bring out what is important to the child. Here are examples:

> *What happened first?*
>
> *What happened next?*
>
> *Were you sitting or standing when he hit you?*
>
> *What do you think she wanted from you?*
>
> *What did he say?*

Simple, direct questions are suitable for children who have some verbal ability to respond, even with limited words or phrases. If they can coherently describe simple experiences when there is no crisis, they should be able to benefit from answering simple questions about incidents. They may emphasize one aspect of the event but leave out other details. The important point is that the child is sharing perceptions with you. The session may be short, and a full investigation of the incident may not be appropriate. But this first exchange teaches you to listen to the child.

In this step, it is not necessary to correct distorted ideas, confront lies, or tell your view of the problem. Repeat the details as described, and reflect what the child is feeling. This helps you gain understanding of the incident from the child's point of view.

Storytelling as an Alternative for the TALK Phase. For children who are not ready to share information freely, try putting the talk into a story narration that parallels the incident. This is a useful alternative when a child cannot tolerate or accept reality because of too much mental or emotional confusion, guilt, or difficulty comprehending the incident. With this strategy, the teacher reconstructs a story with make-believe characters in a make-believe situation with a similar event.

Begin with a standard story opener like, "This reminds me of a story about ..." Ask questions to obtain the child's input and use this to construct the story, touching on the important points of the real incident. Join your words to the child's perceptions, however limited or strange the child's view of the incident may be. In fantasy, some children are able to recognize the problem and the alternative behaviors required to resolve it. During the story, weave the story line around the hero or heroine going to a private place to talk about solving the problem (FIX IT) with an adult. End the story with a return to reality and the real situation. With this strategy, children are able to transfer the make-believe solution to the real incident and can more easily describe the changes needed in their own behavior.

Reverse Role Play. Another variation of this approach is reverse role play. The teacher (T) begins the role play as a narrator of a story and then change to the child's role in portraying the crisis. Encourage the child to take the adult role. Here is an example, using Donna's (D) incident during the music activity described previously.

T: (As narrator) *We are sitting on the rug for music.* (Teacher sits on floor and indicates for Donna to sit also.)

T: (As narrator and then as Donna) *Donna says, "I don't want no tambourine!"* (Teacher mimics the action of throwing the tambourine.)

T: *Now, Donna, you are the teacher. What do you say to this student?*

D: (In teacher's grown-up voice) *Stop that!* (Notice how quickly Donna is able to become the adult.)

T: (In Donna's baby voice) *Why, Teacher?*

D: *'Cause. I said to stop that!*

T: *I don't want to play this dumb thing!*

D: *Well, why didn't you tell me?*

T: *I don't know.*

D: (Long pause.) *You need to tell the teacher when you don't like what you have.*

T: *Okay, Teacher. I'll remember that. I'll say, "Teacher, let me have the drum." Is that okay, Teacher?*

D: *That's good!*

By participating in reverse role play, a child verifies the events of the real incident and begins the process of learning to sequence events. It also encourages some independent effort from the child for a workable solution. When this happens, the child "owns" the solution by putting it into words or actions.

Other Creative Forms for the TALK Phase. Creative materials provide excellent alternatives for communicating during the TALK phase. Drawing materials, chalk, music and rhythms, puppets, dolls, animals, and tape recorders stimulate some children who have no use for other avenues of communication. Structure the activity so that the child is given sufficient content and direction to explore the incident. The material should already be familiar and preferred by the child. Many young children will communicate through creative media to relive or expand on a crisis. This is an excellent opportunity for teaching them to symbolize a critical event and then to use words to describe what they have created and experienced.

Step 3: Find the Central Issue and Decide on a Goal

When the student has talked about the incident and you understand the student's views and feelings about it, you are ready for Step 3. Now it is time to ask yourself, *What is really behind the incident,* and *What do I want the student to learn from it?*

As you begin this step, try to determine if there is another issue behind the incident. Consider what the student may be trying to express with the behavior. Could it be frustration? Insecurity? Anger and payback for unfairness, bullying, or rejection by others? An attempt to avoid looking like a failure? Jealousy? Need for more attention or time with the teacher? The more accurate you are in recognizing a student's real concern, the greater the possibility that you will be effective in guiding the talk to greater personal insight and responsibility by the student.

Try to put the issue as you see it into a single sentence and see how the student reacts. If you are correct, the student will agree, sit silently, nod, or elaborate further on what you said. On the other hand, if the child responds to your statement by talking again about the incident or continuing the emotional behavior, you probably missed the real issue. Repeat Step 2 to get more details and greater understanding of the feelings involved.

When you have some indication from the student that you have accurately identified the real issue, pick a goal that will help the child to face similar incidents more successfully in the future. The goal you choose will shape how you conduct the next phase in the process. Figure 6.4 summarizes the goal choices. If a child is disorganized or in fragile touch with reality, the goal might be to help the child see things more realistically. For a child who knows what is expected but views himself or herself as someone who is "bad," the goal could be to emphasize positive personal characteristics to use for greater self-control. For a child who is in touch with reality, is aware of what happened, and has the desire for more successful ways to behave, the goal would be to teach more acceptable behavior. There are also children who have the capacity for more acceptable behavior and simply misbehave without thought of the consequences. For them, the goal would be to focus on potentially unpleasant results if such behavior continues. Finally, there are occasions when a student is being victimized by another child and is not aware that something can be done to change this. In such situations, the goal is to teach the student different ways to respond.

- Help the student see things more realistically?
- Reinforce the student's good qualities to strengthen self-control?
- Teach the student new, more acceptable ways to behave?
- Emphasize unpleasant results of using unacceptable behavior?
- Help the student see that the action of another child may not be in the student's best interest?

FIGURE 6.4. As the talk continues, think about the outcome (goal) that would be best for the student.

Each of these goals is appropriate at one time or another. The choice among the goals rests with your understanding of the student and the particular incident. The more information you have about the student's ideas, concerns and feelings, the greater insight you will have. The time you spend in listening, questioning, reflecting, and supporting in the previous steps should pay off now as you finish the TALK steps and together begin to focus on how to FIX IT.

The FIX IT Phase

Step 4: Choose a Solution

This step begins the FIX IT part of the process. The focus is on finding a solution that will make things better for the student. This step may be fairly brief, with the solution almost always guided by the teacher. However, the student should be encouraged to contribute to the greatest extent possible. During this step, it is your task to help the student understand that there are many other ways to behave, that better choices bring benefits, and that things will improve when the problem is solved.[5]

[5]Encourage the student to think of many different ways to deal with the incident. Then, together, make a choice about the idea that may have the best results for the student.

You may recall from the discussion of the existential progression in Chapter 4 that age plays a significant part in a child's idea of who solves problems. By age 5 and still in the pre-existential phase of development, children expect adults to take care of problems, although many children should be able to suggest other ways to behave. By age 8, they are usually in the existential crisis phase of development where they begin to see themselves as having responsibility for problem solving. They can come up with many ideas about ways to solve problems, and they are ready to practice taking responsibility for choosing a solution that will have a satisfactory end. Note, however, that talking about how to behave and then actually doing it rarely happens spontaneously. Children will need help from teachers to try new solutions and new behaviors. They seldom successfully implement alternatives without support.

As you and the student talk about alternatives, one solution will begin to take shape as the most satisfactory. For the student, it will be a choice that provides relief from the stress surrounding the incident. For you, it will be a solution that strengthens the goal you selected for the student in the previous step. When possible, the student should come up with the solution and a course of action. If the student is not able to do this, provide guidance in choosing an alternative that will be satisfactory.

Values Are Important in Choosing the Right Solution. Children value different things. A satisfactory solution to a problem is one that is personally "owned" because it fits what an individual values. It is necessary to know what a student usually considers desirable, and then guide the discussion to a solution that fits that value. If the solution the student chooses seems superficial, trivial, or produces little motivation to change, you may want to direct the talk to alternative solutions at the next higher level of values. Emphasize the benefits that come with the choice. Here are statements that focus on benefits (values) that may be gained from attempting a selected solution:[6]

[6]Refer to Chapter 4 for a review of the sequence of values as they typically develop in children from preschool through the teen years.

When you do this, you'll feel really good. (Value: the child's own need)

I'm proud of you for the way you handled this. (Value: teacher approval)

Others will want to do things with you when they know you play fair. (Value: fairness)

When you handle things this way, people will say you are a person they can count on. (Value: adult/peer approval)

Depending on the incident and the selected goal, solutions will vary. A solution may be fixing something that was broken, apologizing to someone whose feelings were hurt, or helping clean up a mess. A solution may involve learning to signal the teacher when a problem begins, or to seek the teacher's help before a small problem gets to be a big one. It also may be planning ways the teacher can change an activity so that the child can be more successful. Several types of frequently used solutions are summarized in Figure 6.5.

- Realistically observe what others do and say.
- Use words instead of unacceptable behavior when facing a troubling situation.
- Consider new ways of behaving for better things to happen.
- "Own" the solution.
- Attempt the solution with confidence.
- Believe that the solution can be successful.

FIGURE 6.5. A solution should help a student achieve these goals.

As you complete this step, it is essential that a student state the solution that has been agreed upon. It can be extremely brief, but it should be to the point. Here are several examples from children who were able to summarize a simple behavioral solution such as,

Sit down.

Tell teacher.

Listen to the teacher.

Do what the teacher says.

Share.

Don't hit. Ignore him.

Tell him, "Stop it."

Wait for a turn.

Find another toy.

Use words to let teacher know.

Be friends by …

Step 5: Plan for Success

Once a solution has been selected, ask yourself, "Will the solution really work for this student?" This is the time to prepare the child for actually carrying out the solution and avoiding a repeat of the unacceptable behavior in the future. Emphasize the positive benefits that can come from trying the new way of handling a problem. It is time to stop when the child feels good about the talk and the choices made, believes that you understand the feelings involved, and is ready to carry out the selected solution with confidence. You can be supportive with statements like

It's not always easy to do what we've been talking about.

You've got a good plan here.

You can do this—just like we talked about it.

Your help is also needed to prepare the child to realistically anticipate problems that may happen when returning to the group. There may be negative reactions from others involved in the incident. If an unpleasant climate was created, the student should be prepared to respond to the other students in an acceptable way. Try role-playing again to practice using the new behaviors instead of old ones when future incidents happen. Ask questions like,

What will you say if …?

If I were that person, what would you say to me?

The next time you start to get mad, what will you say?

Figure 6.6 includes several indicators to help you determine if the FIX IT phase is complete and the child is ready to end the talk. The fewer surprises and the more comfortable the student is with what will happen next, the more likely there will be a smooth transition. Usually a child is eager to put the problem aside and rejoin others with a new way to behave and confidence that the solution will work.

Finally, before the FIX IT phase ends, prepare to rejoin the others. Provide supportive statements like,

What were you doing before all of this started?

Where are the others now?

They're probably expecting you to join them.

Structure a student's reentry into the classroom or ongoing activity carefully so that it is clearly understood how and when to use the new behavior. Encourage a student to rehearse what should actually be said and done before re-joining the group. The student must also be reassured that you will help with the resolution and reentry. Here are several statements to convey this idea of ongoing support:

I'll be beside you when you …

I'll be there, and I know you will do this really well.

When you go back, you can remember just how well you did it here with me. It will work again.

Each time this trouble comes up again, remember that you know how to handle it now!

The student can …

- state the expected behavior,
- actually perform the expected behavior in a real situation, and
- show confidence that everything will be all right as a result.

FIGURE 6.6. Indicators that the FIX IT phase is over.

The SMILE Phase

Step 6: End on a Positive Note

Each child who goes through the TALK and FIX IT steps should have a sense of relief and accomplishment at the end, with the knowledge that he or she had a problem and solved it! When a problem is resolved, celebrate! This is the final part of the TALK, FIX IT, SMILE problem-solving process.[7] The smile itself is not the requirement for this last phase. It only serves as a symbol for feelings of pleasure and accomplishment. The smile is used to end the process because it is an effective way to emphasize the sense of pleasure a child actually experiences with mastery of a new skill—solving a problem in a successful way. When children are encouraged to smile, it helps them get in touch with positive, pleasurable feelings. It is intended to heighten the child's awareness of the elation that comes with solving a problem. If you watch carefully, almost every young student with whom you use it successfully will show a smile, distinctly or fleetingly, as he or she completes the process and reenters the peer group.

[7]A smile provides practice in increased awareness that things are really better when a problem is solved.

Permanent, positive changes in children's behavior occur only when they are *aware* of what they have accomplished and how much better they feel as a result. Because children are often unaware that their emotions have changed during a talk, it is necessary to alert them to the positive shifts in their feelings. They need to know that good feelings happen when they manage a problem with responsibility and self-control. No child is too young or too old to learn this lesson and a smile is one way to emphasize this outcome.

Helping students to have a sense of accomplishment and to be aware of their own feelings of relief and pleasure in resolving an incident is based on the idea that self-regulated behavior must include the ability to control and direct emotions that fuel behavior. No child is too young to begin to learn this lesson, but the form this instruction takes must be suited to the age and developmental stage of the student. For young children, preschool education instructs in the meaning of feeling words such as *happy, sad,* or *mad.* In this way, teachers begin to teach words for these feelings and their behavioral expressions.[8]

There are numerous ways to let children know that they handled a problem in a satisfactory way. Smiles, approving looks, and positive words convey this in a genuinely meaningful manner. Some teachers use an interactive way, such as "Let's shake!" Children automatically respond with similar behavior—a shared moment. Other teachers end with food or snack to nurture and comfort. They accompany this with words that reflect the well-being and pleasure for the satisfactory end to the crisis. Still others provide proximity and a sense of psychological closeness that conveys support and caring, along with words of positive feelings. In all of these endings, the intent is to obtain similar verbal statements of well-being and pleasure from the child.

You may be asking, "Why go through all this effort after you have resolved the crisis and developed a new, alternative behavior for the child?" This emphasis on positive feelings as a last phase of problem resolution is essential for permanent behavior change as well as for greater social and emotional growth. As explained in Chapter 4, emotional memory is where thoughts, feelings, and anxieties are stored. Recognizing that emotions drive behavior and mold self-esteem, it is not sufficient to merely modify behavior. Stored emotions and feeling responses must also change if there is to be lasting change in a child's self-concept, self-esteem, and in the behaviors that express these attitudes toward self and others.

As you use TALK, FIX IT, SMILE, you will find your role and responsibilities adjusting to the particular incident, behaviors, anxieties, and developmental individuality of each student. The roles and messages you will be required to deliver are complex. The variations are endless. Sometimes you will need to be an adult authority who enforces rules, order, and justice. At other times you will be the benevolent nurturer, the teacher, and the sympathetic supporter (see Chapters 2 and 6). Sometimes you will protect a student from situations too overwhelming to handle; at other times, you will back off from a central role to allow experience to teach—the hard way.

Through all of this, you must remain the source of support, affirming belief in the student, whatever age, stage, behavior, or problem arises to produce crises and unacceptable behavior. Then you can be sure that your talk with a child has been a success if you see indications such as those listed in Figure 6.7.

[8]A problem-solving experience has credibility with a child when the result is clearly positive.

The student can ...

- use words instead of unacceptable behavior to deal with feelings,
- show increasing responsibility for choosing acceptable behavior,
- begin to see how behavior affects others, and
- indicate confidence that problems can be solved.

FIGURE 6.7. Evidence that there is a successful outcome.

Transcript of "The Yellow Towel Incident"

Sam's Incident

Five-year-old Sam walks into the day care center, sobbing his heart out. His mother leaves after a quick explanation that Sam wants a yellow towel for the swimming trip today, but she has no yellow towel to give him. Sam's teacher tries to console him and redirect his attention to his beautiful blue towel. The strategy doesn't work. Sam's sobs increase, and tears stream down his cheeks. He is in an emotional spiral that quickly turns into a tantrum. Between gasps, sobs, and tears, Sam blurts out, "But I want a *yellow* towel!" He breaks down again in racking sobs. Sympathy and reassurance have no effect on him. "I want a *yellow* towel! I *have* to have it!" Sam declares. More sobs and another outburst follow.

The teacher tries another strategy, reminding Sam of the fun they will have at the pool and reflecting on Sam's previous accomplishments in swimming. "We're going to have a really good time at the pool today, Sam. Last time, you were the one to jump in and swim to the other side. Remember that? Everyone clapped when you got to the other side." Sam responds with another flood of tears interspersed with, "I can't go without a yellow towel!" Sam's teacher then tries the "reality" approach. "Well, Sam, I guess you'll just have to use a blue towel if you want to go swimming today."

With that, Sam disintegrates into uncontrollable sobbing. "I don't want to go swimming." By now, Sam's emotional state is having a contagious effect on the other children. They stop their play, staring at Sam and the teacher. Thumbs go into mouths; tears well in eyes. One child pushes another. A blanket of unhappiness sweeps through the room. It is time to reverse the rapid disintegration of the emotional climate in the classroom. A break is needed in the conflict cycle occurring with the interactions between Sam and his teacher. The teacher, finally recognizing the need to divert Sam from emotionally driven behavior to a rational, problem-solving mode, chooses to use TALK, FIX IT, SMILE with Sam. As the teacher (T) begins, she knows that the first step is to get Sam (S) to shift his emotional outburst from sobbing to words.

The TALK Phase with Sam

Step 1: Focus on Sam's Incident

T: Do you know that we can do something about this problem?

S: (*Shakes head to indicate no, but sobbing slows and he glances at the teacher*)

T: Sam, let's do something about this problem. Let's talk about a yellow towel, with words, not tears.

S: (*Looks again at the teacher, with some interest, then breaks down*)

T: We can fix things if we can talk about it … with words, not tears.

S: (*Sobs continue, but less intensely*)

T: I can tell your words are wanting to come out and are waiting for you to put away your tears.

S: (*Sobs end*)
T: Good work! Now we can figure out a way to fix things so you will feel better.
S: (*Sobs begin again*)
T: Tell me in words, Sam, not tears.
S: (*Haltingly*) I *have* to have a yellow towel to go swimming! (*Tears begin again, but teacher interrupts*)
T: Use *words,* Sam, to tell me about it.
S: (*Demanding*) I need a yellow towel.
T: Where do children get yellow towels?

Step 2: Encourage Sam to Describe the Incident[9]

[9] Teacher helps Sam recall and describe details about what happened.

S: (*Silence*)
T: Did you pack your towel in your bag before you went to bed last night?
S: Yes, but it wasn't a yellow towel. I didn't like it!
T: What color was the towel you packed?
S: Not yellow!
T: You like yellow. I can understand that. It is your favorite color, right?
S: Yes! And I'm not going swimming.
T: Did you take a bath before you went to bed last night? (*Redirection*)
S: Yes.
T: Think about last night. Can you remember the color of the towel you used?
S: No. But it wasn't yellow. I hate it!
T: Could it have been this blue towel?
S: No! It was white. I hate that blue towel!
T: So, let's see what you did when you got up this morning. Your mom brought you to school?
S: Yes.
T: And did she fix breakfast for you before you left?
S: Yes.
T: What did you have?
S: Cereal and raisins.
T: Sounds delicious. Your mother really takes care of you, giving you a good breakfast like that. (*Motivate with interesting ideas*)
S: (*Nods and looks directly at teacher*)[10]
T: So, your mom took care of you this morning. She fixed you a delicious breakfast. Then she helped pack your bag for our swimming trip today?
S: (*Looking guarded now*) Yes, but I *told* her I didn't want that towel.

[10] Teacher notes Sam's responsiveness to the idea of being cared for.

Step 3: Find the Central Issue and Decide on a Goal for Sam[11]

[11] The teacher thinks about what Sam needs to learn from this talk and how to achieve that goal.

T: Sam, where do children get towels?
S: (*Silence, but looks at teacher hopefully*)
T: To get a towel, we have to know where towels are kept.
S: (*Nods agreement*)
T: Now, what I hear you saying is that you like yellow towels and you do not have one today. Is that right?
S: Yes! I want a *yellow* towel.

The FIX IT Phase with Sam

Step 4: Choose a Solution with Sam[12]

T: To get any kind of a towel, we have to first find the place where towels are kept. (*Structuring the action*)[13]

S: Right! (*Leans toward teacher and conveys interest in the idea*)

T: Do you know, we keep towels here at school for children who sometimes forget their towels?

S: (*Shakes head*) I don't know where the towels are.

T: Can you think where they may be, in this building?

S: (*Now very interested*) Maybe in the office?

T: If not there, where else should we look?

S: Maybe in the supply room? Maybe in the bathroom?

T: Good ideas on how to fix this problem, Sam!

S: (*Beaming*) Let's go look![14]

T: Sam, look what we've found!

S: The towels … we found the towels!

T: Right! Let's look at them.
(*Rummage through the stack of towels, naming the colors as they go: Blue, green, pink*)

T: What funny color is this, Sam?

S: I don't know.

T: Some people may call it white, but I wouldn't, would you?

S: No, that's not white.

T: Then, what color is it?

S: I don't know.

T: Some people call this color "cream" or "beige."[15]

S: (*Listening, but looking disappointed*)

T: Do you know how people make this color called "beige"?

S: (*Shakes head but looks interested*)

T: You mix white and yellow to make beige. So we have found a towel that is made of white and yellow.

S: But I want a yellow towel.

T: Now we have found a towel made with yellow and white, so you have fixed the problem of no yellow towel! Now you can go swimming with us!

Step 5: Practice for Sam's Success[16]

T: When your friends tell you what color towels they have, what will you tell them about your towel?

S: (*Thinks about question, looking cautious again*)

T: How many colors are in your towel?

S: Two! My towel is two colors!

T: That's right. Your towel is a special color made of two colors. That's something they will be interested in. Before we came down here to hunt for towels, we had a problem. Do you remember?

S: (*Nods*)

T: What did we do about it?

S: We found the towels.

[12]Teacher and Sam have moved through the TALK phase, so they begin to plan how to decide how to FIX IT.

[13]Teacher knows there are no yellow towels at school, but she also knows that Sam is ready to consider a way to resolve this problem.

[14]Sam and teacher go to the places he has suggested. The last stop is the supply room where the school keeps a few clean towels on hand for emergencies.

[15]Teacher singles out a grayed-yellow towel that had once been white. Sam looks at it doubtfully. But the teacher knows that Sam is curious and has previously shown interest in using new, "big" words.

[16]Sam's love of swimming overcomes his resistance. He reluctantly takes the towel and hugs it to his chest. He is ready to return to the classroom now, but he needs to practice first.

T: And before that?

S: We talked about it.

T: That's right! We talked about it, and then we fixed the problem! Now there is something else we need to do, so you will feel good.

S: (*Clutching towel; impatient now to rejoin the group for swimming*) I want to go swimming!

T: Before we go back, let's see how you can tell the other children about fixing a problem. When you have a problem, what do you do first?

S: Talk!

T: Right. Then what do you do?

S: Find the towels.

T: That's it! How did you fix the problem?

S: My towel's white and yellow. (*Grinning happily*)[17]

[17]Sam has accomplished the five steps involved in the TALK and FIX IT phases and has stated the solution in his own limited way.

The SMILE Phase with Sam

Step 6: Sam Ends on a Positive Note[18]

T: And after children fix a problem, they feel better! I can see that you really feel better now because you are smiling.

S: (*Thinks about it and gives teacher another faint smile*)

T: What will you tell the others about how they will feel when they fix a problem?

S: Smile!

T: Sam, you have learned something important today that the other children in the group will want to hear about—how to take care of a problem. Everyone has problems, but not everyone knows how to fix them.

T: (*To other children*)[19] What do you do if there is a problem? Sam had a problem and now he knows what to do. Sam, tell them the three steps you use to take care of a problem.

S: (*Beaming with pride and eagerness*) First you TALK about it. Then you FIX it. Then, SMILE!

[18]Teacher begins the final phase, sensitizing Sam to a new feeling of satisfaction, and giving him practice that will carry over into the next activity.

[19]As Sam and the teacher return to the room, the other children come over to him with great interest. They also had been caught up in Sam's emotional outburst and have a need to be reassured that everything is all right now.

Summary

One talk does not usually change a student's way of behaving. If the same or similar problems happen again, don't be discouraged. View each talk as one exchange in a series for building these skills. Lasting change comes slowly and in small ways. Each time you and a student go through the steps summarized in Figure 6.8, you are building toward genuine change. You will gradually see

- improvement in self-esteem,
- increased insight,
- greater awareness of feelings,
- better impulse control,
- positive feelings about others, and
- more self-regulated behavior.

The TALK phase includes Steps 1, 2, and 3.
- Draining off intense feelings so that perceptions of reality dominate behavior
- Using words (instead of behavior) to describe these events and actions of self and others
- Ordering the events into a sequence that conveys what came first, next, and last
- Discriminating between relevant information and elements that confuse or cloud the incident

The FIX IT phase includes Steps 4 and 5.
- Understanding that something can be done to fix a problem
- Learning a new way to make it better
- Stating the new behavior in words
- Wanting to try the new way of behaving
- Rehearsing the new behavior

The SMILE phase includes Step 6.
- Acknowledging that better feelings have resulted from the solution
- Practicing new, positive feelings to carry into the next activity and in the future

---

FIGURE 6.8. The abbreviated LSCI phases.

Solving one crisis or incident is not the end in itself. Life presents one crisis after another; and the solution to one problem does not necessarily free a student from having another, and another, and another. The important point is to teach students to deal with crises in ways that are within their capacities to use. When they try new behaviors with successful and pleasurable results, the motivation is there for retaining the new behavior. If the talks expand a student's self-confidence, with increased insight and ability to change behavior, your efforts will have produced a child who becomes increasingly responsible.

Practice the Process

Are you ready to try the TALK, FIX IT, SMILE process? Check yourself with these questions:

1. What is the purpose of talking with students in crisis?
2. Why it is necessary to use an abbreviated form of LSCI with some children who are young or developmentally delayed?
3. Which children described in Chapter 1 will probably benefit from this modified LSCI process?
4. What are the behavioral characteristics of those who can benefit?
5. This process is most suitable for students in which stage of development?
6. What are the three general phases of the process?
7. What conditions indicate that emotional first aid should be provided first?
8. What should occur in a child after an emotional incident and *before* beginning the process?
9. Which DTORF–R learning objectives can be included?
10. How many steps are in the TALK phase and what is the intent of each?
11. For students with limited verbal abilities, what alternatives can be used during the TALK phase?

12. What are five alternative goals to consider as you decide on a goal so that you can move from the TALK phase to the FIX IT phase?
13. What is the difference between deciding on a goal and choosing a solution?
14. How many steps are in the FIX IT phase and what is the intent of each?
15. If a child continues to talk about the incident in an emotional way when you have moved into the FIX IT phase and are attempting to find a solution, what should you do?
16. Why are rehearsal and role play so important during the FIX IT phase?
17. What single accomplishment by the child is necessary before ending the FIX IT phase?
18. What is the intent of the SMILE phase and the developmental reason for this phase?

Teachers and the Skills They Need

Students want teachers who know young people, who care deeply about their development, and who listen and respond to what is important to them. They want teachers who know teaching and learning and are willing to learn from their students as well as teach them. Students appreciate teachers who make learning both challenging and fun, who remain passionate about their subject matter and curious about the world, and who see learning as a way to improve the world. Young people want teachers who have a deep commitment to fairness and justice. Students often have a strong sense of right and wrong and of ethical and fair behavior, and they expect their teachers to be exemplars of these ideals.

Arturo Pacheco (2004, p. 136)
Professor of Education Research
University of Texas at El Paso

As you watch a teacher with a group of students, you can sense the climate for learning—the "tone" of the group. In healthy learning groups, there is spontaneous interaction between the students and teachers. You hear encouraging statements and a minimum of negative ones. Students show interest in the activities and support each other. Teachers clearly convey respect and regard for the students, and the students seem to absorb these attitudes and reflect them to each other. In such a climate, bullying does not happen, and students are willing to participate because the environment promotes comfortable interpersonal relationships and personal satisfactions, which foster success.

To create such an environment, the most important element is the proficiency of the teachers (Owens & Dieker, 2003), who should have a clear sense of goals and objectives for each student. They must also understand what motivates their students, the values that guide them, how they respond to authority, manage anger, resolve conflict, and cope with success and failure. And because the realities students face in their daily lives outside of school have a significant impact on school performance, teachers must also understand the values and the expectations peers, families, and communities place on students.[1]

If you teach students with social, emotional, or behavioral challenges, you must also have qualities that help you guide students who will not engage in learning, disrupt the lessons you have planned, blame others for their problems, or turn on you in anger to dump their failures and frustrations. When this happens, controlling your personal feelings and responding in helpful ways become top priorities. If you can do this, you will be able to keep your students on the path toward the goals and objectives established for them. This requires a depth of emotional maturity, self-confidence, empathy for others, dedication, self-discipline, compassion, and understanding. The result is a healthy learning environment, but it is not an easy task!

This chapter is about the skills needed by teachers if they are to maintain a developmentally and emotionally healthy environment that encourages learning, in general or special education. Figure 7.1 is a summary of the essentials teachers need to know to be effective with Developmental Therapy–Developmental Teaching. The content is organized around five topics: phases of skill development for teachers (and student teachers), lead and support teachers as a

[1] The most important tool you have for fostering students' learning and development is yourself—what you know and how you put that knowledge into action.

- How typical social, emotional, and behavioral characteristics change with age
- How attitudes, feelings, and anxieties influence students' behavior
- Individual developmental paths of each student
- Group dynamics in the family, neighborhood, and school
- Students' views of adults and authority
- Strategies that strengthen adult–student relationships
- Strategies that encourage student's participation in learning
- Forms of social power—yours and theirs
- Adult attributes that convey needed role models

FIGURE 7.1. What teachers need to know.

team, how teachers use forms of social power to influence students' actions, personal characteristics that influence teacher's effectiveness, and how teachers can gain the needed skills.

At the end of the chapter, there is a review of two tools for teachers to use independently as they expand their own proficiency at using this approach: Developmental Teaching: Rating Inventory of Teacher Skills (DTRITS; see Folder 3 in the CD that accompanies this book) and *PEGS for Teachers* (Developmental Therapy Institute, 2003a, b). The DTRITS is a rating inventory for teachers to check themselves on their use of the specified practices. *PEGS* is a series of three interactive CD-ROMs (CDs) that offer an effective and engaging way for teachers and teaching assistants to obtain independent skill training in using the behavior management strategies described in Chapter 5.

Phases of Skill Development for Teachers (and Student Teachers)

There are three rather distinct phases in skill development for teachers. The beginning phase provides survival skills—how to manage a class in an orderly and positive manner. In the middle phase, teachers increase their abilities to maintain healthy learning environments in which students participate willingly and make progress in achieving their program objectives. Teachers progressing to the demonstration phase are highly proficient in all of the Developmental Therapy–Developmental Teaching practices. They use exemplary practices consistently, even with students who are extremely difficult to teach. Each phase has particular practices that are important for teachers to acquire. Use the charts in this section to check your own practices and those you want to add. When you concentrate on achieving one set of skills at a time, the task does not seem so difficult.[2]

[2]Some teachers move rapidly through all of these phases. Others find that it takes a year or more. It is helpful if they receive ongoing feedback and team support as they learn to apply these practices in their classrooms.

Beginning Phase of Skill Development

During the beginning phase of learning to apply the recommended practices, teachers often ask, "What are the most important things for me to learn first?"

The essentials are summarized in Figure 7.2. Experienced teachers will recognize many of their own practices and should find it fairly easy to add those that they do not already have. For teachers who are new to this field, the material is introduced gradually, step by step. First,

- Know how to use the DTORF–R to identify developmental competencies each student has achieved and those competencies that are the current learning objectives.
- Prepare a group DTORF–R to identify similar objectives selected for all.
- Plan group lessons that include each student's individual DTORF–R objectives.
- Plan lead and support role strategies for the teaching team.
- Identify adult role(s) typically needed for each student's age and stage of development.
- Identify characteristics for the stages just above and below each student's current stage, to recognize any unexpected regression or gains.
- Plan schedule and keep it the same every day, but change content daily.
- Select motivating content based on experiences and interests of the students.
- Plan strategic locations for each lesson. Place materials in easily accessible locations.
- Arrange the room in ways that promote socialization and minimize opportunities for behavior problems.
- Greet students entering and leaving class.
- Understand how each student responds to stress and success.
- Assume a pleasant attitude both verbally and with your body language.
- Be physically alert and move about to convey interest or to prevent problems.
- Make verbal or nonverbal contact with every student frequently (as often as every 5 minutes).
- Avoid asking questions that could be answered by refusal, (e.g., "Don't you want to do your work?")
- Make positive statements about students' behavior and their work.

FIGURE 7.2 In the beginning phase of teachers' skill development, these are basic skills.

learn to use the Developmental Teaching Objectives and Rating Forms–Revised (DTORF–R; see Folder 2 in the CD that accompanies this book) accurately to assess each student's individual social, emotional, and behavioral status. An accurate assessment provides the structure for establishing each student's IEP, IFSP, or ITP objectives. These objectives are the guideposts for teachers' instructional practices. Ask yourself, "Why am I doing this?" You should be able to answer this question with at least one specific DTORF–R objective that is the focus of the lesson for an individual student or for the group.

The same question applies to behavior management strategies. In moments when a student is in crisis or loses control, ask yourself, "What do I do now?" Your immediate response should be based on quickly recalling that student's specific objectives and developmental stage.[3]

After learning to use the DTORF–R accurately, plan lessons, materials and activities that help students achieve their specific objectives. Most teachers focus first on academic areas such as reading, language arts, spelling, and arithmetic to begin this targeted instruction. These subjects seem to be easier to organize into sequential learning experiences than objectives for socialization, communication, or behavior. When students' objectives are the focus of your planning and teaching, you will be able to say, "I know exactly what I should be doing."

As you select content and design lessons, learn more about your students' out-of-school interests and concerns. When lessons have age-appropriate interests and motivating value, they are usually received with enthusiasm—an important ingredient to obtain willing student participation. Include art, music, storybooks, creative writing, drama, role plays, and puppetry as motivating activities in your lessons. With older students, adult heroes, sports stars, and entertainment figures are also sources for motivation.[4]

Another important part of the first phase in learning to apply developmental practices is to match your own style as a teacher to the type of adult role model typically needed for the ages

[3]Instant recall of a student's DTORF–R objectives is a big help, particularly in a crisis.

[4]Chapters 2 and 4 include information about values that typically emerge at particular stages of students' development.

and stages of the students you teach (Wood, 1996b). Consider the many different roles teachers must fill as they work with students in different age groups and in different stages of development (described in detail in Chapter 2). Then examine the type of adult role you portray as a teacher. Which among these roles, listed in Figure 7.3, is comfortable for you, and which roles will you need to learn so that you can more fully meet the needs of your students?

In time, you should be able to portray any of the essential role characteristics that may be needed by a student. However, it is not always easy to change teaching roles from one type of adult to another. It requires practice in using a broad range of responses on your part and an understanding of the type of adult needed by your students. Even experienced teachers—and parents—have trouble making these shifts at first. But the effort has long-term benefits.[5]

[5]Effective teachers and parents can switch to different roles for students of various ages and stages of development. Chapters 2 and 5 describe these roles.

- Nurturer and satisfier of basic needs (for students in Stage One)
- Encourager of individual successes (for students in Stage Two)
- Upholder of law and order (for students in Stage Three)
- Group facilitator and individual advocate (for students in Stage Four)
- Counselor, adviser, and confidant (for students in Stage Five)

FIGURE 7.3. Adjust your role to your students' stages of development. See Chapter 2 for more about these roles.

Middle Phase in Teachers' Skill Development

This phase of skill building fine-tunes instructional practices. Teachers are increasingly aware of their students' emotional and developmental needs. This requires refining instructional practices to meet these needs, and teachers often say, "There is so much to learn. What should I do next?"

As shown in Figure 7.4, the focus during the middle phase of skill development for teachers is on decoding behavior—understanding emotions and motivations that influence a student's thinking and actions. When decoding, look for the ways students gratify their own emotional needs in their interactions with peers and adults. Determine how they respond to authority, frustration, and stress. Also identify their anxieties, interests, values, and concerns. This information will guide you in selecting the most motivating content, effective instructional strategies, and a broad range of management strategies to match students' emotional and developmental needs.[6]

[6]In the middle phase of skill expansion, teachers become increasingly aware of their students' emotional needs. They are then able to draw on their own maturity, insights, and creativity as never before.

The critical skill for this phase is simultaneously using the decoding information in precisely targeted instruction in four developmental areas—DOING, SAYING, RELATING, and THINKING. Effective teachers are able to do this for individual students within group instruction. They also become proficient in using repeated DTORF–R ratings at scheduled intervals to adjust program objectives and practices as students change. The result is increased individual student effort, group participation, reduction in disruptive behavior and conduct problems, and gains in achievement of learning objectives documented by improved DTORF–R scores.[7]

[7]Suggestions for interpreting DTORF–R results are included in Chapter 3.

This is also a phase to expand skills for effective teamwork with colleagues. Teachers become increasingly capable of making independent contributions to a team effort on behalf of their students. They learn to work with other teachers, parents, mental health professionals, and paraprofessionals to provide the best possible program for each student. Often, the effectiveness of students' programs is directly influenced by the extent to which their teachers are collaborative team members. Each day represents a new challenge in planning and implementing program strategies.

- Plan motivating lessons and activities from students' DTORF–R objectives.
- Understand the community and family values each student lives with daily.
- Anticipate students' behavior and respond according to their stages of development.
- Adjust your words to developmental and cultural characteristics of each student.
- Use body language to convey positive nonverbal messages.
- Recognize students' anxieties, and respond in ways that reduce anxiety.
- Convey necessary social power to ensure psychological and physical security for all in the group.
- Maintain an adult role model typically needed for students' stages of development.
- Be calm, dependable, and competent—even under stress.
- Make your own needs secondary to those of your students.
- Adjust your actions and instruction for maximum participation by all.
- Be an advocate for your students, their programs, and their parents.
- Assist other teachers for successful inclusion of your students.
- Work with mental health professionals and other educators on interdisciplinary teams to assist students and their families.

FIGURE 7.4. Essential skills for the middle phase of teachers' skill expansion.

Demonstration Phase of Proficiency

Teachers who are experienced and skilled in using Developmental Therapy–Developmental Teaching are usually in the demonstration phase of skill acquisition. They often acknowledge, "I know I am being truly effective now!"

Their skills are summarized in Figure 7.5. They monitor themselves and their students so carefully that every moment together is constructive, positive, and therapeutic. In addition to demonstrating the skills required for the previous phases, they are superb at motivating students for active participation in learning, and they include therapeutic goals in academic instruction. Because their students' social and emotional needs, IEP goals, and developmental objectives are high priorities, demonstration level teachers are able to plan and conduct highly therapeutic instruction while also guiding students' academic progress.

These teachers are known for their expertise in successful management of students who have severe social, emotional, and behavioral disabilities. They have knowledge about group dynamics, crisis intervention, management of violence, ways to blunt the power of anxiety, and the profound impact of adult actions on students. They use creative arts and language arts—reading, writing, music, dance, movement, storytelling, sociodrama, dramatic play, and graphic arts—to help students resolve anxieties, experience successes, and expand self-confidence.[8]

Teachers at this level of proficiency also seem to be keenly aware of their responsibility to ensure that their students achieve the competencies needed to function successfully in other places. These teachers provide numerous opportunities for students to use newly learned skills successfully at school, at home, in the neighborhood, and at work. This is an extremely difficult task, often requiring teamwork with parents, community agencies, the business community, other educators, policy makers, and mental health professionals. It requires expert use of the DTORF–R data to interpret students' gains (or lack of gains) for others to understand. To be successful doing this, a teacher also needs considerable understanding of the cultural and emotional conditions of a student's current situation. This understanding is the foundation for designing and implementing advanced school placements as rapidly as a student shows gains.[9]

[8] When academic content is used in ways that are highly meaningful to each student, instruction becomes therapeutic.

[9] Demonstration level teachers find themselves asked to design and implement new program initiatives with professionals in interdisciplinary efforts with other students.

- Know your students' anxieties, defense mechanisms, group dynamics, and roles in groups to plan individualized programs and conduct strategic instruction in groups.
- Design creative, expressive, and imaginative curriculum materials for academic lessons to motivate students to participate with enthusiasm.
- Conduct every lesson, including transitions and free time, as if each was the single most important moment of the day for each student.
- Maintain a psychologically healthy climate in the room, in which you provide the necessary amount of social power and personal energy to motivate and sustain each student's participation without fostering dependence on you.
- Monitor each student's progress carefully so that you can facilitate advancement to new objectives and competencies as rapidly as possible.
- Change your intervention strategies to adjust to each student's changing program needs.
- Use repeated DTORF–R ratings at each grading period to interpret progress.
- Make changes in your instructional groupings if needed to accelerate student progress.
- Lead team efforts in daily debriefings to fine-tune instruction and behavior management.

FIGURE 7.5. Skills that teachers need at the demonstration phase (in addition to those acquired in previous phases).

These expert teachers are frequently asked to use their skills as master teachers, supervisors, and consultants for general and special education programs. They provide the best possible models for others who are learning to implement developmental practices. They have the ability to manage even the most catastrophic crises (among students, other professionals, or families). This calls for personal maturity, disciplined responsibility, and emotional stability. It requires empathy, interpersonal perspective taking, and skill in crisis resolution. Experienced and skilled teachers also find themselves cast as parent surrogate, counselor, demonstration teacher, program consultant, conflict mediator, family advocate, mental health expert, in-service provider, and friend. The expectations are endless because the needs are enormous![10]

Lead and Support Teachers as a Team

The task of a teaching team is to ensure that the entire group is motivated to participate and that each member feels recognized, enjoys participating, and is successful. To maintain participation of all students, teachers and teaching assistants have specific responsibilities as team members. A lead teacher conducts the lessons, leads group activities, makes decisions, and maintains the rules. If there is a second teacher, assistant teacher, specialist, or volunteer in the classroom, these individuals have support teacher responsibilities. Support teachers give students individual assistance when needed.[11]

This separation of lead and support responsibilities is intended to provide students with clear expectations about which adult is really in charge. The lead teacher keeps instruction flowing smoothly in spite of any disruptions that may be caused by an individual student. Generally, the lead teacher does not take care of a student who needs individual assistance. This is the responsibility of the support teacher to provide individual help as needed. If a lead teacher forgets this basic rule and deals with an individual for an extended time, the result is almost always deterioration in group behavior because this teacher has slipped into a supporting role with one individual, leaving the remaining students on their own.[12]

[10]As your proficiency increases, you will see results in the progress of your students. And once you have mastered the skills, you will find yourself thinking developmentally in every aspect of your teaching.

[11]These lead and support roles apply to any adult teams responsible for groups of young people—parents and families, coaches with athletes, therapists with counseling groups, and school faculty with students.

[12]If a lead teacher interrupts group instruction to attend to the needs of a disruptive student, the learning process breaks down for everyone else and behavior problems often increase rapidly.

Building an effective lead–support team requires major attention. There must be shared responsibility for smoothly coordinated teamwork. Examples of the needed team skills are listed in Figure 7.6. Team members must actively communicate with each other verbally and nonverbally. Students need to be made aware of what each teacher does. They must see the team interacting seamlessly to keep instruction and group activities moving smoothly. The actions of the team are carefully and consistently executed to convey this. Students always see the lead teacher backed by the support teacher. The teachers seldom shift responsibilities unless there is clear communication with the students that the teachers have decided to do this. If there is confusion between lead and support over who-does-what-when, or if each teacher holds different expectations for the students, some students will use this as an excuse to avoid doing what is expected.[13]

[13]Chapter 5 includes a discussion of verbal interaction between adults, a major management strategy used with students of all ages.

- Know which strategies are appropriate for the lead teacher and which are appropriate for the support teacher.
- Anticipate where you should be physically at a given moment.
- Know which students need immediate attention and which can be managed without individual adult support.
- Select appropriate verbal and physical strategies for individual students.
- Know when to interact with the other team members and when to remain silent.
- Use open, supportive teamwork between the lead and the support teachers.
- Plan ahead—anticipate when to change a strategy.

FIGURE 7.6. Skills that a member of a teaching team should have.

Responsibilities of the Lead Teacher on a Team

The lead teacher is in the psychological power position and is the adult in charge. Figure 7.7 outlines the lead teacher's responsibilities. The lead initiates, conducts, and ends each lesson. The lead maintains group motivation and keeps the learning process going. In short, an effective lead teacher sets the general psychological climate for a group, pacing and timing every activity to maintain maximum participation and investment in every activity by all of the students. The success of the group, and of every individual in the group, depends upon the lead teacher's skill in maintaining a comfortable climate for learning and recognizing each individual's success.

- Keep the lesson going and the students participating.
- Provide smooth transitions from lesson to lesson.
- Involve every student in every activity.
- Convey expectations and maintain them.
- Ensure successful outcomes from each lesson for every student.
- Provide abundant encouragement and positive feedback.
- Create an accepting and supportive atmosphere for every student.
- Manage routines and activities in ways that make each student feel secure.
- Ensure successful or pleasurable outcomes for all.

FIGURE 7.7. Skills and duties of the lead teacher on a team.

[14]The decision about which team member will function as lead and which as support is a team decision, based on group dynamics and the needs of the individual students in that class. It is not intended to designate which adult has the highest certification or educational level.

The lead is also in an advocacy role, so that each student believes that the teacher can be depended upon to take care of issues that the student cannot handle.[14]

Almost all students want to believe that the teacher in charge is glad to see them. The lead must establish an individual connection with each student in order to be viewed as a valued adult. One way to do this is to begin the first activity of the day by locating yourself in a strategic place where you will be able to interact with each student as entering the classroom. Then, as the lesson begins, motivate and hold students' attention by your introduction to the task, your demonstration of the materials to be used, and your voice quality.

When your class or group moves to a new area for a change in activities, be the first to the new location to provide leadership there. By structuring transitions this way, you provide the motivation for engaging students in the next activity. This also helps students anticipate the changes expected in their conduct for the next lesson (more about this later in the chapter).

Responsibilities of the Support Teacher on a Team

[15]When there is a student who is severely disturbed in a group, the more experienced teacher is often the support person on the team, to provide skilled one-to-one crisis intervention. An aide then leads group lessons.

Successful educational programs frequently have a second adult in the classroom. This is especially important in programs for young children and for students with special needs or challenging behaviors. A support teacher may be another teacher, teaching assistant, special services professional, community volunteer, mental health provider, or parent. In fact, anyone assigned to work in a classroom with a teacher can learn to be an effective support teacher.[15]

The responsibilities of a support teacher are listed in Figure 7.8. Two major tasks for the support teacher are: to actively interact with the lead teacher as a role model for students, and assist individual students who need one-to-one help to maintain participation. By paying attention to the lead teacher, asking and answering questions when students seem confused, or by demonstrating how to respond to the teacher's directions, a support teacher provides students with a model to imitate.

- Back the lead teacher.
- Keep individual students involved in participating as group members.
- Provide individual attention to a student in need.
- Respond to the lead teacher as a model for students to imitate, if needed.
- Give abundant encouragement and positive feedback.
- Offer words and actions as models to help students participate.
- Maintain routines and activities in ways that make each student feel secure.
- Interact with the lead teacher to let students know you are on the same team.
- Respond to students in crisis.
- Ensure successful or pleasurable outcomes for all.

FIGURE 7.8. Skills and duties of a support teacher on a team.

[16]Within any group of students, at any age, we estimate that there will be at least three who require attention from a support teacher during a lesson. The team plans ahead for them.

Enthusiasm about an assignment or activity encourages students to stay involved. A support teacher also may deal with students in crisis, those who resist participating, and those with special needs. This minimizes the opportunity for one student to monopolize the lead teacher's attention and diminish learning opportunities for others in the class.[16]

A support teacher must use basic management strategies, especially encouragement and praise, positive feedback, reflection, and redirection. By refocusing a student's attention on the lead teacher's instruction when the student's interest lags, these strategies often are all that is needed to keep students participating. Physical proximity, without direct intervention, is also an important strategy to use selectively. It can provide sufficient adult presence to prevent further loss of control by a student. Proximity gives students a sense that their efforts are being noticed (and approved) by the teachers. When support teachers use this management strategy skillfully, they move about the classrooms quietly—as background to the main lesson—and are generally unnoticed by the students.[17]

A frequent problem for support teachers is allowing students to manipulate them into talking about something else as a way to avoid participating in an assignment or activity. This undermines the message that participation is the important focus. Although support teachers do not intend this to happen, individual assistance can easily become a student's escape from responsibility. However, there are also circumstances when it is essential to provide individual support to a student. Determining just how much assistance to give is a major issue for every support teacher and should be a topic for team discussion.

Daily Team Debriefings

This is the time each day when all members of a team get together, preferably immediately after the students leave. Each team develops its own debriefing style, but certain topics, shown in Figure 7.9, should be covered in the daily team meeting. It is the responsibility of the team's lead teacher to ensure that debriefing occurs and to set the pace for the team discussion. Follow-up lessons are planned for the next day, and changes made in the way lessons will be conducted. There are discussions about possible modifications in the management of individual students. The result is a highly effective team that plans together and then conducts classroom instruction and manages students' behavior in a smoothly coordinated manner.

Time spent debriefing about lessons and strategies that worked (or did not work) is time well spent. During debriefings, there are also opportunities for each team member to ventilate feelings. Problem solving should follow, with open discussion, and all members of the team should be comfortable expressing ideas, feelings, and attitudes. The knowledge of team members will be enhanced by their contributions during debriefings. They should also be receptive to constructive suggestions and be willing to try something new.[18]

- At what time during the day were the students most successful? Why?
- What specific statements were used that achieved the desired results?
- Which strategies were most effective for each student?
- What verbal and nonverbal communication between teachers was effective?
- Were there negative reactions from students toward teachers, or from teachers to students?
- Were the lessons on target for the students' stages of development?
- Were behavioral expectations, rules, and procedures consistent, appropriate, and clear?
- If a student had to be removed from the group for time-out, what was the precipitating event? Was the resolution therapeutic?

FIGURE 7.9. Cover these points in daily team debriefings.

Teachers' Social Power Affects Students' Behavior

Many adults are not aware when they use "social power" to influence others, yet everyone does so. Social power is the ability to influence others to do something that they would not ordinarily

[17]A support teacher should learn to use all of the management strategies described in Chapter 5; however, this will take time, practice, teamwork, and encouraging feedback from the lead.

[18]Teachers who use debriefing profitably are also viewed by their students as competent adults who understand students and each other.

do on their own. Four universal sources of social power—expertise, coercion, manipulation, and likability—affect the actions of others. These are summarized in Figure 7.10. People everywhere use these forms of social power, deliberately or unknowingly. The topic is included here because students respond with increased participation to a teacher who uses social power to influence them in positive ways. Experienced teachers establish and maintain healthy relationships with students by using social power. They are also able to use and vary their forms of social power to meet the needs of their students and the conditions of the moment. Each basic type of social power is described in the following sections.

Expertness: ability to help students solve problems that they cannot handle alone

Coercion: verbal or physical confrontation or overpowering psychological control, with an implied threat of punishment

Manipulation: covert control of situations in which the results are not directly linked to the teacher

Likability: positive personal characteristics that students admire and respect

---

FIGURE 7.10. Be able to use several forms of social power to influence your students.

Teachers as Experts

Students generally seem to prefer teachers with high levels of expertise, if there are no immediate problems. And when a student feels overwhelmed by failure or cannot cope with a situation, expertise on a teacher's part is essential. Students are quick to recognize teachers who have knowledge that can help them. They also recognize teachers as experts who understand their feelings or successfully manage other students who are out of control. When teachers are effective in helping students solve their problems in positive ways, the result is trust, admiration, positive identification with the teacher, and greater confidence to try again.

The ability to help your students solve problems that they cannot handle alone requires expertise. By talking through their frustrations, recriminations, remorse, panic, or anger, together you can make a plan to cope more comfortably. A higher level of trust and greater psychological security will result when you use your expertise skillfully.

Coercion, Another Form of Social Power

Coercion is a form of social power that conveys the threat of undesirable consequences or punishment. It is a way to control students' actions with confrontation, reprimand, rules with stated consequences, or overpowering psychological control with some punishment implied or actually stated. To provide a safe climate for learning, you may find it sometimes necessary to resort to coercion. The important issue is when to use it, with whom, and for how long. Students must know that they are physically safe (from others or from themselves), and the teacher is in charge. Stern reprimands with younger children will often stop those who are behaving in unacceptable ways. Criticism and verbal confrontation are forms of coercion that are sometimes useful with older students to help them gain insight into nonproductive attitudes or behavior. Enforced rules provide structure for what is expected. Many structured reinforcement systems for managing students' challenging behaviors are sophisticated versions of coercion—that is, privileges are withheld by teachers to make students conform to rules and expectations. Reality Therapy, in which possibly painful natural consequences are sanctioned although not directly administered by the adult, is yet another form of coercion for older students. It is based on the idea that there is little payoff in continuing behaviors that result in greater trouble. College professors use coercion in the form of grades to motivate students to study and learn. Some parents also employ coercion by withholding love, privileges, or approval in order to make their children behave in acceptable ways.

Coercion puts an individual in a less empowered, losing position. Students who lose repeatedly to teachers (or parents) may develop strong negative reactions and become psychologically defensive against further coercion. You can see it in students who make comments like "Who cares!" "Try and make me." "Shove it." Those who have experienced coercion as the primary discipline in their lives will usually respond to adult coercion with some form of their own coercion such as bullying, cruelty, aggression, stealing, violence, or use of weapons. When a student has learned to respond in these ways, it may be necessary to use coercive strategies yourself, as a first step in maintaining safety and order in the classroom. However, other forms of social power will prove more effective over time.[19]

Influence by Manipulation

Manipulation is covert control of events without the role of the controller being evident. To encourage students' independence and personal responsibility, teachers sometimes use manipulation of events to help students see themselves as central players in learning. Teachers also use manipulation as a social power base when they design highly motivating lessons, so that students participate because they believe they have a good chance to succeed on their own, without depending on the teacher. The Montessori method of using materials to provide intrinsic feedback is a successful example of manipulation of the learning environment, and which is a subtle form of social power. Self-correcting lessons such as those provided through computer software or on the Internet also are examples of manipulation of the learning environment without obvious control by a teacher.

Manipulation has negative connotations for many adults. Perhaps this is why it is not used as frequently as it should be by teachers as a strategy for helping students. It is an effective way for teachers to influence students who have learned to distrust adults or adult authority, because the role of the adult is not evident in the situation. It is also an effective way to help students who are passive–aggressive. They use manipulation as a social power themselves, and are experts at outmaneuvering adults. When a teacher's role is not boldly evident, these students have no direct adult target to try to control, so they tend to relax their own defensive controls and are more likely to participate voluntarily.[20]

Likable Characteristics Give Teachers Influence

Likability is using positive, personal characteristics to influence students' actions. Students respond to teachers who have likable attributes such as humor, warmth, helpfulness, respect, approval, and fairness. Often, such characteristics are the very elements that promote imitation of an admired teacher. This personal appeal is evident when a teacher says to a student, "Do this for me." Or, when a student calls to a teacher, "Look at this. Do you like it?" Or, "I made this for you."

Likability is effective as a form of social power when it is used selectively in combination with the other three forms of social power. It adds a personal, positive, respectful dimension to the learning environment. But if it is a teacher's primary means of influencing students, it can

[19]See Chapter 5 for recommendations about managing students' aggressive (coercive) behavior.

[20]A discussion of strategies for managing students with severe passive–aggressive behavior is included in Chapter 5.

result in personal bonds that are unacceptable in school. It can also restrict a student's progress toward independent emotional maturity. In these situations, student–teacher relationships merge into person-to-person bonding in which the teacher neither exercises authority nor allows the student the psychological space to become independent. When this happens, separation may become difficult for teacher and student. If this personalizing continues, both the teacher and the student may come to feel that other adults (including parents) cannot provide what this teacher can provide. This is not an acceptable outcome. The best guideline is to keep personal characteristics within boundaries and shift to using other forms of social power to influence students.

Expand Your Power Options

If the idea of social power is new to you or you do not already use all four forms as needed, identify those you use naturally outside of school. You probably use the same ones when working with students. This will give you an indication of what you rely on instinctively when trying to influence others. Consider also the types of social power you seldom use. Practice verbal and nonverbal ways to use these less familiar forms. Try them out first in neutral situations where students will not be confused by sudden changes in your interpersonal style. Then observe the way they respond to the different styles. This information can help you to decide which form of social power to use with each student in particular incidents.[21]

Here is an example of how these multiple options can be used: A teacher takes a middle school student into the counselor's office to discuss a fight on the bus. The teacher and the counselor have several social power options for dealing with the issue. By discussing bus regulations and ways to solve the bus problem, the counselor's social power takes the form of expertise (knowing how to solve a problem with rules). If there is a point system in place for good behavior, they could remind the student that bus points bring privileges—a form of manipulation (the adults are not directly causing the consequence). Or, the counselor could discuss what happens to students who get in trouble on the bus and break the rules. This latter approach is coercion (the threat of punishment if the student doesn't change his behavior on the bus). Another approach would be to indicate their disappointment in the student's actions (an appeal based on likability). This assumes that their personal disappointment will be effective with this student. Notice also that by taking the student to the counselor instead of dealing directly with the issue, the teacher may have diminished the amount of influence she has with the student (through lack of expertise to manage the situation by herself). The teacher and counselor should consider all of these social power options when they respond to the incident.[22]

Personal Characteristics Influence Effectiveness

This section reviews personal characteristics that can be among the most powerful tools you have for effective teaching. Personal characteristics of a teacher often have a greater impact on students than instructional skills. If you can make an objective assessment of your own personal characteristics and carefully monitor how your actions are viewed by your students, you should have a realistic appraisal of what you are doing that works, and what is not as effective as you had hoped. Then, consider making changes in your personal characteristics such as voice, appearance, manner of movement, emotional control, or personal habits, if such changes could be helpful for your students. Although not always easy to do, the result is worth the effort. It should foster helpful teacher–student relationships—exactly what students need for success in school.

[21] Behind every form of social power, the message must be, "Teachers care about students, and teachers can be depended upon to help."

[22] See Chapter 4 for a discussion of decoding the social power of students.

Conflicting Values

Many problems in a classroom are related to a teacher's inability to understand students' personal, cultural, or family values. This frequently leads to serious difficulties in anticipating and managing classroom behavior. Students' values are the product of their emotional needs or environmental influences, which may not always be in their best interest. For example, students who grow up in an environment where value is attached to being physically strong, appearing to be sexually active, coercing others, using drugs, skipping school, or stealing may adopt such behaviors to meet their needs to be accepted by others. In addition, there may be other emotional drives such as anxieties concerning abandonment, inadequacy, guilt, conflict, or identity.[23]

Effective teachers understand the balance of representing school and community standards and their personal values, which may be different. Conflicting values also become increasingly difficult when a teacher's values are different from the values of a student. Differences may include beliefs about religion, politics, sex, clothing, stealing, lying, illegal drugs, authority, work ethics, conduct and manners, styles of dress and speech, or forms of entertainment—to mention only a few. When these values conflict, students do not need to be in the crossfire. Students need assistance in learning to balance and resolve differences in cultures and experiences, personal values, beliefs held by their families, and the values represented by the school's standards for acceptable behavior.

If you find your personal values challenged by differing perspectives on what is desirable and right, respect others' points of view while keeping a perspective on your own beliefs. If these differences cannot be balanced comfortably, carefully consider the choice between remaining at or leaving a school where the standards and values are significantly at odds with your personal values.

[23]Chapter 4 has a discussion of these developmental anxieties and how they shape a student's behavior.

Nonverbal Style

Students rely on unspoken messages from the teacher's body posture, tone, gesture, and facial expressions. Figure 7.11 contains examples of effective nonverbal skills for the classroom. Body language can communicate respect and approval. It may also convey the teacher's anxieties, tensions, or insecurities. Monitor yourself to be sure you are not communicating nonverbal messages to students that you do not intend. By standing over a student, a teacher conveys authority and control. Physical proximity or touch can evoke feelings of closeness that some students crave, while others may misinterpret it as judgment or authority, which they cannot handle. In times of crisis, your choice of a relaxed body stance may give students a sense of security and confidence. A calm face and a smile may neutralize a panic reaction in a student.

- Calm logic
- Competence
- Confidence
- Enthusiasm
- Fairness
- Firmness
- Humor
- Interest
- Positive attitudes
- Respect

FIGURE 7.11. Examples of messages communicated by nonverbal skills and body language.

If you are a person who relies on words with your students, you may also be missing a more effective way to communicate with them. Try expanding your body language by practicing in front of a mirror in private. With gestures, body posture, and facial expressions, try to communicate confidence, power, concern, and enthusiasm without using words. As you increase your skill in doing this, practice with other adults. Then try role playing in pantomime with your students until you and the students can communicate simple ideas without any words being exchanged. It is fun for them and can become one of your most effective strategies—use it!

Eye Contact (or the Opposite)

A glance between two people is a universal sign of contact. In school, it is used to communicate with students of all ages and stages of development. Teachers should be confident in themselves and comfortable enough with their students to look at them and catch their attention visually. Many students are responsive to a quiet, steady gaze from their teacher, and eye contact can be effective in building relationships with them.

Use visual contact regularly during every lesson to obtain students' attention, communicate your interest, send a warning about misbehavior, or signal approval for a student's positive action. If a student accepts your look, it will be interpreted as a personal contact, and it will be returned. However, there are times when avoiding eye contact may be a better strategy. Some students are taught at home that it is disrespectful to look directly at adults. They will avoid your attempts at eye contact. For others, a direct gaze from a teacher is seen as an encroachment on their personal spaces. Provide the needed distance in these circumstances. Give a brief glance and then look elsewhere as you continue your communication with the student. There are also students who feel that they must maintain their disruptive behavior when an adult is watching. By avoiding watching them, you provide a cooling-off time until emotions recede. Then the student may be able to communicate with you.

With very young students and those who are developmentally delayed, a gently touch on the chin can be used to direct the student to look at you. This technique is effective in helping the student focus on what you are saying or asking. It also is a way to help a student who is learning to speak by imitating lip movements. A few students may react negatively to this approach or actively try to avoid you. Avoid direct eye contact with them until they begin to watch you on their own, when they think you are not watching them. This watching often indicates that they are interested in some form of contact with you but are uncertain of it. They may be beginning to trust you, but cannot bring themselves to show it by looking. In such situations, make your glances brief, supportive, and nondemanding. Gradually lengthen your glances into smiles, and then add the student's name as you look and smile. Do not expect a response at first. But eventually, your glance will be returned. It will often happen during a motivating activity. The student may reach out suddenly to show you what has been done in the activity or to call for your assistance. When the student spontaneously seeks contact with you, a major developmental milestone for social communication has been reached.

Voice Quality

Many students rely on "reading" messages in a teacher's tone of voice rather than on listening to the words the teacher uses. Be aware of the effect your voice can have, and learn to communicate with your voice quality as well as your words. There are examples in Figure 7.12. By varying volume and tone of voice, you can attract and hold students' attention. Few students can resist listening to a teacher whose voice suddenly drops to a whisper, or who conveys a questioning tone with surprise or excitement in both face and voice. When a student is upset, a slow and soothing tone conveys that you are not upset and can be trusted. A relaxed voice reflects ease and approval. An emphatic, matter-of-fact voice depersonalizes a situation and communicates that you expect the student to respond as requested. With your voice you can also communicate enthusiasm, warmth, pleasure, encouragement, authority, power, leadership, or guidance.

- Increase or decrease a student's anxiety
- Encourage or discourage effort
- Indicate approval or disapproval
- Avoid or fuel a crisis
- Motivate or squelch participation
- Reassure or threaten
- Signal respect or disrespect
- Offer security or insecurity

FIGURE 7.12. Possible effects of a teacher's voice quality.

Some students will not respond to a simple request unless firmness is conveyed through voice tone. This does not mean shouting or demanding. Firmness lets the student know very clearly what is expected. If you do not firmly state your expectations, some students are more likely to test your limits. On the other hand, a tone that is too firm or strident can be mistaken by a student to be anger or tension, and it may trigger a defensive, negative response.

Teachers with soft, high pitched, or tentative qualities to their voices frequently seem to trigger negative responses from students. Perhaps it is the thinness of the sound that raises doubts about the teacher's ability. The message may be interpreted as lacking authority, pleading, or insecurity, which arouse anxiety in some students and disrespect in others. Invariably, these teachers have behavior management problems with their students. A teacher can overcome this voice problem by using a deep, full tone of voice to communicate firm confidence. Here is an example: A teacher performed her instructional responsibilities adequately, but the students' responses to her were getting progressively worse. Her program coordinator observed that although she was dedicated, bright, aware, and knowledgeable, her voice was consistently soft and barely audible to students. She seemed to keep her voice as low as possible to respect each student's need for private exchanges with her. The teaching team was increasingly uncomfortable about her lack of effectiveness with the students. They recognized that her soft voice was her personal style with students, and had not discussed it as a possible factor in her problems with the students to avoid hurting her feelings. When the problem was brought out into the open, the team talked about how to help her gain more effective verbal communication skills. Initially, she felt that she might not be able to change her voice and was self-conscious when she tried to vary her pitch and volume. But she learned to control her voice qualities to convey her expectations effectively. She did this through practice outside of the classroom with role play, and then focused her attention on her own voice quality in the classroom.[24]

To work on your own voice qualities, we recommend a series of simple exercises to practice varying the message by changing inflection and pitch. Try saying "Good morning," four different ways:

- As an authority figure
- Kindly but distant
- Absentminded or preoccupied with something else
- Intensely personal and focused

Then try another familiar expression, such as: "You have to leave the group until you can get yourself together." As you make this statement several different ways, try to convey these messages:

- Support and confidence that everything will be all right
- Toughness and authority

[24]Sometimes teachers' personal characteristics need to be changed when interacting with students. This may require effort, but it can make a huge improvement in the classroom climate for learning.

- Uncertainty about whether or not the student will leave without a fight
- Rejection and disgust toward the student

These simple exercises are merely the calisthenics of staying in shape for communicating effectively with students. You might have noticed that the words themselves are not nearly as important as how they are said. If you have sufficient control over your voice quality to convey each of these nonverbal messages with the same set of words, you have the skill necessary to convey a range of other messages that are important for students to hear.

Sarcasm, Teasing, and Slang

When teachers use sarcasm, teasing, slang, or other ways of veiling messages, students are left with feelings of helplessness or confusion about how to respond. This lack of confidence in how to respond to teachers does not foster success. Students may also take such remarks as personally disrespectful or as evidence of disregard by the teacher. Students who have difficulty developing adult and peer relationships are particularly sensitive to how others view them. They often interpret even the most casual, unintentional comment as a statement of scorn or ridicule.

Teachers who persist in using sarcasm or teasing with students often try to defend their choice by declaring that this is their natural way of relating to people. Although their intent may be the best, this type of communication shows a lack of sensitivity to how their words and actions are received by their students. We find that the adult role is so critically important in fostering students' progress that if a teacher's need to be "natural" overrides being the type of adult needed by a student, student progress is generally limited.

However, there can be situations in which cultural speech and slang expressions are useful. Informal speech can be a casual, relaxed means of communicating if a student easily understands it. It can also create camaraderie between teacher and student that may foster their relationship. This is particularly effective with older students.

Several subtle problems can arise if teachers use informal speech extensively. First, students may interpret the use of slang as sloppiness. Students with this view seldom accept the teacher as a respected authority. Second, an equal relationship between teacher and student can sometimes be conveyed unintentionally. This is inconsistent with teachers' primary responsibilities to teach and to be acceptable role models for their students.

Professional Appearance

Good judgment is important in choosing how you dress for work in any setting. Personal appearance conveys a clear message to students, parents, and your colleagues. Understandably, conditions of dress and appearance will vary with local standards, and many schools have specific or implied dress codes.[25]

In some schools, teachers must sometimes sit on the floor with students, participate in outside play, or be a part of potentially messy projects. Such activities require practical clothing and shoes that allow freedom of movement. The wrong shoes can slow you down or be a hazard. Few teachers of young children have avoided getting juice or paint on their clothes. And anyone who has attempted to assist a student who is out of control knows how important it is to wear durable clothes. Also, it should not be necessary to remind responsible teachers to avoid seductive or revealing clothing.

Teachers who display unconventional appearance can unintentionally impede communication with parents and other professionals who may have different standards for dress and appearance. When attending meetings with professional colleagues or parents, maintain a conventional appearance because this tends to focus on the work at hand and not on personal

[25]It is not necessary to make a personal statement in dress to convey a professional look.

characteristics. This also shows respect for differing cultural styles among participants. If a teacher has an unkempt, unprofessional appearance, the confidence of parents and other educators in the ability of the teacher to help a student can be undermined.[26]

Accepting Support from Others

Most problems teachers have can be solved. Be open to support from others; they often can help when your own solutions do not produce the positive changes you hope for. However, accepting suggestions from others is not always easy. Their comments may imply failure. They may offer ideas that you have already tried with no success. Many times, others will inadvertently convey the attitude that what you are doing is wrong. Even your effective practices may come under criticism. At that point, it is easy to give up and become defensive or critical of their ideas.

Teachers who can overcome these feelings by understanding their own issues, anxieties, and defenses will be able to use the suggestions of others for positive outcomes for themselves and their students. Supportive colleagues can help. Suggestions can grow out of discussion about what practices are effective, what emotional needs the students are expressing, what procedures need to be changed to respond more precisely to address these needs, and what changes can be expected as a result. Most of all, others can provide support by conveying confidence that what you are trying will be effective.

In situations where there is uncertainty about what is appropriate or needed, a carefully calculated response is more beneficial than an impulsive, emotional one. Avoid the temptation to "let yourself go" emotionally. Such responses may put you into a conflict cycle with the student (Long, Wood, & Fecser, 2001, Chapter 2). You may find it more constructive to focus on a change in the social power base used with your student, modify your role, or select different management strategies. As you consider your options, be prepared with a wide array of management strategies, know how to convey many different adult roles, and be skilled in using each type of social power.[27]

For a summary of these suggestions about personal style in the classroom, see Figure 7.13. A final comment may be helpful here about how much of a teacher's personal reactions and feelings should be revealed to students. It is not usually helpful for teachers to display personal emotions in the classroom. This is especially true for students with social, emotional, and behavioral challenges. They should not have to bear the additional burden of a teacher's own

[26]When meeting parents or other members of the community, teachers should take care that what they do, how they look, and what they say will enhance acceptance of their students by others, and will not impede cooperative efforts.

[27]Try to communicate dispassionate compassion when faced with students whose problems seem overwhelming to you.

- Let your actions be a model for your students.
- Use speech and voice tones that are appropriate for the age of the students.
- Dress and behave in a manner that is professional and nonseductive.
- Control your emotions.
- Use body language to communicate a professional but supportive relationship.
- Respect each student's personal space.
- Avoid personal ties to a student who tries to bond to you emotionally. It is not in the best interest of the student.
- Avoid creating a relationship in which a student becomes dependent on you for behavioral controls.
- Maintain a balance between necessary control of a student in the short run and the need for eventual self-direction by the student.
- Keep differences in your values from creating conflict with a student.
- Do not try to be a surrogate parent to a student.

FIGURE 7.13. Summary of personal style in the classroom.

emotional needs. A skilled and dedicated teacher summed it up this way: "Personal feelings must simply be put aside for the benefit of the social and emotional growth of our students."

How Teachers Gain the Needed Skills

The skills described in the preceding section are not always acquired easily or rapidly. The process requires considerable personal insight, teaching skills, and self-monitoring. Most importantly, it requires a depth of emotional maturity, self-confidence, and empathy for others. Review the specific competencies contained in the DTRITS. Figure 7.14 lists several ways this inventory can help a teacher. The DTRITS contains the basic practices recommended for teaching students at each stage of development. Use it to assess your own skills. Identify practices that you want to add or improve, and monitor your own progress.

In addition, explore the simulations provided in *PEGS (Practice Effective Guidance Strategies) for Teachers* CD-ROM series (Developmental Therapy Institute, 2003a, b). This is an interactive computer game for teachers to practice using the core management strategies included in the DTRITS and reviewed in Chapter 5. *PEGS* contains simulated classroom activities and lively student characters with challenging behaviors. Both the DTRITS and *PEGS* are tools to expand your proficiencies. They are described in the sections that follow.[28]

[28]The four forms of the DTRITS are in the separate CD included with this edition.

- Review the recommended developmental practices that match students' stages.
- Identify instructional practices and management strategies already used with proficiency.
- Select practices and strategies that need to be added.
- Self-monitor progress in skill acquisition.

FIGURE 7.14. Reasons a teacher might want to self-rate with the DTRITS.

The Rating Inventory of Teacher Skills (DTRITS)

There are four forms of the DTRITS. Choose the one designed for the age group and stage of development of the children you teach. See Figure 7.15 when selecting the correct age-referenced form. If you teach toddlers and young children under age 2, use the Stage One form. For teaching preschool children in childcare or early childhood programs, use the form for Stage

---

- When teaching infants and toddlers, use DTRITS Stage One form with 59 items.
- When teaching preschool children, use DTRITS Stage Two form with 83 items.
- When teaching students in primary grades, use DTRITS Stage Three form with 84 items.
- When teaching upper elementary/middle school students, use DTRITS Stage Four form with 78 items.

FIGURE 7.15. DTRITS forms guide practices to match students' ages and stages of development.

Two. When teaching primary grade students in K–3, use the Stage Three form. For teaching upper elementary and middle school students, the Stage Four form contains the basic practices. If you teach students with developmental delays, select the DTRITS form that most closely matches the students' current stages of functioning (Robinson, 1982/1983; Wood, Davis, & Swindle, 1998).[29]

The same rating system is used for each form, whether by the teacher when self-assessing and self-monitoring or by a trained observer. Each DTRITS item is rated *Yes* (Y), *No* (N), *Partially* (P), *Not Needed* (NN), or *Not Seen* (NS) to indicate the extent to which the teacher applies the skill item. A total score is the sum of Y divided by Y + N + P × 100. Effectiveness standards for the scores were established at the time of the first demonstration project and have been used consistently since.[30] Refer to Figure 7.16 for these performance criteria.

[29]The DTRITS is a way to monitor your own classroom skills. It can also be used to measure proficiency in applying teaching practices.

[30]The DTRITS minimum performance criterion for proficiency is > 70 (effective).

> 95 = Highly Effective

71–94 = Effective

51–70 = Adequate

31–50 = Less than Adequate

< 31 = Poor

FIGURE 7.16. Performance standards indicated by DTRITS scores.

DTRITS Content Validity

During the development of this instrument, it was important to verify that a DTRITS score represents a measure of skill in using Developmental Therapy–Developmental Teaching. It was also necessary to determine if it contained the specific practices for teaching children in developmental stages rather than toddlers to young teenagers. To do this, the items in each form were cross-referenced to the Developmental Therapy–Developmental Teaching sourcebook for practitioners and to the instructor's manual for teacher trainers (Robinson, 1982/1983).[31]

[31]For a discussion of internal and external validity, see Cook and Campbell (1979) and Shadish, Cook, and Campbell (2002).

This procedure revealed that several practices from these source materials had been overlooked and were subsequently added. A few items that were judged to be less than essential were dropped. Then a panel of five experts knowledgeable in the theory and practice of this approach individually reviewed each item to determine if it was *essential* for proficiency with Developmental Therapy–Developmental Teaching. Members of the panel rated the items on a 4-point scale from *essential* (4) to *not desirable* (1). Any item receiving a mean rating less than 3.0 (*very desirable*) was discussed by the experts as a group and then either rewritten or deleted by consensus agreement. This procedure resulted in the four forms of the present DTRITS, included in the CD-ROM.

A second study was conducted to verify the practical validity of the DTRITS for teachers and supervisors using it to guide their practices in the daily educational programs for students with challenging behaviors (Robinson, 1982/1983). Ten teachers responded to statements about the stage forms they were using on a 5-point scale from *almost always* (5) to *seldom* (1). The statements were these:

- The DTRITS reflects recommended practices for children I teach.
- It includes the important competencies needed by teachers.

- It provides an accurate description of a teacher's performance.
- It helps a teacher maintain or improve proficiency.

The teachers' average responses to these four statements were 4.9, 4.9, 4.6, and 4.4. Using *t*-tests at a .05 confidence level to compare their ratings to a chosen midpoint (3), results indicated that the ratings on each statement were significantly above the acceptable level of 3.0. For these teachers, the DTRITS proved to have sufficient practical validity as an instrument for guiding them in their classroom practices.

In another field trial, 15 program coordinators judged the practicality of using the DTRITS in their supervision of teachers. They judged each of the four stage forms independently using a 5-point scale from *almost always* (5) to *seldom* (1) in response to these statements:

- The DTRITS is useful in supervision.
- It avoids ambiguity in items.
- It includes necessary content.
- The rating system is easy to use.
- Observers need DTRITS training for reliable use of the instrument.

The supervisors consistently rated each form of the DTRITS high on all these statements. Their average ratings were 4.4 for Stage One; 4.5 for Stage Two; 4.6 for Stage Three; and 4.5 for Stage Four. These ratings were compared to a midpoint of 3.0 using dependent *t*-tests with the .05 confidence level. On every statement for each form, the ratings were significantly above the chosen midpoint. These findings, summarized in Figure 7.17, indicate that this group of supervisors judged the DTRITS to be a practical instrument for classroom supervision (Robinson, 1982/1983).[32]

- Easy to use
- Useful for supervision
- Sufficiently specific about teachers' performance
- Accurate and reliable following training in the rating procedure

FIGURE 7.17. Characteristics of the DTRITS. Supervisors report that the DTRITS is a practical and accurate performance measure.

DTRITS Reliability

A series of field studies was conducted to examine the degree of objectivity and accuracy of DTRITS ratings when used by trained observers. Measures of both interrater agreement and interrater reliability are necessary because of the subjective judgments required in rating a teacher with the DTRITS (Robinson, 1982/1983; Tinsley & Weiss, 1975). Initially, six trained supervisors were randomly divided into pairs to observe and rate six teachers for a 2-hour period using a DTRITS stage form corresponding to the students' stages of development. Raters were instructed to observe together but to rate independently, without discussing their observations. With this small sample, interrater reliability was supported with a Pearson *r* of .83. Two weeks later they repeated the procedure. Each rater's first rating was compared with his or her own second rating. The result was a Pearson *r* of .70, providing moderate support for test–retest (intrarater) reliability.[33]

[33]Interrater agreement indicates the extent to which two observers assign the same value when rating the same teacher at the same time. Interrater reliability is the degree to which their ratings differ from their mean ratings.

To obtain additional measures of interrater reliability using the same procedure, 19 trained raters were randomly assigned in pairs to observe 25 teachers of students with social, emotional, or behavioral disabilities. Several observer pairs rated more than one teacher. A Pearson r of .89 was obtained when the overall scores of each rater were compared, indicating that they used the DTRITS within an acceptable level of reliability (Robinson, 1982/1983, p. 98).

Over the next 3 years at four different schools, DTRITS interrater agreement and interrater reliability were studied using 26 trained raters and 22 teachers. The intent was to obtain further reliability information by comparing their item-by-item ratings on the overall score and on each stage form. They observed for 2 hours in pairs and then rated a teacher on the appropriate form independently. They made 65 pair observations following this procedure. When their item-by-item ratings were compared across the four forms, there was 75% agreement. Comparison of their ratings on each item for each form confirmed their high degree of agreement (Robinson, 1982/1983, pp. 96, 183; Wood, Davis, & Swindle, 1998, p. 58):

Stage One form, 84% agreement ($SD = 12$)

Stage Two form, 78% agreement ($SD = 12$)

Stage Three form 72% agreement ($SD = 19$)

Stage Four form, 69% agreement ($SD = 11$)

Finally, the scores were reanalyzed by obtaining the mean percentage scores of the first raters in each rater pair for comparison to the second raters in each pair (Robinson, 1982/1983, p. 184). Their two groups were within 3 points of each other on each form. Overall, their ratings were almost identical: 81.07 ($SD = 8.9$) and 81.51 ($SD = 10.2$).

During the same period, interrater reliability estimates were also made. Ten trained rater pairs used the Stage Two form to observe and rate 10 teachers of preschool children. They made 57 repeated paired observations for 2 hours each and then independently rated the teacher using the same scoring procedure. The result was a Pearson r of .79 for the Stage Two form. Similarly, 7 rater pairs used the Stage Three form during the same period to observe and rate 12 teachers of primary grade students. They made 43 paired observations, resulting in a Pearson r of .94 for the Stage Three form (Robinson, 1982/1983, p. 185).

Although random assignment of rater pairs was not possible in the Robinson study, results collectively provide evidence that a DTRITS score has acceptable reliability and validity as a measure of a teacher's proficiency in applying the specified practices, when observed by a trained observer. Figure 7.18 summarizes the findings and conclusions indicating that the DTRITS is an effective, performance-based measure of teachers' skills for Developmental Therapy–Developmental Teaching.[34]

[34]Results of studies about content validity, interrater agreement, and interrater reliability suggest that the DTRITS can be used with confidence by trained observers. Both total proficiency scores and item-by-item ratings are accurate measures of teachers' performance when using the specified practices in their classrooms.

- Has valid content for teachers using Developmental Therapy–Developmental Teaching practices
- Measures actual classroom performance
- Contains observable competency items
- Provides reliable procedures for measuring performance
- Requires both high and low inference rater judgments
- Contains qualitative and quantitative information about teachers' classroom performance
- Enables teachers to self-monitor their own skill development
- Offers a practical tool for supervisors to use with reliability
- Applies schoolwide for assessing staff skills

FIGURE 7.18. The DTRITS meets these standards as an effective, performance-based measure of teachers' skills.

[35]The *PEGS for Teachers* series includes *PEGS for Preschool, PEGS for Elementary,* and *PEGS for Secondary.* Information about the series is available on the Internet at http://www.pegsforteachers.com.

PEGS for Teachers CD-ROM Series[35]

The three computer-based interactive CD-ROM programs in the *PEGS for Teachers* series were developed to provide general and special educators with independent practice in using basic behavior management strategies. Among the many educators and related professionals who have used and evaluated *PEGS* are those listed in Figure 7.19. The strategies are described in Chapter 5. With *PEGS*, users learn to

- identify students whose behavior needs improving,
- select strategies that help students participate in acceptable ways and keep them participating,
- apply the strategies to students with various problem behaviors, and
- explore how students' responses vary when a strategy is applied in different activities.

The *PEGS* series, in a game format, contains animated child characters in age groups from 3 through 16 years. These characters behave in ways familiar to teachers, from typical behavior problems to those that are highly disruptive and difficult to manage. For the player, the goal is to increase participation of the child characters in a selected educational activity by choosing strategies to manage disruptive behavior in ways that will increase students' participation in the activity and decrease their unacceptable behavior (Developmental Therapy Institute, 2003a).[36]

[36]*PEGS* development and evaluation projects were supported by the Developmental Therapy Institute, Inc.; LetterPress Software, Inc.; The University of Georgia; the Georgia Department of Education State Improvement Grant from the U.S. Department of Education, contract no. H323A990012; and by the Office of Special Education Programs, U.S. Department of Education, CFDA 84.325N, grant no. H325N990015.

As an activity begins, an animated simulation shows a group of children behaving in characteristic ways. The player selects an individual and then chooses among the management strategies to address the behavior portrayed. The child then responds to the choice. If the strategy meets the needs of the child, there will be an increase in participation. If it is not a good match, problem behavior increases. While the player attends to one child, the other children continue

- Beginning teachers
- Childcare providers
- Experienced teachers
- Head Start teachers
- Paraprofessionals
- School administrators
- School psychologists
- Special educators
- State-level educators
- Student teachers
- Substitute teachers

FIGURE 7.19. People for whom *PEGS* CDs provide practice in behavior management.

to display a range of behaviors. If ignored for too long, the others begin to exhibit negative, non-participative behavior, and the player may lose the game.

The player can explore alternative responses by repeating the same activity but choosing different strategies. Each time the game is played, a randomly selected group is presented, each with a different configuration of behavior problems. The game can be played at three levels of difficulty. At the easy level, there is immediate feedback that flashes on the screen. At the most difficult level, feedback is delayed until the end of the game. Text resources are also available for more information about the child characters, their challenging behaviors, and the recommended strategies. The game is won when all are participating with enthusiasm, and the player has maintained full participation of the group. At the end, the program provides feedback and an analysis of the management strategies used by the player.

Skill with a computer is not needed. Nor is it necessary to have an instructor. However, users must have access to a computer with CD capability, either MAC or PC versions, preferably with sound and a printer. These features enable the user to print feedback and recommendations to use alternative strategies, if indicated. This latter option also provides a record of an individual's practice, which can be of benefit to supervisors or to in-service instructors providing credit for staff development training.[37]

How *PEGS* Was Developed

The project goal was to develop a tool for independent adult learning in an easy-to-use format with content that teachers, assistant teachers, and preservice teachers find engaging, effective, and relevant to everyday classroom behavior management. Recognizing that educators face a broad range of behavior problems in their classrooms, an extensive list of frequently reported problems was compiled as a first step. The list included a range of behaviors from no manifest problem to highly disruptive or severely withdrawn behavior. The list then was reviewed by educators, parents, and mental health professionals serving as advisors to the project. Their task was to identify behaviors that were faced by most educators on a daily basis. The final content, reported in Figure 7.20, includes 11 challenging behaviors unanimously selected by the advisors.

[37]The Georgia Department of Education has the complete *PEGS for Teachers* series available for in-service training to individual educators or school-wide through the Georgia Learning Resource System (GLRS).

- Agitated or upset by others
- Destructive to materials or toys
- Frequently unhappy
- Overly sensitive
- Hurtful to self or others
- Hyperactive
- Irritable
- Chronic physical complaints
- Listening difficulties
- Physically or verbally aggressive
- Restless, short attention span
- Talks or behaves like a younger child
- Uncontrolled anger or temper tantrums
- Withdrawn

FIGURE 7.20. Students' behavior problems selected for the *PEGS* CD series.

A matrix was then prepared as an outline for designing child characters whose actions would portray the selected behaviors. This provided a guide for writing brief vignettes about each child, developing supplementary case materials, and preparing preliminary graphics for animated movements. To do this, a separate matrix was prepared for each of three age groups—early childhood, elementary grades, and secondary schools. Each group of characters was balanced for gender, general level of intelligence, personality, attitudes toward adults and peers, defense mechanisms used, developmental anxieties, and race. From these outlines, extensive case files were written. In all, 18 child characters were developed along with their case records as informational text files.

The materials were reviewed by child psychologists, project advisors, and independent educational experts. These groups reviewed the text content and the graphic animations to reach consensus that the portrayals included all of the selected problem behaviors and the specified characteristics of children. They also reviewed the materials to verify that they were culturally sensitive, with multi-ethnic representations among the characters.

To create authentic simulations of all possible interactions between a player and a child's response, five individualized actions were designed to indicate increasing degrees of positive participation for each student in an activity. There were also seven negative actions designed to indicate declining participation, with increasingly disruptive behavior. Customized graphics then were designed for the characters and the responses each would make to the behavior management strategy options in each of four different school-related activities.

Evaluation of *PEGS* by Teachers

There were 55 teachers and assistant teachers in early childhood, elementary, and secondary schools who volunteered to participate in evaluating *PEGS* For the early childhood version, there were 11 teachers and 13 assistant teachers, working with 393 young children in the 2- to 5-years age range. Their programs included a university demonstration school, a private childcare facility, and a Head Start. For the elementary school version, 12 teachers in three schools volunteered. They taught 387 students, ages 4 to 9 years in Pre-K through 3rd grade. The secondary school version was evaluated by 19 teachers and assistant teachers with 118 students in two middle schools for students in grades 6, 7, and 8. The teachers in one school taught both inclusion and resource room special education for students with mild to moderate learning or behavioral disabilities. The other school was an urban special education program for middle and high school students with severe social, emotional, or behavioral disabilities. The teachers and paraprofessionals in this latter program taught part-day, self-contained special education. Additionally, 57 university students evaluated the *PEGS*. Of these, 16 were preservice teachers in a behavior management class who evaluated the elementary school version, and 41 were education majors in instructional technology using the secondary version.

Participants were given a version of *PEGS* for the age group of the students they taught and a logbook. They were asked to use the CD independently as frequently as their free time allowed for a 2-week period. They recorded activities they selected, the names of the child characters in the groups presented, levels of program difficulty they chose, and any embedded text material they used. At the end of the 2 weeks, they rated the CD using a 24-item rating form shown in Figure 7.21 to evaluate the CD's potential usefulness and effectiveness.

The teachers' ratings indicate that the three CDs exceed the standards for "relevant content," "a helpful learning experience," and "easy to use." They reported that it offered an independent learning format with content they found useful and relevant to their everyday behavior management problems. They judged the information to be clear, professional, and sufficient. The management strategy options and simulated behaviors were familiar ones for them, and the portrayed activities were typical of real school settings. Ratings by the university students were equally high on these same criteria (Developmental Therapy Institute, 2003b; Georgia Department of Education, 2001; Quirk, 2003).

About the Content
- The *PEGS* children have behaviors that I have seen in real children.
- Their difficult behaviors are real-life challenges.
- The activities are typical for educational settings.
- The strategies are ones I have heard of.
- The child characters responded to the interventions in real-life ways.
- The responses of the child characters were appropriate for ages and individual needs.

About *PEGS* as a Learning Opportunity
- The child characters held my attention.
- Some behaviors were easy to guide to participation.
- Other behaviors were challenging to guide to participation.
- The program choices allowed for my preferences.
- There was enough information about the children.
- Information about the children was presented in a professional way.
- The information about the strategies was helpful to me.
- The strategies are practical for real-life situations.
- Feedback at the end provided me with useful information.
- The suggestions for improving my management style were helpful.

About Using *PEGS*
- It can be used with very little computer experience.
- Operating the program presents no problems.
- The format is easy to follow.
- Information about how to play is clear.
- It is easy to change from one activity to another in the program.
- Stopping and reentering later is not difficult.
- Feedback is quick and to the point.
- I used this program without assistance.

FIGURE 7.21. Criterion statements used by teachers and university students to rate the *PEGS* series.

While this preliminary field evaluation provides evidence that *PEGS* was well received by the teachers, there are several limitations. First, the small, self-selecting samples were not randomly chosen and may not be representative of other educators who might use the CD. Repeated studies with randomly selected participants could determine if these responses are typical of educators in other programs. Second, there may be an experimental effect created by the novelty of using a CD game for training that might not be transferred to sustainable classroom practice over time.[38]

Follow-Up Studies in Teachers' Classrooms

From this group of educators who evaluated *PEGS*, 37 also volunteered to participate in follow-up studies of classroom carry over. There were 14 from the early childhood group, 12 from the elementary school group, and 11 from the secondary school group.

Two pairs of independent evaluators obtained classroom performance data during 30-minute observations in each participant's classroom. One observer used a time sampling procedure to record the frequency of strategies observed and the responses of students to a teacher's strategies (or to ignoring by the teacher) in 1-minute intervals. This provided information about how frequently participants used the strategies in the program and how a student responded to the strategy. Every strategy and student response was recorded, minute-by-minute, during the observation.

[38]Teachers, assistant teachers, and preservice teachers consistently rate the three *PEGS* programs high for relevance to their day-to-day experiences in behavior management. They also indicate that it is easy to use and provides valuable practice.

During the same observation, a second evaluator used the *Adult Rating Scale* to measure participants' skills as they applied the strategies. This 54-item observation rating scale contains qualitative descriptions of the basic strategies contained in the *PEGS* series. Three forms of the scale were developed: one to use when rating early childhood educators, another for elementary school teachers, and one for those in middle or high school programs.[39]

After the baseline observation, time-sample data were summarized for each participating teacher, indicating frequency of strategies used, instances of ignoring, and negative student responses. Skill ratings were also totaled to obtain a participant's skill score. Participants were then given a CD and logbook for independent practice. The same two evaluators repeated the process 2 weeks later for post-*PEGS* observations.

Reliability of Data Collection

Because observation and data collection require reliable rater judgments, operational terms were defined and rating protocols were reviewed in detail before the evaluators visited the classrooms. They also received a 2-hour training program together, where they viewed videotapes of other classrooms and practiced using the coding protocols for accuracy. The evaluators were not involved in the project to develop *PEGS*. Each evaluator had extensive prior experience in educating children with emotional and behavioral disabilities, and more than 25 years experience in general and special education as a program supervisor and as an early childhood program specialist.

Changes in Teachers' Classroom Practices

The early childhood teachers improved their classroom management skills 41%; the elementary school teachers increased their skills 41%; and the teachers in secondary schools, 42%. For statistical analysis, one-tailed dependent *t*-tests were calculated using an alpha level of .05. The gains were statistically significant (Table 7.1). Magnitude-of-effect measures taking sample

[39]The 54-item instrument used to assess teachers' classroom practices was modified from the DTRITS. A copy of the version used in this study may be obtained from the Developmental Therapy Institute, P. O. Box 5153, Athens, GA 30604.

Table 7.1

Teachers' Behavior Management Skill Scores Improve Significantly After Using a *PEGS* CD-ROM Program

Teacher	Pre-*PEGS* Skill Score	Post-*PEGS* Score	% Change	*t*	*p*	r_m
Early childhood (*n* = 14)						
M	3.31	4.67	+41%	2.53	.01*	.57[a]
SD	1.26	1.81				
SE	.48	.34				
Range	1.9–6.0	2.4–8.1				
Elementary school (*n* = 12)						
M	1.43	2.01	+41%	3.19	.004*	.69[a]
SD	.90	.95				
SE	.26	.27				
Range	−.22–2.79	+.36–3.18				
Middle/high school (*n* = 11)						
M	2.49	3.53	+42%	1.91	.04*	.52[a]
SD	1.73	2.86				
SE	.52	.86				
Range	0–5.54	.96–8.53				

[a] Large effect (> .50) for sample size

*< .05

size into account were obtained with Friedman's (1968, p. 245) correlations (r_m) and Cohen's standards (1988, p. 96). The large r_m values for the gains in the teachers' skill scores provide additional confidence in the findings.[40]

Correlation between the time participants spent with the CD and their post-CD skill scores was also examined. The relatively small relationship ($r = .33$) suggests that their gains in skills were not influenced by the time they spent with the CD. Some of the participants may have been experienced teachers who mastered the game quickly. Others may have played longer because they enjoy computer games. Still others (possibly inexperienced teachers or those less comfortable with computer games) may have needed extended time to master the game. Future studies are needed to explore the extent to which these variables influence time needed with the program.

Effects on the Students

As the teachers' management skills increased, both the frequency of negative student responses and instances of ignoring of students by teachers declined significantly. The pre-CD baselines of 1-minute time-samples reflected a total of 435 negative student responses to the participants' strategies—an average of 12 instances per teacher during a 30-minute observation. Post-CD time samples revealed a total of 213 instances of negative responses by students—a 50% decrease, for an average of 6 per teacher (Table 7.2). Among the 393 preschool children, instances of negative behavior decreased by 64%, by 55% among the 203 elementary school students, and by 28% among the 118 secondary school students. Although the gains of this latter group were not statistically significant, the practical significance of this decrease in negative behavior among older students, some with severe behavioral disabilities, in a 2-week period is notable.[41]

Another interesting finding in these studies is the significant decrease in the frequency with which these teachers ignored their students' behavior after using *PEGS* (Table 7.3). The early childhood teachers decreased their ignoring of children by 90% and the elementary school teachers by 47%. In contrast, there was a nonsignificant change in frequency of ignoring students among secondary school teachers.

Table 7.2

Students' Negative Responses Decrease Significantly After Teachers Use a *PEGS* CD-ROM Program[a]

Negative Student Responses	Pre-*PEGS*	Post-*PEGS*	% Change[b]	t	p	r_m
Early childhood students (*n* = 393)						
Mean per teacher	4.14	1.50		1.76	.05*	.44[c]
SD	5.64	1.95				
SE	1.51	.52				
Range	0–19	0–6				
Total negative responses	58	21	−64%			
Elementary school students (*n* = 203)						
Mean per teacher	24.08	10.75		2.34	.02*	.58[d]
SD	36.20	20.91				
SE	10.45	6.03				
Range	0–104	0–64				
Total negative responses	289	129	−55%			

(continues)

Table 7.2 *Continued.*

Students' Negative Responses Decrease Significantly After Teachers Use a *PEGS* CD-ROM Program[a]

Negative Student Responses	Pre-*PEGS*	Post-*PEGS*	% Change[b]	t	p	r_m
Middle/high school students (*n* = 118)						
Mean per teacher	8.00	5.73		.71	.25	.22
SD	18.09	10.96				
SE	5.45	3.31				
Range	0–61	0–30				
Total negative responses	88	63	−28%			

[a] Observation time 5 30 minutes per teacher

[b] Decrease is desired

[c] Moderate effect (. .30) for sample size

[d] Large effect size (. .50)

*p < .05

Table 7.3

Teachers Ignore Students Significantly Less Often After Using a *PEGS* CD-ROM Program

Teacher	Pre-*PEGS*	Post-*PEGS*	% Change[a]	t	p	r_m
Early childhood (*n* = 14)						
M	3.43	.36		2.00	.03*	.48[c]
SD	6.08	.84				
SE	1.63	.22				
Range	0–17	0–3				
Total ignoring	48	5	−90%			
Elementary school (*n* − 12)						
M	10.00	5.33		2.12	.03*	.54[d]
SD	8.68	5.61				
SE	2.50	1.62				
Range	0–28	1–14				
Total ignoring	120	64	−47%			
Middle/high school (*n* = 11)						
M	12.09	12.73		.15	.40	.05
SD	10.67	9.25				
SE	3.22	2.79				
Range	0–39	0–29				
Total ignoring	133	140	+5%			

[a] Decrease is desired

[c] Moderate effect (> .30) for sample size

[d] Large effect (> .50)

*p < .05

Another study by Grizzard (2004) in third- and fourth-grade classrooms used the same observational procedures and found statistically significant increases in the skill scores for 18 teachers using *PEGS*. The teachers in schools with low and high socioeconomic designations improved their skill scores at approximately the same rate. Initially high levels of negative responses from students decreased dramatically. The initial range of negative student responses was 0 to 15 instances at the school with low socioeconomic status, and a range of 0 to 3 instances after the teachers received *PEGS* training. In contrast, at the school with high socioeconomic designation, the range of negative student response was 0 to 2 initially, with no instances of negative student responses observed after training.

Follow-up research with randomly selected subjects is now needed for greater precision in determining who can benefit from *PEGS*. For example, there may be differences among the practices of beginning and experienced teachers. Prior experience, existing skills, and educational levels should be studied to determine if similar carryover effects occur. Precise analysis of variations in time spent with the CD could enhance understanding of the time needed with the CD to achieve maximum effectiveness in the classroom. Additionally, there should be an examination of possible shifts in management strategies used by teachers at the beginning of a school year as opposed to later in the year when students and teachers have spent an extended time together. Furthermore, analysis of the interaction effects among multiple characteristics of teachers and students might be considered in evaluating the quality of classroom applications of the strategies.[42]

Conclusions About the Effectiveness of *PEGS*

Although the results are extremely encouraging, it should be noted that the content does not provide practice for structuring students' transitions between lessons, peer social interactions, or talking with a student in crisis. Nor is it intended to provide practice in fostering relationships among children and teachers. Similarly, specific multicultural activities and motivating materials are not identified. While these are all essential elements for a successful behavior management program, they require complex interactions beyond the scope of the graphic interactions and simulations offered in *PEGS*.

Despite these limitations, it is clear that *PEGS* offers independent skill training opportunities to educators, both teachers and assistant teachers. The benefits are summarized in Figure 7.22. It minimizes difficulties in traditional in-service training such as scheduling time for group training, the need for applied practice with direct feedback in the classroom, diverse

[42]While research with *PEGS* continues, these preliminary field trials hold promise that it is an effective, in-service training tool for independent adult learning and that it can result in significant carry over into teachers' classroom practices.

- Meets the needs of educators to use positive behavior management strategies skillfully.
- Provides teachers and assistant teachers with virtual learning experiences for independently practicing intervention strategies shown to be effective in reducing negative behavior of children.
- Offers individualized feedback about the learner's behavior management styles, thereby assisting users in independently self-monitoring and learning at their own rates.
- Fosters shared knowledge of developmentally and emotionally appropriate management strategies between general and special educators through mutual training experiences.
- Gives university students a way to practice managing difficult and disruptive student behavior before their student teaching begins.
- Facilitates coherent program coordination between educators and other child-serving agencies, thereby implementing IEPs in collaborative ways.
- Enables administrators to offer timely in-service training when new personnel or substitute teachers are employed, thereby addressing a need for repeated basic training in programs with staff turnover.
- Provides in-service training tools on an individualized basis for efficient use of supervisors' and teachers' time.
- Meets the needs of students with and without challenging behaviors for supportive learning environments in which they are willing participants.

FIGURE 7.22. Facts about the *PEGS for Teachers* CD series.

levels of skill among teachers, individual differences in their background preparation, different rates in skill acquisition, and variation in prior exposure to a range of students' behavior problems.

Additionally, *PEGS* is useful for training in the basics for beginning teachers and substitute teachers, periodic updating of skills for others, and repeated training sessions necessitated by teacher attrition and staff turnover. There is little prerequisite information needed to use it, and it requires no group instructor and no meetings, thereby avoiding numerous difficulties associated with group training. It offers guided skill practice, repeated practice, and individualized feedback. It is a highly useful approach to adult learning—a cost-effective and time-efficient way to provide opportunities for skill building in basic behavior management.[43]

[43]See Figure 5.11 in Chapter 5 for a summary of the practice experiences *PEGS for Teachers* provides.

Summary

An outline of the Developmental Therapy–Developmental Teaching inservice course content for teachers and paraprofessionals (www.hga.edu.dttp) provides a summary for self-guided skill improvement.

Phase 1: Apply DTDT in Your Classroom
- Look at the developmental and instructional needs of students from early childhood through the teen years.
- Use the DTORF–R to develop a preestablished reliability standard for a functional behavioral assessment (FBA) that identifies a student's achieved and missing academic and developmental competencies.
- Cross-reference DTORF–R results to state performance standards under NCLB/IDEA and translate them into IEP objectives to meet each student's IEP needs.
- Plan and conduct lessons to enhance students' achievement of IEP objectives.
- Document and report student change with repeated DTORF–R assessments.
- Self-assess skills needed to implement instructional and behavioral strategies effectively with students at various ages and stages of development.

Phase 2: Refine the Match Between Instructional Strategies and Individual Student Needs
- Design a behavioral intervention plan (BIP) matched to a student's assessment results.
- Select instructional and behavioral strategies that are individually, developmentally, emotionally, and culturally motivating for individual students.
- Recognize emotional needs conveyed by students' behavior (decoding).
- Implement strategies that encourage willing participation.
- Identify teacher skills that produce mentally healthy learning environments.

Phase 3: Acquire Accelerate Student Progress
- Apply principles of group dynamics to achieve IEP objectives.
- Select curriculum content that evokes enthusiastic student participation.
- Select content that can alleviate and help resolve real-life anxieties and concerns.
- Interpret student gains or losses to plan IEP adjustments and placement options.

Practice: Pick a Role and a Power Option

In practice at the end of previous chapters, you applied developmental information to one age group of students introduced in Chapter 1. Now, select one of those students from each age group. Then apply what you have learned about their developmental needs to choose the corresponding adult roles for yourself. The roles you pick should reflect each student's stage of social, emotional, and behavioral development and the information you gained from decoding the brief amount of information provided in that first chapter. Then consider which social power options you should use with each individual to make your selected role effective in guiding the student toward achieving his or her targeted objectives.

Pick a student in each age group.	What role will you use with this student?	Which social power option will you choose to foster the student's progress toward achieving objectives?
Preschool child:		
Elementary school student:		
Secondary school student:		

Getting Started in Your Own Classroom

CHAPTER

By the end of our first day [of training] we were elated: finally, a proven approach to working with troubled children and an aid to their teachers and caregivers in acquiring skills to foster their social-emotional development.... This approach shaped our entire philosophy and interventions.

Kelley Simmons-Jones
Teacher and Adoptive Parent
Therapeutic Learning Center, Lacey, WA
(personal communication, 2004)

In every classroom, each student has abilities, problems, and particular family situations and lifestyles. Some students are so well developed that they almost teach themselves. Others lack needed skills for negotiating the challenges they face every day, in and out of school. Then there are those who have social, emotional, behavioral, or learning problems. Your task as teacher is to build an effective program around each student's unique characteristics.

Developmental practices have applications whether you teach in early childhood, elementary, middle, or high school. You should find the basics easy to add to your current curriculum and instruction. The practices will also be flexible as you adapt them for your students in various school activities and programs, settings for full inclusion, partially inclusive resource rooms, or in self-contained classes (*Inclusion of Troubled Children* [Special Issue], 1994). Then, as your students make developmental gains, you will find the practices transportable and adjustable from grade to grade and stage to stage.

This chapter explains how to begin using the practices described in the previous chapters. It reviews essential content for getting started with students of any age or stage of development, in any educational setting. The first topic introduces two important considerations before you begin to use developmental practices: your own beliefs about teaching and learning, and a realistic appraisal of how much change this will require of you.

The second general topic includes the basic content needed to put developmental practices in your classroom. This section details how to gather information about your students to establish learning objectives; group students for strategic instruction; plan lessons that target the objectives; choose learning content and materials that target objectives; unify lessons around a central theme; use reading and writing lessons to accelerate competence; and structure teaching for an effective lesson. The chapter ends with suggestions about how you might go about extending developmental practices with schoolwide implementation.

Although the chapter focuses specifically on applications in general and special education classrooms, the same processes apply in child care and community mental health settings. Parents who are home schooling should also find useful applications. When practices are developmentally focused and used by parents, teachers, or therapists consistently, in the same way,

[1]Developmental practices can be used in any program for students, with or without disabilities, who need instruction to gain social and emotional competencies and increasingly responsible behavior.

you will have the best chance for effectively meeting your students' educational, emotional, and developmental needs—a solid foundation for responsible behavior.[1]

Before You Begin

Consider Your Basic Beliefs About Teaching and Learning

There is no single "right way" to begin. However, there should be compatibility between your beliefs about the educational process, your personal mission as a teacher, and the practices you use. Compare your ideas with the four basic beliefs summarized in Figure 8.1 and described below. These are guiding principles for this Developmental Therapy–Developmental Teaching approach to teaching and learning. Be certain that there is a fit with your own beliefs and teaching style.

- **Belief 1:** Focus on students' individual strengths.
- **Belief 2:** Follow developmental guidelines.
- **Belief 3:** Provide lessons that bring pleasure and success.
- **Belief 4:** Make school experiences positive and individually relevant.

FIGURE 8.1. Consider four basic beliefs about successful teaching and learning with this developmental approach.

Belief 1: Focus on Strengths

A strength-based view of students fosters their self-esteem, encourages behavior that is healthy and typical, and promotes their identification with positive values, rather than negative ones.[2]

[2]Positive learning experiences that bring satisfaction and success strengthen a young person's identity as *one who can succeed.*

How can this belief affect a student's program? Adults often generalize about a child being a "bad kid," viewing most of the child's behavior as "difficult" while overlooking age-appropriate behavior. If a child is labeled this way, positive aspects of behavior frequently go unnoticed. This type of bias affects how children view themselves as unsuccessful losers with limited potential. In contrast, an instructional program that focuses on teaching to their strengths promotes a view of students as participants who are making contributions and using acceptable behavior, thus shifting attitudes to a celebration of competence.

Belief 2: Follow Developmental Guidelines

Typical development follows a predictable and orderly pattern, with biosocial factors and previous experiences contributing to the uniqueness of each student's journey along this developmental path.[3]

[3]A teacher can be effective in promoting learning by following benchmarks for typically developing peers as guideposts, while remaining sensitive to each student's individual pattern of development and the cultural values of family and community.

How can this belief affect a student's program? Students who are instructed inappropriately for their current stage of development frequently become bored, rebel, or disconnect from participation. If too little is expected, a program maintains a student at a plateau. This can happen when a program is not changed after a student is successful and demonstrates mastery of a task. An example is the young child who has learned to stack blocks and is allowed to continue stacking blocks each day without a challenge to explore new play materials. Without new learning experiences, the child may remain at the old level of performance, and progress is not likely. At the other extreme, if too much is expected, children are less able to meet demands placed upon them; they experience failure after failure and may simply give up. In contrast, when programs are planned to reflect each individual's unique pattern of development (strengths and gaps) while also following the general course of typical development, the comfortable, familiar ways of responding are blended with new ideas and new challenges, within students' abilities to grasp. This stimulates growth and progress.

Belief 3: Provide Pleasure and Success

Positive changes in behavior occur when students' efforts bring personally satisfying results. Students' willingness to continue to participate in acceptable ways depends upon their anticipation that the task will have satisfactory results.

How can this belief affect a student's program? It seems obvious that success produces success. But look at the number of negative experiences children and teens have in their schools, homes, and neighborhoods. If experiences are confusing, difficult, meaningless, or failure producing, students tend to avoid participating. In contrast, if experiences are pleasurable and successful, they will be motivated to participate and keep trying. When recognized for each accomplishment, students feel the pleasure of success. The more often they experience pleasure and success, the more likely they are to continue to focus on the part of themselves that others see as acceptable or desirable. As a result, students continue to focus their energies to accomplish even more when they see themselves as having done something valued by others, especially when it also is personally satisfying.

Belief 4: Make School Experiences Relevant

Students willingly participate in learning experiences that have personal and cultural value. Lessons have relevance for students when connected to their experiences with family, peers, and significant adults, both in class and away from school.

How can this belief affect a student's Program? If schoolwork fails to connect with students' real-life concerns and values, contradicts their families' cultural standards, or is seen as irrelevant, there is little incentive for them to become involved. In contrast, students willingly participate when instruction has relevance for their own unique experiences. But to build confidence and competence, teachers must also acknowledge students' gains in responsible behavior and socioemotional maturation. The result is invested student participation, generalization, and transfer of learning to new situations.[4]

These four basic beliefs emphasize every student's capability to acquire valued, success-producing behavior. They commit educators to personalized learning strategies within a group context. The beliefs also recognize the importance of culturally sensitive teaching. This requires instruction that is in harmony with a student's personal needs, peers and family members, cultural expectations, and the demands made of the student by others. When these beliefs are followed, there are positive outcomes for students. As a foundation for how you teach, these beliefs offer an anchored approach for guiding students to willingly engage in learning (McCarty & Quirk, 2003). If you and your teaching team share similar beliefs about teaching and learning, and these beliefs are consistent with those of Developmental Therapy–Developmental Teaching, there will be a good fit.

[4]When culturally sensitive practices are a part of all lessons and management strategies, students respond.

How Fully Do You Want To Experience Change?

Before you begin applying developmental practices in your classroom, give thought to how intensely you want to immerse yourself. Be realistic about how much change you want to experience. Do you want to make radical or rapid changes in your teaching style? Or do you want to expand your skills gradually? Consider also the characteristics of your students. How much and how rapidly can they adjust to new procedures?

The gradual "add on" approach is the easiest way to start. Pick just one of the basic topics such as assessment of developmental competencies (the DTORF–R); lessons, curriculum materials, and activities; decoding behavior; positive behavior management; or teachers' roles that meet students' developmental needs. Review the chapter that describes the area you select.

Then, give it a try in your classroom and observe the results. As you become comfortable with one topic, gradually add another and, again, observe your students' responses. A slow approach offers opportunities to thoroughly explore each dimension and to gradually blend it into your own teaching style.

The "insertion" option is a slightly more difficult way to begin. With this approach, provide Developmental Therapy–Developmental Teaching in 1 period a day for a single group of students. This requires learning to apply all of the components with that group. Begin by learning to use the DTORF–R accurately to assess each student. With individual learning objectives identified, pull together all available information about the students to understand their emotional and developmental needs (decoding behavior), and provide lessons and activities to meet the selected objectives. Also include stage-appropriate behavior management, and practice the suggested role options and various social power bases to you. In time, you will see that even the 1-hour-a-day approach will produce positive changes in the students and in your teaching style.

The "infusion" option is the most complex but flexible way to get started. The process involves getting foundation knowledge about how children's personalities develop and how life experiences, including school, impact their learning. This information will help you to understand the significance of the developmental milestones in the DTORF–R, and why they must be included as learning objectives for your students. Begin to apply the many components of Developmental Therapy–Developmental Teaching simultaneously. With persistent practice, support and feedback from others, and background understanding of why you are doing what you do, developmental applications will become an automatic part of your classroom style. You will be able to give reasons why the applications work with the students you teach. And, you will notice your own skills expanding as you design new learning experiences that are developmentally and emotionally appropriate for each student and manage difficult classroom behavior in positive ways.

As you consider which approach works best for you, think also of the learning climate in your school, the general curriculum already in place, standards for achievement and conduct, attitudes toward students, and achievement requirements. Support from administrators and supervisors is essential. When they back your efforts, your task will be easier. The same applies if you are part of a teaching team with a support teacher. Teaching is a team effort. To introduce a developmental dimension in your program, your teaching team needs to sign on, too![5]

[5] Lessons have relevance for students when connected to their experiences with family, peers, and significant adults—both in class and away from school.

Developmental Practices in Your Classroom

Gather Information About Students To Establish Learning Objectives

Once you have made the decision to use developmental practices, several planning steps are necessary when teaching students of any age and stage of development. Begin by reviewing the ages of the students in your classroom. This age reference will give you the characteristics and competencies of a student's age peers. Age offers clues for ways of motivating students and suggests how long a student has had to learn about school and life. It also indicates how peers may influence the student. With increasing age there is generally increasing peer influence. Keep your students' ages in mind as you gather information to plan their instructional programs.

Next, determine if your students have each achieved the competencies for DOING, SAYING, RELATING, and THINKING needed for their age group. The *S–E–B Quick Profile* (see Chapter 3) can be of help in determining competencies as the profile identifies the sequential goals for competence in these learning domains. Each student has an individual pattern of achievement and lags in acquiring these competencies. Use individual profiles as the foundation for planning your teaching and your students' learning. Also, review school records and information from other evaluations and test results. It is extremely important to have as much information as possible to understand how to assist students in achieving their needed competencies.[6]

Functional Assessment

If most of your students are making good progress in acquiring these general competencies, the *S–E–B Quick Profile* may be a sufficient base to begin planning. However, if a student has failed to achieve a general age–stage competence, and there is a notable discrepancy between the student's performance and that of age peers, a DTORF–R assessment is essential. Accurate assessment of each student's unique developmental pathway reveals which competencies are present and which need to be developed. The team assessment procedure is described in detail in Chapter 3. The DTORF–R identifies specific learning objectives, developmentally sequenced for the student. These selected objectives are the target for your strategic instruction and developmental practices. Figure 8.2 summarizes the initial process, which is done in collaboration with the student's other teachers, parents, and those who provide special student services.[7]

- Review each student's school records.
- Collect additional home, neighborhood, and clinical information, if available.
- Make a preliminary estimate of each student's individual competencies (with the *S–E–B Quick Profile*).
- Prepare a baseline DTORF–R for each student (with their other teachers and parents).
- Identify specific learning objectives from their DTORF–R.
- Compile a group DTORF–R.

FIGURE 8.2. Begin with assessments of your students. Assessment is described in Chapter 3.

For students in need of special education, the information gathering process includes psychological, educational, observational, clinical, and developmental assessments. Parents and teachers are equal partners in the assessment and planning process (Rock, 2000). They work together to identify individual program goals and expectations. They identify the student's strengths and vulnerabilities with the DTORF–R, considering achievement, cultural experiences, developmental trajectories, anxieties, interests, values, and concerns (see Chapter 4).

The resulting information is used to plan an Individualized Education Program (IEP), Individualized Family Service Plan (IFSP), or Individual Transition Plan (ITP), with services provided in a group setting, in a separate room, or in an inclusive program with age peers. The amount of time scheduled in these various settings depends on a student's age, developmental stage, and the severity of the needs. Learning objectives for the IEP, IFSP, or ITP determine the schedule, group assignments, and time requirements.

A functional behavioral assessment (FBA) may also be needed when a student's conduct in school is so disruptive that special planning is required (Murdick, Gartin, & Stockall, 2003). This requirement is established by law. An FBA is the basis for a behavioral intervention plan (BIP). Both the FBA and the BIP are then folded into a developmental assessment to assure that the behavioral interventions are developmentally appropriate for that student. In this way, the resulting IEP contains personalized learning objectives for achieving competencies and targets objectives for increasingly responsible behavior. This process is described in Figure 8.3.

- Review management strategies for the students' developmental stage(s).
- Identify students who need targeted intervention and select strategies to focus on achieving their DTORF–R objectives.
- Anticipate students who may need intensive intervention and plan developmentally appropriate strategies for their DTORF–R objectives.
- Consider how a student's disruptive behavior may be serving as an emotional defense.
- Analyze group dynamics, roles, and social power of individual students.
- Determine each student's current view of responsibility (the "X factor").
- Plan with other teachers on your team to be consistent in using the selected strategies for each student.
- Anticipate how you and your team will manage severe behavioral problems and individual students in crisis.

FIGURE 8.3. Tasks for developing a behavior management plan for your class. (Review Chapter 5.)

Planning

After you complete the developmental assessments and understand something of the students' life experiences, feelings, concerns, and current situations, it is time to plan strategic instruction. To begin the planning process, summarized in Figure 8.4, prepare a summary of the selected learning objectives for every student in the group. The group DTORF–R form is helpful way to do this (see Chapter 3). It will highlight objectives that students share. Equally important, it will identify objectives that are uniquely different among the students. This information enables a teacher to target precise instruction for individuals as part of a group process.[8]

[8]At the end of this chapter, there is a format for organizing and summarizing information to use in planning strategic instruction for each student.

- Target your students' individual DTORF–R objectives.
- Make a daily class schedule with time to focus on all of their selected objectives.
- Organize small group sessions for students with similar objectives to work together.
- Include daily lessons for individual objectives in each of the four competency areas.
- Design lesson plans in academic subjects to capture students' interests and concerns.
- Select materials and activities to encourage participation by every student in the group.
- Plan weeklong units around unifying themes for sustaining their interest in learning.
- Arrange your classroom spaces and furniture to accommodate teaching to the objectives.
- Consider the minimum number of classroom rules you plan to use and state them in positive terms.
- As their teacher, review the role you need to provide for their developmental stages.

FIGURE 8.4. Plan your developmental instruction strategically. (Refer to Chapters 2, 4, and 6.)

Plan carefully with your teaching team how students should be grouped for instruction. Consider how their objectives can be addressed in the daily schedule and within the academic curriculum. Look for motivating themes that can provide continuity among lessons for an entire week. To engage and sustain students' involvement, plan lessons that build on their existing competencies and values. Consider materials and activities that will hold everyone's attention. And, make certain that each individual will have success with the lessons.

Plan how your teaching team will convey the lead and support roles (see Chapter 7). Remember that the lead teacher provides motivating instruction and assures the well-being of the entire group. The support teacher responds to individuals when their participation lags or they are in need of special assistance to continue participating. All members of the teaching team have responsibility for creating a classroom climate of psychological security and optimism. This environment happens when there are reasonable, motivating expectations, built on skills students already have. It requires lessons designed to be achieved with success and respect for each student's effort. Every student should have the conviction that *I can do it!*—in every lesson, every activity, every day.[9]

Group Students for Strategic Instruction

Traditionally, the most commonly used criteria in grouping students for instruction have been age, grade, academic achievement, intelligence, or special abilities. A criticism of grouping by age or grade is that individual differences can become so great that instructional needs of individuals are overlooked. Students who lack prerequisite skills cannot keep up. Putting them in a group with others who have more advanced skills may leave them feeling that it is impossible to participate successfully or be part of the group. Problems also invariably arise when students are so far behind their peers that successful participation in group activities with their peers is unlikely. For them, the peer group often produces social isolation. This can lead to more negative responses as psychological defense. When this happens repeatedly, it creates a climate of insecurity and distrust among group members, and the student is increasingly rejected or isolated by the group. Developmentally based groups offer a solution to this problem.[10]

To plan developmentally based groups for instruction, consider two requirements: (a) there are students who can be acceptable behavioral models in the group, and (b) the group offers genuine opportunity for a student to be a successful, contributing member. The group DTORF–R shows which learning objectives they share and which objectives reveal their diversity. Also consider group dynamics and the roles your students have in their peer group. The more information you have about how they interact with each other, the more precise your grouping decisions will be. Positive group dynamics lead to successful lessons, especially when students with similar learning objectives are grouped together and lessons are designed for success by everyone.[11]

Finally, do not expect all group members to achieve at the same rate. As one student masters targeted objectives, consider assignment to a new group. In a different group, with students at a more advanced developmental level, a student has new peer role models and greater learning opportunities. By regrouping students frequently as tasks change, you can move students from group to group without having one individual feel singled out.

Developmental Groups for Children in Early Childhood, Preschool, and Childcare Settings

In typical early childhood programs, children are gaining Stage Two social, communication, emotional, and behavioral skills. When they need no special assistance to continue making

[9]Educational success usually can be traced to precise planning by teachers and parents, based on their knowledge of how a student is developing. This information is the foundation for developmental instruction to achieve missing competencies.

[10]Be cautious about grouping students who have behavior problems with students who may be at risk for problems themselves.

[11]The group DTORF–R summary is in Chapter 3 and information about group dynamics is in Chapter 4.

progress, grouping them with others of the same age provides a natural developmental climate for learning. However, if young children are at risk, have special needs, or fail to maintain developmental progress, they benefit from concentrated instruction in brief, pull-out groups daily, in addition to less intensely focused learning experiences in larger, inclusive groups. In these inclusive programs, teachers also use developmental practices and focus on the same learning objectives in the inclusive setting during the remainder of the day (Buysse, Skinner, & Grant, 2001).[12]

[12]Refer to Stages One and Two in Chapter 2 for descriptions of instructional needs of children during early childhood.

For group experiences to be effective, a group of about five or six young children with special needs is about the maximum number for an inclusive program. With toddlers just beginning Stage Two, and with older students who are developmentally in this stage, plan to spend about 25% of the time on individual tasks. Use the remaining time for group activities to teach skills for interacting successfully with each other. Limit an activity to about 10 minutes to maintain peak involvement. Then end it before interest fades. The length of time for an activity increases as students mature and attention spans increase. At the most, limit the total small group time to 30 minutes with several short, structured activities and highly motivating materials. During that time, alternate between quiet and active learning experiences, with little or no waiting for turns.

Unison activities promote simultaneous, active participation by everyone in a group. Unison activities also avoid extended periods in which one child has a long turn while the others have "down time," waiting to participate in the lesson. Unison activities also promote learning by imitating others who are participating—an effective way to acquire new skills. At this stage of development, children can expand their vocabulary, social skills, and success with materials by imitating others. A small, developmentally based group provides the most focused way to provide these opportunities.

Developmental Groups for Students in Elementary School

During the first three grades of elementary school, students are typically in the process of acquiring Stage Three competencies. Daily inclusion in a regular education program is essential for their progress. The benefits are clear: peer modeling, participation in the general curriculum, and practice with new social and communication skills. However, it is often difficult to provide strategic instruction to meet individual needs of some students in large classes. Small group instruction provides a flexible solution. By grouping students with similar targeted learning objectives, you will find you can target your instruction to be directly applicable for each of them.[13]

[13]Refer to Chapter 2 for a description of students in Stage Three.

If you have students who have failed to achieve the competencies in the previous stage, they will need instruction that continues to focus on readiness skills. You may also have students who are less delayed, but need targeted instruction to achieve Stage Three objectives. Consider having at least two groups for these students—one for teaching Stage Two skills and the other for Stage Three. As students gain competencies, you may find that you can shift the focus of the groups to coincide with their changing instructional needs—by regrouping for beginning Stage Three and advanced Stage Three objectives.

Time spent for small group instruction will vary from 15 minutes for a single lesson to an hour when several learning experiences are provided for intensive and sustained intervention. Be sensitive to how long your students can pay attention with interest. Students just beginning Stage Three usually have sufficient attention span for productive work that lasts about 15 minutes, whereas students completing Stage Three can maintain a high level of attention in a lesson for as long as 30 minutes. By limiting your small group instruction to brief periods, there will also be time for the students to participate in the larger, inclusive group activities, where developmental practices continue but in a broader and less intensive way.

In a developmental group for students in Stage Three, divide the time equally between individual assignments and group activities. Independent tasks allow them to work at their own pace, while group lessons provide the opportunity for collaborative learning in academic and creative endeavors. Both types of lessons can teach traditional in-seat behavior such as sitting quietly, following directions, working independently, and answering questions when called upon. However there is equal need for students at this stage to experience success in group interactions, where they earn to regulate their own behavior. These skills carry over into less structured situations such as the playground, cafeteria, bus, restroom, gym, and halls. For this reason, systematically include both structured and unstructured activities as you plan lessons for the group. Base your decisions about the portion of time allotted for individual and group instruction on each student's individual learning objectives. Many objectives specify new skills associated with interactions with others. Students usually do not gain such skills from solitary assignments. Also weigh the gains to be made by learning with typically developing peers in inclusive groups.[14]

Developmental Groups for Students in Upper Elementary and Middle School Grades

Typical students in upper elementary school are beginning to achieve Stage Four competencies, while students in middle school are achieving advanced competencies in this same stage. There will also be a few students experiencing such difficulties with social, emotional, or behavioral development that they will still be in Stages Two or Three. This three-stage spread (Stages Two, Three, and Four) is not unusual in upper elementary and middle school. It reflects the range of severity of students' problems. For example, older students who have only progressed to Stage Two usually have severe disabilities such as psychosis, thought disorder, autism, severe passive aggression, or severe depression. They may be violent toward themselves or others, and often are far behind their peers in academic skills. In these classes, there will also be (a) students with mild social or behavioral problems; (b) those who are experiencing a severe transient crisis in their lives such as death, divorce, illness, or abuse; (c) those with special needs for short periods of intensive help; (d) those with moderate to severe delays in achieving needed competencies; and (e) students from special education programs who are in need of a general education program for part of the day.[15] Providing effective grouping for students with this broad range in social, emotional, and behavioral skills requires both small, developmentally based groups and opportunities for associations with age peers in larger, inclusive classes. Use Figure 8.5 to identify key characteristics to consider as you group students in upper elementary school for targeted instruction.

The range of time allocated to small group instruction in upper elementary and middle school is as varied as the diversity in students' development. Some students benefit from a fully integrated program in their regular school. Lessons that are about 30 minutes long generally hold their sustained attention. Of course, some lessons may be shorter or extend for longer periods of time.

Other students need as little as one 45-minute small group daily where they can receive targeted instruction, usually provided in several short lessons during the session. There also will be students developmentally in Stages Two and Three needing sustained, intensive intervention. They may require 2-hour, half-day, or full-day programs. In a 2-hour period, six different

[14]In a small group, lessons should include time for both academic and creative learning, individually and as a group.

[15]Chapter 2 contains descriptions of the developmental diversity and instructional needs among students who are typically in Stage Four and in upper elementary or middle school.

Students who have mastered Stage Three competencies have learned that

- they can obtain approval from adults,
- they can make choices that bring benefits,
- adults have authority to set and enforce rules of conduct,
- there are rules of conduct that must be followed,
- positive behavior produces respect from others,
- personal ideas can make a contribution,
- they can be accepted by peers, and
- they can participate in a group without being embarrassed.

Now in Stage Four, students are learning these basics of being a successful group member:

- Behavior is a personal responsibility.
- Some rules can be made and changed by group consensus.
- Other people deserve fair treatment and consideration.
- Others may have views different from one's own.
- There are many choices to be made with varied consequences.
- They can make and keep friends.
- They can be a valued friend and group member.

FIGURE 8.5. Key characteristics to consider when grouping students who are in Stages Three or Four.

lessons can be scheduled, averaging about 20 minutes each. Plan their instructional time as you would any other class—by instructional objectives. Then, watch for the opportunity to regroup the students as they show progress. Additionally, be prepared to support them as they try to maintain themselves for the remainder of the day in the inclusive program. Flexible groups allow you to respond to individuals who suddenly need crisis support or guidance while participating in a general education class.

Developmental Groups for High School Students

Most typically developing high school students are beginning to achieve Stage Five competencies. For them, developmental practices are simply woven into the general education program daily, as a part of each class. However, it is not unusual to find a three-stage spread in the development of troubled teenagers. Some will have only reached Stage Four, indicating moderate delay in achieving needed competencies. For them, targeted interventions are needed. There will also be a few students with a range of moderate to severe problems who will be in Stage Three. These students require intensive intervention, but they are also able to participate in selected general education classes, although they present unique challenges to their teachers and will have difficulties with peer relationships.[16]

Because of this wide range of development and program needs for students in high school, both inclusive and small group placements are necessary. Research shows that inclusion is beneficial for some students in special education when teachers spend more than 75% of their time in direct instruction and interacting with their students, especially those with special needs (Wallace, Anderson, Bartholomay, & Hupp, 2002).

Some small groups may also be formed in a general education class. Assign students to these groups according to learning objectives and the task. Then, reconfigure the groups as les-

[16]Refer to Chapter 2 for learning characteristics and instructional needs of high school students who have reached Stage Five in their development. The chapter also contains descriptions of teenagers who have not yet reached Stage Five.

sons change. For example, consider having two developmentally focused groups—one for students needing to acquire missing competencies from Stages Two and Three and another for students working on competencies for Stages Four and Five. Then, as progress is made during the school year, regroup students according to the objectives they achieve.

Students with greater developmental delays may require groups that provide a more intense focus on their stage characteristics and targeted objectives, usually in Stage Three. Only one such class period a day may be sufficient for some of these students. Others should have small group instruction twice a day, once a week, or on a drop-by basis. There are others who benefit from a two-period time block, half-day, or full-day programs. For those in the latter programs, different small groups can be formed throughout their daily schedule to obtain the best fit with group members who share similar learning objectives. These students have regular homeroom teachers and usually spend at least half of each day in inclusive settings where developmental practices provide support in subject areas where they can be successful. The IEP details how their schedules should be designed and which learning objectives should be targeted in each individual's program.

A well-designed, hour-long group session can provide considerable help to a troubled teen. A small group fosters exchanges of ideas and different points of view. It also provides a setting where an individual's interpersonal skills can be polished. Many times, these special peer groups are the means for students to "find themselves"—to validate their new emerging identities. This is where they also can deal with the remnants of old, unresolved anxieties.

While teenagers can typically stay focused and involved in a lesson for a full 45 minutes to an hour, it is important to be systematic about providing a variety of learning experiences during that time. If only 1 hour is available, include at least three essential activities during that time. Spend about a third of the time in independent work and another third in group discussions, sharing issues and concerns that are important to them. Group support can help each individual find solutions. Divide the remaining time between planning together, discussing events that affect the group, and having a wrap-up session.

Figure 8.6 is a summary of guidelines for building and maintaining a successful group. It is important to recognize that small group sessions do not take the place of naturally developed friendships and peer relationships that typically occur during the teen years. There is insufficient time in a small group schedule to build genuine friendships. Relationships are usually temporary, but are an important step in practicing new skills in relating to others. Close friendships and other significant relationships will probably happen in other groups (homeroom groups, clubs, home, sports, neighborhood gatherings, and leisure groups). However, it is important to have a "drop-in" arrangement for students seeking advice or guidance and to be available for those in crisis.

- Emphasize the value of the group.
- Encourage noncompetitive achievements of individuals.
- Clarify the individual member's responsibility to the group.
- Encourage group verbal interactions (communication skills).
- Communicate expectations (structure, goals, objectives, procedures, contracts).
- Maintain standards that have been set.
- Comment on students' positive behavior toward each other.
- Minimize negative labeling.
- Protect individuals' psychological space.
- Encourage acceptance of individuals' constructive self-disclosure.
- Stop destructive self-disclosure.
- Reflect feeling conveyed by talk or actions (interpretation).
- Confront group behavior that has negative consequences (reality).
- Guide the group in positive evaluation of individuals' efforts in the group.

FIGURE 8.6. Use these guidelines to build and maintain a successful group. *Note.* From *Interpersonal Helping Skills,* by E. K. Marshall and P. D. Kurtz, 1982, p. 327. Copyright 1982 by Jossey–Bass. Adapted with permission.

Provide Lessons with Content and Materials That Target Objectives

Nowhere is the interaction between behavior, cognition, motivation, and emotions more evident than in students' responses to lesson content, activities, and materials. Figure 8.7, which is an image from the CD-ROM that accompanies this text, illustrates this point. Several students may react to the same material in very different ways. The significance of the content is a matter of how it is interpreted by an individual, connecting to past experiences. This can dramatically influence how a student responds.

The task is to have sufficient understanding of your students to help them acquire the targeted learning objectives. This requires careful and systematic planning. Activities and materials play a big part in how successful a student will be. Although effective planning is time consuming and requires considerable effort, the dividends are well worth the effort and time.

Begin by identifying the specific objectives and the needed prerequisite skills. Then sequence the steps a student must go through to master a lesson. A task analysis is helpful in doing this. Anticipate the responses of individual students to each step. Next, consider which activities, materials, and special conditions will make mastery of the steps easy, rapid, and pleasurable for each student. Look for ways to include several similar learning objectives within the same lesson because students have the opportunity to work on several objectives simultaneously.

Content and materials should have the explicit purpose of motivating students to achieve specific learning objectives in the least possible amount of time. Therefore, content and materials also should be suited to the developmental skills of each student in the group, so that everyone can participate and be personally successful. Effective instructional materials encourage participation and involvement by everyone. The result should be a positive outcome for each student. Success should not depend upon the teacher's providing a reward, but should have an intrinsic value. The student should believe that, "There's something in it for me!"

Well-chosen materials are the catalysts for catching students' attention and sustaining their involvement at every age and developmental stage. Materials should have motivational elements and intrinsic qualities that do not need much salesmanship to interest the students. Generally, materials that hold the interest of all students in a group are more useful than those that interest only a few. Materials also should be selected for their potential to elicit active, not

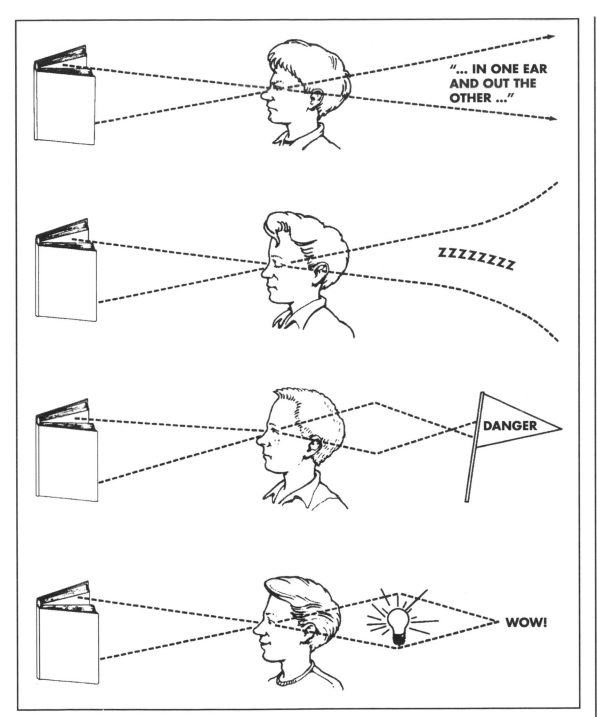

FIGURE 8.7. Same material, four meanings, four behaviors.

passive, participation. When a material also allows for individual exploration, it encourages students to experiment with ways to use it creatively. For example, merely listening to a story is not as effective as being asked to respond, role-play an event, create a new ending, describe characters, or design a new sequence of events. As you select specific materials, ask yourself questions such as those listed in Figure 8.8.

Some materials can be used with students of any age when modified to the developmental characteristics of students in their particular stages. Other materials are effective only for a particular stage or with a specific age group. Figure 8.9 shows how learning materials differ when adjusted to the developmental needs of students. Those in lower stages need simple, manipulative, concrete materials that teach basic skills. These skills become the building blocks

Effective materials are rated "Yes" on each of these ten questions.

- Does the material have qualities that attract your students?
- Does the material contribute to mastery of a particular objective?
- Does the material provide opportunities to work on several objectives simultaneously?
- Do your students have the prerequisite skills needed for a satisfactory outcome?
- Can the material be used by all members of the group?
- Does the material encourage socialization among students?
- Will the material expand their language and social communication skills?
- Can students use the material independently?
- Will the outcome be something each student can value?
- Will the result provide a sense of accomplishment?

FIGURE 8.8. Questions to ask about materials for students of any age or stage.

	Stage One	Stage Two	Stage Three	Stage Four	Stage Five
Purpose of material	Mobilize responses.	Stimulate individual skills.	Increase individual effectiveness in groups.	Increase understanding of others.	Explore broad human issues and personal choices.
Type of material	Sense-arousing properties.	Exploratory, semi-abstract activities.	Regular school materials, adapted as needed.	Regular school materials, adapted as needed.	High school materials, adapted as needed.
Content	Tangible associations with nurture and comfort.	Exploratory associations from personal experience.	Emphasis on group and team collaboration.	References to ideas and values of self and others.	References to universal values and principles.
Source of control	Teacher organizes and controls materials.	Teacher assists individuals in control of materials.	Teacher encourages group to use materials cooperatively.	Group develops and controls materials.	Individual responsibility for group and independent materials.

FIGURE 8.9. Use this chart for developmentally targeted learning materials. See Chapter 5 for discussion of teachers' control of materials as a management strategy.

for higher, more abstract, and more expressive skills at later stages, which require materials with fewer manipulative elements but content that is more complex.

Your students' development will also affect the way you manage and control learning materials. For children in Stage One, it is necessary to control and organize most learning materials for them. They need to be taught acceptable ways to use and enjoy materials. They also need assistance in learning to return things to the proper place at the end of an activity. As their skills increase, gradually shift management and control of materials from yourself to them. By Stage Four, students should be able to select needed materials, plan how to use them, regulate their use, plan ahead to obtain or replace materials to complete a lesson in the future, evaluate the process, and store materials properly at the end of a lesson.

Unify Lessons Around a Central, Motivating Theme

For students in any stage of development, lessons should be connected by a motivating theme that unifies the content during an entire day or week. This allows students to expand and generalize what they have learned from one lesson to the next. Sometimes a theme can reflect a school-wide interest or an academic topic, but most effective themes resonate around specific characteristics of the students in a particular group and developmental stage. Refer to Figure 8.10 for characteristics of effective unifying themes. See Appendix C for a summary of major motivational systems associated with each stage of development.

- Motivate students by building on their own experiences, ideas, interests, or feelings.
- Apply to their targeted learning objectives.
- Fit the daily schedule of lessons and curriculum topics they are studying.
- Build on their previous knowledge and skills to ensure individual and group success.
- Offer opportunities for independent, student-directed exploration within the scope of the theme.
- Have carry-over relevance beyond the classroom.
- Result in purposeful effort and invested learners.

FIGURE 8.10. Characteristics of unifying themes for effective units of study.

Selection of effective content themes comes from understanding students as individuals, their values, anxieties, previous experiences, and cultural backgrounds. Listen as they play or talk with friends during their free-time discussions about after-school and weekend activities. Notice how they choose to play, and learn about their preferences for toys, books, and games. Find out what they watch on television and what they say about what they see. Favorite group activities, movies, musicians, film stars, and sports heroes are other sources of theme material. Also seek similar information from their parents.[17]

Weave these interests into unit themes that address their unique characteristics, interests, and concerns. The closer a theme comes to students' vital interests and emotions, the greater the opportunity to connect a lesson to the realities they face every day. When a theme embodies a concern, emotional problem, fear, or developmental anxiety, it can be used to help students address their own concerns (real and imaginary), cope with them vicariously, and find resolutions. An understanding of universal symbols that evoke distinct associations among most children is helpful when searching for themes that can do this. Themes are readily available in stories from literature, the language arts, and television. Analyze the content for how the story lines, symbols, and associations meet your students' concerns and developmental anxieties: abandonment and loss of attachment, inadequacy, guilt, conflict, and identity. Then use them in the themes and lessons in ways that always offer a resolution that is comfortable and satisfying for the developmental stage of the students. Examples of themes which address developmental anxieties are in Figure 8.11.[18]

Once a general theme is selected, adapt it to the developmental stage of the group and the specific objectives for each student. Add dramatic tone to ensure that the topic holds the students' interest. Then, creatively weave the theme into daily academic lessons and extend the carryover by using variations on the theme throughout the week.

[17]With older children and teens, have discussion sessions during the first week of a school year to identify their interests, especially what they like to watch on television.

[18]Chapter 4 provides a guide for selecting themes that meet students' emotional needs and have motivating values.

Developmental Anxiety	Theme	Example in Children's Classics
Abandonment (loss of attachment)	Hunger	"Stone Soup"
	Stolen child	*Outside Over There*
	Left alone	"Hansel and Gretel"
	Evil forces	"Sleeping Beauty"
	Vast, unknown places	"Little Red Riding Hood"
	Orphan	*Bambi*
	Sibling rivalry	"Cinderella"
	Lost	*Finding Nemo;* "Little Lost Lamb"
	Angry or rejecting parent	"Snow White"
	Divorce	*The Parent Trap*
Inadequacy	Feeling unworthy	*The Little Engine That Could*
	Demanding standards	"Rumpelstiltskin"
	Overwhelming challenge	"Jack and the Beanstalk"
	On your own	"Three Little Pigs"
	Things going wrong	*Olivia; Finders Keepers*
	Being undesirable to others	"Ugly Duckling;" *Dumbo; Beauty and the Beast*
Guilt	Need to be punished	*Pinocchio*
	Out of control	*Where the Wild Things Are*
	Doing something wrong	*Sylvester and the Magic Pebble*
	Bad behavior	*The Cat in the Hat*
	Being different	*Crow Boy*
	Disappointing parents	*Sarah, Plain and Tall*
	Running away	*The Little Mermaid*
Conflict	Strive for independence	"Dick Whittington and His Cat;" *Caddie Woodlawn*
	Seeking recognition	*Black Beauty*
	Good versus evil	*Superman; Harry Potter; Lord of the Rings*
	Knowing but keeping silent	*Shiloh*
	Rewards for doing right	*Anne of Green Gables*
	Freedom from demands	*Peter Pan*
	Search for security	*Swiss Family Robinson; Island of the Blue Dolphins*
Identity	Being oneself	*Amos Fortune, Free Man*
	Self-discipline	*Treasure Island*
	Choosing to fight evil	*Star Wars*
	Compassion for others	*The Diary of Anne Frank*
	Making hard decisions	*The Giver*
	Betrayal	*The Lion King*
	Rejected love	*The Thousand and One Nights*
	Courage	*Call it Courage; I Have Lived a Thousand Years*

FIGURE 8.11. Examples of themes that reflect students' developmental anxieties. Note that age and reading levels are not addressed in these examples. This is a small sample of the numerous resources in the language arts. Content usually touches on more than one developmental anxiety, making the reading relevant to more than a single theme.

Use Reading and Writing To Accelerate Competence

Reading and writing are essential, symbolic ways to communicate. Reading opens the door to new ideas, and creative writing produces something new. These subject areas provide the means for students to gain information, express ideas, find solutions to concerns, and verify themselves as individuals who can learn and achieve. Sometimes reading and writing lessons simply bring pleasure: *Look what I can do!* Sometimes they reveal new insights for a student: *I never thought about it that way before.* Most often, they provide students with immense satisfaction in themselves: *I didn't know my ideas were that good.* In each instance, opportunities to read and to write creatively are essential for all students.[19]

When reading and writing lessons are planned with sensitivity to students' developmental characteristics *and* include a broad range of creative communication and thinking activities, academic skills increase. Perhaps even more importantly, there is a noticeable acceleration in socioemotional competence and responsible behavior. The following examples illustrate a few of the ways to use a developmental progression as you plan reading and writing lessons.[20]

Reading and Writing Readiness for Children in Early Childhood

The best readiness activities for children who are developmentally in Stage One are those that encourage pleasurable involvement with people—watching, listening, and responding. When they participate in reading readiness activities, children learn to do the following:

Listen	Talk
Look	Imitate
Respond	Pretend

In this way, very young children learn actions and sounds by imitating others. These skills lead naturally into forms of meaningful play and become building blocks for achieving more formal readiness skills.[21]

Lessons focused directly on more formalized readiness activities begin for children in Stage Two. The first and most important readiness skill they must learn is to put thoughts and actions into words. Put your emphasis on building a broad communication base for them by connecting words to experiences, ideas, events, and people. Without abundant opportunities to communicate during these preschool years, children are less likely to have the readiness skills for effective reading and writing when they enter elementary school.

Whether they begin this process by learning to use speech and movement in storybooks, play, or art materials depends upon their individual skills and interests. Experiences such as those listed in Figure 8.12 help them acquire habits of verbal spontaneity. But eventually, they

[19]Reading and writing have broad applications for fostering students' social and emotional competence. They help students understand *what is* and then to explore *what can be.*

[20]Follow a developmental sequence when you plan lessons to accelerate reading and writing skills. Chapter 2 describes how students' learning characteristics change in this progression.

[21]If an older child with special needs is in Stage One, the same competencies are relevant, but they are taught using materials appropriate for the older child's chronological age and peers.

- Create dramatic plays.
- Listen to stories in picture books.
- Imagine events.
- Tell stories with puppets.
- Role-play story characters.
- Design titles for drawings.
- Play games with letters and numbers.
- Find letters, numbers, and words in everyday places.
- Make group experience stories.
- Play games with rhyming words.
- Tell about the weather.

FIGURE 8.12. Plan readiness-to-read lessons like these for children in Stage Two.

need to expand their skills to include all of these forms of communicating. Some children in Stage Two simply need opportunities to interact in satisfying ways with other children to gain these readiness skills naturally. Other children need more structured teaching to achieve the same skills. However, they all need teaching to move them steadily forward in mastering the sequence of developmental milestones for school readiness.

As they learn associations between letters, numbers, and meanings, children in Stage Two are ready for beginning-to-read lessons. These include activities such as alphabet and number games, telling stories, drawing and painting their ideas, talking about pictures, dramatic play, and make-believe. All have important places in a Stage Two developmental curriculum. The point of these prereading lessons is to help them to organize their own thoughts into words and to share those ideas with others. These competencies are the foundation for recognizing words and understanding their intended meanings. With this, the reading process begins in earnest.

The Developmental Progression in Reading and Writing for School-Age Students

As they begin school, typical students are in Stage Three and are learning skills to be successful in reading and creative writing. This is the primary focus during the primary grades. With a third-grade academic level, they have the skills to comprehend meanings in paragraphs, and use written forms to communicate their own experiences, ideas, and feelings. To be independently successful with these skills, they need abundant and varied opportunities to use them. Writing and reading short essays, very short stories, brief book reports, letters and notes to friends, riddles, jokes, and open-ended adventure stories written for TV are a few examples of assignments to help them increase their skills. Also include other communication activities, such as those listed in Figure 8.13, in which they learn to organize their ideas for others in group role play, character games, plays, and collaborative projects.

For students in Stage Four, academic lessons are most effective when woven into group activities. Because of their motivation to participate successfully and to be accepted as respected group members, they are often willing to risk themselves in a group if they are confident of success. Involve them in selecting lesson themes, the focus for assignments, and group projects in academic subjects. This ownership sustains their interest and resolve to maintain control if provoked by others.

Reading and creative writing are natural ways to search for new ideas and to express them independently in the group. Lessons and writing formats are similar to those for students in Stage Three, but with distinctly different content. Assignments explore meaning in experiences, feelings, and problems in greater depth for themselves and with others. They learn to

---

- Construct a group story.
- Role-play characters and events.
- Pantomime ideas and messages.
- Dramatize a story.
- Read "first readers."
- Write stories with primary words.
- Read "chapter books."
- Write a book report.
- Keep a journal.
- Write letters.
- Make a code and use it to send messages to friends.
- Write reports about events and weather.

FIGURE 8.13. Accelerate reading and creative writing with activities like these for students in Stage Three.

use rules of grammar, and work on style and structure in organizing ideas into cohesive units of thought. Examples of ways to expand their skills for thinking and communicating in depth are listed in Figure 8.14. These students need abundant opportunities for a wide range of reading and creative writing lessons, such as biographies, adventure stories, news, and the Internet. Lessons are also needed to encourage writing original poetry, letters, news reports, essays, and diaries.

By high school, typically developing students are beginning Stage Five. Provide lessons that require written forms of communication to expand their increasingly complex understanding of themselves, others, and the global community. They need many opportunities to explore the questions, *Who am I?* and *Where do I fit in?*

Reading and creative writing are major tools for accelerating academic and cognitive competence for students in Stage Five. Examples of the types of lessons they need are found in Figure 8.15. Ideas, values, attitudes, experiences, and logic are all ingredients to be woven into reading, analysis, and creative writing assignments. For teens in this developmental stage, creative writing serves the same purposes that storybooks, puppets, storytelling, role-play, and dramatic play do for younger children. Creative writing provides a satisfying means for independent learning, self-understanding, and expansion of a behavioral repertoire.

- Read fiction and write a review.
- Analyze story characters.
- Read and write biographies.
- Read and write poetry.
- Write short stories.
- Tell a story through dance, pantomime, music, and movement improvisations.
- Explore problems and solutions with dramatic role-play.
- Write letters to the editors of newspapers and magazines.
- Write and produce newsletters.
- Write and produce vignettes for video filming.
- Research and report current events using the Internet.
- Debate issues in mock trials.
- Write and produce video info and docudrama programs.

FIGURE 8.14. Expand reading, writing, and thinking skills with lessons like these for students in Stage Four.

- Read and critique fiction and biographies.
- Read and analyze news.
- Write fiction and poetry.
- Write news articles for local papers and magazines.
- Write, produce, and act in TV programs.
- Write, produce, and act in plays.
- Prepare research reports.
- Write travel articles from Internet research.
- Intern in publishing or news offices.
- Analyze famous works of art.
- Critique popular music.
- Debate ideas.
- Research and report on controversial local issues.

FIGURE 8.15. Accelerate academic competence with lessons like these for students in Stage Five.

Adjust Reading and Writing Lessons to Individual Differences

Teachers sometimes express concern about the wide range of academic skills in groups of students. Several steps to provide for these individual differences are outlined in Figure 8.16. First, select content themes based on the most representative socialization stage for the entire group. Plan the form and length of a lesson according to the predominant academic skills of the group. Be sure each individual has the same general assignment, uniquely designed for that student's skill and motivational level. In this way, every member of the group has the same general assignment without focusing negatively on the limitations of a particular student. As the lesson begins, individualize further or restructure the task as needed for success.

Another concern of some teachers is how to respond to a student's poor academic product when there has been creative, independent effort. The work may lack adequate content or be technically below standards for spelling, grammar, or sentence structure. When responding to creative works, keep a focus on content rather than mechanics. Each assignment should be a real "turn on" for a student. Without a burning need to get involved, an assignment becomes drudgery and creative thinking fails to emerge. In time, a motivated student will master the mechanics.

- Select a topic of interest to everyone.
- Provide the title as a focus for everyone.
- Stimulate thinking about the topic with group discussion before individual writing begins.
- List key words on the chalkboard to make spelling easy.
- Limit the length of the assignment (two sentences, one paragraph, one page).
- Circulate among the students as they do their independent writing.
- Help with spelling, talk over a point, or remotivate a student who runs out of ideas.
- Respond to the content of each student's work in an individual way.
- Provide a separate folder to save each student's writings.

FIGURE 8.16. An example of steps to provide for individual differences in creative writing lessons for students in Stages Two through Four.

Structure Teaching for Effective Lessons

A chapter that reviews essential ingredients for beginning a program with students of any age would be lacking if it did not include a discussion of rules and describe a process for teaching lessons effectively. In previous sections, there is information about ways students can be grouped developmentally for instruction. There are also suggestions for using developmental information to select activities, materials, and curriculum content to target objectives. In this section, the focus is on the structure inherent in every successful lesson, to ensure that the instruction is welcomed. Without this climate, it is likely that even the most creative lesson plans will be ineffective.

Rules Are Expectations Stated Clearly

Structure your instruction by first establishing a few, significant rules (expectations) stated in positive ways. Distinguish between building rules that apply to everyone, classroom rules for all students in the class, and individual rules that assist individuals to be successful in special ways. Make rules that are reasonable and meaningful for the students' stages of development. For older students, identify ways to get them involved in planning rules. If you keep rules simple, reasonable, and positive, you will be less likely to have consequences that cause conflict between students and authority.[22]

[22]Chapter 5 reviews how the use of rules should change as students develop.

Students expect teachers to hold limits with fairness and firmness. They admire teachers with these characteristics. They also respond to teachers who will help them with their problems. And, at every age and stage, students trust teachers who do not embarrass them in front of others. Where behavior problems may erupt, design strategies for positive management. Anticipate how each student can be taught to respond successfully to expectations. Choose strategies that are developmentally appropriate for the students' ages and stages. Identify ways to guide them to use words rather than actions, and help them to seek solutions rather than fights when they react to stress, anger, or conflict.

Think of conducting lessons and activities in four distinct phases: (a) the introduction, (b) step-by-step teaching, (c) an ending with closure, and (d) the transition to the next activity. By adhering to this structure, you should find your students responding with increased attention and higher levels of participation. Should their participation decrease and behavioral problems increase, you may find it helpful to review the way you are conducting each of these phases of instruction.

Introduction to a Lesson

A highly motivating introduction is essential. It catches students' attention and conveys the purpose. It sets a tone of confidence that the activity will have a legitimate purpose and a satisfactory outcome. An effective introduction also engages the students with an age- and stage-appropriate connection to build on their interests and experiences. There are examples in Figure 8.17.

Begin with a simple statement, idea, question, demonstration, or material that heightens each student's desire to participate. Be certain that there is something of value in it for each student. An easy way to check the motivational quality of an introduction is to ask yourself, *If I were a student performing this activity, how would I answer the question, "What's in it for me?"*

An introduction should also convey basic information (an overview) about what is to happen, the steps to follow, and the materials to be used. Indicate that the anticipated task has some definite boundaries. Convey expectations about time, place, space, or materials involved.

Stage One: The teacher holds up a brightly painted box and rattles the contents, saying, "Look! What is in the box?"

Stage Two: The teacher holds up a storybook, saying, "Remember the 'wild things' in the story yesterday? What color were their eyes? What did they do? After we read the story today, we will pretend to be Max, who knows how to control the 'wild things'!"

Stage Three: The teacher, introducing a creative writing lesson, shows a news photo and says, "Did you see this picture in the newspaper yesterday? This is the boy who found a bag with a million dollars in it. This will make a great story! Think about a good title and write it on the first line. Then write a sentence that tells where he found the bag. After that, think about what the boy would say to his friend to tell him about the bag. If you need help with spelling, let me know and I will write the word on the chalkboard."

Stage Four: The teacher, introducing a math lesson, says, "What would you do with $100,000?" After the resulting discussion, the teacher teaches a lesson on budget planning.

Stage Five: For a literature class, the teacher begins a new unit by saying, "The person we will be studying this week wrote the story of her own life. As you read this autobiography, look for what she says about her lowest moment and how she resolved it."

FIGURE 8.17. Examples of introductions to lessons at each developmental stage.

A good way to end the introduction is to describe a tangible way that the students can tell when the lesson is almost over. This establishes the lesson expectations clearly. When an introduction contains motivational and organizational elements, initial participation by students is almost always ensured.

Step-By-Step Teaching

A task-analysis format for teaching a lesson or activity provides organization, structure, and sequence that generally lead to students' success. When they have been motivated by the introduction and have a clear idea of each step in the assignment, most students move into an assignment with considerable spontaneity. They know how to begin, what to do next, and how the assignment should end.[23]

During the step-by-step part of a lesson, it is important to observe the extent to which students maintain their attention and involvement. These are times when motivation may lag or they become distracted. It may be necessary to repeat, redirect, or remotivate them to continue. Sometimes restructuring the step or providing praise and positive comments gives the needed boost for a student to continue. Also, watch for signs that a student has completed one step and is beginning the next step. This may be the moment to intervene briefly and acknowledge the student's progress—however slight it may be.

Every student needs some personal contact from a teacher during the step-by-step portion of a lesson or activity. As a general practice, make positive contacts with all students several times during a group lesson. During independent assignments, this is also necessary. Provide positive feedback to each individual, but pick the opportunities carefully so that your involvement does not interrupt a student's independent attention to the task. By being nearby, you may be able to provide reassurance to a student to continue independently to the next step.[24]

End with Closure

End every lesson with a summary discussion that describes, reflects, or questions the students about what they have just done. When students are involved in a lesson, they are usually not evaluating what they are actually doing as it happens. Yet this is what they need to learn: to reflect on what they just did. A good ending transforms their actions and accomplishments into appraisals of what occurred. A look back gives closure to the activity and a synthesis of what has happened. It should be an analysis of what happened and the value of the activity, rather than a focus solely on praise for performance.

You can help them learn to do this retrospective self-evaluation by first recalling the content and sequence of steps yourself. Then teach them to do this. Focus on tangible, positive aspects:

> *What did you do first?*
> *Next? Last?*
> *Who did that? How?*
> *Why is this important?*

For continuity, you may want to end by making a link between the lesson and past lessons. Or, you may link it to the next activity. In either case, an effective ending provides a summary that reinforces what has just been learned. It also encourages students to remember, sequence, and then generalize about what they have done. It helps them become more focused and more confident as they gain greater understanding of the lesson content and their own contribution. It also ties the completed activity to related information and broader experiences of the students.

Students in any stage of development can participate in ending activities for their lessons. Figure 8.18 has examples of endings, adjusted for each stage of development. Younger children learn to recall the activity sequence. Older students begin to think about the meaning of what they have just done. With increasing skills for review and evaluation, they make more contribu-

[23]Every student should understand the steps that must be followed in a learning task.

[24]Encourage maximum possible self-direction by students during a lesson by minimizing your role unless you are needed to instruct or to sustain students' participation.

Stage One: The teacher reopens the brightly painted box and, as each student returns an object to the box, repeats, "It goes in the box!"
As each student does this, the teacher asks, "What did we do?" and models a unison response: "We put it in the box!"

Stage Two: The teacher ends the roleplay by saying, "Max knows how to control the 'wild things'! When we were Max today, how did we control the 'wild things'?"

Stage Three: The teacher collects the writing paper from each student and says, "There were some very imaginative ideas from this group today. Some of you wrote about the person who lost the money. And others wrote about what the boy did with the money. Tomorrow, for writing, we will see if we can use all of these ideas together in one story that will tell about the picture. Then we can put our story on the bulletin board in the hall."

Stage Four: The teacher ends the math lesson with a group meeting in which each student reports an individual budget "big ticket" item. The ensuing discussion includes estimates of how long it would take people with different income levels to earn the items.

Stage Five: The literature reports are shared among group members, with the teacher facilitating discussion and insight by asking questions such as, "How often do people we know have the same experience? Have you ever had to face a situation like that? How did you handle it? How did the people you know respond?"

FIGURE 8.18. Examples of endings for lessons at each developmental stage.

tions to ending activities. In the process, they learn how to synthesize information and communicate ideas, attitudes, feelings, values, or new insights as a result of a lesson. As this happens, they seem to gain involvement that is more personal in learning and greater confidence in their own abilities.[25]

[25]An effective ending is an evaluative activity. It is the way to transform *doing* into *understanding*.

Transition to the Next Lesson

A successful transition gives students the idea that the next lesson will be interesting and of value to them. As the organizational and motivational bridge from one lesson to the next, transition is an essential part of each. Transitions have a distinctly different purpose than lesson endings, but each is necessary for success of a lesson. Where an ending serves to wrap up an activity and give closure to students, a transition takes advantage of students' investment and success in the closing activity and uses it to motivate them for the next activity.

During transitions, students are typically expected to take responsibility for their own conduct as they go from one place to another or from one assignment to the next. However, unless they have learned how to make transitions smoothly, they typically mill around, wander off, begin to display insecurities and anxieties about what to do next, or get into trouble. Most students need structure and guidance from teachers to make acceptable transitions. The task is to teach them to be self-directed and use self-control independently for transitions, without structure or control by the teacher.

Plan your transitions carefully. As one lesson ends and another begins, an effective transition offers students a bridge of ideas to the next assignment. It can motivate, challenge, or simply prepare them to make a mental shift for changing expectations in the next lesson. These are teaching opportunities at the end of every lesson. The expectations for what makes a smooth transition should reflect students' developmental characteristics.

Figure 8.19 contains examples of the way transitions should reflect students' stages of development. For those at lower stages, transitions are highly organized, and physical movements to the next activity are carefully directed. Early childhood and special education teachers often use music, chants, imitative movements, or make-believe actions to propel their students from one place to the next, using simple directions to let them know what is next. For students at higher stages, transitions are more cerebral than physical. Preview "what's next" for them. This creates anticipation. Give reminders of how much time they have between the lessons, or remind students of where they are expected to be. This provides boundaries for time and space.

Stage One: The box of materials disappears as the activity comes to an end. The students clap to the rhythm of the teacher's simple chant, "We're going to the playground," as she begins the movement of the group toward the door.

Stage Two: Students are sitting on the floor as the role play ends. The teacher says, "Now that we know Max can control those 'wild things,' we are going over to the art table to make a wild thing! Think about the color you want for the eyes of your wild thing while we walk to the table."

Stage Three: The teacher ends the writing lesson and prepares the students for math by saying, "We can see that money is interesting to people. I have put a money problem in your folder for math today. As soon as you have your folder, we'll talk about these money problems."

Stage Four: As the math period ends, the teacher says, "Let's take a short break and then discuss how we can use some of these good ideas to do our video project next."

Stage Five: The literature class is over and the teacher says, "Tonight, give some thought to this person's life. Why did she take the trouble to write her autobiography? We'll follow up on this tomorrow."

FIGURE 8.19. Examples of transitions between lessons at each developmental stage.

Because students tend to fluctuate in their interest in participating, readjustments in a lesson may be necessary. If a lesson fails to hold students' interest or participation, be prepared to redirect or restructure the lesson. Consider whether it is so easy that it is boring or is too difficult to do successfully. Be sensitive to the possibility that the content was unfamiliar or that there was too much new information, overwhelming the student. When this happens, be prepared with alternative activities or materials as backup.

Figure 8.20 is a list that summarizes these practices for effective instruction. You may find this list helpful as you prepare lessons and schedules. Then, anticipate how you will obtain ongoing, daily evaluation of the results. Use the students' individual objectives as reference points. These set the focus for each day and shape the activities for the following day. During the lesson, continually estimate each student's investment and attention span, how thinking and emotions are involved, and whether or not progress has been made toward mastery of the target objectives. Follow closely the mental processes each student uses in the activity to identify what the next step should be. It may be necessary to repeat a lesson with a variation, to drop back to a less difficult step, or to move forward to the next, more complex step.[26]

When an objective is mastered, go back to the DTORF–R and select the next objective in the sequence to replace the one that has just been achieved. This process keeps 4 to 16 objectives (at least one but not more than four in each competency area) as the current focus for a student's program. As illustrated in Figure 8.21, this change may require a new task analysis of the steps and processes involved in mastering the new objective. It may also require new activities, new materials, and new strategies. In fact, instructional changes are essential as a student achieves one set of competencies and new learning objectives are added.[27]

[26]Inform students about where they are in the process of achieving an objective. Immediate, positive feedback is an effective way to do this.

[27]Chapter 3 describes the procedure for selecting instructional objectives from a DTORF–R assessment.

- Choose materials and activities to accomplish targeted learning objectives.
- Design lessons that provide success and ways for everyone to enjoy school.
- Provide time each day for activities that foster rational problem solving.
- Include time to stimulate social communication and socialization skills.
- Design creative activities that include art, music, and play to encourage the expression of ideas, values, and concerns.
- Conduct all lessons in ways that encourage participation of each individual.
- Alternate lessons requiring physical movement with those requiring less physical action and more quiet attention.
- Provide opportunities for everyone to make choices and practice new skills independently.
- Select materials that capture the specific interests and objectives of each individual.
- Communicate a plan for each day.
- Convey steps and expected behavior needed to carry out an activity successfully.
- Keep an alternative strategy available as a substitute if a planned lesson proves unsatisfactory or unworkable.
- Never allow a lesson to extend beyond its peak of motivation for a group or individual.
- End each lesson with a focus on positive aspects of what has happened.

FIGURE 8.20. Tips for effective developmental instruction for students of any age and stage.

Schoolwide Implementation

As you become increasingly effective—especially with difficult-to-teach students—you can anticipate interest from other teachers in your school. They will want to know how you get such noticeable gains in student performance. And, you will want to know if they are willing to use the same practices to create a schoolwide climate in which each student has a successful, personalized education. Sugai and Horner (2002, p. 45) offer four important standards to consider in schoolwide planning:

- Clearly defined and socially important outcomes for students and their families and teachers
- Research validated practices
- Data-based decision-making processes
- Systems that support high fidelity implementation

Set Goals and Priorities

The goal to expand the use of developmental practices in your school can be accomplished in several ways. However, it is essential to first establish a schoolwide priority to improve programs and practices for all students, including those with special needs, those requiring targeted interventions, those needing intensive intervention, and those at risk. (See Chapter 1 for definitions of these terms.) Present an introductory review of this developmental approach to the entire staff—teachers, assistant teachers, specialists, support staff, bus drivers, cafeteria supervisors, administrators—and parents.

Begin with the basic beliefs described in the start of this chapter. These beliefs offer a mutual beginning point. Agreement on the fundamental "rightness" of the beliefs should lead to

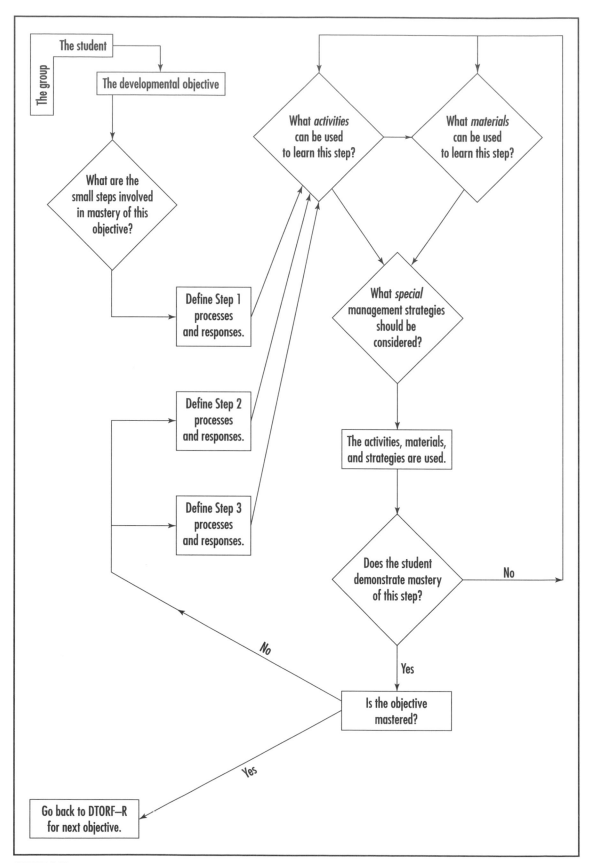

FIGURE 8.21. A strategic way to plan and evaluate instruction for a selected objective.

a growing consensus that students' academic achievements are dependent on social, emotional, and behavioral competencies and must be addressed simultaneously in curriculum planning, instruction, and daily school life. It is essential to have staff agreement that these practices should be explored in greater depth. Describe several ways to go about doing this, as discussed at the beginning of this chapter. Provide time for participation by everyone. Then, build a leadership team with a staff member who has designated responsibility and assigned time for leading this effort to implement developmental practices throughout the school.

Schoolwide Goals

The next step is to target changes selected by the staff to be critical indicators of schoolwide progress. A review of school records can be of great help in doing this. Gather several years of school data. For student performance, look at data such as attendance and absentee rates, academic achievement records, office discipline referrals, promotions, grades repeated, dropouts, suspension, referrals for special services, and transfers to alternative schools. Summarize the data trends for several years to determine whether they reflect acceptable progress or progress that needs to be improved.

During this process, teacher variables might also be considered, such as employment turnover, extent of substitute teaching, educational levels, degrees, certifications, years of experience, skills in discipline, team skills, absenteeism, or other performance indicators. Analyze the data to consider how these may have influenced student performance trends. A thorough review may also suggest concerns not always considered in school performance studies, such as architecture and spaces, social systems, daily routines, resource allocations, and support networks in the school system and community (Carr et al., 2002). The result will be a data-based profile that reflects the school's strengths and weaknesses and indicates where change is needed and how success will be measured.

An Action Plan

For comprehensive schoolwide planning consider (a) schoolwide issues, (b) nonclassroom settings, (c) classroom settings, and (d) support systems for individual students needing targeted or intensive interventions. The *Effective Behavior Support Survey* (EBS) is a useful way to identify these areas within each system in need of change (Lewis & Sugai, 1999; Sugai & Horner, 2002). Other methods for assessing school climate and culture are the *Comprehensive Assessment of School Environment* (CASE) and the *Organizational Climate Descriptive Questionnaire* (OCDQ). The point is to use multiple sources to describe school climate when planning for schoolwide changes (Roach & Kratochwill, 2004).

A multi-year plan requires collaborative efforts to assure that each identified concern will be addressed. This will involve a shared knowledge base among faculty, staff, and parents. Use the EBS school profile to build agreement for priorities. Then obtain administrative and parent council commitment to bring about changes to achieve the targeted goals. Consider time needed for staff development and co-training with parents, ways data will be collected, and how substitute staff and new staff members will be brought into the plan. Also include estimates of resources needed annually to implement the plan. Figure 8.22 is a checklist to use as a guide to assuring that the plan is comprehensive.

Conduct Staff Training and Implementation Activities

The developmental approach, successfully used, can be complex. But an entire faculty and staff can increase skills, improve instruction, and achieve schoolwide changes with sufficient time and training. The basic practices can be initiated effectively during one school year, with clearly documented student progress. However, it is difficult for a schoolwide program to be fully

- There is a staff member with designated responsibility and assigned time to coordinate plans to implement developmental practices.
- The plan for change is based on schoolwide data targets.
- The entire school staff has made the plan a priority.
- There is schoolwide agreement that students' behavior and academic progress are interdependent and must be addressed simultaneously in curriculum planning and in practice.
- Each staff member has a peer partner for yearlong mutual support during training.
- School goals are operationalized with measurable objectives.
- Students' IEP goals include social–emotional–behavioral objectives with specified outcome measures.
- There is planned time for group and self-directed study sessions.
- There is a system for periodic schoolwide evaluation of targeted changes and student progress.
- There is administrative commitment and resources to support these criteria.

FIGURE 8.22. Use these criteria to check the quality of plans for schoolwide change.

[28]Chapter 9 reports research studies of sustained practices over several years, as teachers become increasingly skilled in providing developmentally based instruction.

[29] As teachers identify their students' developmental stages and developmental goals, the range of individual differences they must deal with becomes glaringly apparent.

[30]Staff development consultation and in-service training are available through the University of Georgia, Developmental Therapy–Developmental Teaching Outreach Unit: http://www.uga.edu/dttp

implemented during the first year. Field research has shown that teachers continue to increase their proficiency and many can achieve demonstration level skills during second and third years of staff training (see Chapters 7 and 9).[28]

Begin self-study with a series of small group sessions in which teachers and staff review the developmental competencies typically needed by the students they currently teach. For example, all primary grade teaching teams might form a working group; the groups could be smaller if organized by the grades they teach. In every group, use the *S–E–B Quick Profile* (see Chapter 3) to identify the general stage of development for each student. This will also indicate each student's current goal in all four competency areas of DOING, SAYING, RELATING, and THINKING.[29]

When a teaching team identifies the predominant developmental stage of all of the students in a class, this stage will also reveal the particular students who are falling behind. They are the ones in need of targeted or intensive support systems. They will require more precise developmental assessments provided by the DTORF–R (see Chapter 3). Following the assessment, information gathering, and program planning sequence described previously, the teams will be able to complete an IEP for each student in need of individual support. One such summary planning form is included at the end of this chapter.

As the actual process gets underway, form a staff support group to outline a sequence of self-directed study topics that cover the basic developmental content described previously in this chapter. Topics frequently selected by teaching teams for in-depth study include behavior management; assessment of students' social-emotional and behavioral development; roles of lead and support teachers; building an effective teaching team; functional behavioral assessments; group dynamics; decoding behavior; social roles in groups; and curriculum practices that address emotional needs of students. The assistance group can also provide invaluable in-class support as members begin to use developmental practices in their classrooms. If staff indicates a need for additional resources or consultation, such as those in Figure 8.23, the group can obtain outside consultation for individual teaching teams or for the entire school's faculty and staff.[30]

The schoolwide training can be individualized if each teaching team analyzes its own skills using the phases of skill acquisition outlined in Chapter 6. This process accommodates the needs of beginners, those with different amounts of educational preparation and experience, those with varied assignments, and those who may have challenging students in their classes. It is also a way for teams to maintain a focus on the developmental needs of their particular students, while focusing on their own expanded skill acquisition at the same time.[31]

As a school staff begins to use developmental practices independently, it is important to provide resources and a support system to help make adaptations for each set of unique classroom conditions that may arise. It will also be necessary to develop a process for integrating new and substitute personnel into the program with inservice training at the time of employment, to sustain the quality of the program.

- On-site consultation, workshops, and seminars.
- Teleconferencing about solutions to difficult problems.
- Video consultation on specific issues.
- Online courses for credit.
- Software for independent simulated practices in behavior management.
- Software for IEP and student progress records.
- Observations of teaching teams in their classrooms, with debriefings and feedback.
- Data analysis, evaluation, and recommendations.
- Leadership training.
- On-site technical assistance about progress toward achieving the targeted changes.

FIGURE 8.23. Ways in which outside consultation and resource assistance can augment self-study.

Evaluate Effectiveness for Students, Staff, and the School

A system for periodic schoolwide evaluation, monitoring, and staff review of targeted changes should be planned *before* beginning a schoolwide effort to implement developmental practices. Preferably, this plan would be designed for quarterly appraisals of progress. At a minimum, there should be at least three points for evaluation of progress toward goals, at the beginning, mid-year, and end of the school year. And the process should be repeated regularly every year during the schoolwide staff development phase. At the end of a year, the staff should reevaluate the data, review the process, redefine new goals, and identify ways to sustain the successes.[32]

Because evaluation has both formative and summative dimensions, consider multiple evaluation perspectives: students' progress, expanded staff skills, and improvements in schoolwide data trends. Here are suggestions for ways to do this.

First Evaluation Question

Do students show significant progress in responsible behavior, developmental competencies, and academic skills during the schoolwide implementation effort?

To evaluate the impact of implementing this approach with typically developing students, track their stage progress in achieving competencies in each of the four areas from beginning to end of the school year using the *S–E–B Quick Profile*. For individual students in need of targeted or intensive interventions, collect repeated measures of their progress in achieving specified IEP academic and DTORF–R objectives in evaluation measures routinely used (see Chapter 3).

Second Evaluation Question

Does staff proficiency increase during implementation of developmental practices?

There are several ways to answer this evaluation question. One way is for individual teams to focus on recommended practices for the general developmental stage of the group. The DTRITS is helpful as a guide for self-assessment. A team then can identify practices already in use in a classroom and those that need to be added. With repeated ratings, a team can chart its progress, using DTRITS standards such as Highly Effective, Effective, Adequate, Less Than Adequate, or Poor (see Chapter 7 for the optimum phases of skill training and a self-evaluation procedure).

A teaching team can also self-evaluate by focusing on specific management strategies, such as those summarized in Figure 8.24 and discussed in depth in Chapter 5. In this self-monitoring approach, a team might make a plan that specifies the following:

- Strategies we use successfully now
- Strategies we use sometimes

Write the number that closely corresponds to your response to each question. Then if you want a score, tally the numbers.	How often do you use this strategy? Never = 1 Seldom = 2 Occasionally = 3 Often = 4 Almost always = 5	How well does this strategy work with your students?* Never = 1 Hardly ever = 2 Sometimes = 3 Usually = 4 Always = 5
Encourage and praise		
Motivate students with interesting lessons and ideas		
Assist students in getting organized		
Explain procedures (structure)		
Establish or review rules		
Model expected behavior and relationships		
Move close to signal awareness (proximity)		
Redirect to refocus student on task		
Reflect positive words and actions		
Connect actions to feeling (interpretation)		
Confront or reprimand		
Time-out		
Remove from room to talk		
Hold firmly (for young children only)		
Ignore student's behavior		
Tally your own ratings		

FIGURE 8.24. Check yourself on the strategies you use. *A strategy works well if it reduces a student's problem behavior *and* increases the student's participation.

- Strategies we want to improve
- Strategies we do not want to use

The checklist can be used by a team at repeated intervals to track its own changes. In this way, the team can see changes in frequency with which certain management strategies are used and how well they are working with the students.

Or, a teaching team might choose a different approach by selecting classroom performance goals for individual students who are difficult to discipline. To do this, identify students with current behavior problems. Ask questions like these:

- Which disruptive behaviors do we see most often in our classroom?
- What does the behavior tell us about a student?
- What ideas do we have for improving this behavior?
- How will we know if our interventions are successful?

The skill of a team can be measured by the progress of individual students when the team considers questions like these, then specifies desired changes, precise strategies to use, and documents the responses of the students to these practices.

Teachers who have peer partners often use these self-evaluation strategies by mentoring each other, exchanging observations in each other's classrooms, recording student responses to selected practices, and providing feedback with ideas for improving student participation, using questions like these:

- What are we doing that's working?
- What can we do differently?
- What is going on with this student (decoding)?

If a student is not showing the desired progress, ask the peer partner to observe the student during a 15-minute period. See Figure 8.25 for an example of a form to help structure the observation. Discuss the results and share ideas about steps that might be taken. Implement the changes and then repeat the observation and rating.

 ### Third Evaluation Question
Did the school achieve the targeted changes after adding developmental practices schoolwide?

This evaluation question is addressed by returning to the original data collected during the schoolwide planning sessions. Annual data should reflect changes in each of the four key schoolwide systems targeted for change. If the process is repeated at the end of each school year, adjustments and corrections can be made for the following year. Over time, data trends will emerge to document progress of the school, the staff, and the students.[33]

Perhaps the most difficult part of evaluation is assuring collection of accurate data and maintaining records carefully. It is essential that all staff receive sufficient training with the DTORF–R to assure reliable assessment of student progress. Reliable ratings are particularly difficult to obtain if raters lack sufficient understanding of the instrument or of the student. Results also can be questioned when ratings are carelessly done or incomplete. Untrained staff participating on a team rating can also jeopardize reliability.

When summarizing data for statistical analyses, sampling procedures may be necessary to assure practical validity of conclusions. Related record-keeping problems arise when a student moves away, new students enter without a baseline assessment, students are transferred among classes, or students were absent during the scheduled assessment. In short, acceptable evaluation is quite complex and time consuming. It may be necessary to have a program

[33]Chapter 9 illustrates several ways to report the effectiveness of the developmental practices by classes, groups of students, teachers' skills, or schoolwide changes.

Student's initials: _____ Grade: _____ Date: _____

Lesson/task (e.g., reading): _____ Beginning time: _____ Ending time: _____

Name of student's teacher: _____ Name of observer: _____

Directions: Observe the student for 15 minutes. For each minute of observation, circle the number that most accurately describes the student during that minute. Evaluate the student's level of participation in the activity or task. Do not evaluate the quality of the student's work (e.g., the correct number of answers.) When the observation is complete, record the score for each minute in the column on the right and total the combined scores.

Minute	The student is not participating in the activity or task and is using unacceptable words or actions.*	The student is not participating but is quiet.	The student is participating somewhat but is using unacceptable words or actions.*	The student is participating somewhat, in acceptable ways.	The student is enthusiastically participating in acceptable ways.	Write the score here.
A	1	2	3	4	5	
B	1	2	3	4	5	
C	1	2	3	4	5	
D	1	2	3	4	5	
E	1	2	3	4	5	
F	1	2	3	4	5	
G	1	2	3	4	5	
H	1	2	3	4	5	
I	1	2	3	4	5	
J	1	2	3	4	5	
K	1	2	3	4	5	
L	1	2	3	4	5	
M	1	2	3	4	5	
N	1	2	3	4	5	
O	1	2	3	4	5	
					Total	

FIGURE 8.25. A way to check a student's level of participation. *Note.* During subsequent observations, ensure that the *same* lesson or task are observed at the same time of day, if at all possible. *Unacceptable words or actions are those that are disruptive to the learning environment of self or others.

evaluation specialist as part of the schoolwide effort. Support for this is the responsibility of school administration.

Finally, informal responses of participating staff to the implementation are essential. Gather their ideas about their own skill levels, responses of their students, the usefulness of the specified practices, and the effectiveness of the interventions with their students. Their satis-faction with the support they received and recommendations for changes will reflect their confidence in continuing to use these developmental practices successfully.

Now, Try This in Your Own Classroom

Previous chapters have reviewed basic content needed to begin a developmental approach to teaching. This chapter has attempted to integrate the information in a way that you can use as a starting point in your own classroom. With the summary form shown in Figure 8.26, select one student in your group and go through the process of information gathering and planning.

Student's name: _____ Age: _____

Date: _____

Typical developmental stage of peers in student's age group: _____ (Refer to Chapter 1.)

Summary of Current Competencies
(Refer to Chapters 1 and 2.)

Behavior (DOING)
(Check the one that currently applies best.)

☐ Instincts and drives dominate behavior.

☐ Needs adults to control impulsive behavior.

☐ Recognizes behavioral standards but expects adults to enforce them.

☐ Tries to conform to standards approved by peers and accepted adults.

☐ Uses principles and inner controls to regulate behavior.

Communication (SAYING)
(Check the one that currently applies best.)

☐ Has fundamental ways to communicate needs and relate to others.

☐ Uses language to convey information to others.

☐ Expresses ideas and describes experiences to others.

☐ Communicates to establish relationships.

☐ Relies on communication for problem solving and sustaining relationships.

Socialization (RELATING)
(Check the one that currently applies best.)

☐ Depends on adults to provide for needs.

☐ Seeks adults (or other power sources) for problem solving and confirmation of worthiness.

☐ Seeks recognition and admiration from peers and adults.

☐ Values being an accepted group member.

☐ Builds reciprocal friendships and uses them as a source for personal problem solving.

(continues)

FIGURE 8.26. A way to organize and summarize information as you plan for each student's IEP.

Cognition (THINKING)
(Check the one that currently applies best.)

☐ Relies on sensory information and simple perceptions of tangible objects and familiar people.

☐ Uses concrete information as defined by characteristics, function, and use.

☐ Applies semi-abstract information and symbols in cause and effect, seriation, conservation, and simple reasoning.

☐ Finds abstract symbols and ideas to gain knowledge, generalize, and evaluate consequences.

☐ Evaluates principles, values, ideas, and actions of self and others.

Summary of Background Information

Interests (List and highlight those that are age appropriate.)

Role models and attachments (List and circle those that are strong.)

Concerns (List and circle those that are intense.)

Friends (List and circle those that are age appropriate.)

Values (List and circle those that appear to motivate.)

My needs

Please adults

Be fair

Fit in and be responsible

Do what is right and care for others

(continues)

FIGURE 8.26. *Continued.*

Summary of Emotional Needs and Behavioral Defenses
(Refer to Chapter 4.)

How does the student view authority and responsibility?

☐ Preexistential phase?

☐ Going through the existential crisis phase?

☐ Postexistential phase?

(Based on the student's age, what developmental anxiety is typical for this age group? Mark it 1. Then, in descending order, rank other anxieties that may be unresolved and cause problems for this student.)

☐ Abandonment or attachment (No one cares.)

☐ Inadequacy (I can't do anything right.)

☐ Guilt (I'm so bad I should be punished.)

☐ Conflict (They're making me and I don't want to! Or, I want to and they won't let me.)

☐ Identity (Who am I? Or, What am I to become?)

In stressful moments, how does the student use behavior for emotional defense? Describe defense.

☐ Denies a problem exists? _____

☐ Escapes to avoid facing it? _____

☐ Substitutes another behavior that is more acceptable? _____

What types of social power is the student using? (Check all that apply.)

Type(s)?	Level(s) (High? Medium? Low?)	Change Needed?
☐ Coercion		
☐ Likability		
☐ Expertise		
☐ Manipulation		

What group role(s) does the student have?

Roles in Peer Group?	Change Needed?	Roles in Family Group?	Change Needed?

(continues)

FIGURE 8.26. *Continued.*

Summary of Objectives and Instructional Plan
(Refer to Chapter 3.)

Highest areas and stage where student has achieved 80% or more of the DTORF–R competencies.

_____

_____

_____

General developmental stage where instruction for objectives should begin (the stage with a majority of the objectives marked X based on the DTORF–R): _____

Instructional stage for DOING: _____   Objective: _____

Instructional stage for RELATING: _____   Objective: _____

Instructional stage for SAYING: _____   Objective: _____

Instructional stage for THINKING: _____   Objective: _____

Based on the student's developmental stage, which adult role should the teacher convey? (Refer to Chapters 2 and 7.) _____

Based on this student's interests and values, what materials and activities could be used in lessons to motivate and encourage participation? (Refer to Chapters 2 and 4.)

_____

_____

_____

What themes may catch and sustain the student's interest in a unit of study? (Refer to Chapter 8.)

_____

_____

_____

List management strategies recommended for most frequent use in this student's developmental stage. (Refer to Chapter 5.)

_____

_____

_____

FIGURE 8.26. *Continued.*

You may want to choose a student who is typically developing or one who is challenging to teach. As developmental strengths and lags become clear, you should begin to see the student's instructional needs clustering in a particular developmental stage. Review the stage characteristics in Chapter 2 to verify how your planning fits with the snapshot summary of that stage. When you feel that you have been successful in planning strategic instruction for this student, go on to try it with others. Soon, you can have your entire class benefiting from developmental teaching.[34]

[34]This form is also available in Folder 5 on the CD-ROM that accompanies this text.

Effectiveness

9

CHAPTER

There is increasing interest in identifying and widely implementing the most effective prevention practices ... thereby increasing confidence in and commitment to the use of tested and effective programs and policies to promote positive youth development and prevent health and behavior problems among young people and the general population.

J. David Hawkins (2005, p. 2)
President, Society for Prevention Research

Scientifically based research is a federal program priority emphasized in the No Child Left Behind Act of 2001 (NCLB; P.L. 107-110). The objective is "Research that involves the application of rigorous, systematic, and objective procedures to obtain reliable and valid knowledge relevant to education activities and programs" (U.S. Department of Education, 2005, pp. 4–5). Several defining characteristics of research provided in Section 99101 (37) of this law include the following:

- Employs systematic, empirical methods
- Involves rigorous data analyses
- Relies on reliable and valid measurements or observational methods
- Uses experimental or quasi-experimental designs
- Presents procedures in sufficient detail and clarity to replicate
- Has been reviewed and approved by a panel of independent experts

This chapter reviews how Developmental Therapy–Developmental Teaching meets these standards as it evolved and was evaluated in multiple field-based, quasi-experimental research studies. The approach has repeatedly been shown to be an effective, scientifically based intervention. It has been validated as an "Education Program that Works" by the U.S. Department of Education's National Institute of Education, Joint Dissemination Review Panel (JDRP), the National Diffusion Network (NDN), and the Program Effectiveness Panel (PEP), Office of Innovation and Development.

Several of these validation studies are presented in detail with evidence of progress made by students and gains in classroom skills by teachers and paraprofessionals. Additional studies provide further evidence about the sustainability of students' gains 1 and 2 years after the intervention. There is a report of the maintenance of teachers' skill levels several years after completing the training program. There is also a brief review of a study involving the performance of university interns who received the same teacher training program. The chapter ends with a summary of performance data about program effectiveness at replication sites, which added to the growing body of evidence about significant, positive effects of this approach on teachers' skills, the gains of the students they teach, and the effect of administrative support on teachers' performance.

How This Approach Evolved and Was Validated

The Original Demonstration Project

The initial Developmental Therapy model was developed at the University of Georgia in collaboration with seven local school districts and mental health programs. The task was to provide a comprehensive and effective educational intervention program for children with severe mental health or behavioral problems and for their families. Seeking ways to foster learning, healthy personality development, and responsible behavior, the project began with an extensive review of multiple theories and various interventions that had evolved from them. These theories include developmental psychology, motivational psychology, social and psychosocial psychology, linguistics, individual (ego) psychology, and learning theory. It became evident that the project must translate these theories and practices into a coherent framework with practical classroom applications to be successful with students of many ages, different stages of development, and with a wide range of emotional and behavioral problems. The pivotal framework was provided by the cognitive/structural principle that development typically occurs in hierarchical sequences that change in form and complexity with neurobiological growth and experience. From psychodynamic and social psychology, constructs regarding the power of people, emotions, and anxiety in shaping how children learn and behave were then integrated into this approach, as were principles of reinforcement and replacement from behavioral research. Additionally, theories about age-related dimensions of motivation, social knowledge, moral development, and interpersonal understanding contributed to the framework. This organizational approach accommodated the integration of a wide range of instructional and behavioral interventions into classroom practices in a developmental context with age-, grade-, and stage-relevant guides. Figure 9.1 illustrates this expansion of theories into applied practices. (See also Appendixes A and C.)

The result was a classroom-based instructional model built on four developmental domains that consistently reoccurred among the theories. These domains were behaving, communicating, relating, and thinking. Each domain has specific, sequential milestones through which competence in that area develops from birth onward. Sometimes called developmental stepping-stones, they are markers for a healthy, well integrated personality. If these milestones are evident in a student's behavior, it is assumed that development is progressing in a typical way. If lacking, these same milestones become specific teaching and learning objectives. The idea is to provide teachers with observable examples of what to look for so that they can target instruction for students' social, emotional, and behavioral growth along these developmental pathways.[1]

History over Four Decades

Since the original project, the scope of this approach has expanded over the decades, with continuing formative and summative evaluations of students' assessed needs and effective instructional practices. Figure 9.2 shows this expansion. From the first group of severely disturbed young children, the practices are now used with older elementary age children, young teenage students, those with other disabilities or autism, and those at risk, abused, or developmentally delayed. Typically developing children with adjustment problems are also included. Various educational settings were evaluated to identify those that appear to related to students gains. The studies indicate that this approach is effective in many settings beyond the original special

[1]Appendix B contains a summary of the theoretical foundations of this approach across multiple domains and stages of development.

(text continues on p. 242)

Essential Human Processes →	Global Theories	→	Focused Theories →	Resulting Interventions
Behave	Learning theory		• Behavioral theory • Neuropsychology	• Behavior modification • Applied behavior analysis • Replacement training • Reinforcement principles • Sensory integration
Feel	Individual/ego psychology		• Personality theory • Psychodynamic theory • Emotional intelligence	• Play therapy • Psychotherapy • Bibliotherapy • Movement, art, music therapies
Think	Developmental psychology		• Cognitive theory	• Rational–emotive therapy • Cognitive restructuring • Academic therapy • Reality therapy
Value	Motivational psychology		• Moral development • Empathy and altruism	• Faith-based therapies • Values clarification
Relate	Social and psychosocial psychology		• Gestalt theory • Ecological theory • Social knowledge • Interpersonal understanding	• Social learning curriculum • Transactional therapy
Communicate	Linguistics		• Psycholinguistic theory	• Social communication therapy

FIGURE 9.1. Multiple theories have evolved into coherent contemporary practices integrated in Developmental Therapy–Developmental Teaching.

	The Seventies: 1st demonstration programs	The Eighties: Multistate replications	The Nineties: International adaptations	The 21st Century: Technical assistance and training worldwide
Focus	Combined mental health and special education service delivery prototype.	Set quality standards for documenting fidelity in practices.	Redefined developmental goals for inclusion with typically developing peers.	Provide self-directed and distance learning for educators and parents to use developmental practices.
Target populations	Served children with severe emotional disturbance (ages 3–8).	Extended to students with autism and developmental delays, 18 mos.–12 years.	Extended to abused, at-risk, and typically developing children with adjustment problems, to age 16.	Train leadership personnel responsible for staff development and teacher preparation.
Settings	Located services in school-sponsored, community-based psychoeducational programs.	Expanded to Head Start, childcare, early intervention, and residential programs.	Expanded to inclusive settings, therapeutic childcare, foster care; schoolwide, multi-level needs of students.	Offer Internet preservice, in-service, and self-directed teacher training in developmentally based practices.
Teachers' practices	Designed individual educational and treatment plans with developmentally based intervention strategies and instructional materials.	Expanded positive management strategies; decoding behavior; creative arts, music, art, movement activities. Designed in-service training program.	Adjusted management strategies for use in inclusive general education; matched developmental/emotional needs to general curriculum.	Develop and evaluate software and Internet resources for use in online, self-directed training in developmental practices.

(continues)

FIGURE 9.2. History of Developmental Therapy–Developmental Teaching over 4 decades.

	The Seventies: 1st demonstration programs	The Eighties: Multi-state replications	The Nineties: International adaptations	The 21st Century: Technical assistance and training worldwide
Family services	Involved parents in decision making and in classroom implementation as partners.	Designed home-based programs with parents as participants and mentors for other parents.	Focused on empowering parents to meet developmental needs of children and families.	Expand training for foster families and family service providers.
Evaluation	Developed DTORF for assessment of healthy socioemotional development, ages 0–14. **1st national validation**	Revised DTORF–R to age 16; new reliability training program. DTRITS developed to measure teacher performance. **2nd national validation**	4th edition DTORF–R with examples for rating reliability. Used DTRITS to study teachers' skills and training needs. **3rd national validation**	Refine measurement procedures and reliability of data collectors. Conduct quasi-experimental studies of variables affecting program effectiveness.
Dissemination	Established network of 24 psychoeducational programs in Georgia; technical assistance offered statewide.	Responded to requests with training, textbooks, audiovisual training materials, newsletter, and brochures.	Responded to increased demand for training internationally. Opened www.uga.edu/dttp Web site. Established European Training Institute and Trainers' Network in the U.S.	Encourage continuing international translations and adaptations. Expand Internet access to training materials and information on developmental practices.

FIGURE 9.2. *Continued.*

education programs. These settings include general education classes, Head Start, residential programs, childcare, foster care, and home-based programs.

An inservice training program was also designed and evaluated for teachers and paraprofessionals planning to use this approach. The program provides training to use the DTORF–R to assess the student's social, emotional, and behavioral competence. It also teaches teachers to use the DTRITS to self-monitor their own classroom performance and to guide their instructional practices. As these instruments were developed and refined for validity and reliability, they became central measures to evaluate program effectiveness in a series of quasi-experimental studies over several decades.[2]

Program Validation

When complex phenomena such as the development of social, emotional, and behavioral competence were examined, descriptive and exploratory studies allowed for increased insight into the process, the issues, and conditions relevant to successful educational outcomes. Then, repeated quasi-experimental evaluation research was conducted to examine variables that influence results. Over time, repeated empirical studies resulted in program validation and a growing body of field-based evidence about the effectiveness of the program. These validation studies are cited in Figures 9.3 and 9.4 and described the following sections.[3]

[2]Development of the DTORF–R is described in Chapter 3; the DTRITS development, in Chapter 7. The latest versions of both instruments are included as reproducible instruments in the accompanying CD.

[3]The University of Georgia, through the Developmental Therapy–Teaching Programs Outreach Unit, continues to provide consultation, staff training, online distance learning for teachers, program evaluation, and collaborative research.

- Developmental skills of children with severe emotional and behavioral disorders increased significantly in a combined mental health and educational program using the Developmental Therapy curriculum (U.S. Department of Education, Joint Dissemination Review Panel No. 75-63).
- Teachers and teaching assistants with varying levels of skills before training made significant gains in classroom performance and achieved certification level proficiency after participating in the Developmental Therapy–Developmental Teaching in-service program for 30 contact hours, and they attained accuracy in assessing socioemotional development of their students with severe emotional or behavioral disabilities (U.S. Department of Education, Joint Dissemination Review Panel No. 81-19).
- Children with mild, moderate, or severe social/emotional, speech/language, or developmental disabilities made significant gains in socioemotional competence when receiving Developmental Therapy–Developmental Teaching during a school year. Similar gains occurred in full or partial, inclusion and in special education settings (U.S. Department of Education, Program Effectiveness Panel, National Diffusion Network).
- Teachers, teaching assistants, and student teaching interns achieved proficiency in demonstrating the specified practices and sustained the gains after training (U.S. Department of Education, Program Effectiveness Panel, National Diffusion Network).

FIGURE 9.3. This approach has received multiple validations from the U.S. Department of Education as "an educational program that works."

"In recognition of an innovative and well-researched program that applies the Developmental Therapy model in the treatment of emotionally disturbed children, resulting in outstanding clinical care and professional development."

FIGURE 9.4. Another certificate of significant achievement. *Note.* From "Significant Achievement Awards," by the American Psychiatric Association, 1993, *Journal of Hospital and Community Psychiatry, 44,* 994–996. Copyright 1993 by APA. Reprinted with permission.

The First Validation of Effectiveness

The first lines of inquiry (The National Diffusion Network, JDRP No. 75-63, U.S. Department of Education, 1975) included descriptive, qualitative, and correlation research to document program effectiveness for 49 young children, ages 2 to 7 years (average: 4 years, 11 months), with severe social, emotional, or behavioral disabilities (Hoyt, 1978). At entry, the children had 24% to 34% of the skills typically expected of age peers. During 5 months of receiving a daily Developmental Therapy program in an educational setting, they acquired greater than 50% of the targeted skills expected for their ages. The gains were evident in all four domains, as measured by an earlier version of the DTORF–R: behavior, communication, socialization, and sensory–motor/cognition. The results of this original demonstration study indicated that the developmental skills of children having severe emotional and behavioral disorders increased with participation in a combined mental health and educational effort using the Developmental Therapy curriculum (Wood & Swan, 1978).

Sustained Effects of Children's Gains 1 and 2 Years After the Intervention

Following the original validation study, there was an opportunity to examine the extent to which the gains by 73 of the participating children were sustained upon completion of their programs. For this study, parents' ratings of their children's behavior problems were obtained during referral and again after their children completed the program. All had severe emotional or behavioral disabilities when they were referred. The exit rating was done for some at the time the child had made sufficient progress to participate in a less intensive program. For others, a rating was done approximately 2 years after exiting, as part of a scheduled follow-up. These differences in time between the exit ratings were used to establish two groups (Kaufman, Paget, & Wood, 1981).

Group A was composed of 37 children whose progress during the intervention was evaluated. Group B was a tracking group composed of 36 children rated 2 years after exiting the program to examine sustained effects. Children in Group A ranged in age from 3 to 11 years; 65% were boys and 35% girls; 62% were White, 35% were African American, and 3% were unreported race. The average length of intervention was 11 months. Children in Group B ranged in age from 4 to 12 years; 64% were boys, 36% girls; 50% were White, 47% were African American, and 3% were unreported race. The average length of intervention for this group was 10 months.

Parents identified problems that they considered severe at the time of their child's referral. They used a 32-item checklist containing problem behaviors most frequently mentioned when students are referred for special help. Factor scores for the checklist indicated that the list had three dimensions of problems: aggressive/hostile (14 items), inadequacy/immaturity (9 items), and anxiety/withdrawal (9 items). The mean number of severe problems for Group A at the time of referral was 15 ($SD = 7$); for Group B the mean was 13 ($SD = 8$).

At the time they completed the program, the 37 children in Group A had an 89% reduction in the number of severe problem behaviors, as reported by their parents. Dependent t values indicated that statistically significant decreases occurred in all three factor dimensions ($p < .005$). Results were similar for the 36 children in Group B, showing an 81% decline in number of severe problems from referral until 2 years after completing the program. In view of the 10 months that Group B spent receiving the intervention and the follow-up rating 2 years later, 3 years had actually elapsed since the referral rating.

Although this study confirmed the effectiveness of the original demonstration program in measuring gains made by students during intervention, it also left many unanswered questions. Multitrait analyses and longitudinal studies were necessary next steps. Most notably, this study led to examination of relevant variables that may affect intervention outcomes, such as the type and severity of students' disabilities, age, gender, race, program settings, and skills of their teachers. As applications of the approach expanded, field-based program evaluation and research continued with studies of many of these variables.

The Second Validation of Effectiveness

The in-service training component for Developmental Therapy–Developmental Teaching received the second program validation (Sontag, personal communication, 1981). This validation (JDRP No. 81-19, U.S. Department of Education, 1981) was based on a study to evaluate the performance of 33 teachers and 12 teaching assistants who received inservice training to use the specified developmental practices while teaching school age students with severe emotional or behavioral disabilities. Research questions focused on (a) proficiency levels demonstrated by the personnel after training, (b) the amount of training time needed by teachers to attain proficiency, and (c) the optimal administrative support necessary for a quality replication (Wood & Combs, 1981; Wood, Combs, & Walters, 1986).

Participating Teachers

The teachers were in 13 public schools where this approach was being introduced with concurrent, year-long inservice training. Their average age was 31 years (range = 21–61 years). There were 8 males and 37 females; 34 were White, and 11 were non-White. A high school diploma was the highest degree earned by 6 of the participants, while 9 had an educational degree above the baccalaureate level. The group averaged 2 years of prior teaching experience in special education and 2 years in general education. All of their students had severe emotional or behavioral disabilities.

The In-Service Training Program

The teachers received training from experienced instructors who were certified as demonstration teachers, and who had implemented Developmental Therapy–Developmental Teaching practices themselves with high levels of expertise in classrooms for troubled children or teens. The teachers used a newly developed training manual that contained 63 modules, each with an instructional objective, introductory content on the topic, several group exercises and activities for applying the concepts, discussion questions, explanatory notes, a summary statement, and an assignment to be completed before the next scheduled session (Wood, 1981). At the end of every unit there were both knowledge-based and performance-based evaluations. The instructors also observed the participants individually in their classrooms to evaluate and rate their performance with the DTRITS and to provide individual feedback after an observation. They then prepared a written summary for each participant, which reinforced observed strengths and targeted specified performance skills needing improvement.

Research Design

Pre- and posttraining classroom performance scores were compared at the beginning and end of training. Three subgroups of 13 participants each were identified using pretraining DTRITS scores to examine the effects of initial proficiency on level of skill attainment after training. A low skills group had scores below the passing level. A middle skills group had scores at the passing level or beyond, and a high skills group had scores at the certification level or above. A 3 × 2 analysis of variance (ANOVA) was used to compare performance of the three groups at Time 1 and Time 2.

The six project instructors also received additional training as evaluators. For this reliability training, they observed different classrooms in pairs and their trial ratings were compared, item by item. When there were differences among raters for an item rating, they talked about what they had observed and the intent of the item. This procedure continued until there was a high level of agreement. The procedure resulted in high interrater agreement, item-by-item, of

95%. Interrater correlations were also high for total scores ($r = .79$ for Stage Two early childhood form; .94 for the Stage Three primary grade form; and .81 for the Stage Four upper elementary form).

Each instructor was responsible for conducting the training and using the rating as a guide in direct feedback during the year. However, final ratings were completed by a different instructor who had not been involved in the training at that school. DTRITS scores were the proportion of items correctly demonstrated in the classroom, normalized with an arc sine transformation for inferential analyses.

Results of In-Service Training

After training, 80% of the teachers and teaching assistants demonstrated certification level practices or greater in their classrooms as measured by their post-training DTRITS scores. Of these, 38% also reached the highest demonstration level. On a written test of knowledge about the specified practices, 84% passed; for accuracy in using the DTORF–R to assess students' development, 100% achieved the passing level and 83% achieved the certification level.[4]

As a group, their gains in classroom skills from the beginning ($M = 56$, $SD = 22$) to the ending of training ($M = 81$, $SD = 20$) were significantly improved. The ANOVA also revealed significant differences among the mean scores of the three skill groups, $F(1, 42) = 21.92$, $MSE = .06$, $p < .01$, and from the beginning to ending of training, $F(2, 93) = 51.958$, $MSE = .41$, $p < .01$. The graph in Figure 9.5, which is an image taken from the CD-ROM that accompanies this text, shows the effect of training on participants who differ in skill levels as they begin the training program. The low skills group started below the passing level with an average skill score of 32 and achieved an average score of 70. The middle skills group started with an average score of 57 and achieved a score of 88. The high skills group began with a score of 83 and ended training with a score of 87.

Training Time Needed To Achieve Proficiency

To answer the question of how much training was needed before proficiency improved, repeated measures of performance were sampled for 9 participants three times during training: after 11 hours, 23 hours, and 30 hours. The analysis was a repeated measure (time) one-way ANOVA. Simple effects were then examined with one-tailed dependent t-tests. Results indicate that these participants' scores changed significantly during the three time measurement

[4]Classroom performance skills improved significantly for teachers and teaching assistants after completing the in-service training program.

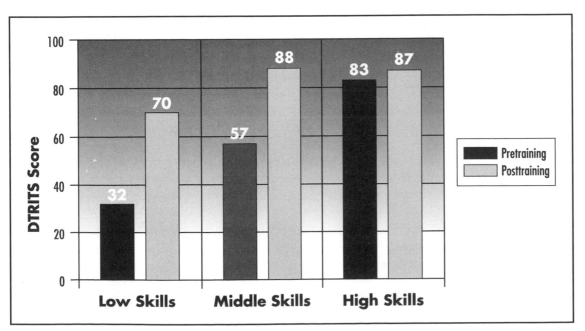

FIGURE 9.5. Gains of 45 teachers following in-service training.

periods, $F = 10.23$, $p < .001$. After a nonsignificant change in mean score of 36 ($SD = 19$) after 11 hours of training ($t = 1.27$), significant improvement occurred between 23 and 30 hours of training ($M = 48$, $SD = 23$, $t = 3.89$, $p < .001$). Their skills continued to improve as training progressed. At completion of 30 hours of training, participants in this group had increased their skill scores significantly from the beginning of training to a mean score of 75 ($SD = 28$, $t = 3.51$, $p < .001$).

Effect of Administrative Support on Teachers' Skills

Administrative support was measured at each site using the *Administrative Support Checklist*. This checklist was completed in a consensus rating by each program administrator and inservice instructor. The list contains 41 support elements considered desirable to support the effectiveness of a program using Developmental Therapy–Developmental Teaching. The score is the number of elements present. Criteria used for judging the quality of support are listed in Figure 9.6.[5]

[5]The *Administrative Support Checklist* is included in the accompanying CD, Folder 4, and may be reproduced.

At each of the 13 schools, administrative support scores ranged from 6 to 33 items present out of a possible 41. Participants' DTRITS performance scores were then correlated with the administrative support scores for their own schools. A Pearson product–moment correlation of .52 indicated that there was a relationship between the quality of administrative support and the teachers' classroom skills. Nine of the 13 schools (69%) had scores of moderate to high quality support (more than 15 items present). In these schools, all of the teachers reached the Certification level of proficiency or higher. The remaining four schools had scores below the minimum support level (more than 10 items present). None of the teachers in these schools reached certification level of proficiency. These findings suggest that a school should provide at least moderate administrative support to the program if personnel are to reach a certification level for performance in the classroom.[6]

[6]Teachers' skill scores were correlated with the levels of administrative support in their schools and were shown to be significantly related.

Controls for Threats to Validity of the Findings in the Study

An additional cohort design was used to rule out the effect that 1 year of teaching experience might have on these performance results. For this comparison, the mean posttraining DTRITS performance score of teachers with no prior teaching experience (Group 1) was compared to the mean score of teachers who had 1 year of prior teaching experience (Group 2) (Cook & Campbell, 1979, pp. 195–196). Group 1 (training alone) had a higher mean DTRITS score of 74 ($SD = 22.3$) after training than Group 2 (experience alone) with a mean score of 54 ($SD = 33.4$) at the beginning of training. The t-ratio of 1.81 occurred at a probability level of less than .05 (one-tailed). This finding rules out the effect of teaching during the training year and adds confidence to the conclusion that the training program contributed to the significant improvement in classroom skills of participants.

Because all of the personnel were required to participate, random selection was not possible and there was a chance of selection effect. However, if so, it would have been toward participants who were inexperienced or insufficiently trained (therefore needing training), thus creating the need for an in-service program. Demographic data on the participants revealed that

---

26–41 items = *High Quality* support (items present and used consistently)

16–25 items = *Moderate Quality* support (sufficient number of items to support implementation)

10–15 items = *Basic* support (essential items provided)

FIGURE 9.6. The *Administrative Support Checklist* provides criteria for rating the resources available to a program. A copy is included in the CD.

the majority had not been trained to work in this field prior to the study. As a group they were young and inexperienced; more than a fourth were employed in low-paying paraprofessional positions, yet were expected to perform effectively on the job with these extremely challenging students.

Summary of the Findings

The evidence supported the conclusion that about 30 hours of in-service training was effective in preparing personnel to use this approach with students who have severe emotional or behavioral disabilities. Unskilled participants became proficient, while those who were already skilled also made gains. When characteristics of the participants such as age, gender, race, years of prior teaching experience, and educational level were correlated, results indicated that these were not significant variables in performance results. However, high quality administrative support was necessary for teachers and teaching assistants to achieve certification level proficiency.

Sustainability of Teachers' Skills 1 and 2 Years After Training

Among the teachers in the study, there were 20 for whom repeated measures were available 16 months after the initial training. These repeated measures allowed for exploration of the stability of their skills over time. Their original DTRITS scores were compared to new ratings, and dependent t-tests with an alpha level of .05 were used to compare the mean scores for the group. Results indicate that there had been no loss in performance ($M = 84.80$, $SD = 9.82$, $t = .55$, $p = .59$). Then, after another 16 months, 14 members of the group remained and were rated again. At that time, a statistically significant gain occurred ($M = 90.07$, $SD = 9.74$, $t = 4.42$), $p < .000$). Surprisingly, the group had reached the Demonstration standard of proficiency (DTRITS score > 90) with no further in-service training.[7]

There are several explanations for this finding. First, it suggests that there may be long-term stability in teachers' performance once skills are acquired. Second, attrition of less skilled teachers may have occurred during the following years, leaving teachers with greater skills in the study group. Third, it is possible that several years of implementing the practices are needed for a teacher to achieve the demonstration level. Further research is needed to clarify how teachers continue to advance in their skills over time.

The Third (Re)Validation

To continue accumulating evidence about the effectiveness of Developmental Therapy–Developmental Teaching, a 7-month study was conducted in Kentucky, Georgia, Washington State, and the Virgin Islands (U.S. Department of Education, 1995). These locations were selected to evaluate effectiveness across varied geocultural areas of the country and in programs with different special education placement options (Davis, 1995). The study compared the effects of full inclusion, partial inclusion, and self-contained special education placements on the progress of troubled children with or without other disabilities. Performance data were also collected on the quality of the intervention they received from their teachers during the study period. The findings were reviewed by the Program Effectiveness Panel of the U.S. Department of Education and resulted in approval of this model with "significant evidence of effectiveness" (Turnbull, personal communication, 1996). The evidence is summarized in this section.

Participating Schools

From a pool of 22 schools using this approach, a stratified sample of 5 sites was selected to represent different cultural and economic characteristics (Table 9.1). Program administrators provided descriptions of geocultural characteristics of the communities where the schools were located. Three broad economic classifications were established for each school neighborhood

[7]This study revealed that teachers could maintain their skills 16 months after training and then continue to gain proficiency to a demonstration level within 32 months after training.

using the U.S. Census Bureau median annual household income statistic, with *low* as income below $20,000, *low–middle* between $20,000 and $40,000, and *upper* income above $40,000.

Initially, 79 children and 12 teachers were in the selected programs. This pool represented all of the children at these five schools who were receiving the program and had identified social, emotional, or behavioral disabilities. The teachers were all those participating in in-service training to implement the program at the schools. From this group, the final analyses excluded data of 21 children because they lacked either pre- or post-DTORF–R ratings, leaving a sample of 58 children, ages 2 to 12 years.

Because of the wide age span of the children, four age groups were established: 2 to 4 years, 4 to 6 years, 6 to 8 years, and 8 to 12 years. The ratio of boys to girls was 5 to 1. Some diversity of race was represented, with half reported as mixed race, African American, or Native American and half as White. Among the primary disabilities, 36% had identified emotional/behavioral problems, 31% were identified as having developmental delay (including intellectual disabilities), and 33% had speech or language problems (Table 9.2).

Because of constraints on collecting data about teachers in some school districts, demographic data were not compiled. However, a previous study of teachers' proficiency after in-service training indicated that neither gender, highest degree earned, race, previous experience in general or special education, nor age correlated significantly with proficiency scores at the end of training.

Table 9.1
Characteristics of Selected Sites

Location	Site 1: Kentucky	Site 2: Washington	Site 3: Virgin Islands	Site 4: Virgin Islands	Site 5: Georgia
Predominant Characteristics					
Geocultural	Rural/ Southern	Migrant/ Multicultural	Caribbean/ West Indian	Caribbean/ West Indian	Suburban/ Metropolitan
Income	Low	Low	Low–middle	Low–middle	Middle–upper
Type of Program					
Preschool		✓	✓	✓	
Head start	✓				✓
Primary grades					✓
Upper elementary					
Type of Service					
Full inclusion	✓				
Partial inclusion		✓	✓	✓	✓
Special classes					
No. of teachers participating	3	1	2	2	4
No. of children participating	13	8	13	10	14

Table 9.2

Characteristics of 58 Children Participating at the Selected Sites

		Site 1 n = 13	Site 2 n = 8	Site 3 n = 13	Site 4 n = 10	Site 5 n = 14
Age at	Range	40–61	39–68	38–57	38–51	60–119
Preintervention	M	50.0	57.7	45.1	43.9	95.8
(months)	SD	7.3	10.5	5.8	4.4	18.8
Age at	Range	42–66	42–71	43–59	44–57	69–127
Postintervention	M	55	61.0	50.1	52.4	105.2
(months)	SD	7.7	10.4	5.8	4.3	19.7
Gender	Boys	11	5	8	8	14
	Girls	2	3	5	2	0
Race	White	13	4	0	0	12
	Mixed race	0	1	13	10	0
	African American	0	1	0	0	2
	Native American	0	1	0	0	0
	Not reported	0	1	0	0	0
Primary disability	Emotional–behavioral	7[a]	0	0	0	14
	Developmental[b]	6	8	4	0	0
	Speech–language	0	0	9	10	0

[a] Five of these children had no diagnosis but are included in this group because they were receiving services for emotional or behavioral problems. When there was a dual or secondary diagnosis, children were included in the emotional/behavioral group because their programs addressed this disability.

[b] Data for children with a specific diagnosis of intellectual disability were included in the group with developmental delay.

Research Design for the Third Validation Study

The DTORF–R was used in a pre–post intervention design to study the progress of children during a single school year. The study compared performance at each site and examined possible effects of age, gender, type of disability, and severity of developmental delay at entry on children's progress. Rater reliability for using the DTORF–R was established in four ways, as summarized in Figure 9.7. For each analysis, mean DTORF–R scores were used for dependent t-tests with an alpha level of .05 to compare groups. Power analysis for estimating the magnitude of effect, taking sample size into account, was obtained with Friedman's (1968, p. 245) point-biserial correlations (r_m) and Cohen's (1988, p. 88) power tables. Effect size criteria were $r_m = .10$ for small, $r_m = .30$ for medium, and $r_m = .50$ for large effects. To control for possible maturation effects, scores were also transformed using a proportional change index (PCI). This permitted comparison of mean rate of item mastery during intervention to the rate before intervention. The procedure is a way to pool gains during intervention for a group mean when children are at different stages of development, different ages, and with different disabilities (Wolery, 1983).[8]

Procedure

Children were rated with the DTORF–R at the beginning of the school year (or at the time of entry, if later). Ratings were repeated at the end of the school year without reference to

[8]For more information about DTORF–R reliability and validity and about the PCI calculation, refer to Chapter 3.

- Internal item consistency: $r = .99$ for each subscale.
- Interrater agreement, item-by-item: 93%, 94%, 94%, and 96% (four subscales).
- Standard error of measurement: Pretest = .62, posttest = .74 (95% confidence band).
- Ratings require item-by-item consensus by three-person team.

FIGURE 9.7. Four ways in which reliability of DTORF–R scores was established. DTORF–R reliability and validity information is described in Chapter 3.

the original ratings. The average intervention period between pre- and post-measures was 6 months ($M = 6.3$ months, $SD = 3.1$). For children entering late and continuing for a second year, the initial rating at entry was used as the baseline and the next rating during the following school year served as the posttest measure.

To examine possible effects of severity of developmental delay on outcomes, a severity index was calculated for each child by dividing the actual score at entry by the expected score (score corresponding to the child's chronological age at entry). Actual scores less than 26% below expected for the age indicated a mild developmental delay. Scores between 26% and 74% below age expectation indicated moderate delay, and scores 75% or more below were designated as severe delay.[9]

Rating teams, preferably a parent and two others working with a child at the program site, completed the DTORF–R ratings. At least one member of the rating team was trained specifically in use of the instrument. Together, they provided a consensus rating of items already mastered, those needing work, and those for which a child was not yet ready. The research staff then reviewed the DTORF–R ratings for procedural accuracy. If a rating appeared to be less than accurate, the rating team reconvened for a review, and a revised consensus rating was made when indicated.

During the year, the teachers participated in an ongoing in-service training program that included seminars, individual tutorials, and follow-up observations as they began to implement the practices in their classrooms. At the end of the school year, observations and ratings of each of the 12 teachers were made by the in-service instructors using the DTRITS to assess the extent to which the teachers demonstrated the specified practices in their own classrooms. These instructors had received training to use the instrument with reliability and had achieved 90% or greater item-by-item agreement when paired with another instructor to observe and rate a teacher at the same time.[10]

Gains Made by Children

As a group, the 58 children made statistically significant gains in DTORF–R scores during the intervention period ($M = 10.05$, $SD = 7.00$, $t = 10.94$, $p < .000$, $r_m = .82$). Similarly, they made significant gains in each subscale domain: DOING ($M = 13.21$, $SD = 16.11$, $t = 6.24$, $p < .000$); SAYING ($M = 11.98$, $SD = 16.03$, $t = 5.69$, $p < .000$); RELATING ($M = 8.65$, $SD = 12.86$; $t = 5.69$, $p < .000$); and THINKING ($M = 8.50$, $SD = 9.39$, $t = 6.89$, $p < .000$).

When scores were analyzed separately for the five schools, the findings showed that significant gains occurred at each site (Table 9.3). Calculation of effect sizes exceeded the Cohen standard of $r_m > .50$ overall and for each subscale. The correlations were also considerably above a common standard used in meta-analysis of $r_m > .80$ (Shadish, Cook, & Campbell, 2002, p. 446).[11]

Gains Analyzed by Disability, Severity of Developmental Delay, Age, and Gender

In this same study, DTORF–R gains scores were also examined on several child variables. Statistically significant t values, probability levels, and correlations for effect size indicated

[9]A procedure for calculating severity of developmental delay from a DTORF–R score is described in Chapter 3.

[10]More information about the reliability and validity of the DTRITS is included in Chapter 7.

[11]When teachers use the specified practices with skill, students show statistically significant gains in social, emotional, and behavioral competence.

that gains were made whether children had speech–language, developmental, or emotional/behavioral disabilities. Similarly, when scores were re-analyzed according to severity of delay, age, or gender, significant results were obtained at high confidence levels. These findings indicate that the children, both boys and girls, with varying levels of delay, and in each age group made statistically significant gains from pre- to postintervention, supporting the claim of program effectiveness for children in preschool through upper elementary school (Table 9.4).

Table 9.3

Gains of Children Receiving Developmental Therapy–Developmental Teaching in 1 School Year at Five Schools

	n	Months in Program	DTORF–R Mean Gains	SD	t	r_m	p
Site 1	13	5.2 (2–8)	12.15	8.56	5.1	.82	.000
Site 2	8	3.2 (3–4)	10.75	4.65	6.54	.91	.000
Site 3	13	5.1 (2–9)	7.38	6.40	4.16	.77	.001
Site 4	10	8.5 (5–17)	13.30	8.19	5.13	.87	.000
Site 5	14	9.4 (3–15)	7.86	5.10	5.77	.85	.000
TOTAL for group	58	6.3 (2–17)	10.05	7.00	10.94	.82	.000

Note. This sample includes all who were identified with complete DTORF–R ratings and IEPs at each site.

Table 9.4

DTORF–R Gains Made by Boys and Girls of Varying Disabilities, Severity Levels, and Ages

		n	DTORF–R Mean Gains	SD	t	r_m	p
Gender	Boys	46	9.96	6.64	10.17	.84	.000
	Girls	12	10.42	8.55	4.22	.79	.000
Disability	Emotional–behavioral	21	9.86	7.27	6.21	.81	.000
	Speech–language	19	11.00	7.85	6.11	.82	.000
	Developmental delay	18	9.28	5.93	6.64	.85	.000
Severity level	Mild	20	8.60	4.63	8.31	.88	.000
	Moderate	29	11.62	8.27	7.56	.82	.000
	Severe	9	8.22	6.36	3.88	.81	.005
Age	2–4 yrs. (24–48 mos.)	27	11.63	8.59	7.03	.84	.000
	4–6 yrs (49–72 mos.)	19	9.42	4.66	8.81	.90	.000
	6–8 yrs. (73–96 mos.)	5	8.20	5.40	3.39	.86	.030
	8–12 yrs. (97–125 mos.)	7	7.00	5.86	3.16	.79	.020

Maturation Effect

To examine the question of whether these results can be attributed to maturation, comparisons were also made of the students' rates of gain before intervention with rates of gain during intervention. To do this, DTORF–R scores for each child were transformed to a PCI (see Chapter 3). Children with greater rates of item mastery during intervention than before have PCI scores greater than 1.0, while children with slower rates during intervention than before have PCI scores less than 1.0. With the PCI, statistically significant *t*-values indicated that the preintervention rate of item mastery was less than the rate achieved during intervention. This finding supports the claim that the children's gains during intervention were not attributable to maturation (Table 9.5). Results indicate that gains made by the students during one school year were significant and not due to chance or maturation. However, continuing experimental research is needed before causal inferences can be made with certainty.

Table 9.5

Children's Rates of Item Mastery During Intervention Compared to Their Preintervention Rates

	n	Mean Rate[a]	SD	t	p
Site 1	13	5.9	8.1	2.6	.02
Site 2	8	6.4	3.8	4.8	.002
Site 3	13	4.3	3.7	4.2	.001
Site 4	10	5.7	6.4	2.9	.02
Site 5	14	1.3	1.0	4.8	.000

[a] The rate is a ratio comparing rates of gain before and during intervention. Scores > 1.0 indicate a greater gain during intervention.

Gains in Different Program Options

Similar findings resulted when the gains scores were analyzed according to program options. Children made statistically significant gains whether they participated in full inclusion, partial inclusion with pullout sessions, or in self-contained special education classes. It should be noted that some of the children in the self-contained special education option also participated in selected inclusive classes when they were able to be successful. This analysis indicates that positive gains can occur in full inclusion, partial inclusion, or in self-contained special education (Table 9.6).

Concurrent Outcomes

Questions frequently arise about whether students make progress in academic areas while also participating in an intervention program that addresses their social, emotional, and behavior disabilities. In this study, the question could not be addressed with school age students for

Table 9.6

DTORF–R Gains of Children in Different Program Options

	n	M	SD	t	r_m	p
Full inclusion	13	12.15	8.56	5.12	.83	.000
Partial inclusion[a]	35	10.03	6.76	8.77	.84	.000
Special education class[b]	10	7.40	5.04	4.64	.84	.001

[a] In addition to their special groups, children participated daily in programs with others who had no disabilities.

[b] Children participated in selected integrated classes when they were able to be successful.

several reasons. The participating schools used different educational measures of achievement—or none at all—and were reluctant to impose additional testing burdens on the students and teachers. In some schools, these students were also excused from the requirement for standardized testing because their emotional problems were believed to adversely affect their performance on tests. In instances when they were expected to take the tests, their absences frequently coincided with scheduled testing.

A concurrent measure of preacademic achievement was available for the study at two of the participating schools (Sites 1 and 4, shown in Table 9.1). Fifteen preschool children who had measures of gains on tests other than the DTORF–R, obtained at corresponding testing dates. These tests were *the Learning Accomplishments Profile*—LAP-D (Sanford & Zelman, 1981) and the *Brigance Diagnostic Inventory of Early Development, Revised* (Brigance, 1991). Mean pre- and posttest scores were compared using a dependent *t*-test with an alpha level of .05 to determine if gains had occurred concurrently on the DTORF–R and the other measures of progress. The children made statistically significant gains on both measures during the same time period (Table 9.7).[12]

Community Characteristics

As noted previously in Table 9.1, there were 5 sites and 12 teachers involved in this study. Each site was selected to provide a range of geocultural and economic characteristics. Because there were distinct differences from site to site, the DTORF–R gains scores were re-analyzed according to the three broad geocultural groups and again according to the three household income groupings. Using one-way ANOVA with an alpha level of .05, no significant differences resulted between the scores within each geocultural grouping, $F(3, 57) = 1.49$, MSE = 53.16, $p = .23$, or between each economic grouping, $F(2, 57) = 1.23$, MSE = 48.57, $p = .30$. This lack of difference in outcomes suggests that significant child progress can occur in different community settings with cultural and economic diversity.

Quality of the Intervention

At the end of the school year, performance ratings of the 12 teachers were obtained to verify that the interventions had been provided at an acceptable level of fidelity. Their DTRITS scores of 59 to 92 showed that all were performing above the Passing level. At three sites, 100% of the teachers were proficient at the Effective level or greater (scores > 70), indicating the ability to apply the practices independently and consistently. One teacher had a Highly Effective score of 92—a level of proficiency for demonstrating the practices for others in training. For the six teachers at the remaining two sites, all scored above the Passing level and two demonstrated proficiency at the Effective level. Overall, these findings indicate that at each

[12]This finding contributes to the growing body of knowledge about how young children can gain basic cognitive skills while achieving social, emotional, and behavioral milestones of development.

Table 9.7.

Concurrent Gains of 15 Preschool Children on Readiness Skills and DTORF–R Objectives

	Preintervention		Postintervention		Gain				
	M	*SD*	*M*	*SD*	*M*	*SD*	*t*	*r*$_m$	*p*
Site #1 (*n* = 8)									
LAP–D	50	6	52	5	2	1	4.54	.86	.003
DTORF–R	33	11	49	12	15	8	5.24	.89	.001
Site #4 (*n* = 7)									
Brigance	38	10	48	11	10	8	3.22	.80	.02
DTORF–R	32	16	48	15	15	9	5.83	.92	.001

school the quality of the interventions applied by the teachers were at acceptable levels of specificity and proficiency.

As in previous studies, an administrative support score was also obtained to measure the quality of support provided to each school. This checklist was completed in a consensus rating by each program administrator and project instructor. Four of the five schools provided administrative support with scores in the High Quality range (28–34). The fifth school had a score of 24, meeting the Moderate Quality standard (Table 9.8). This finding suggests that teachers can learn to apply these practices at an acceptable level when there is at least minimum administration support available.

Additional Studies of Effectiveness

Training for University Interns

A study involving 37 university interns provided an opportunity to examine the effectiveness of the training program for university preservice training. In addition, the study compared effects of the proficiencies the interns brought to the training. The internship sites were special education locations where the interns worked with a teacher previously trained in Developmental Therapy–Developmental Teaching or independently with small groups of children with varying disabilities. Interns participated in seminars with the same content provided to in-service teachers. They also received individual feedback from the instructor and the classroom teacher (Wood, Davis, & Swindle, 1998).

Participants were from diverse academic fields and had elected an optional 10-week teaching internship following their academic course work. The group was composed of 13 undergraduates, 20 graduate students, and 4 postgraduate students. They were from 13 different major fields, with the largest numbers in general special education, emotional disturbance, and social work.

When they started, the 37 interns had an average DTRITS score of 68, slightly below the minimum Effective criterion of > 70. Upon completion of the 10-week classroom-based training, their gains from pre- to posttraining were statistically significant ($M = 19.59$; $SD = 16.69$; $t = 7.14$; $p < .000$). As a group they had achieved at the top of the Effective standard with an average score of 88. This standard indicates that they demonstrated proficiency in using the

Table 9.8

Quality Indicators at Program Sites

	Site 1	Site 2	Site 3	Site 4	Site 5
Administrative support score	30	30	24	28	34
Quality level	High	High	Medium	High	High
Teachers' DTRITS Performance					
n	3	1	2	2	4
Mean Score[a]	83	86	76	86	66
Range	78–92	—	61–85	85–88	59–73
SD	16	—	15	13	16

[a] DTRITS proficiency criteria: Passing = 51–69; Effective = 70–89; Highly Effective = 90–100.

specified practices successfully without assistance from a master teacher. Thus, the group was prepared to replicate the practices independently after graduation.

Additional analyses were conducted to examine the effect of initial skill level on performance at the end of training. Among the interns, 21 had pretraining skill scores > 70. The remaining 16 had marginal pretraining scores < 52, which indicated that they were relatively unskilled as they began their internships. Both groups made statistically significant gains in proficiency during the training. The mean gain for the unskilled groups was 34.69 (SD = 13.23, t = 10.49, p < .000), and the skilled group gain was 8.09 (SD = 7.01, t = 5.29, p < .000). This finding adds additional evidence that the training program was effective in increasing the classroom proficiency of both groups of interns—those who began training with skills and those who were less skilled.[13]

Program Effectiveness at Replication Sites

During 2001, a coast-to-coast regional trainers network was formed for local leadership personnel from Washington State to Maine. These were experienced educators who were completing training as trainers and were certified to implement the in-service training program in their local educational, childcare, and mental health programs. As they began their staff development work, collaborative agreements were obtained from 11 of the sites to evaluate the progress of students during the teachers' in-service training and program implementation. Results added to the accumulating evidence that the practices can be replicated with significantly positive effects on the progress of students with varying disabilities. The findings also provided new information about how the four major developmental domains—behavior, communication, socialization, and cognition—respond differentially to the intervention among students of different ages. The results are summarized briefly in this section.

The Students

A sample of 279 students in six states was obtained from a pool of 521 students whose teachers were participating in training as they implemented the program. The sample was composed of all students in the pool who had two complete repeated DTORF–R assessments and whose ratings occurred at least 2 months but no more than 11 months apart. The students ranged in age from 8 months to 20.6 years, with an average age of 7.2 years. Overall, 32% were in preschools, 54% in elementary schools, 6% in middle schools, and 8% in unclassified school placements. All were receiving special education services, with 84% in special classes and 15% in full or partial inclusion.

In this sample, 74% were male and 26% female, 37% were African Americans, 51% were White, and 12% were other races. All had at least one recorded primary disability. There were 166 with emotional or behavioral disabilities, 45 with autism, 25 with pervasive developmental delay, and 43 with other disabilities (see Table 9.9).

Procedures at the Replication Sites

Following in-service instruction in the reliable use of the DTORF–R as an assessment and planning tool, teachers, teaching assistants, and in-service instructors collaborated to obtain team consensus ratings for each student. These ratings provided baselines for the study. The teachers used these baseline profiles to group students for instruction, to select individualized instructional objectives, and to plan developmentally appropriate lessons. A second assessment was repeated at the next regularly scheduled grading period for the school, or sooner if determined to be needed by the teaching team. The average time between ratings was 8.8 months (range = 2–11 months).

[13]Two to 3 years after the study, teachers who continued to use the practices achieved the demonstration level as they gained experience in using the practices on their own.

Table 9.9
Characteristics of 279 Participating Students at 11 Replication Sites

		n	**% of Sample**
Gender	Boys	207	74
	Girls	72	26
Primary disability	Emotional–behavioral	166	60
	Autism	45	16
	Developmental	25	9
	Other disabilities	43	15
Severity of disability	Mild	120	43
	Moderate	138	50
	Severe	20	7
	No delay	1	—
Race	African American	103	37
	White	142	51
	All others	34	12
Program level	Preschool	90	32
	Elementary	150	54
	Middle school	16	6
	Ungraded	23	8

Analyses

For the entire sample, DTORF–R scores were used as the dependent variable, with mean pre- and postintervention *t*-tests calculated for each of the four subscale areas. Inferential statistical analyses with the null hypothesis were conducted using analysis of covariance (ANCOVA) to examine the data for differences in mean gains scores by gender and by race, corrected for months in treatment (the covariant). A probability level was set at .05 and an effect size of $r_m >$ .50. Additionally, separate program group analyses were conducted for 105 children who were in preschools, 116 who were in elementary schools (kindergarten through 5th grade), and 16 who were in middle schools (6th to 8th grades).

Pre- and postintervention scores were also compared for possible effects of students' disabilities and the level of severity. A severity index was calculated for each student by dividing the actual baseline DTORF–R score by an expected score (the score corresponding to a child's chronological age at entry). Three standards had been previously defined for this severity index: Developmental delay of no more than 25% is classified as mild, scores between 26% and 74% indicate moderate delay, and scores greater then 75% are designated as severe. Of the 279 children in the sample, 120 (43%) were classified as mild, 138 (49%) as moderate, and 20 (7%) as severe. One student had no severity rating because the baseline score was comparable to typical age peers.[14]

[14]There is more about calculating the severity index in Chapter 3.

Gains in Students' Competencies

The 279 students as a group made statistically significant gains in all four DTORF–R subscale domains (see Table 9.10). These findings indicate that their behavior, communication, socialization, and cognitive skills increased as the teachers participated in in-service training and applied the practices in their classrooms. Using Cohen's (1988) suggested standard of $r_m > .50$ to judge the magnitude of the effect given the sample size, the r_m values for each subscale were $> .50$, adding confidence to the findings.

Significant gains were made in all four developmental domains for the 166 students with emotional/behavioral disabilities (see Table 9.11) and for the 25 students with pervasive developmental delay (see Table 9.12). Significant gains were also made by students with autism in two of the four subscales: RELATING and THINKING (see Table 9.13). The other types of disabilities were not analyzed separately because of the small sizes of the groups.

When the scores were re-analyzed by severity of students' delay at time of entry, the t-tests for the pre- to postchanges for each subscale indicated that there were statistically significant gains made by all—those with mild, moderate, or severe delay. All of the t-values were significant with a probability $> .05$. Corresponding r_m values indicate that the effect sizes were large ($> .50$), with several exceeding an r_m of .60.

Table 9.10

Gains of 279 Students in 1 School Year at 11 Replication Sites

DTORF–R Subscale Domain		Mean Score	SD	t	r_m^*
DOING (Behavior)	Preintervention	11.30	5.03		
	Postintervention	13.77	5.76	11.18**	.56
SAYING (Communication)	Preintervention	10.91	5.69		
	Postintervention	13.32	6.26	11.68**	.57
RELATING (Socialization)	Preintervention	13.60	6.27		
	Postintervention	16.48	6.59	12.41**	.60
THINKING (Cognition)	Preintervention	20.75	14.60		
	Postintervention	24.94	14.90	10.36**	.53

*Estimates of magnitude of effect using Friedman's point-biserial correlations and Cohen's standard for power size of $r_m > .50$
**$p < .000$

Table 9.11

Analysis of Students' Gains by Primary Disability: Emotional/Behavioral ($n = 166$)

DTORF–R Subscale Domain		Mean Score	SD	t
DOING (Behavior)	Preintervention	12.37	4.57	
	Postintervention	15.43	5.36	11.05*
SAYING (Communication)	Preintervention	12.68	5.05	
	Postintervention	15.46	5.35	10.93*
RELATING (Socialization)	Preintervention	15.43	5.56	
	Postintervention	18.50	5.93	10.10*
THINKING (Cognition)	Preintervention	25.20	13.34	
	Postintervention	30.22	13.01	10.73*

*$p < .000$

Table 9.12

Analysis of Students' Gains by Primary Disability: Pervasive Developmental Delay ($n = 25$)

DTORF–R Subscale Domain		Mean Score	SD	t
DOING (Behavior)	Preintrvention	9.16	5.26	
	Postintervention	10.24	4.61 *	2.16*
SAYING (Communication)	Preintervention	8.84	5.58	
	Postintervention	10.92	5.66	3.74**
RELATING (Socialization)	Preintervention	10.72	6.50	
	Postintervention	12.92	5.61	4.46***
THINKING (Cognition)	Preintervention	17.60	13.34	
	Postintervention	19.96	12.23	3.73**

*$p < .05$
**$p < .001$
***$p < .000$

Table 9.13

Analysis of Students' Gains by Primary Disability: Autism ($n = 45$)

DTORF–R Subscale Domain		Mean Score	SD	t
DOING (Behavior)	Preintervention	9.71	5.87	
	Postintervention	10.78	5.56	1.70
SAYING (Communication)	Preintervention	7.02	5.79	
	Postintervention	7.73	5.71	1.19
RELATING (Socialization)	Preintervention	10.07	6.51	
	Postintervention	12.09	5.93	3.43*
THINKING (Cognition)	Preintervention	14.58	12.94	
	Postintervention	16.98	13.58	2.39**

*$p < .001$
**$p < .02$

Gender and Race Differences in Program Effects

To examine possible gender and race differences, analysis of covariance (ANCOVA) was used, with time in treatment as the covariant to partition variations as much as possible. Results showed that there was no significant gender differences on any of the four DTORF–R subscales, indicating that the intervention was equally effective for boys and girls. As was expected, months in treatment was a significant variable in these outcomes.

The initial ANCOVA to examine intervention outcomes by race indicated no statistically significant differences between the five racial groups in the sample. Because three of the groups (Hispanic, Asian, and multiracial) were too small for separate analyses, ANCOVA was repeated with only the African American ($n = 103$) and White ($n = 142$) groups. Time in treatment was again statistically significant. However, there were no statistical differences between these two racial groups, indicating that the intervention was equally effective with both African American and White students.

Another potentially significant variable was the impact of the intervention across program levels. Students in preschools (see Table 9.14) and elementary schools (see Table 9.15) made statistically significant gains on all four DTORF–R subscales. Those in secondary schools (see Table 9.16) made gains in SAYING but not in DOING, RELATING, or THINKING. Effect sizes for t values in this latter group varied considerably (from r_m of .31 to .60) across the four subscales. Considering the smaller sample size, these findings raised questions about a number of intervening variables that may have affected outcomes. Among the possibilities considered by administrators of these programs were the severity of the students' disabilities, the extent of inclusion, skills of the teachers, administrative support for the program, and the interaction among these variables. Additionally, the teachers and administrators discussed problems arising

Table 9.14

Analysis of Students' Gains by Program Level: Preschool
($n = 105$)

DTORF–R Subscale Domain		Mean Score	SD	t
DOING (Behavior)	Preintervention	8.53	2.85	
	Postintervention	10.42	3.49	7.74*
SAYING (Communication)	Preintervention	8.34	4.14	
	Postintervention	10.49	4.06	8.71*
RELATING (Socialization)	Preintervention	10.53	4.47	
	Postintervention	13.10	4.32	9.26*
THINKING (Cognition)	Preintervention	15.71	8.55	
	Postintervention	20.15	8.67	8.67*

*$p < .000$

Table 9.15

Analysis of Students' Gains by Program Level: Elementary School
($n = 116$)

DTORF–R Subscale Domain		Mean Score	SD	t
DOING (Behavior)	Preintervention	8.53	2.85	
	Postintervention	10.42	3.49	7.74*
SAYING (Communication)	Preintervention	8.34	4.14	
	Postintervention	10.49	4.06	8.71*
RELATING (Socialization)	Preintervention	10.53	4.47	
	Postintervention	13.10	4.32	9.26*
THINKING (Cognition)	Preintervention	15.71	8.55	
	Postintervention	20.15	8.67	8.67*

*$p < .000$

Table 9.16

Analysis of Students' Gains by Program Level: Middle School
($n = 16$)

DTORF–R Subscale Domain		Mean Score	SD	t
DOING (Behavior)	Preintervention	16.50	4.77	
	Postintervention	18.50	5.85	1.86
SAYING (Communication)	Preintervention	15.69	5.21	
	Postintervention	18.06	6.60	2.89*
RELATING (Socialization)	Preintervention	20.56	6.25	
	Postintervention	21.81	6.75	1.26
THINKING (Cognition)	Preintervention	30.81	17.79	
	Postintervention	35.94	17.34	1.64

$p < .01$

when the secondary academic curriculum receives a preemptive priority over instruction for social, emotional, and behavioral competence.

Quality of Administrative Support at Participating Schools

The administrative checklist (described previously) containing 41 basic program elements desirable for effective replication was used by project instructors and site administrators to determine the extent to which administrative support was provided for the implementation efforts. Administrative support scores for each of the 11 schools ranged from 13 to 37, indicating that basic administrative support or better had been available during the implementation. Six schools were rated at the Quality support level with scores ranging from 13 to 25, and five schools had provided Moderate Quality administrative support with scores from 28 to 37. These results supported the conclusion that the schools had met the specified standards for quality replications and that outcomes of the implementations and staff training had positive effects on the students.[15]

[15] As evidence accumulates about the effectiveness of Developmental Therapy–Developmental Teaching, it provides increased confidence that this is a program that works.

Summary

Countless numbers of educators and parents concerned about the social, emotional, and behavioral development of children and teens have learned to use Developmental Therapy–Developmental Teaching effectively over the past 3 decades. Because evaluation is built into the core of this approach, every time it is used correctly the documented results contribute to a growing body of field-based evidence about program effectiveness. The essential measures of effectiveness are (a) students' increased social and emotional competence with increasingly responsible behavior as measured by gains on their individual DTORF–R learning objectives, and (b) teachers' proficiency in using the specified practices as measured by their DTRITS scores for classroom performance.

Cumulative evidence about the effectiveness of Developmental Therapy–Developmental Teaching indicates that troubled students, who may or may not have other disabilities, can make statistically significant gains in achieving individual objectives for social, emotional, communication, and behavioral development within 1 school year when their teachers use the specified practices with skill. The results also indicate that students make significant annual yearly progress whether they are in full inclusion, partial inclusion, or self-contained special education programs. These gains do not appear to be influenced by the type or severity of their disabilities, gender, race, age, or by geographic, economic, and cultural differences in the communities where the programs are located. The evidence also indicates that teachers, teaching assistants, and student teachers in internships who participate in the in-service training program can improve their skills in using the specified practices during a single year and maintain their proficiency for at least 2 years. Further, these skills tend to increase as personnel gain additional experience in using the practices independently.

As an extensively researched intervention over 3 decades, Developmental Therapy–Developmental Teaching has been effective for students with emotional and behavioral disabilities from ages 2 to 18 years, across grade levels, and in intensive, targeted, or preventive programs in diverse educational settings. Guided by quality indicators for group experimental research and evaluation standards required by the No Child Left Behind Act of 2001, repeated studies at numerous replication sites consistently report significant annual yearly progress of students and increased classroom proficiency of teachers.

Epilogue on International Applications

To support educators and communities as they expand educational opportunities for troubled children and youth, a Developmental Therapy–Developmental Teaching consortium is developing a worldwide resource network. This organization is dedicated to expanding international and intercultural applications of the approach. It assists educators in adapting the practices to local cultures, languages, and educational standards. It also provides coaching, staff training, consultation in program design, technical assistance for documenting program effectiveness, and demonstration of effective practices (Bergsson, 2001).

The educational inclusion movement of the last decade has focused on every child's right to participate in education—with freedom from isolation or exclusion—and every child's need for healthy mental as well as physical development. As nations become increasingly conscious of these rights of students and the contributions that can be made by those with disabilities, inclusive special education is becoming an increasingly accepted part of international educational opportunity. Yet the conduct of troubled children and youth with social, emotional, and behavioral disabilities continues to work against this goal.

During a time of heated discussions about the new inclusive legislation, a school for students with behavioral disabilities was established in Essen, North Rhine–Westphalia, Germany. The school program was designed to provide intensive program support and extend into general education settings. In search of a suitable educational program for the students, Karl-Heinz Benkmann, professor of special education at the University of Dortmund, and Marita Bergsson, director of the school, introduced Developmental Therapy–Developmental Teaching to German educators (Benkmann & Bergsson, 1994; Wegler, 1997). It seemed to have many features they had been looking for:

- An approach that adapts theories from a variety of psychological backgrounds and integrated them with developmental concepts
- A turning away from deficit models and a focus on strengths and assets for students' social and emotional development
- Logical derivations from theory to educational practice that allow close linking of diagnosis, teaching in the classroom, and evaluation
- Explicit methods for in-service training to further increase proficiencies within an educational team
- The possibility of applying the program in inclusive as well as in special school settings
- An intercultural compatibility that offers the possibility of adjusting the content and organization to local needs and standards

The German version was named Entwicklungstherapie–Entwicklungspaedagogik (ETEP). Dr. Bergsson initiated the first demonstration program at the school in Essen, trained the teachers, and prepared the German translations of the textbook and assessment instruments (Bergsson, 1995, 1997, 1999b). She also authored and edited several curriculum resource books with her colleagues for use by teachers in their ETEP programs (Bergsson, 1999a; Bergsson & Luckfiel, 1998; Doeller-Fleiter, 2004; Erich, 2002, 2003a, 2003b, 2003c, 2004; Erich, Guelden, & Stemmer, 1999).

As ETEP applications expanded, it was also becoming a part of the curriculum in several German universities and departments of special education, among them the universities in Leipzig, Halle, Munich, Oldenburg, and Potsdam. Information about the suitability of the approach for inclusive settings had spread and within 2 years, requests for staff training in this approach increased to the point where it was difficult for the demonstration school staff to respond to all of the requests for technical assistance in establishing similar programs in other German school districts.

With assistance from the teachers at the school in Essen, other schools, institutions, and teachers soon initiated similar programs for their students with behavior problems. There were also general education teachers who used this approach for children and youth at risk, most of them in grades 1 through 6 or in vocational training courses. It became clear that an increasing number of teachers regarded the special educational needs of their students as their responsibility, and they needed additional skills. They also indicated greater understanding of the nature and meaning of behavioral problems in children and saw their task as the achievement of a balance between individual developmental needs of the students and the expectations of public education in regular classrooms. Furthermore, they understood the importance of preventive work concerning behavior in schools.

These teachers also provided many important insights to guide future replication efforts. They assessed the overall usefulness of the training as high because it increased their sensitivity to the needs of their students; changed their perceptions toward a learning resources-orientated point of view; and increased their proficiency in assessment, classroom planning, and behavior management. The teachers emphasized that a professional standard in the application of behavior management strategies was critical for the success of the whole program. The training topics for teachers, which they regarded as the most important for successful assistance to students with behavior problems in inclusive settings, were as follows:

- Encouraging students with helping attitudes toward their behavior problems (the beliefs and philosophy)
- Understanding (decoding) behavior
- Assessing social and emotional levels of competence of a student
- Selecting instructional objectives for social and emotional development
- Planning objective-based classroom instruction for these students
- Using specified positive intervention strategies (behavior management)
- Collaborating with the families of the students

By the turn of the millennium, critical questions had to be addressed by ETEP staff. It was obvious that training for the increasing number of requests from schools and other institutions could not be provided from the original school and staff in Essen. A training institute was needed that would dedicate its resources solely to teacher training. In response, an international group of educators convened in Düsseldorf, Germany, in October 2000 to explore ways to further expand European training opportunities for teachers of troubled children and youth (Bergsson, 1998, 2001). Among those attending were educators from Russia, Norway, Germany, and the United States. The multinational goal was to offer special and general education teachers training opportunities that meet mutually acceptable standards while encouraging local adaptations for unique cultural and educational differences. The result was the formation of the Institut fuer Entwicklungstherapie–Entwicklungspaedagogik—ETEP–Europe (Institute for Developmental Therapy–Developmental Teaching—Europe).

During the conference, participants reached agreement on guidelines and standards for international training programs in Developmental Therapy–Developmental Teaching. The group also noted that it was imperative for trainers to be present in each teacher's classroom—observing, demonstrating strategies, encouraging, and giving feedback as these practices were implemented. They identified core content and a set of proficiencies essential for teachers using this approach in both general and special education. While establishing mutually acceptable standards across national boundaries for quality of practice, they also encouraged local interpretations and applications (Developmental Therapy Institute, 2000a, b; ETEP–Europe, 2001a, b). The resulting universal standards for practitioners include the following:

- Accurate developmental assessment to identify a student's current social, emotional, and behavioral status
- Individualized learning objectives based on each student's developmental assessment
- Instructional strategies designed from each student's developmental assessment
- Instructional programs provided in inclusive settings whenever possible and for early childhood, academic, and vocational programs
- Knowledge of core theoretical content that provides the foundation for this approach, including developmental stages of social, emotional, and behavioral development, the existential crisis, decoding behavior, motivating values, developmental anxieties, psychosocial roles, social power, and group dynamics
- Team roles and collaborative skills specified for implementing the practices successfully
- Self-monitoring procedures so that a practitioner can independently maintain skills
- Processes to monitor and document each student's progress during a school year

The conference participants also developed standards for licensure of academies to encourage other educational institutions inside and outside of the European Union to provide coaching, consultation, technical assistance, and training in this approach. An academy was to be responsible for exploring with local colleagues the relevance of this approach and philosophical fit with their educational standards. Translations of Developmental Therapy–Developmental Teaching textbooks, instructional materials, and assessment instruments were also necessary. In addition, each academy would be encouraged to develop its own sequence for a course of study and educational materials reflecting local customs, values, and procedures for meeting their own educational standards. Further, the consortium specified that an approved academy should also certify practitioners who successfully acquire the core skills and knowledge. This certification will require recertification training for every 5 years.

Following formation of ETEP–Europe, a demonstration program began in Jorpeland, Norway. The program is offered entirely in an inclusive setting in a general education school (Grades 1–7). It provides inclusive programs for children with almost all types of disabilities, as is customary for Norwegian schools. Students with mental health and behavior problems receive intense support from social workers, counselors, and special teachers at their schools. Yet, the school found that the needs of students with social, emotional, or behavioral problems were not met as well as they needed to be. Therefore, they invited ETEP–Europe to assist in training a group of teachers in the relevant skills during a period of 8 months.

After preparing a translation of the DTORF–R into Norwegian (*ULDiB Utviklingsbasert Laeremal-Diagnose-Bok*), two teachers from the school observed programs using ETEP at several German demonstration sites. They returned to Norway and started the first group of students in spring 2001 with on-site instructors from ETEP–Europe. At that time, an informational meeting was also held for the entire staff of the school and guests from other schools. Training was designed along three major lines: (a) ongoing training and observation for the original group, (b) beginning training for new members of the school staff, and (c) selection and training of a few teachers to function as future trainers. Teachers from other schools are now showing increased interest in gaining similar skills for the support of the students in their regular classrooms. An institute similar to ETEP–Europe is being planned as a future resource for Scandinavian educators after the program has had sufficient time to be evaluated for its effectiveness with students in Norway.

The first demonstration program in Italy—Terapia dello Sviluppo–Pedagogia dello Sviluppo—began in a children's home, Il Faro, in Nicosia, Sicily. Unlike most Italian children's homes, this one is organized in family-type groups with children of different ages and genders living in a group. This organization allows for sisters and brothers who were taken from their parents by the youth welfare office to stay together. Most of the children had suffered extreme ill treatment in their original families and had severe mental health and behavior problems. All of the children attend regular schools. Italy, one of the first countries in Europe with complete inclusion of children with disabilities, is regarded as a model for inclusion. But this inclusion does not mean that the social and emotional needs of students with mental health and behavior problems have always been met, due to an intense focus on academic matters.

The residential staff of Il Faro asked ETEP–Europe for training, with two goals. First, staff members wanted skills to use the developmental approach in their daily work with the children; and second, they wished to apply this knowledge for collaboration with a local clinic for psychiatry and psychology and with the schools their children attended. The first phase of training has been completed, with the DTORF–R (*Schede Diagnostiche Obiettivi della Pedagogia dello Sviluppo*–SDOPS) and instructional materials translated into Italian by the staff.[1]

These first demonstration programs revealed several necessary elements for successful implementation. At the school level, implementation should begin with a small group of educators who indicate a genuine commitment to explore and try these new practices. Collaboration with a university faculty in teacher education is extremely helpful. Specific goals for implementation must be mutually constructed. Then, the actual implementation begins—gradually— with on-site coaching and knowledgeable backup support from a small network of local colleagues who have used the approach successfully.

As educators in other countries seek effective ways to include troubled children and youth in their educational programs, new demonstration programs are started. Each has its unique characteristics, constraints, and goals. Together, these programs represent the nucleus of a growing international network of mutual support for introducing this approach and maintaining the highest possible quality standards across national boundaries. Programs no longer focus solely on children's massive behavioral problems, but are beginning to serve children with milder social and emotional delay and those at risk. There is also a growing belief that social and emotional education should be a part of instructional programs for all children.

International, multicultural applications provide growing evidence of the effectiveness of this approach in eight European, Asian, and Latin American countries, Canada, and the Virgin Islands. With multinational collaboration, there is increasing agreement about what constitutes an effective educational program for these students. To implement this developmental approach, a collegial resource network is essential. It must first be perceived as filling a recognized need, which educators are committed to address. There must also be an exploratory period when the philosophy and theoretical foundations of this approach are examined in light of local cultures and language, the meanings of words, and educational policy regulations.

Since May 2004, 25 nations have become members of an expanded European Union. With expansion comes a vision of a unified Europe with greater opportunities for educational excellence across boundaries. The experiences of ETEP–Europe and the Developmental Therapy Institute–USA in offering access to information and training underscore the reality that locally adapted Developmental Therapy–Developmental Teaching practices can be inclusive and highly effective for students with behavioral problems and mental health needs. In this endeavor, it became clear that while there are cultural and national differences, there are universally recognized indicators of troubled students in need of special help. There are also many mutually shared beliefs about how students develop social, emotional, and behavioral competencies.

Worldwide formation of several academies such as ETEP–Europe has potential as the foundation for an emerging international network of ongoing communication and support. With each new academy, establishment of its own demonstration program can provide opportunity to

[1]Portions of this information appeared previously in Bergsson, Wood, Quirk, and DeLorme (2003). They are included here with permission of the publisher.

evaluate the applicability of the approach for the local educational system and a locus for training certified practitioners under the coaching of experienced demonstration teachers.[2]

The effectiveness of this developmentally based education movement for troubled students worldwide will ultimately be judged by what these students do when they leave school and join the adult workforce. Will they be able to achieve their potential to become productive citizens, or will they remain the responsibility of the communities in which they live? With concerned educators who have effective instructional skills, the probability of success is greatly increased for individual students, each community, and every nation.

[2] Additional information about ETEP–Europe can be obtained from the Internet at http://www.etep.org. For information about the program in the USA, the Internet address is http://www.uga.edu/dttp.

Publications Documenting the Developmental Therapy–Developmental Teaching Movement Through Three Decades, 1970–2007, Listed Chronologically

Original Model Development, Program Effectiveness, and Model Validation

Wood, M. M., & Fendley, A. (1971). A community psychoeducational center for emotionally disturbed children. *Focus on Exceptional Children, 3,* 9–11.

Wood, M. M., Quirk, J. P., & Swan, W. W. (1971). *Comprehensive services to children with serious emotional and behavioral problems.* Report to the Governor's Commission to Improve Services for Mentally and Emotionally Handicapped Georgians. Atlanta, GA: Georgia Archives.

Wood, M. M. (Ed.). (1972). *The Rutland Center model for treating emotionally disturbed children* (Unpublished Prototype Report). Athens: University of Georgia. [Sections reprinted in J. Platt (1973), *Exemplary programs for the handicapped* (Vol. 3, pp. 1–25). Cambridge, MA: Abt Associates.]

Huberty, C. J., Quirk, J., & Swan, W. W. (1973). An evaluation system for a psychoeducational treatment program for emotionally disturbed children. *Educational Technology, 13,* 73–80.

Wood, M. M. (Ed.). (1975). *Developmental Therapy: A textbook for teachers as therapists for emotionally disturbed young children.* Baltimore, MD: University Park Press.

Swan, W. W., & Wood, M. M. (1975). Making decisions about treatment effectiveness. In M. M. Wood (Ed.), *Developmental Therapy* (Chap. 3). Baltimore, MD: University Park Press.

Swan, W. W., & Wood, M. M. (1976). Rutland Center supplemental services to day care programs. In *Educational programs that work.* U.S. Office of Education, Division of Education for the Disadvantaged. San Francisco: Far West Laboratory for Research and Development. [Reprinted in D. Pefley & H. Smith (Eds.), *It's Monday morning: A history of twenty-seven handicapped children's early education projects* (pp. 20–22). Chapel Hill: University of North Carolina, The Technical Assistance Development System.]

Wood, M. M. (1977). Interagency response to a troubled child. *Teaching Exceptional Children, 9,* 86–88.

Hoyt, J. H. (1978). Georgia's Rutland Center. *American Education, 14,* 27–32.

Wood, M. M., & Swan, W. W. (1978). A developmental approach to educating the disturbed young child. *Behavioral Disorders, 3,* 197–209.

Crimm, W. L. (1980). *An investigation for a prototypical school: The Rutland Center for Developmental Therapy.* Unpublished master's thesis, University of Pennsylvania, Philadelphia, PA.

Kaufman, A. S., Paget, K., & Wood, M. M. (1981). Effectiveness of Developmental Therapy for severely emotionally disturbed children. In F. H. Wood (Ed.), *Perspectives for a new decade* (pp. 176–188). Reston, VA: The Council for Exceptional Children.

Wood, M. M., & Combs, M. C. (1981). *Inservice training in Developmental Therapy.* Research report submitted to the Joint Dissemination Review Panel of the National Institute of Education, U.S. Department of Education, and approved for national dissemination (JDRP approved #81–19).

Wood, M. M. (1982). Developmental Therapy: A model for therapeutic intervention in the schools. In T. B. Gutkin & C. R. Reynolds (Eds.), *A handbook for school psychology* (pp. 609–629). New York: Wiley.

Wood, M. M. (1986). Developmental Therapy. In C. R. Reynolds & L. Mann (Eds.), *Encyclopedia of special education* (Vol. 3, pp. 499–500). New York: Wiley.

Wood, M. M. (1986). *Developmental Therapy in the classroom* (2nd ed.). Austin, TX: PRO-ED.

Wood, M. M. (1989). Lessons learned and insights garnered. In S. Braaten, F. H. Wood, & G. Wrobel (Eds.), *Celebrating the past: Preparing for the future* (pp. 59–97). Minneapolis: Minnesota Council for Children with Behavioral Disorders and Minnesota Educators of Emotionally/Behaviorally Disordered.

Schuh, D. (1992, December). Peg Wood on today's children. *Athens Magazine,* 78–85.

American Psychiatric Association. (1993). Significant achievement awards: Clinical and special education services for severely disturbed children—Developmental Therapy Program, Rutland Psychoeducational Services, Athens, Georgia. *Hospital and Community Psychiatry, 44,* 995–996.

Davis, K. R. (1994). Rutland Developmental Therapy model. In *Educational programs that work: The catalogue of the National Diffusion Network* (20th ed., p. 12.12). Longmont, CO: Sopris West.

Davis, K. R. (1995). Rutland Developmental Therapy model. In *Educational programs that work: The catalogue of the National Diffusion Network* (21st ed.). Longmont, CO: Sopris West.

Wood, M. M. (1996). Vibes, values, and virtues. *Reclaiming Children and Youth, 5,* 174–179.

Berscheid, L., Cooley, L., & Dier, L. (1998). Assisting students to behave in ways that serve them better in the school environment. *Developmentions Newsletter.* (Available from the Developmental Therapy–Teaching Programs, University of Georgia, P.O. Box 5153, Athens, GA 30604.)

Wood, M. M., Davis, K. R., & Swindle, F. H. (1998). *Documenting effectiveness.* (Monograph available from Developmental Therapy Institute, P.O. Box 5153, Athens, GA 30604.)

Wood, M. M., Brendtro, L. K., Fecser, F. A., & Nichols, P. (1999). Psychoeducation: An idea whose time has come. The Third CCBD Mini-Library Series: *What Works for Children and Youth with E/BD: Linking Yesterday and Today with Tomorrow* (pp. 1–37). Reston, VA: Council for Children with Behavioral Disorders, a Division of the Council for Exceptional Children.

Wood, M. M. (2001). Preventing school failure: A teacher's current conundrum. *Preventing School Failure, 45,* 52–57.

McCarty, B. C., & Quirk, C. A. (2003). An "oasis of hope": The power of thinking developmentally. *Reclaiming Children and Youth, 12,* 105–107.

Staff Development

Wood, M. M. (1971). *Rutland Center staff training: Exemplary early childhood centers for handicapped children.* [Staff Training Prototype Series (Vol. 2, No. 10). U.S. Office of Education, Bureau of Education for the Handicapped; Project Number OEG-0-70-4815-613.] Austin: University of Texas at Austin.

Wood, M. M. (1977). The developmental therapy teacher training program: Review of the components for teachers of children with autistic characteristics. In F. H. Wood (Ed.), *Proceedings of a conference on preparing teachers for severely emotionally disturbed children with autistic characteristics.* Minneapolis: Advanced Institute for Trainers of Teachers for Seriously Emotionally Disturbed Children, University of Minnesota.

Wood, M. M. (1981). *Instructor's training manual for Developmental Therapy* (unpublished training manual). Athens, GA: Developmental Therapy Institute.

Wood, M. M., Skaar, C., Mayfield, G., Morrison, K., & Gillespie, F. (1984). *Psychoeducational computer simulation series for teachers of emotionally handicapped students,* Lessons 1 & 2. (Computer Program. Apple IIE software with accompanying workbook.) Athens, GA: Developmental Therapy Institute.

Wood, M. M., Combs, M. C., & Swan, W. W. (1985). Computer simulations: Field testing effectiveness and efficiency for inservice and preservice teacher preparation. *Journal of Educational Technology Systems, 14,* 61–74.

Wood, M. M., & Gunn, A. (1985, May). *Technical assistance to principals, administrators, and teachers in the Portland, Oregon school system for replication of the Developmental Therapy curriculum.* (Unpublished report to the school district, Portland, OR. Reprinted in the CASE national newsletter, Fall, 1985.)

Wood, M. M., Combs, M. C., & Walters, L. H. (1986). Use of staff development by teachers and aides with emotionally disturbed and behavior disordered students. *Teacher Education and Special Education, 9,* 104–112.

Quirk, C. A. (1993). Skill acquisition in in-service teachers of students with emotional and behavioral disabilities. (Doctoral dissertation, University of Georgia, 1993.) *Dissertation Abstracts International, 54,* 2116A.

Wood, M. M. (1999). *Developmental perspective.* (Transcript of an auditory presentation for the University of Missouri–Columbia project, *Enhancing Teachers' Problem-Solving Skills in Early Childhood Behavior Disorders.*)

Developmental Therapy Institute. (2000). *Developmental Therapy–Developmental Teaching certification standards for associate instructors.* Athens, GA: Author.

Developmental Therapy Institute. (2000). *Developmental Therapy–Developmental Teaching: Core content for practitioners.* Athens, GA: Author.

Atlanta Regional Consortium for Higher Education. (2002). Developmental Therapy–Teaching Programs at the University of Georgia. In *Investing in Georgia's future: Higher education partnerships with public schools* (p. 21). (Available from ARCHE, 50 Hurst Plaza, Atlanta, GA.) Atlanta, GA: ARCHE.

Quirk, C. A. (2002). *Final performance report: Developmental Therapy–Teaching outreach for troubled children and teens through a regional associates training network.* Washington, DC: U.S. Department of Education [grant (CFDA 84.324R), Grant No. H324 R 990008-01].

Developmental Therapy Institute. (2003). *PEGS! for Teachers* CD-ROM Series. (Available from www.pegsforteachers.com.)

Developmental Therapy Institute. (2003). *PEGS! for Teachers: Executive brief and report of field tests.* Athens, GA: Author.

Quirk, C. A. (2003). *Final performance report: project PEGS! interactive CD-ROMs to teach adults positive behavior management skills.* Washington, DC: U.S. Department of Education, Office of Special Education Programs, Projects of National Significance. [(CFDA 84.325N), Grant No. H325N990015. Available through ERIC, EC309782.]

Developmental Therapy Institute. (2004). *PEGS! for Parents*—interactive CD-ROM series. (Available from www.lpsoftware.com.)

Quirk, C. A. (2003–2006). *Final performance report: Regional outreach project to expand the quality and effectiveness of educational programs for students with social, emotional, and behavioral disabilities.* Washington, DC: U.S. Department of Education, Office of Special Education Programs, (CFDA. 84.324R). Web-based staff development courses).

Outreach, Replications, and Service Delivery

Wood, M. M. (1971). A case study in replication. *TADSCRIPT Newsletter.* [Expanded in 1976 in L. Gunn (Ed.), *Outreach: Replicating services for young handicapped children* (pp. 133–136). Chapel Hill: University of North Carolina, Technical Assistance Development System.]

Wood, M. M. (1972). Case study 2: An example of program development and the replication process. In D. W. Davis, B. Elliot, & R. R. DeVoid (Eds.), *Replication guidelines* (pp. 28–36). Chapel Hill: University of North Carolina Technical Assistance Development System.

Dillard, J. W. (Ed.). (1974). *Steps in decision making for teachers of disturbed children, and representative objectives rating handbook.* Tuscaloosa: West Alabama Children's Center, Alabama Department of Education.

Wood, M. M. (1974). The Georgia Psychoeducational Center Network. In F. R. Crawford (Ed.), *Exploring mental health parameters* (pp. 194–203). Atlanta, GA: Paje Publishing.

Swan, W. W. (1975). *An outreach process model* (Tadscript No. 8). Chapel Hill: University of North Carolina, Technical Assistance Development System.

EDGE. (1979). *Expanding developmental growth through education.* (Curriculum guide.) Coon Rapids, MN: Anoka-Hennepin School District No. 11, Special Education Department.

Davis, K. (1983). *Rutland Center Developmental Therapy Outreach Project, 1982–1983 Annual Report.* Washington, DC: U.S. Department of Education (Grant No. G008200730).

Davis, K. (1985). *Rutland Center Developmental Therapy Outreach Project, 1984–1985 Annual Report.* Washington, DC: U.S. Department of Education (Grant No. G00840193).

Swan, W. W., Wood, M. M., & Jordan, J. A. (1991). Building a statewide program of mental health and special education services for children and youth. In G. K. Farley & S. G. Zimet (Eds.), *Day treatment for children with emotional disabilities: Models across the country* (Vol. 1, pp. 5–31). New York: Plenum Press.

Davis, K. R. (1992). *Final performance report: Rutland Center—Developmental Therapy outreach project.* Washington, DC: U.S. Department of Education, Office of Special Education. (Grant No. G00840193.)

Swan, W. W., & Brown, C. L. (Eds.). (1992). *GPN Research Reports.* Atlanta, GA: Georgia Psychoeducational Program Network, Georgia Department of Education.

Wood, M. M. (1999). *Final performance report: Developmental Therapy–Developmental Teaching: An outreach project for children and youth with severe disabilities.* Washington, DC: U.S. Department of Education, Office of Special Education (CFDA No. 84.086U; Grant No. H086U6005497).

Quirk, C. A. (2000). *Final performance report: Developmental Therapy–Developmental Teaching: An outreach project for young children with social–emotional–behavioral disabilities.* Washington, DC: U.S. Department of Education (CFDA 84.024D; Grant No. HO24D70035-98).

Instrument Development

Wood, M. M. (1979). *The Developmental Therapy objectives: A self-instructional workbook* (3rd ed.). Austin, TX: PRO-ED. (Portions reprinted in 1984 in *A user's manual for the structured learning center behavioral classroom,* Portland Public Schools, Portland, OR.)

Developmental Therapy Institute. (1982). *Developmental Therapy Rating Inventory of Teacher Skills* (DTRITS). Athens, GA: Author.

Robinson, J. S. (1982). Construction of an instrument to assess the classroom skills of teachers who use Developmental Therapy with emotionally disturbed students. (Doctoral dissertation, University of Georgia, 1982.) *Dissertation Abstracts International, 43,* 1932A.

Robinson, J. S., Wood, M. M., & Combs, M. C. (1982). *Technical report on the Developmental Therapy Rating Inventory of Teacher Skills* (DTRITS). (Unpublished manuscript, University of Georgia, Developmental Therapy Institute, Athens, GA.)

Weller, D. L. (1991). Application of a latent trait model to the developmental profiles of SED/SBD students. (Doctoral dissertation, University of Georgia, 1990.) *Dissertation Abstracts International, 51,* 3388A.

Developmental Therapy Institute. (1992). *The Developmental Teaching objectives for the DTORF: Assessment and teaching of social–emotional competence* (4th ed.). Athens, GA: Author.

Wood, M. M. (1992). *DTORF Technical Report.* Athens, GA: Developmental Therapy Institute.

Wood, M. M. (1992). *DTORF User's Manual.* Athens, GA: Developmental Therapy Institute.

Developmental Therapy Institute. (1998). *Technical report for the Developmental Teaching Objectives Rating Form Revised—DTORF–R.* Athens, GA: Author.

Developmental Therapy Institute. (1998). *User's manual for the Developmental Teaching Objectives Rating Form–Revised—DTORF–R.* Athens, GA: Author.

Buros Institute. (2001). Developmental Teaching Objectives and Rating Forms–Revised (DTORF–R). In B. S. Plake and J. C. Impara (Eds.), *The 14th mental measurements yearbook.* Lincoln: University of Nebraska Press.

Buros Institute. (2002). *Developmental Teaching Objectives and Rating Forms–Revised.* In L. L. Murphy, B. S. Plake, J. C. Impara, & R. A. Spies (Eds.), *Tests in Print VI* (p. 218). Lincoln: University of Nebraska Press.

Maddox, T. (Ed.). (2003). Developmental Teaching Objectives and Rating Forms–Revised (DTORF–R). In *Tests: A comprehensive reference for assessments in psychology, education, and business* (5th ed., p. 199). Austin, TX: PRO-ED.

Developmental Therapy Institute. (2004). *DTORF–R electronic system for assessment and record keeping.* (Available from http://www.lpsoftware.com/dtorf.)

Interventions and Curriculum Expansions

Behavior Management and Life Space Crisis Intervention

Wood, M. M., Combs, M. C., & Lomax, A. (1976). *Strategies for managing severe problem behavior while fostering emotional growth* (CEC Early Childhood Education Institute Series). Reston, VA: The Council for Exceptional Children.

Wood, M. M., & Weller, D. (1981). How come it's different with some children? A developmental approach to Life Space Interviewing. *The Pointer, 25,* 61–66.

Wood, M. M., Peterson, R. L., Combs, M. C., & Quirk, C. A. (1987). *Crisis in classroom behavior management: A developmental issue.* Paper presented at the 67th annual international conference of the Council for Exceptional Children.

Wood, M. M., & Long, N. J. (1991). *Life space intervention: Talking with children and youth in crisis.* Austin, TX: PRO-ED.

Wood, M. M., & Quirk, C.A. (1993). The "Talking into the Air" LSI. *Journal of Emotional and Behavioral Problems, 2,* 45–53.

Georgia Department of Education. (2000). *Georgia state improvement grant (SIG), final performance report, subcomponent #10b: Behavior management skills enhancement through technology.* Atlanta, GA: Author.

Long, N. J., Wood, M. M., & Fecser, F. A. (2001). *Life space crisis intervention* (2nd ed.). Austin, TX: PRO-ED. (Dutch translation by Franky D'Oosterlinck as *Praten met kinderen en jongeren in crisissituaties.* LannooCampus, Belgium.)

Grizzard, V. P. (2004). *The impact of behavior management training on teacher and student behavior.* (Unpublished doctoral dissertation, University of Georgia.)

Developmental Music, Movement, and Play

Graham, R. M. (1975). Music education for emotionally disturbed children. In R.M. Graham (Ed.), *Music for the exceptional child* (pp. 111–129). Reston, VA: Music Educators National Conference.

Graham, R. M., Swan, W. W., Purvis, J., Gigliotti, C., Samet, S., & Wood, M. M. (1975). *Developmental music therapy.* Lawrence, KS: National Music Therapy Association. (Sections reprinted in *Developmental music therapy conference reports,* Developmental Music Therapy and Special Education Conference, 1975, Tempe, AZ: Arizona Department of Education and Arizona State University Music Department. Sections also reprinted as A developmental curriculum for social and emotional growth, in *The interdisciplinary use of art, music, and literature,* March, 1979. Madison, WI: Wisconsin Department of Public Instruction.)

Purvis, J., & Samet, S. (Eds.). (1976). *Music in Developmental Therapy.* Baltimore, MD: University Park Press.

Wood, M. M. (Ed.). (1981). *Developmental Therapy sourcebook: Vol. 1: Music movement and physical skills.* Baltimore, MD: University Park Press.

Wood. M. M. (Ed.). (1981). *Developmental Therapy sourcebook: Vol. 2: Fantasy and make-believe.* Baltimore, MD: University Park Press.

Developmental Art Therapy

Williams, G. H., & Wood, M. M. (1977). *Developmental art therapy.* Austin, TX: PRO-ED.

Age Extensions

Early Childhood

Wood, M. M. (1975). A developmental curriculum for social and emotional growth. In D. L. Lillie (Ed.), *Early childhood education* (pp. 163–182). Chicago, IL: Science Research Associates.

Wood, M. M., & Hurley, O. L. (1977). Curriculum and instruction. In J. B. Jordan, A. H. Hayden, M. B. Karnes, & M. M. Wood (Eds.), *Early childhood education for exceptional children* (pp. 132–157). Reston, VA: The Council for Exceptional Children.

Wood, M. M. (1978). The psychoeducational model. In N. J. Enzer (Ed.), *Social and emotional development: The preschooler.* New York: Walker & Co.

Wood, M. M., & Swan, W. W. (1978). A developmental approach to educating the disturbed young child. *Behavioral Disorders, 3,* 197–209.

Knoblock, P. (1982). *Teaching emotionally disturbed children* (pp. 110, 215–216, 233–235). Boston: Houghton Mifflin.

Geter, B. A. (1991). Longitudinal study of preschool handicapped children. (Doctoral dissertation, University of Georgia, 1991.) *Dissertation Abstracts International, 52,* 879A.

Zabel, M. K. (1991). *Teaching young children with behavioral disorders.* Reston, VA: The Council for Exceptional Children.

Geter, B. A. (1992). Longitudinal cost study of preschool children with severe emotional disabilities. *GPN Research Report, 5,* 17–30.

National Early Childhood TA Center (2004). Georgia: Pegs for parents! In *Contact list.* Frank Porter Graham Child Development Institute (p. 39). Chapel Hill: University of North Carolina.

Adolescents and Preadolescents

Braaton, S. (1979). The Madison School program: Programming for secondary level severely emotionally disturbed youth. *Behavioral Disorders, 4,* 153–162.

Brown, G., McDowell, R. L., & Smith, J. (1981). *Educating adolescents with behavior disorders* (pp. 148–149). Columbus, OH: Merrill.

Braaten, S. (1982). *Behavioral objective sequencing.* Minneapolis: Minnesota Public Schools, Special Education Program.

Braaten, S. (1982). A model for assessment and placement of emotionally disturbed students in special education. In M. M. Noel & N. Haring (Eds.), *Progress or change: Issues in educating the emotionally disturbed: Vol. 1.* Seattle: University of Washington, Program Development System.

Rich, H. L. (1982). *Disturbed students, characteristics and educational strategies* (pp. 292, 294–295). Baltimore, MD: University Park Press.

Shea, T. M., & Bauer, A. M. (1987). *Teaching children and youth with behavior disorders* (2nd ed., pp. 222, 272–274). Englewood Cliffs, NJ: Prentice-Hall.

Rizzo, J. V., & Zabel, R. H. (1988). *Educating children and adolescents with behavioral disorders: An integrative approach* (pp. 80–81, 276–282). Needham, MA: Allyn & Bacon.

McCarty, B. C. (1993). The effect of race, socioeconomic status and family status on the interpersonal understanding of preadolescents and adolescents with severe emotional disturbance. (Doctoral dissertation, University of Georgia, 1992.) *Dissertation Abstracts International, 54,* 485A.

Disability Extensions

Autism and Developmental Delay

Orange County School District. (1976). *An educational model for autistic children: Vol. 3* (pp. 71–83, 92–106). Orange County, FL: Gateway School.

Bachrach, A. W., Mosley, A. R., Swindle, F. L., & Wood, M. M. (1978). *Developmental Therapy for young children with autistic characteristics.* Austin, TX: PRO-ED.

Wood, M. M., Swan, W. W., & Newman, V. (1981). Developmental Therapy for the severely disturbed and autistic. In R. L. McDowell, G. W. Adamson, & F. H. Wood, (Eds.), *Emotional disturbance* (pp. 264–299). New York: Little, Brown.

Wood, M. M., Hendrick, S. J., & Gunn, A. (1983). Programming for autistic students: A model for the public schools. In C. R. Reynolds & J. H. Clark (Eds.), *Assessment and programming for children with low incidence handicaps* (pp. 287–318). New York: Plenum Press.

Gunn, A. L. (1985). A comparison of behaviors and developmental ratings between mentally retarded autistic and mentally retarded non-autistic children. (Doctoral dissertation, University of Georgia, 1984.) *Dissertation Abstracts International, 45,* 2835A.

Language Delay

Lucas, E. V. (1978). The feasibility of speech acts as a language approach for emotionally disturbed children. (Doctoral dissertation, University of Georgia, 1977.) *Dissertation Abstracts International, 38,* 3646A.

Cultural Diversity

Wood, M. M. (1975). *Terapia Evolutiva* [from *Developmental Therapy,* A. Alegría-Martín, Trans.]. Trujillo, Peru: Escuela Especial Carlos A. Manucci. (Reprinted also as *Revisión por Programa de Educación Especial,* Departamento de Instrucción Pública, Hato Rey, Puerto Rico, 1976.)

Marsé, A. (1980). *Recherche en musecotherapie de development.* (Unpublished master's thesis, Ecole de Musique, Université Laval, St. Damien, Quebec.)

Wood, M. M. (1981). *Terapia de Desarrollo* (from *Developmental Therapy,* I. Cudich, M. del C. Gonzalez, & M. I. Stinga, Trans.). Buenos Aires, Argentina: Editorial Médica Panamericana S.A.

Chowdhry, M. (1982). *A study of the programs of some selected institutions for handicapped children in the United States and their relevance to India.* (Unpublished master's research report, University of Georgia, Athens.)

Wood, M. M. (1986). *Developmental Therapy in the classroom* (2nd ed.). Austin, TX: PRO-ED. [Sections translated into Chinese by Wu Jiajin (1988). Anhui Normal University Library, Wuhu City, Anhui Province, China.]

Wood, M. M. (1989, February). What will become of the "Chinese princess"? *Women of China* (pp. 24–25, 44). Beijing, China: Women of China.

Wood, M. M. (1993). *Entwicklungstherapie im klassenzimmer.* (Translation by M. Bergsson of *Developmental Therapy in the classroom.*) Kettwig, Germany: Sonderpädogogisches Forderzentrum für Erziehungshilfe.

Benkmann, K.-H., & Bergsson, M. (1994). Der entwicklungstherapeutische ansatz einer päedagogik für kinder und jugendliche mit verhaltensstöerungen. In K.-H. Benkmann & K. Saueressig (Eds.), *Fördern durch flexible erziehungshilfe* (pp. 73–100). Dortmund, Germany: Vds Landesverband NW.

Bergsson, M. (1995). *Ein entwicklungstherapeutisches modell für schueler mit verhaltensauffäelligkeiten - organisation einer schule. Praxis der entwicklungstherapie: Vol. 1.* Essen, Germany: Bergsson-Billing-Wiedenhöft-Verlag/Progressus Verlag für Pädagogische Praxis.

Wedel, P. (1996). *Roboter 5 besucht unsere Klasse. Praxis der Entwicklungstherapie: Vol. 2.* Essen, Germany: Bergsson—Billing—Wiedenhöft—Verlag/Progressus Verlag für Pädagogische Praxis.

Bergsson, M. (1997, Fall). News of Developmental Therapy in Europe. *Developmentions Newsletter.* (Available from the Developmental Therapy–Teaching Programs, University of Georgia, P.O. Box 5153, Athens, GA 30604, USA.)

Wegler, H. (1997). Die entwicklungstherapie nach Mary Wood—modell eines integrativen therapiezentrums mit spezialunterricht. In O. Speck (Ed.), *Päedagogische modell für kinder mit verhaltensstoerungen* (pp. 100–137). Muenchen, Germany: Reinhardt.

Bergsson, M. (1998, Spring). Special education is beginning to take shape in Russia and Siberia. *Developmentions Newsletter, 7.* (Available from the Developmental Therapy–Teaching Programs, University of Georgia, P.O. Box 5153, Athens, GA 30604, USA.)

Bergsson, M., & Luckfiel, H. (1998). *Umgang mit "schwierigen" Kindern.* Berlin, Germany: Cornelsen-Scriptor.

Bergsson, M. (1999). Creative programming in Germany: Vocational assessment with EldiB. *Developmentions Newsletter.* (Available from the Developmental Therapy–Teaching Programs, University of Georgia, P.O. Box 5153, Athens, GA 30604, USA.)

Bergsson, M. (1999). *ELDiB - Entwicklungstherapeutischer lernziel-diagnose-bogen sowie Erlaeuterungs - und beispielkatalog des ELDiB für jugendliche.* [This version of the ELDiB (DTORF–R) and the catalogue of examples have been modified in wording from the original version to fit the needs of older youths by the staff of the Jakob Muth-School, Essen, and the Vocational Training Setting CJD, Frechen. Available from ETEP–Europe, Krahestrasse 13 A, 40233, Düsseldorf, Germany].

Erich, R., Guelden, U., & Stemmer, P. (1999). *Neue Abenteuer mit den Superfreunden. Praxis der Entwicklungstherapie: Vol. 4* Düsseldorf, Germany: Bergsson-Billing-Wiedernhoeft-Verlag/Progressus-Verlag für Pädagogische Praxis.

Bergsson, M. (2001, Spring). A worldwide network of Developmental Therapy training institutes. *Developmentions Newsletter.* (Available from the Developmental Therapy–Teaching Programs, University of Georgia, P.O. Box 5153, Athens, GA 30604, USA.)

ETEP–Europe (2001). *Entwicklungstherapie–Entwicklungspadagogik* (ETEP), [Trainer Manual I]. Düsseldorf, Germany: Author.

ETEP–Europe (2001). *Entwicklungstherapie–Entwicklungspadagogik* (ETEP), [Trainer Manual II]. Düsseldorf, Germany: Author.

Erich, R. (2002). Umgang mit verhaltensschwierigen Kindern. *Das Lehrerhandbuch.* Berlin, Germany: Raabe-Verlag.

Bergsson, M., Wood, M. M., Quirk, C., & DeLorme, B. T. (2003). An emerging European model for educational inclusion of troubled children. *International Education, 32,* 5–26.

Erich, R. (2003). Interventionsstrategien im Umgang mit verhaltensschwierigen Kindern. *Das Lehrerhandbuch.* Berlin, Germany: Raabe-Verlag.

Erich, R. (2003). Verhalten beobachten und beschreiben: Methodisches Herangehen als Hilfe zur Versachlichung. *Attraktive Grundschule.* (Hrsg. Dr. Heinfried Habeck). Berlin, Germany: Raabe-Verlag.

Erich, R. (2003). Verhaltensentwicklung diagnostizieren und foerdern. Problemverhalten Entwicklungsrueckstaende erkennen. *Attraktive Grundschule.* (Hrsg. Dr. Heinfried Habeck). Berlin, Germany: Raabe-Verlag.

Doeller-Fleiter, L. (2004). Entwicklungspaedagogische Foerderung von Schuelern mit Verhaltensauffaelligkeiten – ein offenes (sonder-) paedagogisches Konzept. In R. Kollmar-Masuch (Ed.), *Spruenge ueber Klippen.* Osnabrueck, Germany: Der andere Verlag.

Erich, R. (2004). Verhaltensfaehigkeiten einschaetzen und Foerderziele definieren. *Attraktive Grundschule.* (Hrsg. Dr. Heinfried Habeck). Berlin, Germany: Raabe-Verlag.

Developmental Therapy–Developmental Teaching

Content Analysis Charts for Behavior,
Communication, Socialization, and Cognition

APPENDIX

Table Appendix B.1
Behavior Content Grid

Stage	Behavioral Style	Physical Skills	Behavioral Motivators and Regulators	Behavioral Processes	Rule Governing Behavior and Play
Stage One	Affect–motor Impulsive Unorganized	Body management Manipulation of hands Balance, locomotion, coordination	Sensory stimulation Impulses Pleasure Nurture	Impulsive Repetitive movement Motor limitation Fleeting attention span	No awareness of rules
Stage Two	Motor, language, and imagination Expression of personal experience	Basic movement skills Ball manipulation Eye–hand coordination Directionality Spatial awareness (body-in-space) Stunts and tumbling	Adults and physical gratification Punishment orientation to conforming Simple control of impulse	Motor–verbal exploration Imitation of social behaviors of adults Limited interaction with peers Limited attention span	Games played with no rules or simple ones Winning not a priority
Stage Three	Vacillation between self-expression and conformity	Body coordination skills in simple group games Ball manipulation Low-organized games Manipulative games Body movement (rhythm) Laterality	Self-expression and expectations of adults Some inner controls Self-protection Language used to mediate behavior Adult power through approval	Patterns of simple group behavior Feelings expressed with minimal restraints Adults and heroes modeled Increased attention span	Rules represent authority Elaborate rules Inflexible rules Rules to serve own interest Fairness in taking turns Winning is important Losing is intolerable
Stage Four	Conformity to demands	Basic skills for sports Team sports Group games Intermittent growth spurts	Peer groups and adults representing standards of society Models mannerisms of peers and adults Identification with values Mediates behavior Group social interaction skills	Tolerates delayed results and distant goals Cause and effect Identification with others Recognizes roles of leaders and followers	Basic law-and-order orientation Rules can change to suit group Personal justice Equality Golden rules Group winning important Losing is tolerated
Stage Five	Integration of personal behavior into a value system	Personal fitness Group and individual sports skills Major physical–sexual changes	Individual and group values Personal acclaim by others Valued by others Work role	Experimentation with new experiences Sexual activities Sex-role mannerisms Vicarious experiences satisfy	Rights and contracts orientation Universal justice Rules developed and modified in response to need

Table Appendix B.2
Communication Content Grid

Stage	Social Communication Style	Social Purpose	Social Communication

Stage One	Preverbal and beginning speech	Meeting physical needs
		Expressing drives
			Basic receptive language
			Nonverbal language
			  Eye following
			  Body movement
			  Gestures
			  Vocalizing
			  Word approximations
			  Vocal initiation
			  Labeling
			  Word sequences

Stage Two	Spontaneous language	Verbal assertions
		  Thinking aloud
		  Organizing world
		    with words and
		    concepts
			Egocentric monologues
			  Verbal language
			  Action statements
			  Intention statements
			  Exchanging information

Stage Three	Socialized language	Sustained individual
		exchanges and inner
		language
			Social expression
			  Group discussions
			  Describing experiences
			  Expressing pride
			  Describing characteris-
			    tics of self and others

Stage Four	Self-expressive rational language	Extended group social
		exchanges
			Social–affective expression
			  Elaboration of
			    experiences
			  Expressing feelings of
			    self-praise
			  Expressing feelings of
			    others

Stage Five	Abstract, idea-oriented language	Expanded friendships among peers	Ideological and interper- sonal expression

Table Appendix B.3
Socialization Content Grid

Stage	Major Interpersonal Focus	Predominating Developmental Anxieties	Ego Functions	Characteristic Play	Moral Values	Interpersonal Perspectives and Friendship	Problem-Solving Approach
Stage One	Recognition and trust Relational bonds with adult Dependency Primary identification and separation	Abandonment Aloneness Separation The unknown Deprivation	Undifferentiated pre-social instincts and drives	Sensory-based experiences Awareness Pleasure Sameness Touch Imitation Abundance Repetition	Premoral conscience not yet emerged	Unaware of separate self Adults provide for needs Security comes from objects (toys and people)	None
Stage Two	Individuation and autonomy Measuring up and being successful to please adults Beginning independence and initiative through self-assertion	Inadequacy (anxieties from previous stage plus new ones) Fears loss of acceptance and approval Concern for obtaining needs (physical and emotional) Management of body impulses and drives Restrictions from adults Fear of being caught Fear of punishment	Impulsive Identity formed Organization of external cues Emotional security from adults Minimal expression of inner life	Symbolic play about people and animals Play is for self Make-believe Imitation of other children Desires, fears, and impulses projected into play and resolved happily Simple story sequences Creative imagination Imitation of adults	Preconventional/heteronomous Simple schemata, good versus evil Own needs justify actions Fear and respect of adults	Ego-centered one-way relationships Affection for adults as need satisfiers Adult authority dominates Adults imitated Personal characteristics of adults not recognized Best friends change frequently	Problems solved by adults and other powerful sources Magic Pretend

(continues)

Table Appendix B.3 *Continued.*
Socialization Content Grid

Stage	Major Interpersonal Focus	Predominating Developmental Anxieties	Ego Functions	Characteristic Play	Moral Values	Interpersonal Perspectives and Friendship	Problem-Solving Approach
Stage Three	Self-esteem and social uniformity Acceptance and appreciation by others Measuring up to self-standards set by peers and adults Self is worthy or unworthy "Looking good" in the eyes of others Self-protective in response to others Cooperation Independence tested	Guilt (anxieties from previous stages plus new ones) Fear of loss of love or approval because of personal failings Death fears; fatalism Fear of the unknown Realistic fears ("It could happen") Remote fears ("It might be possible") Mystical fears ("Wouldn't it be terrible if")	Self-protective Superego formed Ego ideal emerges Others help solve conflicts Desires and needs expressed View of reality reconstructed to control feelings	Organized social play Group participation and cooperation Concern over nonconformists Attempts to win games Fairness Experiments with direct power (control) over others Dramatic elaboration Imaginative group play Interactions with other children (parallel and interactive play)	Hedonistic Conscience development Fairness for self Adults' values internalized	Differentiated, subjective perspective Friends are close with mutual interests Sympathy for others Adults seen with unidimensional characteristics Adults provide hero image for imitation and identification	Problems solved by others (adults, heroes) Conforming to rules reduces problems Winning enhances self
Stage Four	Social self conforming to social rules Acceptance in groups Interest in helping others	Conflict (anxieties from previous stages plus new ones) Balancing complex inner drives and needs with outer demands of peers and adults	Conformist Self is obscured Feelings modified to others' expectations	Group interactions Group predominates over child's need to control	Conventional Good behavior Rules internalized Fairness and justice for others Law and order	Self-reflective perspective Friends are partners Interest in roles of others	Problems solved by self and peers

(continued)

Table Appendix B.3 *Continued.*
Socialization Content Grid

Stage	Major Interpersonal Focus	Predominating Developmental Anxieties	Ego Functions	Characteristic Play	Moral Values	Interpersonal Perspectives and Friendship	Problem-Solving Approach
Stage Four (*continued*)	Independence–dependence conflict temporarily resolved	Fear of not being accepted by the group versus expressing self Anxiety over re-spondence and making decisions				Sympathy and awareness of others' needs Second-person reciprocity Altruism Adults seen as multidimensional	
Stage Five	Identity "Who am I" (in relationship to modified social standards) Personal convictions and values Security in belonging Goals and ideals Desire for independence Emotional self-reliance	Self-image (anxieties from all previous stages plus new ones) Concern for body Sex-role doubts Sexual expressions Obtaining affection Doubts of future role and earning capacity Conflict about values governing behavior and decision making	Conscientious and individualistic feel-ings expressed within social-cultural framework Inner controls Formalized affect Instinctual anxieties intellectualized	Experiments with alternatives Changes physical style via dress, mannerisms, eating, drinking, and drug experimentation Daydreams Dates (role-playing relationships) Talking about others Cliques, clubs, and groups Imitation of soci-etal roles via TV, movies, magazines, and sports	Justice Justice in social relationships Social contract orientation Individual rights	Multiple perspectives Empathy Mutual respect in relationships Friends are autonomous but interdependent Awareness of pluralistic social groups Personal character-istics of adults recognized	Problems solved by self and close friends

Table Appendix B.4
Cognition Content Grid

Stage	Cognitive Style	Symbol System	Reasoning Process	Schematic Style

Stage One	Sensorimotor
	  Kinetic feedback
	  Use of simple objects
	    as tools
	  Association of motor
	    movements to
	    environment
	    by labeling
	  Imitative
		Concrete
		  Tangible objects and
		    familiar persons
			Simple perceptions
			  Matching similar
			    objects
			  Object permanence
			    (memory forming)
				Unorganized
				  Random movements
				  Scribbling
				  Imitative movements

Stage Two	Egocentric, prelogical
	    learning through
	    motor experience
	    and concrete
	    materials
	  Representative
	    imitations
		Animistic
		  Simple concrete
		    symbols (toys)
		    representing direct
		    experience and
		    images
		  Anthropomorphic
			Egocentric causality
			  Categorizing
			  Visual perceptual
			    skills
			  Sequencing
			  Simple concepts
			    of past and
			    future, relating
			    parts (memory)
				Preschematic
				  Simple form
				    recognition
				  Human figure forms
				  Concepts defined
				    by use
				  Organization of
				    parts

Stage Three	Concrete operations
	  Organization of parts
	    into whole
	  Relational concepts,
	    rigid constructs
	  Decentering begins
		Semi-abstract
		  Pictures
		  Words
		  Numerals
		  Ludic play
			Organized
			  Seriation
			  Simple conservation
			  Simple abstraction
			  Classification
			  Numerical
			    operations
			  Simple time-telling
				Schematic
				  Organized spatial
				    relationships
				  Basic line appears
				  Colors used to ap-
				    proximate realism
				  Primitive human
				    forms

Stage Four	Expanded concrete
	    operations systems
	    and relationships
	  Generalizing
		Abstract
		  Symbols and images
		    organized in
		    systems
			Complex
			  Conservation
			    processes
			  Understands conse-
			    quences of actions
			  Cause and effect
			  Written expression
			    of experience
			  Concepts of
			    distance, time,
			    and volume
			  Rules used to solve
			    problems
			  Sex-role concepts
			  Evaluating ideas
				Drawing Realism
				  Realistic
				    interpretation
				  Use of simple
				    perspective
				  Skyline disappears
				  Attention to detail
				  Human forms
				    elaborated

Stage Five	Formal operations
	  How things work
	  Values assimilated into
	    cognitive style
	  Decisions
	  Producing ideas
	  Metacognition
	  Evaluation
		Conceptual complexity
		  Idological "causes"
		  Logical relations
		  Principles
			Combining systems
			  Distinguishing pro-
			    cess from outcome
			  Group logic and ethic
			  Writing to commu-
			    nicate informal
			    ideas and feelings
			  Inductive processes
				Naturalistic
				  Natural
				    surroundings
				  Proportion
				  Detailed perspective
				  Color for variations

Summary of Major Motivational Systems

Applied to Developmental Stages

Stage One
Sensorimotor equilibration (Piaget, 1972)

Id drives, instinctual energy, pleasure (Erikson, 1956; A. Freud, 1942; S. Freud, 1936)

Attachment (Bowlby, 1982/1997, 1988)

Model warmth, loss, prosocial imitation, nurturing, bonding (Maccoby, 1980; Mahler, 1968/1987; Rutter & Rutter, 1993)

Anxiety preparedness (Brody & Axelrad, 1970/1993)

Temperament (Kagan 2002; Thomas & Chess, 1977)

Physiological and safety needs (Maslow, 1987)

Stage Two
Avoidance of anxiety (Sullivan, 1953)

Reality demands (S. Freud, 1936)

Belongingness and love needs (Maslow, 1987)

Individuation (Mahler, Pine, & Bergman, 1975)

Tension reduction (Rapaport, 1960)

Autonomy (Erikson, 1968)

Egocentricity (Piaget, 1932/1960)

Stage Three
Initiative, fears, guilt (Erikson, 1968)

Internalization through identification (A. Freud, 1973) or observational modeling (Bandura, 1986)

Heteronomous needs (Kohlberg, 1981; Piaget, 1932/1960)

Esteem needs (Maslow, 1987)

Self-protection (Loevinger, 1976, 1987)

Stage Four
Competence (White, 1963)

Industry and self-esteem (Erikson, 1968, 1977)

Conformity (Loevinger, 1976)

Law and order (Kohlberg, 1981)

(continues)

Vicarious rewards, empathy for a positive effect on another (Aronfreed, 1968; Bandura 1986)

Empathy resulting from either intrinsic or extrinsic rewards (Rosenhan, 1972) or from reciprocal role taking (Selman, 1980)

Search for meaning (Ausubel, 1971; Fingarette, 1963)

Stage Five

Interpersonal conformity (Kohlberg, 1981)

Self-actualization (Maslow, 1987)

Conscientious conformity (Loevinger, 1976, 1987)

Ideal self as pacer (Loewald, 1962)

Identity through society's rituals (Erikson, 1977)

References

Achenbach, T. M. (1992). *Manual for the Child Behavior Checklist.* Burlington: University of Vermont, Department of Psychiatry.

Ainsworth, M. D. S. (1973). The development of infant–mother attachment. In B. M. Caldwell & H. N. Ricciuti (Eds.), *Review of child development research:* Vol. 3 (pp. 1–94). Chicago: University of Chicago Press.

Alpern, G. D., Boll, T. J., & Shearer, M. S. (1986). *The Developmental Profile–II.* Los Angeles: Western Psychological Services.

American Psychiatric Association. (1993). Significant achievement awards. Clinical and special education services for severely disturbed children: Developmental Therapy Program–Rutland Psychoeducational Services, Athens, Georgia. *Journal of Hospital and Community Psychiatry, 44,* 994–996.

Anthony, E. J. (1976). The genesis of oppositional behavior. In E. J. Anthony & D. C. Gilpin (Eds.), *Three clinical faces of childhood* (pp. 1–8; 103–110; 165–172). New York: Spectrum.

Arllen, N. L., Gable, R. A., & Hendrickson, J. M. (1994). Toward an understanding of the origins of aggression. *Preventing School Failure, 38,* 18–23.

Arnold, J. (1984). Values of exceptional students during early adolescence. *Exceptional Children, 51,* 230–234.

Aronfreed, J. (1968). *Conduct and conscience: The socialization of internalized control over behavior.* New York: Academic Press.

Ausubel, D. P. (1971). Motivational issues in cognitive development. In T. Mischel (Ed.), *Cognitive development and epistomology* (pp. 357–361). San Diego, CA: Academic Press.

Bandura, A. (1986). *Social foundations of thought and action: A social cognitive theory.* Englewood Cliffs, NJ: Prentice-Hall.

Bandura, A., & Walters, R. H. (1963). *Social learning and personality development.* Troy, MO: Holt, Rinehart & Winston.

Barbour, N. H., & Seefeldt, C. (1993). *Developmental continuity across preschool and primary grades.* Wheaton, MD: Association for Childhood Education International.

Bayley, N. (1969). *The Bayley Scales of Infant Development* (2nd ed.). San Antonio, TX: The Psychological Corporation.

Beckman, P. J., & Lieber, J. (1992). Parent–child social relationships and peer social competence of preschool children with disabilities. In S. L. Odom, S. R. McConnell, & M. A. McEvoy (Eds.), *Social competence of young children with disabilities* (Chap. 3). Baltimore: Paul H. Brookes.

Benkmann, K.-H., & Bergsson, M. (1994). Der entwicklungstherapeutische ansatzeiner päedagogik für kinder und jugendliche mit verhaltensstöerungen. In K.-H. Benkmann & K. Saueressig (Eds.), *Foerdern durch flexible erziehungshilfe* (pp. 73–100). Dortmund, Germany: Vds Landesverband NW.

Benson, P. (1997). Spirituality and the adolescent journey. *Reclaiming Children and Youth, 5,* 206–209, 219.

Benson, P. L., Williams, D. L., & Johnson, A. L. (1987). *The quicksilver years: The hopes and fears of early adolescence.* New York: HarperCollins.

Bergsson, M. (1995). Ein entwicklungstherapeutisches modell für schueler mit verhaltensauffaelligkeiten - organisation einer schule. In M. Bergsson & L. Doeller-Fleiter (Eds.), *Praxis der entwicklungstherapie: Vol. 1.* Essen, Germany: Bergsson-Billing-Wiedenhoeft-Verlag/Progressus Verlag für Paedagogische Praxis.

Bergsson, M. (1997, Fall). News of Developmental Therapy in Europe. *Developmentions Newsletter.* (Available from the Developmental Therapy–Teaching Programs, University of Georgia, P.O. Box 5153, Athens, GA 30604, USA.)

Bergsson, M. (1998, Spring). Special education is beginning to take shape in Russia and Siberia. *Developmentions Newsletter, 7.* (Available from the Developmental Therapy–Teaching Programs, University of Georgia, P.O. Box 5153, Athens, GA 30604, USA.)

Bergsson, M. (1999a). Creative programming in Germany: vocational assessment with ELDiB. *Developmentions Newsletter.* (Available from the Developmental Therapy–Teaching Programs, University of Georgia, P.O. Box 5153, Athens, GA 30604, USA.)

Bergsson, M. (1999b). *ELDiB - Entwicklungstherapeutischer lernziel-diagnose-bogen sowie Erlaeuterungs- und beispielkatalog des ELDiB für jugendliche.* (This version of the ELDiB [DTORF–R] and the catalogue of examples have been modified in wording from the original version to fit the needs of older youths by the staff of the Jakob Muth-School, Essen, and the Vocational Training Setting CJD, Frechen. Available from ETEP–Europe, Krahestrasse 13 A, 40233, Düsseldorf, Germany.)

Bergsson, M. (2001, Spring). A worldwide network of developmental therapy training institutes. *Developmentions Newsletter*. (Available from the Developmental Therapy–Teaching Programs, University of Georgia, P.O. Box 5153, Athens, GA 30604, USA.)

Bergsson, M., & Luckfiel, H. (1998). *Umgang mit "schwierigen" Kindern*. Berlin, Germany: Cornelsen-Scriptor.

Bergsson, M., Wood, M. M., Quirk, C., & DeLorme, B. T. (2003). An emerging European model for educational inclusion of troubled children. *International Education, 32*, 5–26.

Berscheid, L., Cooley, L., & Dier, L. (1998). Assisting students to behave in ways that serve them better in the school environment. *Developmentions Newsletter*. (Available from the Developmental Therapy–Teaching Programs, University of Georgia, P.O. Box 5153, Athens, GA 30604, USA.)

Beyda, S. D., Zentall, S. S., & Ferko, D. J. K. (2002). The relationship between teacher practices and the task-appropriate and social behavior of students with behavioral disorders. *Behavioral Disorders, 27*, 236–255.

Blos, P. (1979). *The adolescent passage: Developmental issues*. New York: International Universities Press.

Bowlby, J. (1982/1997). *Attachment and loss* (2nd ed., Vol. 1). New York: Basic Books.

Bowlby, J. (1988). *A secure base: Parent–child attachment and healthy human development*. New York: Basic Books.

Bowlby, J. (1989). *The making and breaking of affectional bonds*. London: Routledge.

Bowman, B. T., & Stott, F. M. (1994). Understanding development in a cultural context. In B. L. Mallory & R. S. New (Eds.), *Diversity and developmentally appropriate practices* (Chap. 6). New York: Teachers College Press.

Bradley, R., Henderson, K., & Monfore, M. (2004). A national perspective on children with emotional disorders. *Behavioral Disorders, 29*, 211–223.

Brazelton, T. B. (1994). Preface to *Heart Start: The emotional foundations of school readiness* (p. 5). Boston, MA: Zero to Three Project, National Center for Clinical Infant Program, Children's Hospital Medical Center.

Bredekamp, S., & Copple, C. (Eds.). (1997). *Developmentally appropriate practice in early childhood programs* (*Rev. ed.*). Washington, DC: National Association for the Education of Young Children.

Bretherton, I. (1987). New perspectives on attachment relations: Security, communication, and internal working models. In J. D. Osofsky (Ed.), *Handbook of infant development* (*2nd ed.*, pp. 1061–1100). New York: Wiley.

Brigance, A. H. (1991). *Brigance Diagnostic Inventory of Early Development, Revised*. North Billerica, MA: Curriculum Associates.

Brittain, C. V. (1968). An exploration of the bases of peer compliance and parent compliance in adolescence. *Adolescence, 2*, 445–458.

Brody, S., & Axelrad, S. (1970/1993). *Anxiety and ego formation in infancy*. New York: International Universities Press.

Brown, L. M., & Gilligan, C. (1992). *Meeting at the crossroads*. Cambridge, MA: Harvard University Press.

Buhrmester, D. (1990). Intimacy of friendship, interpersonal competence and adjustment during preadolescence and adolescence. *Child Development, 61*(4), 1101–1111.

Buros Institute (2002). *Tests in Print*. L. L. Murphy, B. S. Plake, J. C. Impara, & R. A. Spies (Eds.). Lincoln: University of Nebraska Press.

Buysse, V., Skinner, D., & Grant, S. (2001). Toward a definition of quality inclusion: Perspectives of parents and practitioners. *Journal of Early Intervention, 24*, 146–161.

Cardillo, J. E., & Smith, A. (1994). Psychometric issues. In T. J. Kiresuk, A. Smith, & J. E. Cardillo (Eds.), *Goal attainment scaling: Applications, theory, and measurement* (Chap. 9). Hillsdale, NJ: Erlbaum.

Carr, E. G., Dunlap, G., Horner, R. H., Koegel, R. L., Turnbull, A. P., Sailor, W., Anderson, J. L., Albin, R. W., Koegel, L. K., & Fox, L. (2002). Positive behavior support: Evolution of an applied science. *Journal of Positive Behavior Interventions, 4*, 4–16, 20.

Carter, E. W., & Wehby, J. H. (2003). Job performance of transitional-age youth with emotional and behavioral disorders. *Exceptional Children, 69*, 449–465.

Children's Defense Fund. (2004). *The state of America's children yearbook*. Washington, DC: Author.

Cohen, J. (1988). *Statistical power analysis for the behavioral sciences* (2nd ed.). Hillsdale, NJ: Lawrence Erlbaum.

Coles, R. A. (1990). *The spiritual life of children*. New York: Houghton Mifflin.

Coles, R. A. (1997). *Moral intelligence of children*. New York: Random House.

Congressional Research Service (2005). *Individuals with Disabilities Education Act (IDEA): Analysis of changes made by P.L. 108-446*. Washington, DC: Library of Congress.

Cook, T. D., & Campbell, D. T. (1979). *Quasi-experimentation: Design and analysis issues for field settings*. Chicago: Rand McNally.

Cooper, C. R., & Cooper, R. G. (1992). Links between adolescents' relationships with their parents and peers: Models, evidence, and mechanisms. In R. D. Parke & G. W. Ladd (Eds.), *Family–peer relationships: Modes of linkage* (pp. 135–158). Hillsdale, NJ: Erlbaum.

Coopersmith, S. (1967). *The antecedents of self-esteem*. San Francisco: W. H. Freeman.

Cosmos, C. (2002). Children behaving badly—helping students with emotional disorders. *Today, 9*, 1, 5, 9, 13.

Council for Children with Behavioral Disorders (2003). Special issue: The relationship of language and behavior. *Behavioral Disorders, 29*.

Council for Exceptional Children (2003). Special issue: Management of disruptive behavior. *Teaching Exceptional Children, 36.*

Cramer, P. (1990). *The development of defense mechanisms.* New York: Springer-Verlag.

Cullinan, D., Evans, C., Epstein, M. H., & Ryser, G. (2003). Characteristics of emotional disturbance of elementary school students. *Behavioral Disorders, 28,* 94–110.

Cummings, E. M., Davies, P. T., & Campbell, S. B. (2000). *Developmental psychopathology and family process.* New York: Guilford Press.

Curran, P. J. (2000). A latent curve framework for the study of developmental trajectories in adolescent substance abuse. In J. S. Rose, L. Chassin, C. C. Presson, & S. J. Sherman (Eds.), *Multivariate applications in substance abuse research* (pp. 1–42). New York: Lawrence Erlbaum.

Curran, P. J., & Hussong, A. M. (2001). Structural modeling of repeated measures data. In D. Moskowitz & S. Hershberger (Eds.), *Modeling intraindividual variability with repeated measures data: Methods and applications* (pp. 58–86). New York: Lawrence Erlbaum.

Damasio, A. R. (2003). *Looking for Spinoza: Joy, sorrow, and the feeling brain.* Orlando, FL: Harcourt.

Davis, K. R. (1992). *Final performance report: Rutland Center—Developmental Therapy Outreach Project.* Washington, DC: U.S. Department of Education, Office of Special Education.

Davis, K. R. (1995). Rutland Developmental Therapy model. In *Educational programs that work: The catalogue of the National Diffusion Network* (21st ed.). JDRP No. 75–63. Longmont, CO: Sopris West.

Dawson, C. A. (2003). A study of the effectiveness of Life Space Crisis Intervention for students identified with emotional disturbances. *Reclaiming Children and Youth, 11*(4), 223–230.

Developmental Therapy Institute (1998a) *Technical report for the Developmental Teaching Objectives Rating Form—Revised—DTORF–R.* Athens, GA: Author.

Developmental Therapy Institute (1998b). *User's manual for the Developmental Teaching Objectives Rating Form—Revised—DTORF–R.* Athens, GA: Author.

Developmental Therapy Institute. (2000a). *Developmental Therapy–Developmental Teaching: Certification Standards for Associate Instructors.* Athens, GA: Author.

Developmental Therapy Institute. (2000b). *Developmental Therapy–Developmental Teaching: Core Content for Practitioners.* Athens, GA: Author.

Developmental Therapy Institute. (2001/2005). *Developmental teaching objectives for the DTORF–R: Assessment and teaching of social–emotional competence* (4th ed.). (Available from the Developmental Therapy Institute, P.O. Box 5153, Athens, GA 30604, or from www.dtorf.com)

Developmental Therapy Institute (2003a). *PEGS! for teachers: Practice effective guidance strategies.* (Software available from http://www.pegsforteachers.com)

Developmental Therapy Institute (2003b). *PEGS! for teachers: Executive brief and report of field tests.* (Booklet available from the Developmental Therapy Institute, P.O. Box 5153, Athens, GA 30604.)

Doeller-Fleiter. L. (2004): Entwicklungspaedagogische Foerderung von Schuelern mit Verhaltensauffaelligkeiten – ein offenes (sonder-) paedagogisches Konzept. In R. Kollmar-Masuch (Ed.), *Spruenge ueber Klippen.* Osnabrueck, Germany: Der andere Verlag.

DTORF–R. Internet-based electronic assessment system. (Available from www.dtorf.com)

Dwyer, K. P., Osher, D., & Hoffman, C. C. (2000). Creating responsive schools: Contextualizing early warning, timely response. *Exceptional Children, 66,* 347–365.

Edward, J., Ruskin, N., & Turrini, P. (1992). *Separation/individuation: Theory and application* (2nd ed.). New York: Brunner/Mazel.

Eggbert, L. L. (1994). *Anger management for youth: Stemming aggression and violence.* Bloomington, IN: National Educational Service.

Eisenberg, N. (2000). Emotion regulation and moral development. *Annual Review of Psychology, 51,* 665–697.

Eisenberg, N., Miller, P. A., Shell, R., McNalley, S., & Shea, C. (1991). Prosocial development in adolescence: A longitudinal study. In B. Puka (Ed.), *Moral development* (Vol. 7, pp. 1–7). New York: Garland.

Elmore, R. F. & Rothman, R. (Eds.) (1999). *Testing, teaching, and learning: A guide for states and school districts.* Washington, DC: National Academy Press.

Erich, R. (2002). Umgang mit verhaltensschwierigen Kindern. *Das Lehrerhandbuch.* Berlin, Germany: Raabe-Verlag.

Erich, R. (2003a). Interventionsstrategien im Umgang mit verhaltensschwierigen Kindern. *Das Lehrerhandbuch.* Berlin, Germany: Raabe-Verlag.

Erich, R. (2003b). Verhalten beobachten und beschreiben. Methodisches Herangehen als Hilfe zur Versachlichung. *Attraktive Grundschule* (Hrsg. Dr. Heinfried Habeck). Berlin, Germany: Raabe-Verlag.

Erich, R. (2003c). Verhaltensentwicklung diagnostizieren und foerdern. Problemverhalten Entwicklungsrueckstaende erkennen. *Attraktive Grundschule* (Hrsg. Dr. Heinfried Habeck). Berlin, Germany: Raabe-Verlag.

Erich, R. (2004). Verhaltensfaehigkeiten einschaetzen und Foerderziele definieren. *Attraktive Grundschule* (Hrsg. Dr. Heinfried Habeck). Berlin, Germany: Raabe-Verlag.

Erich, R., Guelden, U., & Stemmer, P. (1999). *Neue Abenteuer mit den Superfreunden.* Düsseldorf, Germany: Bergsson-Billing-Wiedernhoeft-Verlag.

Erikson, E. H. (1956). The problem of ego identity. *Journal of the American Psychoanalytic Association, 4,* 56–121.

Erikson, E. H. (1959/1980). *Identity and the life cycle.* New York: W. W. Norton.

Erikson, E. H. (1964). *Insight and responsibility.* New York: W. W. Norton.

Erikson, E. H. (1968). *Identity, youth and crisis.* New York: W. W. Norton.

Erikson, E. H. (1972). Play and actuality. In M. W. Piers (Ed.), *Play and development* (pp. 127–167). New York: W. W. Norton.

Erikson, E. H. (1977). *Toys and reasons.* New York: W. W. Norton.

ETEP–Europe (2001a). *Entwicklungstherapie–Entwicklungspadagogik* (ETEP) (Trainer Manual I). Düsseldorf, Germany: Author.

ETEP–Europe (2001b). *Entwicklungstherapie–Entwicklungspadagogik* (ETEP) (Trainer Manual II). Düsseldorf, Germany: Author.

Farmer, T. W., Goforth, J. B., Leung, M-C., Clemmer, J. T, & Thompson, J. H. (2004). School discipline problems in rural African-American early adolescents: Characteristics of students with major, minor, and no offenses. *Behavioral Disorders, 29*(4), 317–336.

Feather, N. (1979). Values in adolescence. In J. Adelson (Ed.), *Handbook of adolescent psychology* (pp. 247–294). New York: Wiley.

Feil, E. G., Walker, H., Severson, H., & Ball, A. (2000). Proactive screening for emotional/behavioral concerns in Head Start preschools: Promising practices and challenges in applied research. *Behavioral Disorders, 26,* 13–25.

Fingarette, H. (1963). *The self in transformation.* New York: Basic Books.

Forness, S. R. (2005). The pursuit of evidence-based practices in special education for children with emotional or behavioral disorders. *Behavioral Disorders, 30,* 311–330.

Forness, S. R., Walker, H., M., & Kavale, K. A. (2003). Psychiatric disorders and treatments. *Teaching Exceptional Children, 36,* 42–49.

Freud, A. (1942). *The ego and the mechanisms of defense.* London: Hogarth Press.

Freud, A. (1965). *Normality and pathology in childhood: Assessments of development.* New York: International Universities Press.

Freud, A. (1973). The concept of developmental lines. In S. G. Sapir & A. C. Nitzburg (Eds.), *Children with learning problems* (pp. 19–36). New York: Brunner/Mazel.

Freud, S. (1936). *The problem of anxiety.* New York: Psychoanalytic Quarterly Press and W. W. Norton.

Friedman, H. (1968). Magnitude of experimental effect and a table for its rapid estimation. *Psychological Bulletin, 70,* 245–251.

Gable, R. A., Butler, C. J., Walker-Bolton, I., Tonelson, S. W., Quinn, M. M., & Fox, J. J. (2003). Safe and effective schooling for all students: Putting into practice the disciplinary provisions of the 1997 IDEA. *Preventing School Failure, 47,* 74–78.

Gallatin, J. (1980). Political thinking in adolescence. In J. Adelson (Ed.), *Handbook of adolescent psychology* (pp. 344–382). New York: Wiley.

Gardner, H. (1999). *Intelligence reframed: Multiple intelligences for the 21st century.* New York: Basic Books.

George, H. P., Harrower, J. K., & Knoster, T. (2003). School-wide prevention and early intervention: A process for establishing a system of school-wide behavior support. *Preventing School Failure, 47,* 170–176.

Georgia Department of Education. (2001). *Georgia state improvement grant final performance report, subcomponent #10b: Behavior management skills enhancement through technology.* Atlanta, GA: Author.

Gesell, A., & Amatruda, C. (1975). *Developmental diagnosis* (3rd ed.). New York: HarperCollins.

Gibbs, J. C., Potter, G. B., & Goldstein, A. P. (1995). *The EQUIP program: Teaching youth to think and act responsibly through a peer helping approach.* Champaign, IL: Research Press.

Giedd, J. N. (2000). Dynamic systems: Maps of brain development. In A. W. Toga & J. C. Mazziotta (Eds.), *Brain mapping: The systems.* San Diego, CA: Academic Press.

Giedd, J. N., Blumenthal, J., & Jeffries, N. O. (1999). Brain development during childhood and adolescence: A longitudinal MRI study. *Nature Neuroscience, 2,* 861–863.

Giedd, J. N., & Yurgelun-Todd, D. (2004). *Imaging study shows brain maturing.* Bethesda, MD: National Institute of Mental Health, U.S. Department of Health and Human Services. (Available from http://www.nimh.nih.gov/press/prbrainmaturing.cfm)

Ginzberg, E. (1972). Toward a theory of occupational choice: A restatement. *Vocational Guidance Quarterly, 20,* 169–176.

Glasser, W. (1965). *Reality therapy.* New York: HarperCollins.

Glasser, W. (1968). *Schools without failure.* New York: HarperCollins.

Glasser, W. (1998). *The quality school: Managing students without coercion.* New York: HarperCollins.

Goldstein, A. P. (1997a). *Skill streaming the adolescent.* Champaign, IL: Research Press.

Goldstein, A. P. (1997b). *Skill streaming the elementary school child.* Champaign, IL: Research Press.

Goleman, D. (1995). *Emotional intelligence.* New York: Bantam Books.

Goleman, D. (1998). *Working with emotional intelligence.* New York: Bantam Books.

Gorman-Smith, D., Tolan, P. H., & Henry, D. (1999). The relation of community and family to risk among urban poor adolescents. In P. Cohen, C. Slomkowski, & L. Robins (Eds.), *Historical and geographical influences on psychopathology*. Hillsdale, NJ: Erlbaum.

Gotay, N., Sporn, A., Clasen, L. S., Nugent, T. F., Greenstein, D., & Nicolson, R., et al. (2004). Comparison of progressive cortical gray matter loss in childhood-onset schizophrenia with that in childhood-onset atypical psychoses. *Archives of General Psychiatry, 61*, 17–22.

Gould, M. S., King, R., Greenwald, S., Fisher, P., Schwab-Stone, M., Kramer, R., Flisher, A. J., Goodman, S., Canino, G., & Shaffer, D. (1998). Psychopathology associated with suicidal ideation and attempts among children and adolescents. *Journal of the American Academy of Child and Adolescent Psychiatry, 37*, 915–923.

Greenspan, S. I. (1997). *The growth of the mind*. Reading, MA: Perseus Books.

Grizzard, V. P. (2004). *The impact of behavior management training on teacher and student behavior*. (Unpublished doctoral dissertation, University of Georgia.)

Hawkins, J. D. (2005). SPR President Statement. Cited in B. R. Flay et al., Standards of evidence: Criteria for efficacy, effectiveness and dissemination. *Prevention Science* (DOI:10.1007/s11121-005-5553-y).

Hebb, D. O. (1949). *The organization of behavior: A neuropsychological theory*. New York: Wiley.

Henry, D. B. (2000). Peer groups, families, and school failure among urban children: Elements of risk and successful interventions. *Preventing School Failure, 44*, 97–109.

Hobbs, N. (1994). *The troubled and troubling child* (2nd ed.). Cleveland, OH: American Re-Education Association.

Hoyt, J. H. (1978). Georgia's Rutland Center. *American Education, 14*, 27–32.

Huberty, C. J., Quirk, J., & Swan, W. W. (1973). An evaluation system for a psychoeducational treatment program for emotionally disturbed children. *Educational Technology, 13*, 73–80.

Hughes, D. A. (1998). *Building the bonds of attachment*. Northvale, NJ: Jason Aaronson.

Hyman, I. A., & Snook, P. A. (2000). *Dangerous schools/dangerous students: Defining and assessing student alienation syndrome*. Paper presented at the National Association of School Psychologists, 2000 Annual Convention and Exposition, New Orleans, LA.

Ilg, F. L., Ames, L. B., & Baker, S. M. (1981/1992). *Child behavior*. New York: HarperCollins.

Inclusion of Troubled Children [Special issue]. (1994). *Journal of Emotional and Behavioral Problems, 3*(3).

Izard, C. E., & Ackerman, B. P. (2000). Motivational, organizational, and regulatory functions of discrete emotions. In M. Lewis & J. M. Haviland-Jones (Eds.), *Handbook of emotions* (2nd ed., pp. 253–264). New York: Guilford Press.

Joseph, G. E., & Strain, P. S. (2003). Helping young children control anger and handle disappointment. *Young Exceptional Children, 7*, 21–29.

Kagan, J. (1982). The emergence of self. *Journal of Child Psychology and Psychiatry and Allied Disciplines, 23*, 363–381.

Kagan, J. (1989). *Unstable ideas: Temperament, cognition, and self*. Cambridge, MA: Harvard University Press.

Kagan, J. (2002). *Surprise, uncertainty, and mental structures*. Cambridge, MA: Harvard University Press.

Kaiser, A. P., Hancock, T. B., Cai, X., Foster, E. M., & Hester, P. P. (2000). Parent-reported behavioral problems and language delays in boys and girls enrolled in Head Start classrooms. *Behavioral Disorders, 26*, 26–41.

Kandel, D., & Lesser, C. (1969). Parental and peer influence on vocational plans of adolescents. *American Sociological Review, 34*, 213–223.

Kaufman, A. S., Paget, K. D., & Wood, M. M. (1981). Effectiveness of Developmental Therapy for severely emotionally disturbed children. In F. H. Wood (Ed.), *Perspectives for a new decade* (pp. 176–188). Reston, VA: Council for Exceptional Children.

Kegan, R. (1982). *The evolving self: Problem and process in human development*. Cambridge, MA: Harvard University Press.

Kohlberg, L. (1981). *The philosophy of moral development: Moral stages and the idea of justice. Essays on moral development: Vol. 1*. New York: HarperCollins.

Kohlberg. L. (1984). *The psychology of moral development: Moral stages and the life cycle. Essays on moral development: Vol. 2*. New York: HarperCollins.

Kohlberg, L., & Hersh, R. H. (1977). Moral development: A review of the theory. *Theory into Practice, 16*, 53–58.

Kohlberg, L., & Turiel, E. (1971). *Research in moral development: The cognitive developmental approach*. Troy, MO: Holt, Rinehart & Winston.

Lam, M. S., Powers, S. I., Noam, G. G., Hauser, S. T., & Jacobson, A. M. (1993). Parental moral stage and adolescent moral development. In J. Demick, K. Bursik, & R. DiBiase (Eds.), *Parental development* (pp. 75–85). Hillsdale, NJ: Erlbaum.

Lane, K. L., Mahdavi, J. N., & Borthwick-Duffy, S. (2003). Teacher perceptions of the preferred intervention process: A call for assistance with school-based interventions. *Preventing School Failure, 47*, 148–155.

Larson, R. W. (2000). Toward a psychology of positive youth development. *American Psychologist, 55*, 170–183.

Larson, S., & Brendtro, L. (2000). *Reclaiming our prodigal sons and daughters* (Chapter 5). Bloomington, IN: National Educational Service.

Last, C. G. (1993). *Anxiety across the life span: A developmental perspective.* New York: Springer.

LeDoux, J. E. (1996). *The emotional brain: The mysterious underpinnings of emotional life.* New York: Touchstone.

LeDoux, J. E., and Phelps, E. A. (2000). Emotional networks in the brain. In M. Lewis & J. M. Haviland-Jones (Eds.), *Handbook of emotions* (2nd ed., pp. 157–172). New York: Guilford Press.

Lerner, R. M. (Ed.). (1993). *Early adolescence.* Hillsdale, NJ: Erlbaum.

Lewis, M. (1990). Challenges to the study of developmental psychopathology. In M. Lewis & S. Miller (Eds.), *Handbook of developmental psychology* (pp. 30–31). New York: Plenum Press.

Lewis, M. (2000). The emergence of human emotions. In M. Lewis & J. M. Haviland-Jones (Eds.), *Handbook of emotions* (2nd ed., pp. 265–280). New York: Guilford Press.

Lewis, M., & Rosenblum, L. A. (Eds.). (1978). *The development of affect.* New York: Plenum Press.

Lewis, T. J., & Sugai, G. (1999). Effective behavior support: A systems approach to proactive school-wide management. *Focus on Exceptional Children, 31*(6), 1–24.

Lickona, T. (1985). *Raising good children.* New York: Bantam Books.

Lickona, T. (1991). *Educating for character: How our schools can teach respect and responsibility.* New York: Bantam Books.

Loevinger, J. (1976). *Ego development.* San Francisco: Jossey-Bass.

Loevinger, J. (1987). *Paradigms of personality.* New York: W. H. Freeman.

Loewald, H. W. (1962). The superego and the ego ideal. II: Superego and time. *International Journal of Psycho-Analysis, 43,* 264–268.

Long, N. J., & Long, J. E. (2001). *Managing passive–aggressive behavior of children and youth at school and at home.* Austin, TX: PRO-ED.

Long, N. J., Wood, M. M., & Fecser, F. A. (2001). *Life space crisis intervention* (2nd ed.). Austin, TX: PRO-ED.

Maccoby, E. E. (1980). *Social development.* Orlando, FL: Harcourt Brace Jovanovich.

Madsen, K. B. (1968). *Theories of motivation* (4th ed.). Kent, OH: Kent State University Press.

Mahler, M. S. (1968/1987). *On human symbiosis and the vicissitudes of individuation: Infantile psychosis: Vol. 1.* Madison, CT: International Universities Press.

Mahler, M. S., Pine, F., & Bergman, A. (1975). *The psychological birth of the human infant.* New York: Basic Books.

Maloney, F. P., Mirrett, P., Brooke, C., & Johannes, K. (1978). Use of the goal attainment scale in treatment and ongoing evaluation of neurologically handicapped children. *American Journal of Occupational Therapy, 32,* 505–510.

Margolis, H., & McCabe, P. P. (2003). Self-efficacy: A key to improving the motivations of struggling learners. *Preventing School Failure, 47,* 162–169.

Marshall, E. K., & Kurtz, P. D. (1982). *Interpersonal helping skills.* San Francisco: Jossey-Bass.

Martens, B. K., Peterson, R. L., Witt, J. C., & Cirone, S. (1986). Teachers' perceptions of school-based interventions. *Exceptional Children, 53,* 213–223.

Maslow, A. H. (1987). *Motivation and personality* (3rd ed.). New York: HarperCollins.

Mattison, R. E., Gadow, K. D., Sprafkin, J., & Nolan, E. E. (2002). Discriminant validity of a DSM–IV-based teacher checklist: Comparison of regular and special education students. *Behavioral Disorders, 27,* 304–316.

McAdams, C. R., & Lambie, G. W. (2003). A changing profile of aggression in schools: Its impact and implications for school personnel. *Preventing School Failure, 47,* 122–130.

McCarty, B. C. (1992). The effect of race, socioeconomic status and family status on the interpersonal understanding of preadolescents and adolescents with severe emotional disturbance (Doctoral dissertation, University of Georgia, 1992). *Dissertation Abstracts International, 54,* 485A.

McCarty, B. C., & Quirk, C. A. (2003). An "oasis of hope": The power of thinking developmentally. *Reclaiming Children and Youth, 12,* 105–107.

McLean, M. E., Snyder, S., Smith, B. J., & Sandall, S. R. (2002). The DEC recommended practices in early intervention/early childhood special education: Social validation. *Journal of Early Intervention, 25,* 120–128.

Murdick, N. L., Gartin, B. C., & Stockall, N. (2003). Step by step: How to meet the functional assessment of behavior requirements of IDEA. *Beyond Behavior, 12,* 25–30.

Mussen, P. H., Conger, J. J., Kagan, J., & Huston, A. C. (1990). *Child development & personality* (7th ed.). New York: HarperCollins.

Myers, J. (1993). Curricular designs that resonate with adolescents' ways of knowing. In R. M. Lerner (Ed.), *Early adolescence* (pp. 191–205). Hillsdale, NJ: Erlbaum.

Myles, B. S., & Simpson, R. L. (1994). Understanding and preventing acts of aggression and violence in school-age children and youth. *Preventing School Failure, 38,* 40–46.

National Association of School Psychologists (2005). *Links to IDEA legislative information.* Available from www.NASPonline.org/advocacy/IDEAlinks.html.

National Association of State Directors of Special Education (1998). *Guidance on functional behavioral assessments for students with disabilities.* Available from www.vesid.nysed.gov/specialed/publications/policy/functionbehav.htm

National Center for Clinical Infant Programs. (1992). *Head Start: The emotional foundations for school readiness.* Boston: Children's Hospital Medical Center, Zero to Three Project. (Available from the National Center for Clinical Infant Programs, 2000 M Street, Washington, DC 20036.)

National Center for Education Statistics. (2005). *Indicators of school crime and safety.* Washington, DC: U.S. Department of Education, Office of Education Research and Improvement. (Available from http://nces .ed.gov/pubs2004/crime03/index.asp.)

National Clearinghouse on Child Abuse and Neglect. (2003). *Child maltreatment: Summary of key findings* (Table 3-2). Washington, DC: U.S. Department of Health and Human Services. (Available from http:// nccanch.acf.hhs.gov/index.cfm.)

National Institute of Mental Health. (2000). *Child and adolescent violence research at the NIMH.* Bethesda, MD: National Institute of Mental Health, U.S. Department of Health and Human Services. (NIH publication no. 00-4706.) (Available: www.nimh.nih.gov/publicat/NIMHviolenceresfact.pdf.)

National Institute of Mental Health. (2004). [Summary of NIMH activities] Bethesda, MD: National Institute of Mental Health, U.S. Department of Health and Human Services. Available: www.nimh.nih.gov

National Research Council. (2002). Scientific research in education. In R. J. Shavelson & L. Towne (Eds.), *Committee on Scientific Principles for Educational Research.* Washington, DC: National Academy Press.

Nelson, J. R., Babyak, A., Gonzalez, J., & Benner, G. J. (2003). An investigation of the types of problem behaviors exhibited by K–12 students with emotional or behavioral disorders in public school settings. *Behavioral Disorders, 28,* 348–359.

Nelson, J. R., Benner, G. J., Lane, K., & Smith, B. W. (2004). Academic achievement of K–12 students with emotional and behavioral disorders. *Exceptional children, 71,* 59–73.

Newborg, J., Stock, J. R., Wnek, L., Guidubaldi, J., & Svnicki, J. (1988). *Battelle Developmental Inventory Screening Test.* Allen, TX: DLM-Teaching Resources.

Odom, S. L. (2000). Preschool inclusion: What we know and where we go from here. *Topics in Early Childhood Education, 20,* 20–27.

Osofsky, J. D. (1994). Introduction. In J. D. Osofsky & E. Fenichel (Eds.), *Caring for infants and toddlers in violent environments: Hurt, healing, and hope* (pp. 5–6). (Available from the National Center for Clinical Infant Programs, Zero To Three Project. 2000 M Street, Washington, DC 20036.)

Owens, L., & Dieker, L. A. (2003). How to spell success for secondary students labeled EBD: How students define effective teachers. *Beyond Behavior, 12,* 19–23

Pacheco, A. (2004). The gap between what we say and what we do. In C. Glickman (Ed.), *Letters to the next president* (pp. 134–140). New York: Teachers College, Columbia University.

Parke, R. D., Burks, V. M., Carson, J. L., Neville, B., & Boyum, L. A. (1994). Family–peer relationships: A tripartite model. In R. D. Parke & S. C. Kellam (Eds.), *Exploring family relationships with other social contexts* (pp. 115–145). Hillsdale, NJ: Erlbaum.

Parrott, W. G., & Spackman, M. P. (2000). Emotion and memory. In M. Lewis & J. M. Haviland-Jones (Eds.), *Handbook of emotions* (2nd ed., pp. 476 490). New York: Guilford Press.

Parten, M. (1932). Social participation among preschool children. *Journal of Abnormal and Social Psychology, 27,* 243–269.

Patterson, C. R. (1988). Family processs: Loops, levels, and linkages. In N. Bolger, A. Caspi, C. Downey, & M. Morehouse (Eds.), *Persons in context: Developmental processes.* New York: Cambridge University Press.

PEGS! for Teachers. Interactive CD-ROM series. (Available from www.pegsforteachers.com.)

Peterson, R. L., Miller, C., & Skiba, R. (2004, Spring). A framework for planning safe and responsive schools. *Beyond Behavior,* 12–16.

Piaget, J. (1932/1960). *The moral judgment of the child.* New York: Free Press.

Piaget, J. (1937/1954). *The construction of reality in the child.* New York: Basic Books.

Piaget, J. (1951/1962). *Play, dreams, and imitation in childhood.* New York: W. W. Norton.

Piaget, J. (1952). *The origins of intelligence in children.* New York: International Universities Press.

Piaget, J. (1967). *Six psychological studies.* New York: Random House.

Piaget, J. (1972). Some aspects of operations. In M. W. Piers (Ed.), *Play and development* (pp. 15–27). New York: W. W. Norton.

Piaget, J. (1977). *The development of thought: Equilibration of cognitive structures.* New York: Viking Press.

Quirk, C. (1993). Skill acquisition of in-service teachers of students with emotional and behavioral disabilities (Doctoral dissertation, University of Georgia, 1993). *Dissertation Abstracts International, 54,* 2116A.

Quirk, C. A. (2002). *Final performance report: Developmental therapy–teaching outreach for troubled children and teens through a regional associates training network.* Washington, DC: U.S. Department of Education grant, CFDA 84.324R, No. H324 R 990008-01.

Quirk, C. A. (2003). *Final performance report: Project PEGS! interactive CD-ROMs to teach adults positive behavior management skills.* Washington, DC: U.S. Department of Education, Office of Special Education Programs, Projects of National Significance, CFDA 84.325N, No. H325N990015. [Available through ERIC Document Reproduction Service No. EC309782].

Rapaport, D. (1960). The structure of psychoanalytic theory. In G. S. Klein (Ed.), *Psychological Issues* (Vol. 2, pp. 7–158). New York: International Universities Press.

Rasch, C. (1960). *Probabilistic models for some intelligence and attainment tests.* Copenhagen: Paedogogiske Institute.

Redl, F., & Wineman, D. (1951). *Children who hate.* Glencoe, IL: Free Press.

Redl, F., & Wineman, D. (1952). *Controls from within.* Glencoe, IL: Free Press.

Redl, F., & Wineman, D. (1957). *The aggressive child.* Glencoe, IL: Free Press.

Roach, A. T., & Elliot, S. N. (2005). Goal attainment scaling: An efficient and effective approach to monitoring student progress. *Teaching Exceptional Children, 37,* 8–17.

Roach, A. T., & Kratochwill, T. R. (2004). Evaluating school climate and school culture. *Teaching Exceptional Children, 37*(1), 10–17.

Robins, L. N., & Rutter, M. (1990). *Straight and devious pathways from childhood to adulthood.* New York: Cambridge University Press.

Robinson, J. S. (1982/1983). Construction of an instrument to assess the classroom skills of teachers who use Developmental Therapy with emotionally disturbed students (Doctoral dissertation, University of Georgia, 1982). *Dissertation Abstracts International, 43,* 1932A.

Rock, M. L. (2000). Parents as equal partners: Balancing the scales in IEP development. *Teaching Exceptional Children, 32*(6), 30–37.

Rogers, D. E., & Ginzberg, E. (Eds.). (1992). *Adolescents at risk: Medical and social perspectives.* Boulder, CO: Westview Press.

Rogers-Adkinson, D. L., & Hooper, S. R. (2003). The relationship of language and behavior: Introduction to the special issue. *Behavioral Disorders, 29,* 5–9.

Rosenhan, D. L. (1972). Learning theory and prosocial behavior. *Journal of Social Issues, 28,* 151–163.

Rutter, M., & Rutter, M. (1993). *Developing minds: Challenge and continuity across the life span.* New York: Basic Books.

Ryan, J. B., & Peterson, R. L. (2004). Physical restraint in school. *Behavioral Disorders, 29,* 154–168.

Saarni, C. (2000). The social context of emotional development. In M. Lewis & J. M. Haviland-Jones (Eds.), *Handbook of emotions* (2nd ed., pp. 306–322). New York: Guilford Press.

Salovey, P., Bedell, B. T., Detweiller, J. B., & Mayer, J. D. (2000). Current directions in emotional intelligence research. In M. Lewis & J. M. Haviland-Jones (Eds.), *Handbook of emotions* (2nd ed., pp. 504–520). New York: Guilford Press.

Sanford, A. R., & Zelman, J. C. (1981). *Learning Accomplishments Profile–LAP* (Rev. ed.). Chapel Hill, NC: Training Outreach Project.

Sandall, S. R., McLean, M. E., & Smith, B. J. (Eds.). (2000). *DEC recommended practices in early intervention/ early childhood special education* [Special issue]. Longmont, CO: Sopris West.

Sandall, S., & Ostrosky, M. (Eds.). (1999). Practical ideas for addressing challenging behaviors. *Young Exceptional Children* [Monograph series]. Longmont, CO: Sopris West.

Schoen, S. F., & Nolen, J. (2004). Action research: Decreasing acting-out behavior and increasing learning. *Teaching Exceptional Children, 37,* 26–29.

SEARCH Institute. (1998). *Healthy communities, healthy youth.* (Available from the SEARCH Institute, 700 S. Third St., Minneapolis, MN 55415.)

Selman, R. (1980). *The growth of interpersonal understanding.* San Diego, CA: Academic Press.

Selman, R. (1989). Fostering intimacy and autonomy. In W. Damon (Ed.), *Child development today and tomorrow* (pp. 409–435). San Francisco: Jossey-Bass.

Selman, R. L. (2003). *Promotion of social awareness: Powerful lessons from the partnership of developmental theory and classroom practice.* New York: Russell Sage Foundation.

Selman, R., Beardslee, W., Schultz, L. H., Krupa, M., & Podorefsky, D. (1986). Assessing adolescent interpersonal negotiating strategies: Toward the integration of structural and functional models. *Developmental Psychology, 22,* 450–459.

Selman, R., & Schultz, L. H. (1990). *Making a friend in youth: Developmental theory and pair therapy.* Chicago: University of Chicago Press.

Shadish, W. R., Cook, T. D., & Campbell, D. T. (2002). *Experimental and quasi-experimental designs for generalized causal inference.* Boston: Houghton Mifflin.

Siegel, D. J. (1999). *The developing mind: Toward a neurobiology of interpersonal experience.* New York: Guilford Publication, Inc.

Simeonsson, R. J., Bailey, D. B., Huntington, C. S., & Brandon, L. (1991). Scaling and attainment goals in family-focused intervention. *Community Mental Health Journal, 27,* 77–83.

Simeonsson, R. J., Huntington, C. S., & Short, C. S. (1982). Individual differences and goals: An approach to the evaluation of child progress. *Topics in Early Childhood Education, 1,* 71–80.

Sizer, T. (2004). What we all want for each of our children. In C. Glickman (Ed.), *Letters to the next president* (pp. 207–210). New York: Teachers College, Columbia University.

Smith, A. (1994). Introduction and overview. In T. J. Kiresuk, A. Smith, & J. E. Cardillo (Eds.), *Goal attainment scaling: Applications, theory, and measurement.* Hillsdale, NJ: Erlbaum.

Smith, B. J., Strain, P. S., Snyder, P., Sandall, S. R., McLean, M. E., Broudy-Ramsey, A., & Sumi, C. (2002). DEC recommended practices: A review of 9 years of EI/ECSE research literature. *Journal of Early Intervention, 25,* 108–119.

Snyder, S., & Sheehan, R. (1992). The Rasch measurement model: An introduction. *Journal of Early Intervention, 16,* 87–95.

Sprague, J., & Walker, H. (2000). Early identification and intervention for youth with antisocial and violent behavior. *Exceptional Children, 66,* 367–379.

Stien, P. T., & Kendall, J. (2004). *Psychological trauma and the developing brain.* Binghamton, NY: Haworth Press.

Sugai, G., & Horner, R. H. (2002). The evolution of discipline practices: School-wide positive behavior supports. *Child and Family Behavior Therapy, 24,* 23–50.

Sullivan, H. S. (1953). *The interpersonal theory of psychiatry.* New York: W. W. Norton.

Swan, W. W., & Wood, M. M. (1975). Making decisions about treatment effectiveness. In M. M. Wood (Ed.), *Developmental Therapy* (pp. 39–59). Baltimore, MD: University Park Press.

Thomas, A., & Chess, S. (1977). *Temperament and development.* New York: Bruner/Mazel.

Tinsley, H. E., & Weiss, D. J. (1975). Research methodology. *Journal of Counseling Psychology, 22,* 358–376.

Tobin, T. J., & Sugai, G. (1993). Intervention awareness: Educators' perceptions of the need for restrictions on aversive interventions. *Behavioral Disorders, 18,* 110–117.

Toga, A. W., & Mazziotta, J. C. (2000). *Brain mapping: The systems.* San Diego, CA: Academic Press.

Turiel, F. (1983). *The development of social knowledge.* Cambridge, England: Cambridge University Press.

Turiel, E. (1994). The development of social–conventional and moral concepts. In B. Puka (Ed.), *Fundamental research in moral development.* New York: Garland.

U.S. Department of Education. (1975). *Report of the Joint Dissemination Review Panel.* Washington, DC: Author.

U.S. Department of Education. (1981). *Report of the Joint Dissemination Review Panel.* Washington, DC: Author.

U.S. Department of Education. (1995). *Program Effectiveness Panel.* National Institute of Education. Washington, DC: Author.

U.S. Department of Education. (1997). *Twenty-second annual report to Congress on the implementation of the Individuals with Disabilities Education Act.* Washington, DC: Author.

U.S. Department of Education. (2001). *Twenty-third annual report to Congress on the implementation of the Individuals with Disabilities Education Act* [IDEA; Table AF1]. Washington, DC: Author.

U.S. Department of Education. (2002). *No Child Left Behind Act of 2001,* Public Law 107-110, January 8, 2002 [reauthorized Elementary and Secondary Education Act]. (Available from http://www.ed.gov/policy/elsec/leg/esea02/107-110.pdf.)

U.S. Department of Education. (2005). *Scientifically based evaluation methods.* Federal Register: January 25, 2005. (Available from http://www.ed.gov/news/fedregister.)

Vondracek, F. W. (1993). Promoting vocational development in early adolescence. In R. M. Lerner (Ed.), *Early adolescence: Perspectives on research, policy, and intervention* (Chap. 16). Hillsdale, NJ: Erlbaum.

Wallace, T., Anderson, A. R., Bartholomay, T., & Hupp, S. (2002). An ecobehavioral examination of high school classrooms that include students with disabilities. *Exceptional Children, 68*(3), 345–359.

Wegler, H. (1997). Die entwicklungstherapie nach Mary Wood—modell eines integrativen therapiezentrums mit spezialunterricht. In O. Speck (Ed.), *Paedogoogische modelle fur kinder mit verhaltensstoerungen* (pp. 100–137). Muenchen, Germany: Reinhardt.

Weller, D. L. (1991). Application of a latent trait model to the developmental profiles of SED/SBD students (Doctoral dissertation, University of Georgia, 1990). *Dissertation Abstracts International, 51,* 3388A.

White, R. W. (1963). Ego and reality in psychoanalytic theory. In G. S. Klein (Ed.), *Psychoanalytic Issues* (Vol. 3, pp. 517–649). New York: International Universities Press.

Whittmer, D., Doll, B., & Strain, P. (1996). Social and emotional development in early childhood: The identification of competence and disability. *Journal of Early Intervention, 20,* 299–317.

Wolery, M. (1983). Proportional change index: An alternative for comparing child change data. *Exceptional Children, 50,* 167–170.

Wolery, M. R. (2000). Recommended practices in child-focused interventions. In S. Sandall, M. E. McLean, & B. J. Smith (Eds.), *DEC recommended practices in early intervention/early childhood special education,* (Chapter 3). Longmont, CO: Sopris West.

Wolery, M. R., & Bredekamp, S. (1994). Developmentally appropriate practices and young children with disabilities. *Journal of Early Intervention, 18,* 331–341.

Wolery, M., & Sainato, D. (1996). General intervention and curriculum strategies. In S. Odom & M. McLean (Eds.), *Early intervention/early childhood special education: Recommended practices* (pp. 125–158). Austin: TX: PRO-ED.

Wood, M. M. (1975). *Developmental therapy: A textbook for teachers as therapists for emotionally disturbed young children.* Baltimore, MD: University Park Press.

Wood, M. M. (1981). *Instructor's training manual for Developmental Therapy* (unpublished training manual). Athens, GA: Developmental Therapy Institute.

Wood, M. M. (1986). *Developmental therapy in the classroom* (2nd ed). Austin, TX: PRO-ED.

Wood, M. M. (1996a). *Developmental therapy–developmental teaching* (3rd ed). Austin, TX: PRO-ED.

Wood, M. M. (1996b). Vibes, values, and virtues. *Reclaiming Children and Youth, 5,* 174–179.

Wood, M. M., Brendtro, L. K., Fecser, F. A., & Nichols, P. (1999). Psychoeducation: An idea whose time has come. *The Third CCBD Mini-Library Series: What works for children and youth with E/BD: Linking yesterday and today with tomorrow* (pp. 1–37). Reston, VA: Council for Children with Behavioral Disorders, a Division of the Council for Exceptional Children.

Wood, M. M., & Combs, M. C. (1981). *Inservice training in Developmental Therapy.* Research submitted to the Joint Dissemination Review Panel of the National Institute of Education, U.S. Department of Education, Washington, DC. (JDRP approved #81–19.)

Wood, M. M., Combs, M. C., & Walters, L. H. (1986). Use of staff development by teachers and aides with emotionally disturbed and behavior disordered students. *Teacher Education and Special Education, 9,* 104–112.

Wood, M. M., Davis, K. R., & Swindle, F. H. (1998). *Documenting effectiveness.* (Available from the Developmental Therapy Institute, P.O. Box 5153, Athens, GA 30604.)

Wood, M. M., & Long, N. J. (1991). *Life space intervention.* Austin, TX: PRO-ED.

Wood, M. M., Peterson, R. L., Combs, M. C., & Quirk, C. A. (1987). *Crisis in classroom behavior management: A developmental issue.* Paper presented at the 67th annual international conference of the Council for Exceptional Children.

Wood, M. M., & Swan, W. W. (1978). A developmental approach to educating the disturbed young child. *Behavioral Disorders, 3,* 197–209.

Ya-yu, L., Loe, S. A., & Cartledge, G. (2002). The effects of social skills instruction on the social behaviors of students at risk for emotional or behavioral disorders. *Behavioral Disorders, 27,* 371–385.

Youness, J., & Smollar, J. (1985). *Adolescent relationships with mothers, fathers and friends.* Chicago, IL: University of Chicago Press.

Zeeman, R. (1989). From acting out to joining in. In W. Glasser (Ed.), *Control theory in the practice of reality therapy* (pp. 16–33). New York: HarperCollins.

Acknowledgments from the 1986 Edition
Developmental Therapy in the Classroom,
2nd Edition

—By Mary M. Wood with Carolyn Combs,
Andrea Gunn, and Diane Weller

We wish to acknowledge the important contributions made to the 1986 revision of *Developmental Therapy* by the many talented school administrators and teachers throughout the United States who have worked with us in staff development at replication sites for over a decade and have created educational environments where innovation, evaluation, and revision are welcomed with enthusiasm and understanding. The contributions of these individuals have been enormous, each implementing a significant application of the Developmental Therapy model and participating in the evaluation of effectiveness. Through these efforts, more than 12,000 educators have participated in field applications of Developmental Therapy, and we have been able to study the entire range of effects resulting from widespread implementation of the model with more than 10,000 students. This second edition of *Developmental Therapy* reflects the refinements we have been able to make as a result.

The Developmental Therapy Institute at the University of Georgia has been the focal point for advanced leadership training, material development, field applications, program evaluations, and model adaptations during the 10-year period since the first edition. The Institute staff deserves special recognition for providing the nuclear energy for this revision, especially Julie Hendrick, Michael Hendrick, Bonnie McCarty, Rosalie McKenzie, Joey Thomas, and Constance Quirk.

Similarly, since 1975 the Rutland Center–Developmental Therapy National Technical Assistance Outreach Project, under the able direction of William Swan, Anthony Beardsley, and Karen Davis, has provided major leadership in assisting educators and mental health professionals in replicating the model. The Outreach Project staff and consultants—Mary Beussee, Susan Galis, Joyce Garrett, Ann Long, Faye Swindle, and Sara Jo Williams at the University of Georgia; Mary Bross, University of Wisconsin, Whitewater; Bonnie Eninger, San Diego, California; Mary Leiter, Myrtle Beach, South Carolina; Jennie Purvis-Band, Waynesville, North Carolina; Barbara Reid, Eastern Illinois University; and Geraldine Williams, Ohio University—have provided the fieldwork and outreach activities during this decade.

Both the Institute and the Outreach Project received funding from the U.S. Department of Education, Special Education Programs, and the National Diffusion Network. This support has enabled us to continue evaluation of program effectiveness, personnel training in preservice and inservice, leadership training, instructional material development, and replication assistance to schools and agencies at 102 different sites in 30 states. We are deeply appreciative of the support received from our colleagues who have, through the grant review process, given us approval and sustained encouragement in this effort. This second edition of *Developmental Therapy* reflects the refinements we have been able to make as a result.

The Rutland Psychoeducational Center in Athens, Georgia, has continued as the original demonstration and training site for Developmental Therapy since its beginning in 1969. We especially acknowledge the contributions of its director, Robert Jacob, the Clarke County School District, and the talented, supportive staff who have been partners with us for more than 15 years of program development at the original field-based demonstration site. They also have collaborated in the training of countless numbers of student interns and Institute trainees through the years. In all of this, the Rutland Center staff has maintained a standard of service to severely emotionally disturbed students and a dedication to exemplary demonstration of the model components. Several Rutland Center staff members have been with us since the first model demonstration 15 years ago. They are Leroy Dowdy, James Flanagan, Ruby Ann Free, Barbara Geter, the late Diane Perno, Jacqueline Smith, Patricia Stovall, and Faye Swindle. We have traveled together a long distance!

We are particularly appreciative of the sustained support and encouragement of the late Professor E. Paul Torrance, University of Georgia; and Professors Frank Wood, University of Minnesota; Peter Knoblock, Syracuse University; Kathleen Paget, University of South Carolina; Larry Grantham, Western Carolina University; Gene Plank, Emporia State University, Kansas; Cecil Reynolds, Texas A&M University; Alan and Nadeen Kaufman, Lynda Walters, and William Swan, University of Georgia; and Joby Robinson, Columbia, South Carolina. They have aided us substantially in the difficult tasks involving the evaluation of treatment outcomes.

Special appreciation is extended to Dorothy Chambers of the Portland, Oregon, school system for her imaginative and dedicated leadership. Her insightful questions pushed us to find answers. In the follow-up work we did with her colleagues Pat Bungcayo, Bob Gettel, Judy McArdle, Stephanie Newcomer, and Eileen Uland, we continued the exciting process of seeking new classroom applications of developmental theory.

To our many talented and creative colleagues in Georgia who have been supportive and encouraging over the years we extend a special thanks, especially to Joan Jordan, director of Georgia's special education programs; Donna Davis, psychologist with the Clarke County Schools; Robert Gordon, director of the South Metro Psychoeducational Programs in Atlanta, and program coordinators Dan Burns and Linda Dickson; George Andros, director of the Dalton Psychoeducational Programs, and program coordinators Muncie Cooper and Steve Davis; Juanda Ponsel, director of the Griffin Area Psychoeducational Program; Wayne Moffett, director of the Alpine Psychoeducational Programs; Patsy Hinely, director of the Chatham-Effingham Psychoeducational Program in Savannah, Georgia; the late Bob Clarke; and the late Jim Hall.

In the preparation of this manuscript, we are deeply indebted to Marilyn Perkins, who provided the leadership and adopted this book as her own. Without her determination to bring the finished product to press, it might not have been done. We also wish to acknowledge our appreciation of Libby Johnson, Joyce Oliver, and Isabel Clark who provided typing, editing, and cheerful encouragement. For the secretarial assistance to our projects over the years, we thank Harriet Elder and Joyce Davis, and for expert management of our grant accounts and personal enthusiasm, Connie Morse at the University of Georgia.

Acknowledgments from the 1975 Edition *Developmental Therapy: A Textbook for Teachers as Therapists for Emotionally Disturbed Young Children*

—Contributors: Anthony Beardsley, Livija R. Bolster, Carolyn Combs, Cynthia Cook, Marylyn Galewski, Barbara Geter, Ola Jennings, Andrea Lomax Gunn, Bonnie Lee Mailey, William W. Swan, Diane Weller, Ann Reed Williams, Mary M. Wood, Editor.

The material for this text has evolved over a period of 6 years. During that time, many people have contributed to planning, implementing, evaluating, and modifying the various components of Developmental Therapy. To the families of these many individuals, the authors extend their deepest appreciation for providing a climate where each personal contribution had enthusiastic backing and understanding.

The project has had four consultants who have maintained long, loyal relationships to the effort: James Flanagan in child psychiatry; Carl J. Huberty in research design and evaluation; Arthur E. Alper in clinical psychology; and David R. Levine in social work. Their contributions have influenced every aspect of Developmental Therapy.

The advice, expertise, and assistance of a number of outside consultants have also influenced the philosophy and practices of Developmental Therapy as it emerged at the Rutland Center. The time and interest of these consultants is gratefully acknowledged: Norbert Enizer and Sam Rubin in psychiatry; William Frankenberg and William Bonner in pediatrics; Robert Lange and Herbert Quay in research design and evaluation; Frank Wilderson, Ida Wilderson, and Dorothy Campbell in special education; Jane DeWeerd, Laura Fortson and Glenna Bullis for infant and preschool education; Richard Graham in music therapy; and Milton Blue and William Ambrose in language development and hearing.

Perhaps the most significant contributions to the early formulation of what was to become Developmental Therapy can be attributed to Stanley Ainsworth, Kathryn Blake, and Frances Scott at the University of Georgia; and to Nicholas Long at American University, Hillcrest Children's Center, and the Rose School in Washington, DC.

The Technical Assistance Development System (TADS) at the Frank Porter Graham Child Development Center, University of North Carolina has helped put the entire effort into perspective over a 3-year period. In particular, David Lillie, Donald Stedman, Dan Davis, Patrick Trohanis, and Richard Surles have worked closely with the Rutland Center staff as the model emerged.

Finally, Developmental Therapy, as a transportable model, was tested from 1971 to the present in other centers serving seriously disturbed children. Participating in this effort were the staff at several highly effective treatment centers in other locations in Georgia, notably: Carrollton, Georgia, Peggy Pettit, director; Savannah, Georgia, Mignon Lawton, director; and Brunswick, Georgia, Virginia Boyle, director. Also Ana Alegria in Trujillo, Peru has translated Developmental Therapy for Spanish programs. The contributions of these directors and their staffs have been enormous. Each location has demonstrated that Developmental Therapy can be effective in a variety of locations and can provide a common language among professionals trained in vastly different approaches.

In addition to contributions as an evaluator to the project, Faye Swindle provided editorial review of this manuscript. Eileen Patrick typed and retyped the many drafts. For their careful work and cheerful encouragement, the authors are deeply indebted.

The list of acknowledgments would be incomplete without recognition of the immense talent and effort contributed by every member of the Rutland Center staff during the years of development. The authors recognize that Developmental Therapy is a product of the contributions of each:

James Bachrach
Mary Beussee
Nancy Bonney
William Butler
Robert Clarke
Carmie T. Cochrane
Janis Conlin
John Cook
Allan Crimm
Nancy Cudmore
William Cudmore
Allen Curry
John Davis
Steve Davis
Kathleen Deeney
Leroy Dowdy
Bonnie Mailey Eninger
Amy Fendley
Daisy Fleming
Ruby Ann Free
Joyce Garrett
Clementine Gigliotti
Barbara Goldberg
Harry Goodwin
Belita Griffith
Angela Hiley
Patricia McGinnis Hinely
John Humphreys
Linda Javitch
Ola Jennings
Laura Levine
Tucker McClellen
Karen McDonough

Sarah McGinley
Ann McPherson
David Mendenhall
Marilyn Mendoza
Nora Mitchell
Walter Moore
Ada Mosley
Margaret Obremski
Diane Perno
Jennie Purvis
John Quirk
Kathleen Quirk
Steve Reese
JoAnne Rizza
Dixie Lou Rush
Shelley Samet
Ann Seward
Linda Shackleford
Jacqueline Smith
Peggy Smith
Allan Sproles
Patricia Stovall
Carol Stuart
William W. Swan
Faye Swindle
Judi Trebony
Diane Weller
Sally Westerfield
Lesley Whitson
Geraldine Williams
Patricia Willis
Nedra Zisa

Author Index

Subject Index

A

Abandonment, 33, 98, 155, 216

Absenteeism, 14, 95

Abuse. *See* Physical abuse; Substance abuse; Verbal abuse

Academic success, 19, 26, 30

Acceptance, 25–26, 30, 45

Adequacy/inadequacy, 98, 216

Adequate yearly progress (AYP), xxii, 72, 76

Administrative support, 260

Administrative Support Checklist, teacher performance measures and, xix, xxii

Aggression and violence, *See also* Physical abuse; Verbal abuse

   behavior management and, 146–149

   coercion experiences and, 179

   core competencies and, 209

   elementary school children and, 6, 8–9

   emotional phases and, 147–148

   existential crisis and, 106

   family discord and, 18

   group dynamics and, 110

   high school students and, 11

   passive aggression, 144–146

   preschool children and, 39

Aggressive phase, 147–148

Alcohol. *See* Substance abuse

Anger

   anxiety and, 33

   displaced anger, 17

   high school students and, 10

   intervention and, 26

   neuroscience and, 17

   preschool children and, 3

   stress and, 46

   values and, 95

Anxiety

   abandonment anxiety, 33, 98, 155, 216

   anger and, 33

   behavior management and, 120, 125

   curriculum and, 98-99

   definition of, 33

   developmental anxieties, 30, 36, 96, 98–100,

   99, 216, 280–282

   intervention and, 26

   learning and, xxi

   motivational systems and, 285

   psychological defenses for, xxv, 17, 100–102

   stage of development and, 30, 36, 99

   values and, 95

Approval, 25–26, 30

Arrest, 14

Art therapy, 273

Assessment and evaluation, *See also* specific assessment instruments

   bar graphs and, 81–82

   comprehensive assessment, 59–62

   core competency development, 61, 63, 79

   cultural sensitivity and, 88

   developmental age score (DAS) and, 70–71

   evaluation instruments, xix, xxiv

   functional behavior assessment (FBA) and, xix, xxii, xxiv, 59, 117, 205

   goal attainment scaling (GAS) and, 81

   group assessments, 71–74

   IEP and, xix, xxii, xxiv, 23

   IFSP and, xix, xxiv, 205

   implementation of developmental practices and, 205–206, 229–236

   maturation as effect on, 80–81

   overview of, 59

   proportional change ratio (PCR) and, 81

   rating systems and, 60–67, 69, 71, 77–78

   reassessment, 71–72

   student progress evaluation, 75

At-risk students, 18–19, 55

AYP. *See* Adequate yearly progress (AYP)

B

Babies (in groups), definition of, 108

Bar graph summaries, 81–82

Barney, 100

Battelle Developmental Inventory Screening Test (Newborg, Stock, Wnek, Guidubaldi, & Svinicki), 87

Bayley Scales of Infant Development (Bayley), 87

About the Authors

This book is a collaboration among colleagues who have worked together for years, each specializing in a unique aspect of Developmental Therapy–Developmental Teaching. Throughout the phases of model development and expanding applications of this approach over three decades, they have kept their focus on helping troubled preschoolers, children, and teens. They have worked to provide Developmental Therapy–Developmental Teaching to children and families in special education programs, in daycare and child development settings, in children's homes; in general education; in clinics, camps, and residential programs; and in mental health facilities. Their work has taken them from New England to the Pacific Coast, from Maine to Hawaii, from Minnesota to Texas, to the Southern states, the Virgin Islands, Puerto Rico, and into South America, Europe, and Asia.

They provide consultation to school administrators, university teacher preparation programs, the U.S. Department of Education, and private enterprises seeking better ways of meeting the social, emotional, and educational needs of children. Through all of this work to improve direct services to children and families, and to enhance the skills of those who work with them, this team maintains a commitment to creative communication and networking, translating new findings from research into effective day-to-day practice.

Priority efforts continue on field-based research, collecting data to document the progress of students and studying ways to enhance the effectiveness of the teachers who work with them. Current projects include (a) expanding the national and international networks of certified trainers for Developmental Therapy–Developmental Teaching; (b) the *PEGS! for Teachers* series of innovative, interactive CD-ROMs that provide practice in using effective behavior management strategies for inservice or preservice teachers in early childhood programs, elementary schools, and middle/high schools; (c) *PEGS! for Parents,* a version designed to offer similar practice to parents and foster parents; and (d) a series of e-learning courses in this approach for in-service teachers.

Mary M. Wood currently directs training, research, and publication activities of the Developmental Therapy Institute, Inc. and international expansion of Developmental Therapy–Developmental Teaching. As Professor Emerita of Special Education at the University of Georgia, she serves as Senior Advisor to the Developmental Therapy-Teaching Programs at the University, lectures, consults, and writes about issues that affect the lives of troubled children and their families. Her concerns about the impact of contemporary psychosocial stresses on young people continue to fuel efforts also to use this approach with children who are at risk.

Connecting the best in mental health and special education practices is a continuing endeavor for Dr. Wood. Her academic preparation in early childhood and elementary education, special education, and clinical psychology, with degrees from Goucher College and the University of Georgia, enabled her to translate theory and research across disciplines into current practices that enhance educational competence and life skills of troubled children and teens. To this academic background, she adds 25 years of direct clinical work and teaching children and youth who have social, emotional, and behavior disabilities. The earliest foundations for Developmental Therapy–Developmental Teaching came from her work in establishing the first special education teacher training program and clinic for severely emotionally disturbed children and youth in Georgia. This effort expanded into the Rutland–Developmental

Therapy model for the public school district in Clarke County, Georgia, eventually becoming the prototype for the Georgia Psychoeducational Services Network of 24 programs, serving about 7,000 severely disturbed children and youth each year.

Dr. Wood is author and editor of numerous textbooks and articles on the education of children and youth with emotional and behavioral problems. Her writings have been used worldwide and translated into seven languages. She has received many national awards, including the leadership award for "significant contributions to the education of children with behavioral disorders" from the Council for Children with Behavioral Disorders; the Outstanding Service Award from the Midwest Symposium for Leadership in Behavior Disorders; the Spirit of Crazy Horse award for "creating courage in discouraged youth" from the Black Hills Seminars in South Dakota; and the first annual award for distinguished service to the Georgia Psychoeducational Services Network, named in her honor.

Constance A. Quirk is currently Director of Developmental Therapy–Teaching Programs in the College of Family and Consumer Sciences, University of Georgia. She leads this outreach team in providing staff development training and technical assistance to expand applications of Developmental Therapy–Developmental Teaching nationally and internationally. This effort involves designing inservice training materials and new e-learning courses for inservice teachers. She has written and directed numerous federal grants to provide assistance to schools and other agencies serving troubled children and teens, including Head Start, mental health services, and childcare programs for those with special needs, including autism and other disabilities.

Dr. Quirk has degrees in special education from Florida State University and the University of Georgia. Over the past 20 years, she taught students with varying exceptionalities in public and private schools, in day treatment programs, and in residential facilities in Florida, Maine, Oregon, and Georgia. At the University of Georgia and the Rutland Psychoeducational Services in Athens, Georgia she was a demonstration teacher of Developmental Therapy–Developmental Teaching, in Stages One through Four, for students with severe emotional and behavioral disabilities. Dr. Quirk is also a certified Senior Trainer for the Life Space Crisis Intervention Institute, an advanced, interactive strategy that promotes meaningful change for troubled children and youth with chronic patterns of self-defeating behavior. She continues to use her broad background of understanding about the developmental characteristics of children—especially upper elementary and middle school students—in new applications to blend this approach with the general academic curriculum, especially in inclusive, less restrictive school settings.

Faye L. Swindle is currently consultant to the Developmental Therapy–Teaching Programs at the University of Georgia. For 25 years, she has provided workshops and training in this approach throughout the country and has worked with field-based program evaluators to document program effectiveness. She continues to provide inservice training for teachers and program administrators and to develop instructional materials for teachers, parents, and foster parents.

Dr. Swindle has degrees in Language Education with emphasis on language development. After teaching in general elementary and secondary school, she worked in special education language research at the University of Georgia. This background led to her interest and specialization in language delay of preschool children, those with autism, and young children with communication and sensory-integration problems. As Coordinator of Infant and Preschool Programs at the Rutland–Developmental Therapy Psychoeducational Services in Athens, Georgia for 14 years, Dr. Swindle worked directly with preschoolers, their families, and many childcare agencies. Her skill at involving parents in Developmental Therapy–Developmental Teaching has expanded the effectiveness of home-based programs and applications for foster parents, volunteer mentors, and childcare workers in inclusive settings.